MW01089213

ch

FIRST-YEAR COMPOSITION
FROM THEORY TO PRACTICE

r. 9/6

9/30 - ch 4

10/7 - ch 8
p. 211

10/19 - ch 2

12/2
ch 13

11/11
ch 5

10/26
ch 3

11/18
ch 11
p. 276

The new
Generations

steven Pinkwood (?)
Sense of style

LAUER SERIES IN RHETORIC AND COMPOSITION
Series Editors: Catherine Hobbs, Patricia Sullivan, Thomas Rickert, and Jennifer Bay

The Lauer Series in Rhetoric and Composition honors the contributions Janice Lauer has made to the emergence of Rhetoric and Composition as a disciplinary study. It publishes scholarship that carries on Professor Lauer's varied work in the history of written rhetoric, disciplinarity in composition studies, contemporary pedagogical theory, and written literacy theory and research.

BOOKS IN THE SERIES

First-Year Composition: From Theory to Practice (Coxwell-Teague & Lunsford, 2014)
Contingency, Immanence, and the Subject of Rhetoric (Richardson, 2013)
Rewriting Success in Rhetoric and Composition Careers (Goodburn, LeCourt, Leverenz, 2012)
Writing a Progressive Past: Women Teaching and Writing in the Progressive Era (Mastrangelo, 2012)
Greek Rhetoric Before Aristotle, 2e, Rev. and Exp. Ed. (Enos, 2012)
Rhetoric's Earthly Realm: Heidegger, Sophistry, and the Gorgian Kairos (Miller) *Winner of the Olson Award for Best Book in Rhetorical Theory 2011
Techne, *from Neoclassicism to Postmodernism: Understanding Writing as a Useful, Teachable Art* (Pender, 2011)
Walking and Talking Feminist Rhetorics: Landmark Essays and Controversies (Buchanan and Ryan, 2010)
Transforming English Studies: New Voices in an Emerging Genre (Ostergaard, Ludwig, and Nugent, 2009)
Ancient Non-Greek Rhetorics (Lipson and Binkley, 2009)
Roman Rhetoric: Revolution and the Greek Influence, Rev. and Exp Ed. (Enos, 2008)
Stories of Mentoring: Theory and Praxis (Eble and Gaillet, 2008)
Writers Without Borders: Writing and Teaching in Troubled Times (Bloom, 2008)
1977: A Cultural Moment in Composition (Henze, Selzer, and Sharer, 2008)
The Promise and Perils of Writing Program Administration (Enos and Borrowman, 2008)
Untenured Faculty as Writing Program Administrators: Institutional Practices and Politics, (Dew and Horning, 2007)
Networked Process: Dissolving Boundaries of Process and Post-Process (Foster, 2007)
Composing a Community: A History of Writing Across the Curriculum (McLeod and Soven, 2006)
Historical Studies of Writing Program Administration: Individuals, Communities, and the Formation of a Discipline (L'Eplattenier and Mastrangelo, 2004). Winner of the WPA Best Book Award for 2004–2005.
Rhetorics, Poetics, and Cultures: Refiguring College English Studies Exp. Ed. (Berlin, 2003)

FIRST-YEAR COMPOSITION

From Theory to Practice

Edited by
Deborah Coxwell-Teague
Ronald F. Lunsford

Parlor Press
Anderson, South Carolina
www.parlorpress.com

Parlor Press LLC, Anderson, South Carolina, USA

Printed in the United States of America

SAN: 254-8879

Library of Congress Cataloging-in-Publication Data Application Filed

First-year composition : from theory to practice / edited by Deborah Coxwell-
Teague ; Ronald F. Lunsford.
    pages cm. -- (Lauer series in rhetoric and composition)
  Includes bibliographical references and index.
  ISBN 978-1-60235-518-7 (pbk. : alk. paper) -- ISBN 978-1-60235-519-
4 (hardcover : alk. paper) -- ISBN 978-1-60235-520-0 (adobe ebook : alk.
paper) -- ISBN 978-1-60235-521-7 (epub : alk. paper) -- ISBN 978-1-60235-
522-4 (ibook : alk. paper) -- ISBN 978-1-60235-523-1 (kindle : alk. paper)
  1. English language--Rhetoric--Study and teaching. I. Coxwell-Teague,
Deborah, editor. II. Lunsford, Ronald F., editor.
  PE1404.F55 2014
  808'.042071--dc23
                        2014016004

                          4 5

Cover photo, "Hats for Sale, Williamsburg, Virginia" by Greg Glau. See
gglau.zenfolio.com for more of Greg's photography. Greg Glau is the Official
Photographer of Parlor Press.
Cover design by David Blakesley.
Printed on acid-free paper.

Parlor Press, LLC is an independent publisher of scholarly and trade titles
in print and multimedia formats. This book is available in paper, cloth and
Adobe eBook formats from Parlor Press on the World Wide Web at http://
www.parlorpress.com or through online and brick-and-mortar bookstores.
For submission information or to find out about Parlor Press publications,
write to Parlor Press, 3015 Brackenberry Drive, Anderson, South Carolina,
29621, or email editor@parlorpress.com.

We dedicate this book to the memory
and legacy of Richard Straub—

Deborah's teacher

Ron's student

Deborah's colleague

Ron's co-author

Dear, dear friend to both.

Without Rick, this collection would not be.

Preface

Like many worthwhile projects between colleagues in Rhetoric and Composition (Rhet/Comp), this one began over drinks after a full day attending sessions at a composition conference. We had been acquaintances for many years, having been introduced to each other by Richard Straub. Not long after Rick's tragic, untimely death in January 2002, we became good friends and had talked on and off for years about working collaboratively on a book project, but we had never quite come upon the right topic—one that interested and engaged each of us to the extent that could find the time and energy to make it happen. However, on this particular afternoon, we stumbled upon what we considered the perfect topic—one that would not only fully engage us, but one that we believed would also make a worthwhile contribution to our field.

As we explored collaborative possibilities, we talked about Timothy Donovan and Ben McClelland's *Eight Approaches to Teaching Composition*, published in 1980, and briefly discussed working on a collection that explored the primary approaches composition teachers use today, thirty plus years later. We were not completely sold on the idea that teachers could be pigeon-holed, or categorized according to a single theory or philosophy that informed their pedagogy. We discussed many of the good teachers we know and how they don't strictly adhere to one particular philosophy in planning and teaching their courses.

As our conversation continued, we discussed the contributions other articles and books had made in providing composition teachers with information regarding the theories that inform our pedagogies—publications such as Richard Fulkerson's "Four Philosophies of Composition" (1979) and "Composition at the Turn of the Twenty-First Century" (2005), William E. Coles, Jr. and James Vopat's *What Makes Writing Good: A Multiperspective* (1985), and Howard Tinberg and Patrick Sullivan's *What Is College-Level Writing?* (2006), and a second collection by the same name they edited with Sheridan Blau (2010).

Not just 1 pedagogy

As we talked, our conversation turned toward a discussion of what leaders in our field actually do in their classrooms. Having just spent a couple days listening to brilliant presentations by outstanding figures in Rhet/Comp, we found ourselves talking about and wondering how those figures we think so highly of in our discipline, teach—or would teach—first-year composition courses. Ronald Lunsford and Richard Straub's 1995 collection, *12 Readers Reading: Responding to College Student Writing*, provides insight into the ways Chris Anson, Peter Elbow, Anne Gere, Glynda Hull, Patricia Stock, Ed White, and others who are highly respected in our discipline respond to student writing, but we could think of no collection that captured what actually goes on—or would go on—in our leaders' first-year composition classrooms. Many of those we admire regularly teach composition, but many others have teaching assignments that rarely, if ever, include first-year composition courses. What would the individuals whose sessions we had attended over the past couple of days actually do if they taught semester-long first-year composition courses at their schools and if they knew such courses were to be the only college-level composition course the students would take? What would be their major goals, objectives, and writing assignments? What kinds of outside texts would they bring into these courses? What roles would reading and responding to assigned texts play? How would they use classroom discussion, respond to major assignments, and assess their students' work? What explanations would they provide for the overall structure of their courses? What would their syllabi include?

And so this project began. We composed a dream list of individuals to include in this collection and searched for a publisher that could take on a new project and believed in our idea. Over the coming months, our dream list became reality—one after another of the individuals on our list accepted our invitation to write a chapter for our collection, and David Blakesley of Parlor Press offered us a contract.

In the following collection, we first offer introductory remarks about what we see as key moments in composition theory in the last half of the twentieth century. We then present twelve chapters from our contributing authors and conclude with a final chapter that offers our own reflections on what we see in this sampling. We encourage readers to read the following chapters while imagining their own first-year composition classrooms and to think about how to borrow from and adapt the ideas presented here to use with students at their respective schools.

We sincerely thank our contributing authors—Chris Anson, Suresh Canagarajah, Douglas Hesse, Asao Inoue, Paula Mathieu, Teresa Redd, Alexander Reid, Jody Shipka, Howard Tinberg, Victor Villanueva, Elizabeth Wardle, Doug Downs, and Kathleen Blake Yancey—for making time to share their ideas with all of us; it is our hope that in reading their chapters, you will find yourselves as inspired, re-energized, and excited about teaching composition as we have. We'd like to offer an additional, most sincere thank you to Kathleen Blake Yancey for her support of our project from the very beginning and for the invaluable help she gave us along the way.

—Deborah Coxwell-Teague and Ronald F. Lunsford

WORKS CITED

Coles, William E., Jr. and James Vopat. *What Makes Writing Good: A Multiperspective.* Lexington, MA: D.C. Heath and Company, 1985. Print.

Donovan, Timothy R., and Ben W. McClelland. *Eight Approaches to Teaching Composition.* Urbana, IL: NCTE, 1980. Print.

Fulkerson, Richard. "Four Philosophies of Composition." *College Composition and Communication* 30.4 (December 1979): 343–48. Print.

—. "Composition at the Turn of the Twenty-First Century." *College Composition and Communication* 56.4 (June 2005): 654–87. Print.

Straub, Richard, and Ronald F. Lunsford. *12 Readers Reading: Responding to College Student Writing.* Cresskill, NJ: Hampton Press, 1995. Print.

Sullivan, Patrick and Howard Tinberg. *What Is "College-Level" Writing?* Urbana, IL: NCTE, 2006. Print.

Sullivan, Patrick, Howard Tinberg, and Sheridan Blau. *What Is "College-Level" Writing?* Vol. 2. Urbana, IL: NCTE, 2010. Print.

Contents

Setting the Table: Composition in the Last Half of the Twentieth Century

Deborah Coxwell-Teague and Ronald F. Lunsford

As we enter this project, we would like to offer a brief discussion of what we see as key moments in composition studies during the last half of the twentieth century. No doubt others would choose different moments, and with good reason. We offer our reasons for choosing these particular *moments* below, hoping that readers will agree that they are, indeed, important; however, we offer them not as a history, but as a way of whetting the appetites of our readers for the main course of this study: our contributors' syllabi and their discussions of the theories that give rise to them.

THE FOUNDING OF THE CONFERENCE ON COLLEGE COMPOSITION AND COMMUNICATION

What we think of today as first-year composition can trace its origins to the implementation of a written admissions exam at Harvard in 1874. Given the perceived weaknesses in students' performance on these exams, a composition course—originally conceived of as remedial—began at Harvard in 1885. Although the course was intended as a temporary fix to what some saw as the "illiteracy of American boys," this course did not go away; in fact, within fifteen years, such a course existed at most colleges in America (Connors 11).

The freshman writing courses offered from the mid-1880s until the mid-twentieth century are often characterized as monolithic and uniformly bad—in particular because of their focus on grammar, mechanics, and essay structure. There were surely exceptions to these characterizations, however. For example, in 1922, Allan Gilbert calls for a freshman writing course that deals with content in ways that sound rather modern:

> The teacher of Freshman English must deserve his right to stand on the same level as any other teacher of Freshmen and must deal with big things, ideas and books that hit the intelligence of the students. This does more to improve slovenly sentences than does constant worrying of details. . . . the teacher of Freshmen who gives himself to trivial things and neglects the weightier matters of good literature does not make his course a power for literacy. (400)

We pass over Gilbert's assumption that all teachers of this course are male to note that, while he calls for teachers to focus on big ideas, he assumes that such big ideas are found in literature. That assumption reflects the fact that many, if not most, of those pressed into service in freshman composition were teachers of literature who did, in fact, want to focus on the "big ideas" of literature, but were often forced by the reductive testing students faced at the end of the course to focus on trivial matters related to grammar and mechanics. Such instruction led I.A. Richards to opine in 1936 that the rhetoric course taken during their first year of college was "the dreariest part of the waste the unfortunate travel through" (3).

Robert Connors documents in *Composition-Rhetoric: Backgrounds, Theory, and Pedagogy* that a few teachers and researchers—many of them linguists—began, in the 1930s and the 1940s, to stand against reductive approaches to writing (159). The annual conference of the National Council of Teachers of English (NCTE), formed in 1911, provided a forum for these teachers. In addition, writing teachers began noticing that first-year communication courses had begun to spring up in the late 1930s and 1940s. As a result, they began to find a community with teachers of these courses, teachers who often introduced them to research in rhetorical history and to the research of contemporary linguists. In the 1947 meeting of NCTE, a small group of teachers formed an interest group around the teaching of freshman composition and communication. Modern writing instruction can trace its origins to a conference held in Chicago by members of this interest group in the spring of 1949. That first conference was chaired by

John C. Gerber, and featured papers by such luminaries in the fields of composition and communication as Wallace Douglas, James. M. Mc-Crimmon, Richard M. Weaver, Harold Allen, S.I. Hayakawa, Robert C. Pooley, and Paul Diederich.

In its annual meeting in November 1949, the Executive Committee of NCTE voted to recognize the Conference on College Composition and Communication as a conference for three additional years. At the end of this three-year period, John C. Gerber, the first chair of CCCC, published an article that appeared in the October 1952 issue of *College Composition and Communication (CCC)*, the official journal of CCCC. The article reported the clear success of the CCCC organization, and boasted of 500 members in 1950, representing forty-six states, Hawaii, and the District of Columbia. Gerber's article also notes the success of the first two meetings of CCCC, both of which took place in Chicago, and both of which had over 500 conference attendees (Gerber 17). Clearly, those teaching in composition and communication classrooms across the country felt a kinship with one another, and wanted to meet to discuss what they were doing in their classrooms. The second meeting, in 1950, included workshops as well as general sessions. Reports from those workshops appeared in the May 1950 issue of *CCC*. In a very real sense, with the founding and continued success of CCCC, composition became a subject to be studied, and not just a set of skills that teachers of literature could transmit to students lacking those skills.

The Dartmouth Conference

The next key moment we wish to discuss again involves a meeting of teachers—this time, a meeting comprising teachers of English from Canada, Great Britain, and the United States. Despite the social upheavals taking place in nearly all realms of public and private life during the 1960s, many teachers and researchers of English felt that instruction in college writing classes was little changed. Those organizing the Dartmouth conference that ran for four weeks in the summer of 1966 wanted a re-examination of English pedagogy. The conference was designed to achieve three goals: 1) offering a definition of English; 2) providing an understanding of the proper role of literature in the English classroom; and 3) exploring effective teaching methods in the English classroom (Sublette 348).

The participants' responses to these issues have come to be labeled the "Growth Model of English," in part because of John Dixon's book reporting on the work of the conference. Dixon's book, *Growth in English*, recounts the conference attendees' understanding that English is not defined as literature, but rather as a study of how one grows in his or her ability to use and understand English. As such, the course is not about literature per se, but, to the extent that literature is used in the English classroom, conference attendees pronounced their commitment to Louse Rosenblatt's transactional theory of reading; i.e., to the understanding that readers create the meanings they take from texts via the various contexts (personal and public) that they bring to the reading of texts.

The third principle espoused by conference attendees, especially by those from Great Britain, concerns classroom instruction. In his book, Dixon speaks eloquently and at length against the traditional, authoritarian classroom, where teachers saw their role as imparting information about texts and about writing to students. This "transmission" model of classroom instruction was rejected in favor of one that focused not on the teacher, but on the students and their individual growth.

As we reflect on the lasting influence of the Dartmouth Conference, we must place it in the context of the socially liberal cultures of participants attending this conference as well as other movements that arose from these cultures, movements such as the Affirmative Action program—the first in the nation—adopted at the City University of New York in 1966 and the National Writing Project that arose from the Bay Area Writing Project, begun in 1973. Important also is the fact that while there were differences in emphasis between U.S. participants and British and Canadian participants, the conference marked the beginning of an international interest in the teaching of writing that resulted in the contributions of such scholars as John Dixon, James Britton, Michael Halliday, J.R. Martin, and John Swales.

STUDENTS' RIGHT TO THEIR OWN LANGUAGE

A third key moment reinforces the critical role that linguistic research played in the formation of writing as a discipline in the twentieth century. As is noted above, many who opposed reductive approaches to teaching writing in the 1930s and 1940s were linguists. The influence of linguists on writing instruction continued into the second half of the twentieth century, as Geneva Smitherman recounts in "'Students' Right to Their Own Language' A Retrospective." There she credits the work of such linguists as Chomsky, Labov, Halliday, Hymes, Dillard, and Fishman for supporting those in leadership roles of the Conference on College Composition and Communication in calling for teachers of writing to recognize diversity in language (both spoken and written) as a good thing, as something to be encouraged and nurtured, rather than eradicated by the red pen (Smitherman, "Students' Right" 23).

The key moment arrived in April 1974, when the membership of the Conference on College Composition and Communication passed the following resolution:

> We affirm the students' right to their own patterns and varieties of language—the dialects of their nurture or whatever dialects in which they find their own identity and style. Language scholars long ago denied that the myth of a standard American dialect has any validity. The claim that any one dialect is unacceptable amounts to an attempt of one social group to exert its dominance over another. Such a claim leads to false advice for speakers and writers, and immoral advice for humans. A nation proud of its diverse heritage and its cultural and racial variety will preserve its heritage of dialects. We affirm strongly that teachers must have the experiences and training that will enable them to respect diversity and uphold the right of students to their own language. ("Students' Right")

As might be expected, there were many dissenters to this document both within and without CCCC. As soon as the document was endorsed by CCCC, there ensued an intense struggle to convince the parent organization of CCCC, the National Council of Teachers of English (NCTE), to endorse the "Students' Right" document, a struggle that was ultimately lost: NCTE did adopt a weaker statement affirming students' right to their spoken dialects, but that document took a much more conservative approach to written texts, arguing that students should learn the "conventions of what has been called written edited American English" (NCTE Resolution #74.2, 1974). The "Students' Right" resolution is important because, as Geneva

Smitherman notes, "spelling, punctuation, usage, and other surface structure conventions of Edited American English (EAE) are generally what's given all the play (attention) in composition classroom[s]" ("Students' Right" 23). "Students' Right" called for writing teachers to first and foremost attend to what students had to say, and to do so while recognizing the connection between language and identity, rather than using language norms to eradicate identity.

We see the effects of the "Students' Right" movement far beyond its initial "moment" in 1974. Its insistence that one's native language be valued and validated by our educational system can be seen in the Ann Arbor Decision of 1979, when a United States District Court ruled in favor of black students who were found to have been denied equal protection of the law. The Court ruled that the school district had "failed to recognize the existence and legitimacy of the children's language, Black English" (Smitherman, *Talkin' That Talk* 135). This ruling was a precursor for the National Language Policy that was adopted by CCCC in 1988, a policy that came about as a response to the "English Only" movement. The National Language Policy recognized English as a language that should be taught for its communicative benefits. However, at the same time, and just as importantly, it called for support of "programs that assert the legitimacy of native languages and dialects and assure that proficiency in the mother tongue will not be lost."

We also see effects of the "Students' Right" movement into the 1990s within the resolution passed by the Oakland, California school board recognizing the legitimacy of Ebonics, formerly known as African-American Vernacular English, as a language ("Original Oakland Resolution"). The resolution—that students whose primary language is Ebonics should have some instruction given in that language to validate their native language and to assist them in learning—caused national uproar, the upshot of which was likely to deepen the rift between those valuing language diversity and those looking to use a dominant language as a means of promoting cultural assimilation. At the same time this brouhaha erupted, another group of educators from across North America met, without fanfare, in a small town called New London. The scholars attending that meeting were birthing a movement that would pick up the mantle from the "Students' Right" movement and broaden the issue of diversity to include a range of Englishes from across the world. Before we speak of that moment, there is another key moment that had occurred fifteen years earlier to discuss.

SUMMER RHETORIC SEMINARS AND NEH COMPOSITION/RHETORIC SEMINARS

The next key moment was not actually one moment, but rather a series of moments that took place in the late 1970s and early 1980s. In the summer of 1977, Janice Lauer and W. Ross Winterowd initiated a seminar that ran for thirteen consecutive summers; at the same time, the National Endowment for the Humanities (NEH) sponsored a large number of summer seminars—including one year-long seminar—in composition/rhetoric. We find these seminars important for several reasons, the first being the influential scholars who served as seminar leaders. Among the seminar leaders for the Lauer/Winterowd Rhetoric Seminars were James Berlin, Edward Corbett, Janet Emig, Linda Flower, James Kinneavy, Andrea Lunsford, James Moffett, Walter Ong, Janice Lauer, D. Gordon Rohman, Ross Winterowd, and Richard Young. Notable leaders of NEH seminars were William E. Coles, Jr., Edward Corbett, Ross Winterowd, and Richard Young. The list of names of those attending these workshops is also long, and many of those listed are well-known in recent composition history. It is important to note, as Byron Hawk does in discussing the seminars, that "many of the participants had degrees in literature rather than rhetoric" (21). In a very real sense, these seminars offered post-doctoral work in an area participants had very little training in to date, and was the field they were destined to make their mark in and, at the same time, help create.

In making our case that these seminars represent a key moment worthy of being included here, we pause briefly to note some of the work that came out of two specific NEH summer seminars. The first, "Teaching Writing: Theories and Practices," was offered by William E. Coles, Jr., in the summers of 1977 through 1980 at the University of Pittsburgh. We could list important work done by numerous members of those three summer seminars, but we limit ourselves to two key books that came out of these seminars: (1) *What Makes Writing Good: A Multiperspective* by William Coles and James Vopat (a participant in the 1977 summer seminar); and (2) *Eight Approaches to Teaching Composition*, edited by Timothy Donovan and Ben McClel-

land, both participants in that same 1977 seminar. The other seminar, a year-long NEH seminar entitled, "Rhetorical Invention and the
Composing Process," was offered in the 1978/1979 academic year at
Carnegie-Mellon University. The director, Richard Young, based his
seminar on two influential articles that he had authored, "Invention: A
Topographical Survey" (1976), and "Paradigms and Problems: Needed Research in Rhetorical Invention" (1978). Two influential articles
written by participants in this seminar were James Berlin and Robert Inkster's "Current-Traditional Rhetoric: Paradigms and Practices"
(1980), and James Berlin's "Contemporary Composition: The Major
Pedagogical Theories" (1982).

These two seminars, like the many other NEH seminars and the
thirteen summer institutes of the Lauer/Winterowd Rhetoric Seminar,
were important because leaders in the field (to the degree that it could
be called a field at that time) facilitated the conversations, the upshot
of which was interrogating just what the discipline was, what it was
becoming, and what it could become. In many cases, leaders put their
own imprimatur on the field. For example, in their edited collection,
What Makes Writing Good: A Multiperspective, William E. Coles, Jr.
and James Vopat present actual pieces of student writing as well as
comments from teachers who submitted the writing that explain what
made the pieces good writing. In his preface to the collection, Coles
tells the story of how he and Vopat embarked on the project, because
it was their sense that people who spent a good bit of time talking
about the teaching of writing seldom offered writing from their students as examples of what they hoped to accomplish in their teaching.
Coles' famous mantra for years before and after the publication of
this collection was "Get your money up," by which he meant, "Show
me what your students are doing." He and Vopat did just that in the
collection, and they convinced a veritable "who's who" in the developing discipline to do the same. Coles' fervent beliefs that writing is too
complicated to be reduced to a formula; that all writing grows out of
a context, and must be understood in that context; and that no piece
of writing should be offered as a model for other writers to copy are
clearly stated in comments he makes about the essay included in this
collection:

> The paper is an anomaly. I want to make clear that I under-
> stand this. I do not believe it should be used as a model for
> students to imitate. It is not an example of what I think any

writing classroom ought to teach students to do. But for me it is a paper worth sharing with students and explaining as an enactment of what I have to see the teaching of writing as being about, as having the possibility of involving, if I am to keep going as a teacher at all. (328)

Another seminal collection that traces its beginnings to this seminar is *Eight Approaches to Teaching Composition*. In this volume, Donovan and McClelland extended the categories offered by Richard Fulkerson in "Four Philosophies of Composition," published in *CCC* in 1979. In this piece, Fulkerson identifies four major types of writing instruction practiced by composition teachers of the period: (1) Formalist (emphasizes the text); (2) Expressivist (emphasizes the writer); (3) Mimetic (emphasizes reality); and (4) Rhetorical (emphasizes the reader). As the title indicates, Donovan and McClelland offer eight approaches to writing, with chapters contributed by authors that explain how their theories apply in the classroom: Donald M. Murray (Process); Paul A. Eschholz (Prose Models); Stephen Judy (Experiential); Janice M. Lauer (Rhetorical); Kenneth Dowst (Epistemic); Harvey S. Wiener (Basic Writing); Thomas A. Carnicelli (Conferencing); Robert H. Weiss (Writing Across the Curriculum). Although their approaches are not intended as discrete categories, in the fashion of Fulkerson's types of writing instruction, Donovan and McClelland offer insight into the various theories and methodologies of the developing discipline as well as the institutional needs (e.g., "basic writing" and "writing across the curriculum") the new discipline might be expected to meet. Since they are not offered as categories per se, Donovan and McClelland's approaches have not been used to "map" the field in the way that Fulkerson's and James Berlin's have (discussed further below). We argue, however, that Donovan and McClelland's impulse to allow writing teachers to speak for themselves and talk about the ways in which their theories impact instruction in their classrooms had a very real impact on this developing field. As we noted in our prefatory comments, it was important in the formative stages of our thinking about this collection.

The other NEH seminar, Richard Young's "Rhetorical Invention and the Composing Process," was offered for the entire 1978/1979 academic year at Carnegie Mellon University. In the content of this seminar, and in the articles that provided the framework for the seminar, "Invention: A Topographical Survey" (1976) and "Paradigms and Problems: Needed Research in Rhetorical Invention" (1978), Richard Young places himself at the forefront of a movement to critique what he sees as a stifling an emphasis on form in the then current writing instruction, and offers in its place a return to classical theories of invention.

This seminar was attended by ten young composition/rhetoric scholars, all of whom made important contributions to the developing field. Among a group that included Lisa Ede, David Fractenberg, Robert Inkster, Charles Kneupper, Victor Vitanza, Sam Watson, Vickie Winkler, and William Nelson, James Berlin stands out because of the important work he did in mapping composition studies. In his 1982 publication, "Contemporary Composition: The Major Pedagogical Theories," Berlin offers four categories—three of which are similar to Fulkerson's categories mentioned above: (1) Neo-Aristotelian (Fulkerson's Rhetorical category); (2) Romantic (Fulkerson's Expressive category); and (3) Positivist (Fulkerson's Formalist category). However, in place of Fulkerson's Mimetic category, Berlin offers a new fourth category that became, in its various iterations, his life's work: Epistemic. For Berlin, the Epistemic writing teacher sees it as his/her charge to help students understand the power of language for good—as in the creation of "temporary" knowledge—and for bad—as in the ideologies that one's language reinforces.

In summing up the influence of this key moment, it is difficult to overstate the importance of these NEH and Rhetorical seminars. The work begun in these seminars has rippled in untraceable ways through the remaining years of the twentieth century, and into the twenty-first. The hundreds of seminar participants, and the thousands of composition/rhetoric teachers who have populated the graduate classrooms of these teachers, created the field of composition studies as we know it today.

THE NEW LONDON GROUP

Our final key moment again involves a meeting—this time a week-long meeting of ten prominent scholars from Australia, Great Britain, and the United States. These scholars, representing the academic fields of Education, Linguistics, and Sociology, came together to "consider the future of literacy teaching; to discuss what would need to be taught in a rapidly changing near future, and how this should be taught" (Cope and Kalantzis 3). As a result of this meeting, the group published a jointly-authored article in the *Harvard Education Review* in 1996, entitled: "A Pedagogy of Multiliteracies: Designing Social Futures." From there, the group assigned one another various topics for research and investigation, and expanded the group to include three scholars working in literacy education in South Africa. In 2000, the group published the book, *Multiliteracies: Literacy Learning and the Design of Social Futures*, comprising of the original essay, together with fifteen essays reporting on the research of group members.

We are aware that it may seem premature to call something a "key moment," given that the group's manifesto was published in 2000. We are also aware that we may seem to be expanding the world of composition studies considerably by including the work of a group whose expertise lie is education, linguistics, and sociology—and not composition, not writing studies, or even rhetoric. What we are really doing here is predicting that this will come to be seen as a key moment in composition history, because it marks a critical change in what will count as composition in college writing courses.

Before explaining what we mean, let us pause to note the connections between the New London Group and the history of writing instruction in the last half of the twentieth century. We have already alluded to the connection between the New London Group and the "Students' Right" movement. That connection is made abundantly clear in the following comments about linguistic diversity, found in the introductory section of *Multiliteracies*:

> Gone are the days when learning a single, standard version of the language was sufficient. Migration, multiculturalism and global economic integration daily intensify this process of change. The globalization of communications and labor markets makes diversity an ever more critical local issue. Dealing with linguistic differences and cultural differences has now become central to the pragmatics of our working, civic, and private lives. Effective citizenship and productive work now require that we interact effectively using multiple languages, multiple Englishes, and communication patterns that more frequently cross cultural, community, and national boundaries. (6)

In addition to the "Students' Right" movement, the New London Group also has connections with another important strand of composition theory in the twentieth century, one that we have not identified as a "key moment" because its reach is too pervasive to be labeled as such. When Carolyn Miller published "Genre as Social Action" in 1984, she placed herself at the forefront of a movement that would revolutionize the way composition theorists and practitioners understood the work that writing does. She did so by offering an analysis of forms of discourse that moved writing theory beyond the reach of any attempt to reduce writing instruction to form. The New London Group shows its debt to Miller's work, as well as hundreds of other scholars working in genre theory, and its commitment to literacy education based on writing as social action, in the following comments in the introduction to *Multiliteracies*:

> Accordingly, the starting point of those discussions and now this book is the shape of social change—changes in our working lives; our public lives as citizens; and our private lives as members of different community lifeworlds. The fundamental question is what do these changes mean for literacy pedagogy? In the context of these changes we must conceptualize the "what" of literacy pedagogy. The key concept we developed to do this is that of Design, in which we are both inheritors of patterns and conventions of meaning while at the same time active designers of meaning. And, as designers of meaning, we are designers of social futures—workplace futures, public futures, and community futures. (7)

Clearly, members of the New London Group see writing as social action; but, that is not the only kind of social action they wish to investigate. For them, the term "multiliteracies" has a double meaning:

> We decided that the outcomes of our discussions could be encapsulated in one word, "Multiliteracies"—a word we chose because it describes two important arguments we might have with the emerging cultural, institutional, and global order. The first argument engages with the multiplicity of communications channels and media; the second with the increasing salience of cultural and linguistic diversity. (5)

They go on to outline a literacy program that would be comprised not only of linguistic literacy (what they refer to as Linguistic Design), but also Visual Design, Gestural Design, Spatial Design, and Audio Design. The scope of communication is not limited to these modes only. Their final mode, the Multimodal Design, allows for hybrids that make use of multiple modes of communication.

While the chapters in *Multiliteracies* devoted to Audio, Gestural, Visual, and Spatial design are admittedly exploratory, Gunther Kress's chapter, "Multimodality," reflects years of very productive research into the Visual, and the ways in which the Visual—and, for that matter, all other modes—form hybrids with the Linguistic. In fact, the New London Group argues that the Linguistic, itself, is multimodal:

> In a profound sense, all meaning-making is Multimodal. All written text is also a process of Visual Design and spreads responsibility for the visual much more broadly than was the case when writing and page layout were separate trades. So a school project can and should properly be evaluated on the basis of Visual as well as Linguistic Design, and their multimodal relationships. (The New London Group 29)

Concluding Remarks

We title this section "concluding remarks" rather than "conclusion" because the brevity of our account, focused as it is on "moments" that stand out for us, makes it impossible to draw conclusions. Returning to the metaphor used in our title, our purpose in this introduction is to set the table for the feast (if we may be permitted to sustain the metaphor a bit longer) to come when readers delve into the work of our contributors.

The remarks we make about this brief account will no doubt reveal more about why we have chosen the moments described above than they do about the history of composition in the U.S. Our view of this history is that, from the beginning, it represents something of a tug of war between those who would reduce writing to form and formulas—e.g., those who instituted the first "writing" courses at Harvard—and those who see writing instruction as something more—e.g., those who founded CCCC. From the early days, the search for something "more" has led composition theorists to other disciplines: Early on it was to ancient rhetoricians for invention and style; then it was to linguists, who offered critiques that suggested linguistic diversity was something to be expected and, in fact, encouraged; then it was to linguists who, again, encouraged writing teachers' focus on the power of language to create and control thought; then it was to sociologists and linguists, whose work suggests that language is capable not only of creating identity, but also of being social action itself; finally, linguists, sociologists, and semioticians suggested that viewing writing as the only mode of communicating is extremely limiting.

This last insight, that there are multiple modes of communication, together with the insight that writing itself comprises more than one mode, provides the underpinning for a recent return to the use of "composition" as the name for what we do in first-year courses. We welcome this move because it seems, to us, to be a move that opens rather than closes possibilities, a move that includes rather than excludes, and a move that involves us in uncertainties rather than certainties. In that spirit, we offer the essays in this collection.

WORKS CITED

Berlin, James A. "Contemporary Composition: The Major Pedagogical Theories." *College English* 44.8 (December 1982): 765–77. Print.

Berlin, James A. and Robert P. Inkster. "Current-Traditional Rhetoric: Paradigm and Practice." *Freshman English News* 8.3 (Winter 1980): 1–4, 13–14. Print.

"CCCC National Language Policy." *Conference on College Composition and Communication*. National Council of Teachers of English. 1988. Web. 4 Mar. 2013.

Coles, William E., Jr. and James Vopat. *What Makes Writing Good: A Multiperspective*. Lexington: D.C. Heath and Company, 1985. Print.

Connors, Robert J. *Composition-Rhetoric: Backgrounds, Theory, and Pedagogy*. Pittsburgh: U of Pittsburgh P, 1997. Print.

Cope, Bill, and Mary Kalantzis. *Multiliteracies: Literacy Learning and the Design of Social Futures*. New York: Routledge, 2000. Print.

Dixon, John. *Growth Through English*. Reading, England: National Association for the Teaching of English, 1967. Print.

Donovan, Timothy R., and Ben W. McClelland. *Eight Approaches to Teaching Composition*. Urbana: NCTE, 1980. Print.

Fulkerson, Richard. "Four Philosophies of Composition." *College Composition and Communication* 30.4 (December 1979): 343–48. Print.

Gerber, John, C. "Three-Year History of the CCCC." *College Composition and Communication* 3.3 (October 1952): 17–18. Print.

Gilbert, Allen H. "What Shall We Do with Freshman Themes?" *English Journal* 11.7 (September 1922): 392–403. Print.

Hawk, Byron. *A Counter-History of Composition*. Pittsburgh: U of Pittsburgh P, 2007. Print.

King Junior Elementary School v. Ann Arbor School District. United States District Court for the Eastern District of Michigan. 1979. Web. 5 Mar. 2013.

Kress, Gunther. "Multimodality." *Multiliteracies: Literacy Learning and the Design of Social Futures*. Ed. Bill Cope and Mary Katantzis. New York: Routledge, 2000. 182–202. Print.

Miller, Carolyn R. "Genre As Social Action." *Quarterly Journal of Speech*. 70.2 (May 1984): 151–67. Print.

NCTE. Resolution #74.2. November. 1974. Web. 1 Mar. 2013.

Oakland, California School Board. "Original Oakland Resolution on Ebonics." No. #597–0063. December 18, 1996. Web. 4 Mar. 2013.

Richards, I.A. *The Philosophy of Rhetoric*. New York: Oxford UP, 1936. Print.

Smitherman, Geneva. "'Students' Right to Their Own Language': A Retrospective." *The English Journal* 84.1 (January 1995): 21–27. Print.

—. *Talkin That Talk: Language, Culture and Education in African America*. London: Routledge, 2000. Print.

"Students' Right to Their Own Language." *Conference on College Composition and Communication*. National Council of Teachers of English. 1974. Web. 5 Mar. 2013.

Sublette, Jack R. "The Dartmouth Conference: Its Reports and Results" *College English* 35.3 (December 1973): 348–57. Print.

The New London Group. "A Pedagogy of Multiliteracies: Designing Social Futures." *Multiliteracies: Literacy Learning and the Design of Social Futures*. Ed. Bill Cope and Mary Katantzis. New York: Routledge, 2000. 9–37. Print.

Young, Richard. "Invention: A Topographical Survey." *Teaching Composition: Ten Bibliographic Essays*. Ed. Gary Tate. Fort Worth: Texas Christian UP, 1976. 1–44. Print.

—. "Paradigms and Problems: Needed Research in Rhetorical Invention." *Research and Composing: Points of Departure*. Ed. Charles R. Cooper and Lee Odell. Urbana: NCTE, 1978. 29–47. Print.

First-Year Composition
From Theory to Practice

1 Writing, Language, and Literacy

Chris M. Anson

OH, THE THINKS YOU CAN THINK

In the early 1990s, I noticed with increasing interest how even skilled writers struggled to adjust to new and unfamiliar writing environments. Whenever they faced a challenging paper in a course whose content they hadn't studied before, otherwise skilled students often asked me for advice and shared their frustrations with me. What was the text supposed to look like? What did the teacher mean by "a causal analysis of the historical events" or "an affective response supported by specific details of the painting"? How should the paper be structured, and what style was appropriate? If students felt this helpless writing in an environment designed to support their learning, I wondered what would happen when they traveled into the less nurturing worlds of corporations, small businesses, or non-profit agencies.

Curious, I teamed up with a colleague to conduct research on students' transitions from academic to work-related writing (Anson and Forsberg). Our context was a special writing course enrolling English majors, mostly seniors. In the course, students talked about the writing they were doing in local internships arranged in advance, through the help of my department. As the students tackled their on-the-job writing assignments, they brought artifacts of their work to the class, and shared their experiences and struggles. Over time, our readings, discussions, and analyses of their writing contexts led them to develop a kind of meta-awareness of the complex, multidimensional nature of writing. Along the way, my colleague and I interviewed the students and tracked their adaptation to new, professional settings.

What we found surprised us. These highly successful English majors, most "A" students with excellent track records as academic writers, came back to class after their first week on the job utterly devastated by their performance; they were despondent and crushed by failure. Little of what they had learned in school—strategies and habits that had effectively supported them in the past—was of much use as they started in on corporate histories, PR materials, press releases, or columns for a weekly employee newsletter. At the start of the course, they had glowingly shared their successes with writing in-depth analyses of water imagery in *The Awakening* or research papers on James Joyce, but they had absolutely no idea how to structure a corporate memo or put together a report analyzing viewer ratings at a local television station. Meanwhile, their supervisors simply assumed that these bright, young students would do fine when given an assignment and a desk where they could write.

Over time, our study revealed a series of stages the interns passed through in order to begin writing more successfully and confidently on the job. Immersion in the context, help from supervisors and employees, models of specific genres, and iterative attempts to write were necessary for their eventual success. There was no question that the course also helped, mostly by giving students ways to untangle and make sense of their on-the-job writing: to learn how to "read" their new contexts, and to get help from others in doing so. By studying the role of *language* in their new settings, they started to gain conscious strategies for tackling new, complex writing and speaking tasks.

The problem of "transfer" or "adaptation" has recently become a central concern in writing studies, and is generating burgeoning interest and scores of research studies (see, for example, the Fall 2012 special issue of *Composition Forum*). If a central goal of composition instruction is to provide students with foundational skills that they can then deploy in a range of other college courses, including those in their chosen majors, then "transferring" those skills from first-year composition takes on critical importance. Yet, very little evidence exists that students' experiences with typical genres of writing in composition courses help them to write more specialized genres found elsewhere in the college curriculum. Instead, research on transfer in various contexts shows that learning to write is highly situated, and depends on immersion in communities of practice where the conventions of writing, imbricated with complex aspects of rhetorical purpose, local histories, and subtly evolving norms, are unfamiliar to outsiders. As David Russell puts it, first-year composition usually teaches the equivalent of "general ball-handling skills" that are largely ineffective for playing specific sports (57). This concern has even led some scholars, in composition studies and beyond, to question the necessity of a generic first-year writing course.

A number of compositionists have proposed not junking the first-year course, but re-orienting it. The re-oriented course would focus less on the "ability" to write (learned anew in each new context) than on the nature of writing itself—on thinking about the thinking that writing involves—and on the way that each writer's personal, literate history has shaped his or her beliefs, dispositions, ways of working, and both conscious and unconscious strategies for meeting the demands of writing tasks in various settings. A new kind of course, dubbed "writing about writing" (WAW; see Wardle and Downs in this collection), proposes to facilitate the adaptation to new writing contexts by encouraging students to begin thinking and learning about writing itself while they also work on their writing abilities. Developing "mindfulness" and meta-cognitive awareness becomes one of the most important aims of the course, as it is fueled by the study of writing from theoretical and research-driven perspectives (559-60).

WOWED BY WAW

Although I always try to bring some of what we know in our field into my undergraduate writing courses, it's usually haphazard and occasional—not the grist of the course. When I encountered the work of composition scholars advocating a WAW approach, I was immediately drawn to their ideas and intrigued by their proposed pedagogy. In the context of my work on transition and adaptiveness, the approach *makes sense*. As proponents argue, WAW legitimizes our field, allows those of us engaged in scholarship to make better use of it in teaching undergraduates, and encourages other teachers to begin learning more about what we know, our disciplinary knowledge.

My own history as a teacher might have predicted any number of orientations for the course I contribute here: literature-based courses; courses with a service-learning component; project-focused, basic writing courses; composition courses linked to large, general-education lecture sections in disciplines such as social psychology; theme-based courses; and topical seminars for honors students. Of all the courses I have taught over the past thirty years—including, but not limited to composition—the most enriching were those that focused thematically on *language*. This interest goes back to my earliest years: A child of British parents, I lived near Paris for six years as a young boy and grew up bilingual, attending a local French-speaking school. After we moved from France, our travels exposed me to other languages and cultures, and I experienced a peer-driven, pre-adolescent morphing of my original British dialect to one characteristic of the Northeastern U.S. My eventual fascination with language and writing shaped my choice of a doctoral program that focused on the study of the English language, with a specialization in composition theory and research. My coursework in language and linguistics was extensive. When I was hired at the University of Minnesota in 1984 to help run its large Program in Composition and Communication, there was also a constant need in the English Department to staff a large lecture course: "Introduction to Language and Linguistics." I taught that course almost every quarter for fifteen years, including sections of the course offered in the evening extension program and during summer sessions. Although it enrolled as many as 250 students, I found plentiful ways to build active learning into class sessions, and I assigned extensive, low-stakes and reflective writings (Anson and Beach; Beach and Anson). Beyond the study of the building blocks of language, the course covered topics such as child language development, the history of English, linguistic pragmatics, dialectology, the acquisition of reading and writing ability, and the sociology of language.

Year after year, my excitement about the course came from the way it awakened students to new realizations about language in all its forms and uses. In spite of the central role of language in their lives, students usually hadn't thought very consciously about it. Did they have a dialect? How did they feel about others' dialects? How had they learned to talk and write? What did they read, and why? How did they learn to read? How did they use language in different contexts? Why did they use certain terms, and how did those terms differ throughout the U.S.? Why was it okay in New York for conversants to "overlap" their discourse while in Minnesota such practices were seen as rude interruptions? Why did Minnesotans tolerate silent pauses in their conversations, while, in other communities, pauses would trigger a fear that someone had said the wrong thing? Why was the word "like," as a kind of pause or placeholder, so compelling that it peppered the speech of most students? Was "like" a bad thing? Was it as bad as "um" or "you know"? Who makes the rules of language? What rules of grammar could they remember? How good were those rules? Where did English really come from, and why has it kept changing?

After some years eagerly teaching this course, I became involved in a service-learning initiative and created a smaller-enrollment course that focused on literacy in the United States. Students tutored children in community centers and after-school programs in poor and working-poor areas of the Twin Cities that were populated mostly by under-represented minorities and refugees. As part of their coursework, they read essays about the nature of literacy and also about the experiences of authors who grew up bilingual, experienced prejudice against their own home and community dialects, were forced to give up their linguistic identities and "assimilate" into a dominant white culture, or had to write in a voice not their own. We read Native American authors' narratives of forced assimilation. We read studies of how literacy functions for various groups, such as the Amish, as well as black residents of impoverished, rural Southern communities. We read about language prejudice and about the history and legitimacy of African American English, Hispanic English, and immigrant dialects. We read about illiteracy in poor, white Appalachian households. The students wrote literacy autobiographies that traced their own development and gained insight into their identities and practices as literate people. We listened to interviews with illiterate adults, and talked about how the circumstances of their schooling and upbringing could have denied them access to literacy in what is supposed to be "the greatest country in the world." We read elegantly written essays by homeless people, and tried to understand why they were on the streets in spite of their talents as writers. We explored the functions of literacy in prisons for those who would be paroled and also for those who would die or be executed there. We read about shocking disparities in U.S. literacy education because of unequal school funding. As time passed, I incorporated readings that focused on digital literacies, and we speculated about the ways technology changes the nature of written, oral, and visual communication.

In all these classes—the language-focused general education courses and the literacy-oriented service-learning courses—I observed and often co-experienced the kinds of intellectual transformations that can happen when something tacit is brought into consciousness, is examined critically and thoughtfully, and is supplemented by the voices of people who have reflectively mined personal experiences for something more than just a story. During all the years I taught these courses, some of those voices crept into my introductory composition courses. I often began with a literacy narrative, if only to get students thinking about their writing practices and histories, which were always richly diverse. I drew on the work of Cindy Selfe and other scholars of literacy narratives, and sometimes we read an essay or two about writers' experiences. The program's outcomes, however necessary and well-rationalized as they were, tugged me back toward a focus on the principles of structure, writing processes, revision, research, and other staples of composition. The content focus of my language and literacy courses remained an arm's length from the "improvement of writing" focus of my composition courses. Enhanced ability always seemed to trump increased awareness.

LANGUAGE AT THE CENTER

In contributing to this project, I have been challenged to imagine a course that could fulfill some outcomes of first-year writing, such as those proposed in the *WPA Outcomes Statement for First-Year Composition*, while building in opportunities for the ways that my language-focused courses transformed students' understandings and restructured their knowledge. We typically think of the former as a *process* or set of activities, something practiced and honed. The latter is thought of like genetics or art history, as a body of content to be integrated into existing knowledge. The evolution in our thinking about first-year writing helps: Documents such as the new *Framework for Success in Postsecondary Writing* supplement the usual writing outcomes with various habits of mind, including curiosity, engagement, and creativity—dimensions of students' learning that so intrigued me in my language and literacy courses. The recent development of post-process theories and of the WAW curriculum also helped in providing me the theoretical permission to rethink the balance of what David Jolliffe calls the "whatness" of first-year writing with the development of skill and ability.

I also had to get over thinking of the course in this project as an exemplar for first-year writing. Composition enjoys a rich diversity of instructional approaches, in part because the content that drives students' writing is free of disciplinary constraint. This very collection illustrates that richness. At the same time, I was wary of creating a "boutique" course, one so idiosyncratic and personal that it would lose its possible value to others. Composition teaching always suffers the tension between a desire for pedagogical consistency (i.e., the accountability of shared outcomes) and the need for teachers to be *thoughtful* and *creative* about their instruction, to make informed, principled, and unique decisions about every aspect of their teaching. The course I sketch here represents a patchwork of ideas that try to balance the forces contributing to that tension. Some ideas have stood the test of many hundreds of students, stretching back for decades, while others await the possibilities of success, failure, and revision.

In constructing the course, I draw on principles of a post-process WAW curriculum, and extend its focus to include communication in multiple forms—oral, written, and digital. The course is designed to tie students' own experiences and observations to systematic, scholarly inquiry and an enhanced understanding of the role of language in their lives. One central goal of the course is to heighten students' awareness of how they communicate and what roles writing, reading, and literacies (both print and digital) have played in their own intellectual development. Of increasing importance is the relationship of speech to writing, and what, as Peter Elbow puts it, speech can "bring" to writing (*Vernacular Eloquence: What Speech Can Bring to Writing*). Both the content and processes of the course turn around language; just as students explore language as a uniquely human activity, they also reflect on the ways they use language in the course to communicate their explorations with others.

FLIPPING OUT ABOUT DELIVERY

In thirty years of systematically observing teachers and passing by the classrooms of dozens of colleagues, I've been uneasy with how often and for how long teachers think they need to present information. The ubiquitous "lecture-test" model is at best a weak method of teaching, and is a lousy way to learn, even in discipline-based courses such as history, physics, or biology. Hardly a course lives on in the college curriculum that can justify denying students frequent opportunities for active learning, an assumption massively supported in the educational literature (there is even a journal, *Active Learning in Higher Education*, devoted to the subject). This is why I asked students in those 250-seat sections of "Introduction to English Language and Linguistics" to pair-and-share, write, and engage in active discussion or application of the material frequently during each class session, even as the classroom system (i.e., the tiered rows of chairs, the giant screen in the front of the room, the microphone) was set up to make me the "knowledge teller" who would impart truths to be written down, rehearsed, remembered, and chanted back like a crowd that responds at a political rally.

In writing courses, lecturing is even less defensible. Classes are deliberately kept small with the understanding that students must *practice* and have opportunities to talk about what they've written to keep refining it. Brief presentations on certain principles make good sense in such a context, but only when immediately followed or preceded by methods of engaged learning: truly participatory discussion, small-group work, writing, and active problem-solving. Still, I've seen dozens of writing teachers fill entire class sessions with presentations on style, grammar, and structure, or spend an hour unpacking an assigned reading *for* students, as if they're incapable of being coached to take the reading apart themselves. This tendency to do all the work for the students, to see one's self as the holder and giver of information, increases in relation to how strongly a particular theme or body of content drives the course. This is one reason the "writing about literature" approach received early and justifiable critique in the development of composition studies for being theme-driven (see Lindemann).

In my proposed course, the increased need for "knowing that" (from the course's focus on language) alongside the "knowing how" (from the course's focus on writing) runs the risk of placing students in a passive role. After all, lots of ideas and concepts do need to be explained, including those about the reading process, dialect variation, models of literacy, and research on writing. In spite of my strong beliefs about the value of active learning, like most academics, I enjoy displaying my knowledge and erudition. Lecturing is like a drug, and the more captive the audience, the more addictive it becomes.

For this reason, my design hinges on a method that I call "course delivery reversal" (CDR). Known in the vernacular as "course flipping," it assumes a need for students to be actively engaged in their learning, and is founded on the principles of constructivism (in contrast to the behaviorist principles of objectivism that have dominated education for decades; see Jonassen; Prince). In the traditional lecture model, students are least active when they are the most supervised: in class. Ironically, unless the teacher uses highly interactive kinds of presentations, he or she has little way of knowing what's happening in students' heads. Most lecture classes I pass daily as I walk the halls of my campus open to a similar scene: an academic authority at the front of a room with rows of students, many of them staring with indifferent, glazed eyes, some using laptops or smart phones, and some asleep. At home, then, students are the most active when they are least supervised and potentially confused or frustrated, and they apply principles from a lecture to their homework assignments, conduct research, or write.

CDR involves flipping these two spaces and sets of activities. Whatever lectures would be delivered in class are created digitally and posted online for students to view as homework (perhaps with low-stakes writing assignments for accountability). This validates the teacher's desire to share his or her expertise with students, but it does so when supervision for exposure to that knowledge is least needed. Current technology provides ways for teachers to lecture, show slides, work on virtual blackboards, and record almost anything they might do in a physical classroom. When students come to class, the lecturing is already over; almost everything students do involves active learning with the supervision of the teacher, who is the orchestrator of knowledge integration, and no longer the sole source of that knowledge. Occasionally, very brief presentations help set a context for students' work, or remind them of various concepts or principles; but, the time in class is decidedly not used for teacher-dominated talk (Educause).

Following the provisions of CDR, my planned course consists of multimedia presentations of my own creation (as well as those already available online) that are integrated into students' homework, and includes reading material and other, more common, out-of-class assignments. Class time is devoted to large-group discussion (using student-centered methods, such as those described by Brookfield and Preskill), small-group work, brief writing episodes, peer-group brainstorming and revision conferences, oral mini-presentations, poster creation and "gallery walks," problem-solving through cases and scenarios, and other activities.

Consider, for example, an area of scholarship and a set of concepts about reading known as "schema theory." In a traditional class, the teacher lectures about schema theory by tracing its origins, explaining its mental constructs, and applying it to an understanding of the reading process and the distinction between getting meaning from the words on the page and creating meaning by bringing prior schematic knowledge *to* what's on the page. Students might then go home and read about experiments with schema theory, or work through some activities that reveal the activation or instantiation of schemas. As any glance at a half-conscious student during a lecture suggests, that teacher has no assurance that students are really learning about schema theory. Nor is there be any guarantee that students are fully engaged in the homework activities—at least without some type of repressive pop quiz during the following class period.

In my flipped course, schema theory is explained in a video presentation made as engaging as possible, given the medium. Students can watch the video more than once, pause it to take notes, or break it up into smaller episodes to look at when they are most awake. Students are assigned some low-stakes writing relating to their viewing of the online video that they post to a forum about schema theory; or, that writing could be done on paper and collected or used during the next class. When students come to class, the session is filled with highly stimulating activities that demonstrate the operation of schemas, some of them from fascinating research on reading. For example, students read a passage about balloons, a wire, a musical instrument, or a message that is unable to be carried far enough by voice. "An additional problem," the passage concludes, "is that a string could break on the instrument. Then there could be no accompaniment to the message. It is clear that the best situation would involve less distance. Then there would be fewer potential problems. With face-to-face contact, the least number of things could go wrong" (Bransford and Johnson 719). The passage contains no complex syntax or words that are not able to be "read" (with a lower-case "r"). Yet, when asked what's going on in the passage, students are baffled. Working in groups for a few minutes, students try to interpret the passage—a nearly impossible task. In coordinating these groups, I frequently break in to ask why on earth no one can explain the passage, since it is written so simply. Bewildered, students begin to make wild guesses from the lexical items: a wire, sound, an instrument . . . something transmitted, something about communication, something about a message. . . . A weather balloon? At the peak of their frustration, I reveal a picture on-screen that shows a stick-figure Romeo with a microphone and guitar and amplifier that is plugged into a wall outside a high-rise building. A wire runs up to a speaker that is suspended by helium balloons outside a window, several stories up, where a stick-figure Juliet is looking out. As soon as students see this picture—a demonstration of the missing schema—they "understand" the passage. As we re-read every word of the passage, every sentence pops into place, demonstrating Reading (with a capital *R*); or, reading with comprehension. We then briefly discuss the implications of reading and learning to read, the role of background knowledge in reading, and the problems associated with mismatches between learners' diverse experiences and what they are asked to make sense of. Students share their own memories of trying to read with missing or partial schemas, such as having little knowledge of farms (if they lived in the inner city), or not knowing what's going on in a story about American football (if they grew up playing cricket in India). The concept of the "schema" then maps easily onto the need for writers to provide sufficient orienting information for diverse readers.

Four or five such demonstrations later, students are highly energized and completely immersed in the class. Lest this look like too much gimmickry when "important and challenging concepts must be learned," students' understanding of schema theory and its relationship to the processes of literacy stand as a testament: Not only do they learn the concepts better, but they are far more engaged in the class. Engaged learners are far more likely to persist, succeed, and extend their new knowledge into new contexts.

FORAYS INTO THE FORUM

As in all my courses, students are placed into small, four- or five-person digital forums. Students in each group interact with each other about the readings, class materials and sessions, ongoing projects, occasional assigned scenarios, and phenomena that they notice about language. Their main (required) interactions take place within their group, but they can also visit other group forums and add responses and/or reactions as outside participants. In their totality, forum posts count for 15% of the course grade and offer an excellent way to ensure that students watch and reflect on the multimedia presentations. Imaginative, scenario-based forum assignments coexist with "open" assignments, where students can write about anything related to the course. For example, a literacy scenario designed for forum discussion sketches an imaginary micro-culture of farming families whose members are entirely illiterate, their lives void of print. The families are phenomenally successful at farming, and pass all their accumulated information down orally to their children. Students then write to the forum about whether literacy really matters to this culture by answering, "What is gained by literacy?" Almost always, the exchanges begin by revealing deeply held beliefs about the functions of literacy in societies. This narrative is then opened to new perspectives from lectures and readings, such as theories of literacy as a set of social practices rather than as an essentialist construct that is deterministically tied to individual accomplishment. Some students argue that the farmers could tap into larger and more profitable markets for their produce through literacy, while others argue that literacy "adds" something to a culture only on the basis of its self-determined needs (after all, the farmers are highly successful, and their oral methods for passing on their knowledge already work). Returning to the "meta" functions of the course, the forums also give us an opportunity to reflect on the processes of blogging or writing interactively online as well as differences of register, social function, and rhetorical purpose across multiple contexts and media of written communication.

INTRINSIC MOTIVATION AND INQUIRY PROJECTS

In addition to ongoing forum entries that provide a space for students to experiment with language, react to ideas in the course, write about their own experiences, or dialogue with other students about theirs, the course involves three longer and more formal papers: a language and literacy autobiography, a language and literacy biography, and an inquiry project focusing on some aspect of language and literacy in accordance with the course theme. The first two projects are designed to be written before the end of the first third of the course; the third project takes up the remainder of the course, and is more substantial, as it involves the creation of a project portfolio.

The three projects are also designed to scaffold students' experiences as writers. The literacy autobiography, written while we learn about writing and literacy practices and read personal accounts of the role of literacy in people's lives, offers a way for students to personally reflect on their experiences with writing, reading, and communication. In addition, this project helps students understand some important rhetorical concepts, such as ethos or persona (i.e., who they want to be in the writing relative to their defined purposes and audiences) and elements of the writing process that are explored through readings from composition studies. Like most narratives, it uses students' own resources of memory and experience as content, but challenges them to find ways to represent that content in more than solipsistic, egocentric ways. As a narrative genre, autobiography is also an excellent way for students to focus on the processes of writing, as these processes are brought into consciousness through a combination of online presentations and meta-level discussions before, during, and after writing and revision.

This assignment is also designed to provoke the kind of cognitive dissonance that leads to major and productive revision. In their first drafts, students often invoke culturally dominant tropes about literacy as a key to upward mobility, and they frequently fail the "so what" test by telling about their literacy development in highly generalized ways (e.g., their parents read to them during their childhood, their third-grade teacher fostered in them an interest in books, and so on). When they exchange drafts within their forum group to provide response prior to an in-class revision conference, they read about the distinction between "master narratives" of literacy and "little narratives" that particularize literacy in specific contexts. Kara Poe Alexander's helpful framework, based on a study of literacy narratives, serves to open up complex dimensions of students' drafts as they consider both the "grand" representation of literacy and the "little narratives" that particularize it—cultural narratives of success, being the victim or child prodigy or hero, "winning" something associated with literacy, and so on (see also Daniel). This is also an important occasion to discuss self-representation, voice, ethos, and the relationship between what matters to the writer and why the reader would care about it. Students' revisions often move from sweeping sketches of their entire literacy development to a specific experience that illustrates a broader principle or that raises interesting questions about literacy and its role in people's lives. A "little narrative" can, as Alexander argues, "become the lens through which [students] and others understand their literacy experiences" (629).

By the time they have finished the autobiography, students have explored many new ways of thinking about writing, language, and literacy, and have reflected on their own writing and revision processes. At this point, the focus moves beyond their personal experiences. The

literacy biography scaffolds the experience of writing their own narrative by adding information from interviews they conduct with someone else, giving them practice with integrating outside information
into their own texts, but without all the encumbrances, at this point,
of "research" (see Howard, Rodrique, and Serviss for a critique of student source work). It is no less challenging to incorporate interview
data into their writing than it is to incorporate multiple passages from
several academic sources; but, the singularity of the source and the
need to structure the text as an interesting account of a living person's
experience allows for a greater focus on the processes of source integration and the complex rhetorical decisions students need to make
along the way. It's also an effective way to have students think about
the relationships between spoken and written texts (Elbow). Concerns
over source citation and excusable plagiarism disappear. Crucial here,
though requiring some work in class, is the choice of an interview subject. More importantly, the biographies can be gathered and published
online as a course project, giving students a clearer context and purpose for their work, and allowing for the introduction of some issues
in ethical writing and communication, such as subject identity, IRB,
copyright, and the nature of disclosure.

The third and major project in the course is a hybrid of the famous
"I-search" paper (Macrorie) and the "inquiry project" (Jolliffe). Jolliffe
argues that too often, students in first-year composition courses write
new papers that focus on a new topic, often written in a new genre,
every couple of weeks. We can hardly expect students to write with any
authority after thinking or reading about a subject for just a week, and
to also gain control over a genre that may be unfamiliar to them. Jolliffe's scheme involves immersing students in a semester-long inquiry
project. Over time, students gain authority and expertise on a subject
and then "spin off" writing about that subject in multiple genres for
multiple purposes—public, personal, and academic. In Jolliffe's experience, students' writing improves significantly over the course because
they gain expertise and a fund of knowledge about their subject of
inquiry. In a meta-analytical way, class sessions can focus on the relationship between acquired knowledge and writing or communicating
about that knowledge. Meanwhile, students constantly work on their
projects in class, explore aspects of language, writing, and literacy,
and teach each other about what they are learning, both orally and
through the forum. Continued, online presentations provide students

with further information about multiple genres, the rhetorical dimensions of writing, and writing processes.

As an educator, I have always had great faith that when students are intrinsically motivated, they usually do their best work (Bain). For this reason, I avoid making decisions on all the parameters of students' projects, narrowing their choices of topics, or creating lockstep procedures that do not allow them to use their own best ways of working. Students are coached to produce text about their inquiry projects and to brainstorm new sources of information, including interviews, academic sources, or materials in the public discourse. As they work, students must produce writing in various genres for various rhetorical and pragmatic purposes and, together with all the artifacts of their work, place these materials into a digital inquiry portfolio. During one week, a student might write an editorial about his or her language-related topic for publication in the newspaper, while another student might work on an informative booklet about a reading-related issue to be disseminated to parents in a public school district. Theories of intrinsic motivation support a view of purposeful discourse arising from felt needs and interests. Instead of adding constraints about the types and purposes for writing, the course simply requires that students write a certain amount of polished text in a range of distinct genres, include a reflective introduction to the portfolio, and that they not roam beyond the main thematic focus of the course.

FEEDING BACK

Teachers' response to students' writing comes most often in the form of evaluative comments on final papers. However, much research in the field has shown that constructive, reader-based response during the drafting process can lead students to make substantive revisions that improve a text and help them learn strategies more effectively than final evaluations (Anson; Nystrand). In this course, however, the role of response in revision gets an overt focus as part of the actual course coverage. Students learn about research on response: they read drafts, consider videotapes or transcripts of student response groups, look at revised texts for evidence of where the response worked or failed, and provide frequent response on each other's emerging texts. Digital media also play a role here: Both I and the students provide response using video screen-capture programs to demonstrate some of the ways that digital media are changing the nature of reading, writing, and communication.

Clearly, there is much going on in this proposed course. Students learn about writing and literacy as uniquely human phenomena. They reflect on their own development of these capacities, and gain metacognitive strategies for coping with new writing situations. They think about the role of language and literacy as socially determined practices. They engage in the demanding processes of composing based on personal experience, the experiences of others gained through interviews, and formal investigations on a language-related topic of their choice. They are exposed to new media. They develop skills for working collaboratively. They learn how to manage differences in the language register by moving along a continuum from casual forum writing, to explanatory or persuasive public writing, and to academic, research-based writing. Although this may seem almost too robust a plan for a semester-long course, it also leaves much out. For example, a more deliberate focus on academic genres of writing in different disciplines is not covered. The idea is to not just help students develop "skills" of writing, but to make them far more aware of the complex nature of writing and other forms of communication so that they can meet with greater insight and energy those experiences they will have as they move into, across, and beyond the academic curriculum.

WORKS CITED

Alexander, Kara Poe. "Successes, Victims, and Prodigies: 'Master' and 'Little' Cultural Narratives in the Literacy Narrative Genre." *College Composition and Communication* 64.2 (2011): 608–33. Print.

Anson, Chris M. (Ed.) *Writing and Response: Theory, Practice, and Research.* Urbana: NCTE, 1989. Print.

Anson, Chris M., and Richard Beach. *Journals in the Classroom: Writing to Learn.* Norwood: Christopher-Gordon, 1995. Print.

Anson, Chris M., and Laurie L. Forsberg. "Moving Beyond the Academic Community: Transitional Stages in Professional Writing." *Written Communication* 7 (1990): 200–31. Print.

Bain, Ken. *What the Best College Students Do.* Cambridge: Harvard UP, 2012. Print.

Beach, Richard, and Chris M. Anson. "Using Dialogue Journals to Foster Response." *Exploring Texts: The Role of Discussion and Writing in the Teaching and Learning of Literature.* Ed. George E. Newell and Russell Durst. Norwood: Christopher-Gordon, 1993. 191–210. Print.

Bransford, John D., and Marcia K. Johnson. "Contextual Prerequisites for Understanding: Some Investigations of Comprehension and Recall." *Journal of Verbal Learning and Verbal Behavior* 11 (1972): 717–26. Print.

Brookfield, Stephen D., and Stephen Preskill. *Discussion as a Way of Teaching: Tools and Techniques for a Democratic Classrooms.* 2nd ed. San Francisco: Wiley, 2005. Print.

Council of Writing Program Administrators. WPA Statement of Outcomes for First-Year Composition, 2008. Web. 12 Oct. 2012.

Daniel, Beth. "Narratives of Literacy: Connecting Composition to Culture." *College Composition and Communication* 50.3 (1999): 393–410. Print.

Downs, Douglas, and Elizabeth Wardle. "Teaching about Writing, Righting Misconceptions: (Re)Envisioning 'First-Year Composition' as 'Introduction to Writing Studies.'" *College Composition and Communication* 58.4 (2007): 552–84. Print.

Educause. "Seven Things You Should Know About Flipped Classrooms," 2012. Web. 12 Oct. 2012.

Elbow, Peter. *Vernacular Eloquence: What Speech Can Bring to Writing.* New York: Oxford UP, 2012. Print.

Framework for Success in Postsecondary Writing. Council of Writing Program Administrators, National Council of Teachers of English, and National Writing Project, 2011. Print.

Howard, Rebecca Moore, Tanya K. Rodrigue, and Tricia C. Serviss. "Writing from Sources, Writing from Sentences." *Writing and Pedagogy* 2.2 (2010): 177–92. Print.

Jolliffe, David A. *Inquiry and Genre: Writing to Learn in College.* Boston: Allyn and Bacon, 1998. Print.

Jonassen, David. "Objectivism versus Constructivism: Do We Need a New Philosophical Paradigm?" *Educational Technology Research and Development* 39.3 (1991): 5–14. Print.

Lindemann, Erika. "Freshman Composition: No Place for Literature." *College English* 55.3 (1993): 311–16. Print.

Macrorie, Ken. *The I-Search Paper.* Portsmouth: Heinemann, 1988. Print.

Nystrand, Martin. "Dialogic Discourse Analysis of Revision in Response Groups." *Discourse Studies in Composition.* Ed. Ellen Barton and Gail Stygall. Cresskill: Hampton, 2002. 377–92. Print.

Prince, Michael. "Does Active Learning Work? A Review of the Research." *Journal of Engineering Education* 93.3 (2004): 223–31. Print.

Russell, David. "Activity Theory and Its Implications for Writing Instruction." *Reconceiving Writing, Rethinking Writing Instruction.* Ed. Joseph Petraglia. Hillsdale: Erlbaum, 1995. 51–78. Print.

Appendix: Course Syllabus

WRITING, LANGUAGE, AND LITERACY

Course Overview

What this course is about:

Think about it. Your eyes are passing over a bunch of oddly-shaped symbols—not really much different from these: é " β α ξ φ ¢ < ∞. But the symbols you're reading add up to something and *make sense* to you—with *your* help, they create pictures and concepts and ideas in your mind. And those same symbols allow me, the person putting them together, to communicate my thoughts to you—thoughts that do something, such as welcoming you to this course and giving you information about what we'll do in the next 16 weeks. If you wish, you can also read the symbols out loud and give them the sounds of speech, turning them back into something just as complex, something deep in our bones as a species: an ability to move our vocal apparatus, create odd sounds, and make the same pictures and concepts and ideas in each other's minds.

On a basic level, you've been using these systems for most of your life, through formal schooling, through family educational practices, through work-related experiences, and through daily routines. At a higher level, your experiences have created beliefs in you about the role of writing, language, and literacy in your development, in your plans for your life and career, and in a society that demands these literate abilities and uses them to establish criteria for your success. In a course that focuses on *writing, language, and literacy,* reading those very words calls into play many beliefs you have about our class system, economic and political structures, educational institutions, cultures, and media.

In this course, we'll focus on how you can become a better communicator and thinker, mainly through the manipulation of those little symbols (alone or in conjunction with other communicative media). But that's not all. We'll also focus on the *nature* of written and other forms of communication—how we use them, what we use them for, how they vary in different settings, and how you can learn to "read" those practices as you move across the communicative landscape.

Some of our work will ask you to dig deeply into your own history to mine experiences you've had, and habits you've formed, as you've learned to write, read, and communicate with others. You'll also reach outward and begin analyzing how literacy functions for others, and you'll investigate some aspect of literacy that will bring you to a higher level of awareness of its range and diversity. Think of the course, then, not just as helping you know *how* to do something better, but as helping you to know much more *about* it as well, so that you can figure out how to perform effectively in all sorts of settings.

Outcomes guiding our work:

This course has several important learning outcomes that have structured its design. By the end of the course, you should be able to:

- explain the nature, history, and functions of literacy as a set of complex human activities;
- explain the differences between spoken and written communication and the primacy of the former;
- critically reflect on your own development of written literacy and the way your community uses oral communication, and do so for others;
- apply the course material to specific situations in literacy development, e.g., at home, in schools, in workplaces, and at community organizations;
- articulate the relationships among literacy, culture, social class, education, and politics;
- read, write, speak, communicate digitally, and work with information sources with greater proficiency and with sensitivity to the expectations of different communities.

To gauge how well you think we are accomplishing our outcomes at midterm, take the Anonymous Midterm Course Evaluation (this link will be live at midterm).

What you need:

- All readings will be available in full-text online (linked in the assignment schedule) or through the library's electronic reserves (ER in assignment schedule).
- Depending on your choice of an interview subject for the second project, you may need a mode of transportation for the interview.

- A few dollars (or your own printer and supplies) to print copies for peer-revision sessions and other text sharing; some of this can be done free online.

How we'll spend our time:

Our class meetings will be highly active and participatory. I will spend only a minimal amount of time presenting information to you; instead, you'll view online presentations that provide background on, and explanations of, the readings and various topics we cover in the course. The class sessions will depend on what you glean from the presentations, so please watch them fully, take notes, and think about their content. After each presentation, there will be an informal assignment, usually to be posted to your forum group. Don't try to do these assignments before watching the presentations.

Class sessions will include small-group work and follow-up (reporting your group's discussions to the class); large-group discussion using various formats that encourage everyone to participate; brief writing episodes; small-group revision sessions; group poster creation and gallery walks; brief, individual presentations; a *pecha kucha* presentation at the end of the course; and all sorts of activities. The success of the sessions will depend on your contributions. This is not the kind of course in which you can remain passive or uninvolved.

What you need to do:

- Come to class and participate actively.
- Prepare for sessions by viewing the online presentations or other media and taking notes; doing the readings; engaging in any assigned activities; and posting to the forum.
- Draft and revise a literacy autobiography (see guidelines).
- Draft and revise a literacy biography involving interviews with a subject (see guidelines).
- Create a portfolio of written products based on a sustained exploration of a specific topic relating to language, writing, and literacy (see guidelines).
- During the last week of class, do a *pecha kucha* presentation to share material related to your inquiry project (see guidelines).

How you'll be evaluated:

The course is graded on a point system, with 100 maximum points. The points are tied to the 0–100 grading scale (i.e., 85 points = B, 92 points = A-, and so on). You earn points up to the maximum value of each project or assignment, and these are added to your total score. For example, the first two papers are worth 20 points each; a paper scoring 15 points is roughly equivalent to a C+. Be sure to study the evaluative criteria for each assignment. Here are the more specific requirements:

- Forum postings: Postings to your group's forum will help you to reflect thoughtfully on the course readings and online presentations, give and get feedback on the course projects, and carry on a dialogue with the other members of your group. More information about the forum is included at the assignments page. Reflections are assigned in the daily syllabus; some are "open" reflections (you choose the focus), and others will ask you to respond to specific questions, mini-cases, readings, or items in the news. You will post your reflections to the forum set up for your group. Your reflections should refer to other students' reflections whenever relevant. In this way, your posts will alternate between personal reflection and dialogue with others about your own or their reflections. The forum is designed to be relatively informal, so you won't be expected to write highly elegant, polished entries; however, some attention to structure, readability, and proofreading will be expected. Most importantly, however, it will be read for the insightfulness of your observations and reflections (see separate description and samples at the assignments page). While entries can be loose, exploratory, and tentative, they should connect with the issues we'll be exploring about writing, language, and literacy. All your forum entries are worth 15 points in your final grade. You will receive three assessments of your contributions, at around 1/3 and 2/3 of the way through the course and at the end.

- Literacy autobiography and biography: These papers will be more formal and stylized than your reflections. The papers will be several pages long, carefully focused, thoroughly revised, and thoughtfully written. The objective of the papers is to help you to explore your own literacy history and experience (the first paper) and those of someone else (the second paper) as a way to more richly understand your attitudes and beliefs about writing, language, and literacy, and to find a context for some of the ideas we'll be exploring in the course. Each paper is worth 20 points. See the separate information describing the nature and criteria for each short paper at the assignments page, as well as the annotated samples there. An option is available to create digital papers, especially if you have certain artifacts from your literacy development or artifacts, or video clips and other materials for the second paper that would be effectively presented in digital form.

- Investigative project and portfolio: Over the rest of the course, you will choose a specific question about language, writing, and literacy to investigate. (We will spend considerable time in class brainstorming and refining your question.) As you explore your question and develop expertise in the area you've chosen, you will write at least three texts, of different kinds, for your portfolio. Each text will need a clearly defined purpose and audience. For example, your explorations might lead you to advocate for something, and you could write an editorial convincing general readers to take a claim or idea seriously. Or you could write a full-length, reference-based entry for Wikipedia. We will also spend considerable time in class considering the kinds of texts you might produce, and how you can learn about the standards or expectations for those kinds of texts (how they're structured, what kind of style they're written in, what role you play in them as a writer, and so on). For each text you produce, you'll write a parallel reflective paper explaining these standards and the evidence for them, and how your own paper reflects your attempt to meet those standards. At the end of the course, you'll give a *pecha kucha* presentation on your project. This is a 5-minute presentation in which you create 15 PowerPoint slides that will advance automatically every 20 seconds, so you will need to be highly focused and *thoroughly* rehearsed. We'll look at some *pecha kucha* presentations in class and discuss what can make them effective. They're a chance to be creative and hone your presentational skills.
- Participation: Your active participation in the course is assumed, so that when I determine your final grade, I'll take this into account. Participation includes attending class (see

attendance policy), speaking regularly in class, actively engaging in small-group or paired work, and being ready for class (e.g., doing the assigned reading, watching the online presentations, or doing low-stakes writing). In cases where you have not participated up to the standard, your grade may lose one plus or minus category (e.g., a B could turn to a B minus). I also use participation to determine borderline final grades (for example, strong participation could boost you to the higher of two borderline grades, such as an A instead of an A-).

General Topic Areas

The first 3 weeks of the course will focus on the experience of gaining literacy and culminate in a literacy autobiography. The next 3 weeks will focus on spoken language and its variations, and culminate in your literacy biography (of another person). The remainder of the course will focus on a range of topics in the area of writing, language, and literacy, especially what we know about writing, how it develops, how it varies across contexts, and how you can learn to analyze those contexts. During this time, you'll conduct your investigation, sharing your ongoing expertise with the class. You will write at least three different papers, for specific purposes and contexts, about your investigation, and these will go into a project portfolio along with some reflective writing.

Week 1: Ice breaker: who are we? Introduction to the course. What are "language, writing, and literacy"? The role of language and literacy in our lives. Sample literacy autobiographies.

Week 2: Online presentations: the nature and history of literacy. Classwork: literacy experiences and autobiographies: what we can learn about language, writing, and literacy from others' accounts.

Week 3: Online presentations: the nature of writing and how it develops. Classwork: focus on your own writing processes as you create your literacy autobiography. Literacy autobiography due.

Week 4: Online presentations: Reading: how it works, how it develops, and what we know about it. Classwork: experimenting with reading phenomena.

Week 5: Online presentations: the nature of speaking; dialect variation and the sociology of language. Classwork: exploring our hidden values about speaking and oral language variation.

Week 6: Online presentations: how speaking and writing work together. Classwork: using your interview data to create your literacy biography. Literacy biography due.

Week 7:   Online presentations: a social view of literacy, part one: the varied nature of writing across different professional and academic communities. Classwork: choosing and litmus-testing a focus for your project.

Week 8: Break

Week 9: Online presentations: social views of literacies, part two: blind literacies, deaf literacies; how the concept of literacy is bound up with our values, prejudices, and feelings about others. Classwork: producing and sharing written artifacts.

Week 10: Online presentations: what's a "genre" and what does it mean to learn one? The concept of "transfer" across contexts. Classwork: developing your first written artifact.

Week 11: Online presentations: what are "grammar" and "correctness" and how are they socially constructed? Classwork: producing and sharing written artifacts.

Week 12: Online presentations: the role of technology in literacy, part one. Classwork: producing and sharing written artifacts.

Week 13: Online presentations: the role of technology in literacy, part two. Classwork: producing and sharing written artifacts.

Week 14: Online presenations: information literacy. Classwork: preparing the portfolio.

Week 15: *Pecha kucha* presentations.

Week 16: *Pecha kucha* presentations. Portfolio due.

2 ESL Composition as a Literate Art of the Contact Zone

Suresh Canagarajah

How do we design an English as a Second Language (ESL) composition course that situates language and writing in the contact zone? Traditionally, students (largely from international backgrounds) have been expected to orientate to the norms of "native speakers" of English in their writing. ESL students are expected to develop proficiency in a variety of the English normative in native speaker communities, or the version of it labeled "Standard Written English" (SWE) in writing contexts. These students are considered to be alien to English, and the English varieties they do bring are considered to be unsuitable for formal academic purposes. In matters of writing conventions, these students are considered strangers to the genres, knowledge traditions, and voice treated as normative in American universities. The genres of writing in their communities are considered formulaic, when American universities require rhetorical sophistication and creativity. The knowledge traditions they bring are considered too personal or conformist to serve them well in writing that requires criticality and reason. They are perceived to be disinterested in voice, when American universities require individuality. Not only are these students considered strangers to these expectations, they are also considered to be so influenced by their community norms that they will find it difficult to make the transition to the expectations of American colleges. Though I generalize these assumptions considerably, the pedagogical practices of even well-meaning teachers are often influenced by variations of such assumptions that are meant to remedy what these students lack. An orientation to ESL writing as a contact zone activity requires a reconsideration of these assumptions and practices.

A contact zones orientation first involves treating the identities of these students differently. We must consider these students as not *ESL* but *multilingual*. The acronym *ESL* treats those who speak English as their first language as the frame of reference in assessing the proficiency of the students who speak English as a second language. The label connotes that ESL students are trying to (or should try to) approximate the norms of native speakers. However, multilingual life in the contact zone does not enable us to easily enumerate people's language proficiencies (as first, second, or third). People shuttle in and out of languages, freely borrowing semiotic resources for their communicative purposes and developing equal proficiency in all of them, as relevant for their purposes. Besides, a contact zone orientation makes us treat languages as always in contact, as borrowing from and influenced by each other, often in ways that are not easy to distinguish. Adopting the term *multilingual* would make us perceive ESL students as expanding their repertoires rather than adding something that is missing in their language proficiency. From this point of view, a contact zone writing course is not remedial. In fact, English is often one of the languages international and minority students possess as part of their language repertoire. This realization motivates us to look at these students as already bringing some awareness of English, or at least as bringing multilingual proficiencies that enable them to appropriate English in ways that they have already acquired with many other languages. More importantly, a contact zone perspective redefines our goal as not preparing these students for conformity with American norms, but to critically renegotiate English for contact purposes. Such a competence focuses on communicating in contexts where there are multiple norms of English, appropriating dominant norms according to one's own purposes and values, and even bringing together competing norms for voice—a capacity that is beginning to be called *translingual* (Horner et al.; Canagarajah, "Codemeshing"). While a translingual competence is manifested in different types of written products from both native and non-native speakers, a particularly creative type of hybrid written product is *codemeshing* (Young; Canagarajah, "The Place"). While current pedagogical wisdom holds that students' own varieties may be kept for home, informal, or social uses, while SWE is adopted for formal classroom purposes, codemeshing brings together one's repertoires within a single text for voice. In such texts, writers strategically

better connotation [handwritten marginal note]

laminate their diverse Englishes within the dominant framework of SWE norms to develop a hybrid text that features diverse codes.

The contact zone perspective has other implications for the activity of writing, beyond language concerns. It involves perceiving genres as not already defined according to the norms of specific communities, but as taking new shape in relation to intercultural contact. The genres of the contact zone are therefore not static or homogeneous; rather, they are always kept open to change and reconstruction. This applies to academic genres as well. They take different realizations according to the communities and contexts involved in the writing activity. While students must recognize that there are always dominant norms related to academic genres, they must also remember that those norms can be strategically negotiated in relation to their personal agendas and values. The same applies to knowledge. Though the academy has its definitions of what counts as "scholarly," knowledge is constructed in the contact zones of the personal and the scholarly, the practical and the theoretical, not to mention in various disciplinary boundaries and community traditions. Established scholarly discourses in the academy often occlude the mediation of the diverse factors that go into their production. Multilingual students must realize that the knowledge represented in their writing must be negotiated in relation to the intellectual traditions meeting in the contact zone.

Therefore, a contact zone writing pedagogy treats languages, genres, and knowledge as always contested, but also as taking new shape in relation to the rhetorical objectives and interests of the people involved. While recognizing the reality of power behind established rules in different contexts, contact zone pedagogy also inculcates faith in the negotiability of norms. I describe below how my course is designed to encourage shuttling among languages, genres, and knowledge traditions to develop a translingual writing competence.

WRITING ACTIVITY

The genre I ask students to focus on for this course is itself a hybrid. It permits a range of realizations. It can be rendered as a straight-forward, personal narrative on one end, or as a reflexive and well researched academic article on the other. It is called a *literacy autobiography* in its former version, and *autoethnography* in the latter. Furthermore, it can accommodate different voices and rhetorics within the body of the same text. The genre accommodates the personal and the objective, narrative and argumentation, community discourses and academic constructs. The writing process engages students in activities that are part of academic literacy—such as gathering literacy artifacts, interviewing others for information, documenting one's experiences, reading scholarly publications, and data analysis—as students move their first-person narratives to an autoethnography. The trajectory also takes them through shorter texts that use a diversity of rhetorical modes, including description, comparison, cause/effect, and argumentation. The process of transforming personal experience into an autoethnography develops the language awareness and rhetorical sensitivity needed to engage with the hybrid and layered genres one encounters in the contact zones inside and outside the academy.

This writing activity is also designed to generate a reflexive awareness of students' own literacy backgrounds. In reflecting on their multilingual, literate lives, students analyze the tensions between different language norms and literate practices, their strategies in negotiating them, their efforts for voice, and their trajectories of development. The exercise helps students value their experiences and learn from them. Autoethnographies also often show me that multilingual students are developing valuable skills and strategies for negotiating competing languages and literacies in contact zones outside the classroom (Canagarajah, "Codemeshing"). Teachers should tap into these experiences to develop more reflective and critical writing competencies in the classroom. The writing project also helps students learn from the literacy trajectories of their peers, conduct more reflective analyses of their experiences, and engage in a grounded theorization of language and literacy. More importantly, in traveling between their personal experiences, writing about them, and reading research articles, students will develop a reflective and critical awareness of literacy.

In moving towards the final product—a twelve to fifteen page autoethnography—students also write various, shorter drafts. They start with simple and short narratives that describe their early literacy experiences. As they go further, their drafts parallel the chapters in Chang's *Autoethnography as Method*, a text that orientates readers to the theory, methodology, and rhetoric of autoethnography. After situating autoethnography within different forms of narrative research, Chang leads readers through the processes of gathering literacy artifacts as data, generating memory details, interviewing other sources for information, and storing and analyzing data. Drafts follow the stages of tapping into diverse sources in order to elicit details and experiences from one's literacy trajectory. In the process, students also engage in different genres of writing: comparison, cause/effect analysis, argumentation, description, and narrative. Through these shorter projects, students will discover their thesis for a final product.

Though some might consider this a very demanding genre for multilingual students, it is also a safe genre in many ways. No one is handicapped by this exercise. Every student has a story to share about his or her literacy background. The personal nature of this exercise also makes each person the authority in this writing. It is their story, one only they know best. The final product can be rendered in more complex terms, if one has the motivation and aptitude. Textual complexity can also develop slowly through the process of writing, as students engage in the shorter projects. At the end of the course, different levels of achievement will be seen. However, it is important for teachers to provide spaces for the motivations and possibilities of students at different levels. What is important is that the project enables every student to submit a product, of whatever level of complexity.

READING

In addition to the book by Chang, the second important text for the course is *Rotten English*, by Dora Ahmad. This book brings together creative writing, personal reflections, autobiographical narratives, and semi-scholarly discussions on the ways English is negotiated in the social life of multilinguals. Poems by writers like Louise Bennett, and short stories by those like Grace Patrick, show the ways multilinguals confidently use local varieties of English for expression. Excerpts from novels by Ken Sara-Wiwo and Gautam Malkani show the ways English is mixed with urban dialects in fascinating forms of codemeshing. These confident and dazzling uses of English motivate students to consider how SWE can be appropriated for their purposes, or merged with their repertoires for voice.

The short essays in the book will also encourage students to critically reflect on the attitudes of other multilingual writers toward using English. We start with excerpts from Thomas Macaulay's *Minutes*, revealing the colonial motivations for introducing English in other lands. We then move on to consider personal reflections by those like

Chinua Achebe and Amy Tan on the tensions English generates as they struggle to represent their community experiences. We move on to more strident criticisms by those like Kamau Brathwaite, who expresses a need to resist alien values, and seeks local inspiration for a voice in English. We conclude with an essay from Gabriel Okara that calls for experimentation with a hybrid English that represents local experiences, and an essay from Gloria Anzaldua that enacts such an alternative in a codemeshed text. These essays display a range of responses to using English by multilinguals, and will generate endless debates on the best strategy for voice. More importantly, they acquaint students with linguistic and textual options they can themselves try out in their writing. In fact, some of the texts in this reading, such as those by Tan and Anzaldua, can themselves be considered autoethnographies, and can therefore serve as models for student writing.

An important source of reading in the course is our own writing. Very early in the course, I provide a published example of my own literacy autobiography. Though literacy autobiographies written by better known scholars are available, there is a purpose in prescribing the instructor's own writing. Students have the option of seeing me, another multilingual, as struggling with competing language norms and literacies to develop a hybrid practice for voice. I have heard from past students that this essay has given them confidence that their own multilingual experiences are worthy of being rendered in writing, and perhaps even being published. The essay also motivates students to tap into their experiences for reflection and analysis. Classroom discussion of the essay has generated personal questions that dig deeper into my experiences, probing for the rationale of my writing choices.

In the same vein, students also read one another's drafts throughout the course. This exercise makes their writing purposeful and meaningful. Students become aware that they are writing to a supportive and interested audience. We become a community of practice, involved in a common project, and benefitting from mutual help, learning, and practice.

PEDAGOGICAL PRACTICE

The course is designed to be practice-based: Students learn about writing primarily by writing. Other classroom activities, such as idea generating, research, peer review, and serial revision, also teach students important practices in the writing process. The course is also collaborative. Students interact with each other and with the instructor to interpret readings, help each other in doing research and in collecting data, comment on each other's essays, and revise and edit their writing together.

The electronic instructional system (*Angel*, in my university) helps tremendously in a practice-based and collaborative pedagogy. Each student has a folder into which he or she posts drafts, journal entries, and other coursework. Their peers and I will also post comments on the student's drafts directly into his or her own folder. This arrangement helps in many ways: Everyone always has access to the various artifacts in the course. The folder also provides a record for students on how their own and others' writing is developing. Additionally, students can examine the ways in which their ideas and writings are taking shape, thus serving as a portfolio of their work during the semester and helping them to reflect on their own development. Students often reflexively comment on materials in their folders in weekly journal entries.

The electronic instructional system also enables the class to have online discussions that complement in-class discussions. This medium makes the interpreting texts more participatory, and students build on each other's interpretations to negotiate a consensus on their reading. There is also much sharing of different perspectives and opinions that sometimes lead to debates and arguments that further help in negotiating the meaning of a reading or writing.

In all this, the course is highly interactive. It encourages students to engage with each other to develop interpretations of texts, shape their own written texts, assess their work, and generate ideas and opinions. There are important pedagogical functions behind such practice. Students learn that meaning is co-constructed. They must collaborate to develop a shared understanding of the texts they read and write. Research findings suggest that it is in this manner that communication works and succeeds in multilingual contact zones (Canagarajah, "Lingua Franca English"). Interlocutors do not frame their texts and talk in relation to norms exterior to their interaction; instead, they focus primarily on constructing meaning with each other in relation to the norms they bring to the interaction. Meaning, in this sense, is situational, social, and collaborative. Since there are diverse norms for languages, genres, and literacies in the contact zone, interlocutors must negotiate them situationally for texts and for talk that make sense to each other. This does not mean that multilinguals are insensitive to dominant norms and ideologies of correctness in society. Instead, they consider these norms as open to negotiation, especially in relation to their interests and values. Though this practice is risky, mutilinguals assume that success depends on their creativity and agency to renegotiate dominant norms in their favor. My pedagogical environment provides a space where such attitudes and orientations multilingual students bring from contact zones outside the classroom can be put into practice.

Students also learn that written products are shaped socially and contextually. Not only do they generate ideas collaboratively, in relation to what others think and write, but they also shape the structure, organization, and genre conventions in relation to the uptake of others. Though students may initially come with some strong preferences on what to write, they renegotiate their products in relation to the preferences and suggestions of their peers and the instructor. The text emerges out of the contact between these different expectations and values. The final product may not conform to a rigid notion of genre or the textual conventions of any one community, but it may take a shape that is appropriate to the rhetorical objectives, audience expectations, and authorial interests in that contact zone.

The interactions and responses of the students are not always homogeneous or predictable in these classroom negotiations. They are as diverse as the communities and social backgrounds from which the students come. It is not uncommon for multilingual students to express the dominant ideologies of literacy and language norms, as they have been influenced by socially powerful discourses to treat writing according to established models. Reviewing classroom transcripts of interactions and electronic communications, I have noted how I myself straddle an instructor's voice that favors established norms and that of a multilingual researcher's persona that favors creativity and appropriation. These conflicting responses are important to acknowledge. Contact zone writing occurs in contexts marked by power differences and inequalities. It also occurs in a context of diverse norms that participants bring to an interaction. These tensions of the contact zone have to be negotiated by readers and writers for voice. Successful communication calls for strategic and judicious negotiation of these conflicting norms, according to one's own interests and values.

COURSE EXPECTATIONS

What kind of final product do I expect from this course? Though the syllabus does not say that a codemeshed essay is required, some students produce essays that mesh different varieties of English. As they engage with essays that theorize the possibility of hybrid codes, and with creative writing that performs such codemeshing in the Dora collection, some students gradually become comfortable with meshing codes. Furthermore, their own reflections on their multilingual lives, and increased appreciation for voice in literacy, lead writers to experiment with appropriations of SWE. Often, drafts that initially approximate SWE norms progress to bring in qualified uses of their vernaculars. In some sense, these literacy narratives require such a codemeshing for rhetorical effectiveness. When writers discuss the ways they negotiate their multilingual repertoires and literacies, using SWE uncritically sounds contradictory. Therefore, the writing project itself inspires many students to codemesh.

However, not all students perform codemeshing in their final products. Some students display a reverse trajectory: They start with various forms of codemeshing and proceed to approximate SWE norms. In such essays, what I look for is a critical and creative use of this language variety. The notion of translingual practice focuses more on the language awareness and metalinguistic competence that enables students to negotiate diverse semiotic resources for their own interests and voices, and not on a fixed type of textual product. In fact, SWE itself is not a monolithic variety; it is a social construct that accommodates diverse language resources. SWE is also a hybrid. It can be made to accommodate new registers and discourses. The repertoires of the students therefore have a bearing on their use of SWE. It is possible that some sentence structures and idiomatic expressions may sound atypical. However, I look for the rhetorical appropriateness of that usage in that context, and try to discern the author's design in doing so. Whether students codemesh or approximate SWE, my focus is on developing a critical awareness of the different linguistic and literate traditions students draw from for their writing.

As it should be evident, the course does not aim toward mastery of the conventional, five-paragraph essay with an obligatory thesis statement, topic sentences, and error-free prose. It is difficult for any one-semester course to accomplish as much. My syllabus states the following about what students should expect from the course:

This course will orientate you to the basic processes and practices of academic writing in English. Though you may not
be able to write perfectly structured essays in language free
of errors at the end of this course, you will have developed a
good understanding of the *writing process*, *language awareness*,
and *rhetorical sensitivity* that you will need to keep developing
your proficiency as you continue your education in the university. Spending the whole semester on mastering one type of
essay and language is unwise, as you will find that genres and
registers change in different academic fields and contexts of
writing. The processes this course develops will help you deal
with any type of writing product you encounter and expand
your writing repertoire for different contexts.

The course, therefore, focuses on the following three aspects:

- *Writing process*: A familiarity with the stages of generating
  ideas, outlining the draft, collaborating with peers and the instructor on drafting and revising your text, and treating *writing as an ongoing collaborative project.*
- *Language awareness*: An understanding of appropriate language
  for different contexts, the ways language norms are changing,
  strategies to represent diverse identities in language.

- *Rhetorical sensitivity*: An orientation to effective writing style
  and structure for different contexts, in relation to the diverse
  expectations of one's audience.

I make clear to my students my rationale for adopting this approach. Since the written products that are expected in their fields
of study and in diverse social domains are always heterogeneous, it is
unwise to spend the first semester of writing mastering certain, fixed
norms or forms. I also do not think that there are certain codes or
literacies that can be treated as generic or foundational to prepare students for the communicative challenges they will face later. What is
generative and foundational are the underlying practices—i.e., writing process, language awareness, and rhetorical sensitivity—that the
course focuses on. I make this clear in the syllabus when I articulate
the philosophy behind the course:

The philosophy motivating this course is that writing occurs in the *contact zone*. The idea is that we write and communicate in a context where many languages, cultures, and knowledge traditions meet. Rather than imposing one way of using language or writing, the course aims to teach you how to engage with the diverse norms of the contact zone to construct effective texts. This metaphor of contact zones applies to ESL college writing in many ways. As ESL students, you are bringing language and rhetorical skills that will meet the norms of an American university. Rather than treating one norm (either yours or the university's) as the sole option, you will negotiate both for creative alternatives. The college is itself a contact zone of diverse academic fields and intellectual traditions, with related styles of communication. In addition to this diversity, there are also changes underway in writing, English language, literacy, and communication in the context of globalization and technology. The writing processes, language awareness, and rhetorical sensitivity that this course focuses on prepare you for such diversity in college English writing.

ASSESSMENT

The variable nature of the written products generated by this course might create some difficult challenges for assessment. However, since the focus of the course is not on products, but on linguistic/literate/rhetorical awareness, I grade students on process as well as product.

Process refers to many things in relation to assessment. It refers, for example, to the extent to which students involve themselves in the writing process. Their commitment to outlining, serial drafting, revising, and editing are reflective of such engagement. Their involvement in the collaborative process of writing can be judged on their engagement in reading peers' drafts and by offering constructive feedback. Such involvement also shapes reflections in their journals. The extent to which they engage with their experiences of past literacies and present projects, and develop their perspectives in a sustained manner in their drafts, also demonstrates their engagement in process. Process also relates to the ways in which students negotiate meanings and interpretations of course texts (including peer writing) in collaboration with others.

In assessing process, I hope to gauge the three metacognitive strengths I strive to develop through this course: writing process, language awareness, and rhetorical sensitivity. The grade for process is subjective but fair to the level of involvement students individually display. I grade them along the following three categories: Good, Satisfactory, and Unsatisfactory. I also give periodic feedback to students to indicate where they stand in relation to these categories in their course participation.

The letter grade for the final product conveys to students that metacognitive skills have implications for constructing text. The written product matters. However, I do not look only for formal correctness. Beyond proficiency, I look for aptitude—the promise students display for future text construction in their trajectory of development. There are also rhetorical considerations that outweigh grammatical correctness. We must consider the extent to which the chosen organization and structure of an essay suits the author's objectives, the way the author's voice finds expression in the essay, the confidence and creativity with which the author negotiates competing norms, and the ability to develop a thematically focused text. I also keep in mind that sometimes norms have to be violated for performative reasons, as considerations of voice or expressive purpose often demand renegotiating norms.

All this is not to say that norms are to be ignored. An understanding of SWE and its place in academic writing cannot be overlooked. The power of SWE is impressed upon students through various means in the course, including published texts that use SWE, scholarly essays that discuss their importance, comments from the instructor and peers that (often unconsciously) assume it as the norm for evaluation. More important is for students to engage critically and creatively with SWE. This calls for negotiation. One has to merge his or her desired codes in a qualified way, in relation to dominant norms. A use of one's repertoires without considering the dominant norms will sound naïve and fail to display rhetorical sensitivity or language awareness. Besides, the objective of the course is repertoire-building for contact zones, and SWE is an important part of one's repertoire.

Even when students use hybrid codes that are informed by their local languages, vernacular Englishes, and personal repertoires, instructors should consider such factors as intention, appropriateness, and control in assessing such usage. It can be very difficult to define *error* in hybrid and creative language usage. Is deviating from SWE a sign of creativity, or lack of proficiency? There is text-internal and writer-specific evidence that helps us answer this question. I consider the following questions when I encounter deviations from SWE: (1) Is there evidence that the author is using this feature with awareness? (i.e., If the usages seems contradictory or inconsistent in the same text or in the writer's other drafts, one can assume that it is a mistake or error.); (2) Is the usage rhetorically effective? (i.e., What does the unconventional usage add to the text?). Answering these two questions also shows the writer's level of control over the medium. The language awareness of the writer becomes evident in the extent to which he or she uses language that is rhetorically motivated and textually designed. Not all deviations from SWE are meaningful or grammatical. Not everything goes in the contact zone.

CONCLUSION

There are many questions that might arise on the appropriateness of such a practice-based and collaborative pedagogy of translingual writing for first-year, ESL students. Many instructors assume that ESL students have such low proficiency in the English language that it is idealistic to address issues of voice with them. Even well-intentioned teachers often assume that a course for such students should focus on "the basics." "The basics," for ESL students, is often interpreted as grammatical competence. Therefore, in many institutions, entire first-year ESL courses are focused on teaching basic grammar. This is a pedagogy of deficiency; it underestimates the ability of multilingual students. We must remember that these students often come with advanced metalinguistic competencies that are derived from socialization in contact zones and shuttling between languages. They have the aptitude to develop competence in additional languages. Furthermore, the global status of English for contact purposes means that many students already come with considerable exposure to the language. Rather than thinking that we have to start building competence from scratch, we have to consider how we can build on the strengths and resources multilingual students bring with them. Moreover, issues of voice are not irrelevant for novice writers. Some models of language and literacy acquisition theorize that any learning is entwined with identity development (Norton). They are not separable. The possibility of forming empowering identities motivates students to appropriate a language with agency.

Expecting codemeshed uses of English or hybrid literacies may also be considered by some instructors to be too idealistic for first-year ESL students. Many prefer to have students write short paragraphs, culminating in five-paragraph essays in SWE. Well-intentioned teachers may argue that we can teach codemeshing only after SWE has been mastered. In other words, codemeshing and hybrid literacies might be considered as possible only for advanced writers. However, research in multilingual communities shows that language contact and mixing is the norm for these communities (Canagarajah, "Lingua Franca English"). Notions of standardization, language separation, and linguistic purity are the exceptions. Besides, multilingual students already come with rich traditions of codemeshing. What I have found in beginning-level ESL classes is that students already bring with them a repertoire of Englishes from social media sites and from popular culture. They are already codemeshing, and what they need is rhetorical awareness about what extent of meshing goes where and when. In other words, codemeshing is not a new skill, and does not need to be taught. What needs to be taught is the extent and type of codemeshing that is acceptable in academic settings.

There are also concerns about how such classroom literacies relate to the dominant norms of larger educational and social institutions. By encouraging multilingual students to use English creatively for voice, are we preparing them for failure and stigmatization in educational and social institutions that value privileged forms of English? Contact zone literacies does not mean that students do not develop an awareness of dominant norms. As they shuttle among different varieties of English, students are also developing a keen sensitivity to divergent norms in different social contexts. In other words, my pedagogy is not disinterested in developing an awareness of and a competence for privileged norms. It expects students to go beyond a passive and mechanical use of norms, and to engage in creative appropriations of them. As students engage in translingual practices, they are shuttling in and out of codes and developing a metalinguistic awareness of what is contextually appropriate.

Therefore, the course goes beyond developing competence in only one mode of writing or tradition of literacy. While recognizing dominant norms for various institutional contexts, the course aims to develop competencies for the relativity of norms in global contact zones. As students receive conflicting feedback, read texts with different norms, and compose serial drafts for slightly different rhetorical objectives, they are also developing a rhetorical awareness of what codes are appropriate in what settings. A student who composes only one form of text all the time (even though admirably hybrid) has a poor repertoire. More versatile students recognize and develop competencies for shifting norms in response to the context. The course aims to develop the language awareness needed to recognize fluid contexts and norms, and to perform accordingly.

Is this pedagogical goal eventually helpful for social and educational mobility for mutlilingual students? My assumption is that appropriating texts and codes from one's own perspective gives one a critical edge. It also develops a language awareness and rhetorical sensitivity that helps students engage with the diverse texts, genres, and knowledge they will encounter in global contact zones. Success today requires dealing with unpredictable, changing, and relative norms of language and literacy. It is possible that some students may not succeed in the short term to produce the stereotypical language and literate artifacts expected in some academic contexts; however, in the long run, developing more subtle writing processes, language awareness, and rhetorical sensitivity helps them go far. Moreover, we must prepare students to take risks in contact zones. In fact, all writing is risky. Writing involves making rhetorical and linguistic decisions that are controversial and subjective, relative to one's contextual constraints and rhetorical objectives. While we sometimes miscalculate our strategies and/or face unimaginative audiences who do not measure up to our expectations, in others we find that our risk-taking is richly rewarded. Preparing students for these variable responses and rewards in global context zones is part of the training my collaborative and practice-based writing pedagogy provides. Assuring them success if they master a monolithic product is to lead them up the garden path.

WORKS CITED

Ahmad, Dohra, ed. *Rotten English: A Literary Anthology.* New York: Norton, 2007. Print.

Canagarajah, A. Suresh. "Codemeshing in Academic Writing: Identifying Teachable Strategies of Translanguaging." *Modern Language Journal* 95.3 (2011): 401–17. Print.

—. "Lingua Franca English, Multilingual Communities, and Language Acquisition." *Modern Language Journal* 91.5 (2007): 921–37. Print.

—. "The Fortunate Traveler: Shuttling between Communities and Literacies by Economy Class." *Reflections on Multiliterate Lives*. Ed. Diane Belcher and Ulla Connor. Clevedon: Multilingual Matters, 2001. 23–37. Print.

—. "The Place of World Englishes in Composition: Pluralization Continued." *College Composition and Communication* 57.4 (2006): 586–619. Print.

Chang, Heewon. *Autoethnography as Method*. Walnut Creek: Left Coast, 2008. Print.

Horner, Bruce, Min-Zhan Lu, Jacqueline Jones Royster, and John Trimbur. "Language Difference in Writing: Toward a Translingual Approach." *College English* 73.3 (2011): 303–21. Print.

Norton, Bonny. *Identity and Language Learning*. London: Pearson, 2000. Print.

Young, Vershawn. "Your Average Nigga." *College Composition and Communication* 55.4 (2004): 693–715. Print.

Appendix: Course Syllabus

FIRST YEAR ESL COMPOSITION: WRITING
AT THE CONTACT ZONE

This course will orientate you to the basic processes and practices of academic writing in English. Though you may not be able to write perfectly structured essays in language free of errors at the end of this course, you will have developed a good understanding of the writing process, language awareness, and rhetorical sensitivity that you will need to keep developing your proficiency as you continue your education in the university. Spending the whole semester on mastering one type of essay and language is unwise, as you will find that genres and registers change in different academic fields and contexts of writing. The processes this course develops will help you deal with any type of writing product you encounter and expand your writing repertoire for different contexts.

The course therefore focuses on the following three aspects:

- Writing process: a familiarity with the stages of generating ideas, outlining the draft, collaborating with peers and the instructor on drafting and revising your text, and treating writing as an ongoing collaborative project.
- Language awareness: an understanding of appropriate language for different contexts, the ways language norms are changing, strategies to represent diverse identities in language.
- Rhetorical sensitivity: an orientation to effective writing style and structure for different contexts, in relation to the diverse expectations of one's audience.

The philosophy motivating this course is that writing occurs in the *contact zone.* The idea is that we write and communicate in a context where many languages, cultures, and knowledge traditions meet. Rather than imposing one way of using language or writing, the course aims to teach you how to engage with the diverse norms of the contact zone to construct effective texts. This metaphor of contact zones applies to ESL college writing in many ways. As ESL students, you are bringing language and rhetorical skills that will meet the norms of an American university. Rather than treating one norm (either yours or the university's) as the sole option, you will negotiate both for creative alternatives. The college is itself a contact zone of diverse academic fields and intellectual traditions, with related styles of communication. In addition to this diversity, there are also changes underway in writing, English language, literacy, and communication in the context of globalization and technology. The writing processes, language awareness, and rhetorical sensitivity that this course focuses on prepare you for such diversity in college English writing.

REQUIRED TEXTS

Ahmad, Dohra, ed. *Rotten English: A Literary Anthology.* New York: Norton, 2007.
Chang, Heewon. *Autoethnography as Method.* Walnut Creek: Left Coast, 2008.

SUPPLEMENTARY MATERIAL

Additional essays will be posted online (in *Angel*) in the folder titled "Supplementary Material" as relevant to the themes and tasks that emerge in the course. The following materials are already posted in that folder:

- Canagarajah, A. Suresh. "The Fortunate Traveler: Shuttling between Communities and Literacies by Economy Class." In Belcher and Connor, eds., *Reflections on Multiliterate Lives.* Clevedon: Multilingual Matters, 2001. 23–37.
- Questionnaire for literacy autobiography: Belcher, Diane, and Ulla Connor, eds. *Reflections on Multiliterate Lives.* Clevedon: Multilingual Matters, 2001. pp. 209–211

COURSE REQUIREMENTS

The main writing requirement is a literacy autobiography. This requires writing about the development of your literacy skills in the languages of your proficiency. This is a very fluid genre, taking different shapes according to your interests and abilities. At its simplest, this is a personal narrative on your language and literacy development. At a more advanced level, it takes the form of an autoethnograpy, a genre valued by researchers and scholars. To satisfy the requirements of this genre, you are encouraged to do disciplined research to collect data relating to your development and document literacy artifacts. You will also read research articles that relate to your themes and may help you further analyze and interpret your personal experiences. These components will make this genre of writing very hybrid. It can merge narrative and argumentation, the personal and the academic. In other words, this genre ranges from a simple first-person narrative at one level to a well-researched autoethnography at the other end, allowing you to approximate whichever level based on your motivations and interests.

We will do several short writing assignments that will help you develop your literacy autobiography and then turn it into an auto-ethnography. We will also read and analyze several model narratives, including mine (see Canagarajah in the supplementary reading), to give examples of this genre. We will read an accessible book, *Autoethnography as Method,* to learn more about the academic version of this writing. The chapters in this book will walk you through the research and analysis that will strengthen your narrative.

The second required text for the course is *Rotten English.* The readings from this book will help your writing project and language awareness in many ways. The book features different genres of writing: essays, autobiographies, poems, and fiction. These texts are written by multilingual and second language writers like you. They present diverse views on the role of English in multilingual communities in different points of their history; models of writing by multiliguals who use English creatively to represent their identities; narratives on the role of English in the lives of multilinguals from different lands; and debates on different attitudes and orientations to English in multi-lingual communities. The selections scheduled for each class meeting have to be read before you come to the class.

The course is computer-assisted. You will find on *Angel* a folder with your name, where you will post your assigned work. Your peers and I will have access to your folder. We will comment on your drafts periodically. The web based instructional system will allow us to con-duct online discussions; share our journals; post our drafts, data, and activities; and communicate with each other on writing collaboration, classroom management, and other course issues.

Scheduled writing assignments have to be posted into your folder before the class meeting. You will find my comments in your folder before the following class meeting. In addition to writing your own drafts, you will periodically review the drafts of your peers and post your comments into their folders.

An important requirement is maintaining a weekly journal. You may comment on your reflections on the writing projects, reading assignments, or research activity. Post your journal entry into your folder. Note that your peers and I will read and comment on your entries periodically.

GRADING

Drafts: 35%
Journal: 10%
Research Activity: 10%
Peer Review: 10%
Final Submission of Literacy Autobiography: 35%

The drafts, journal, research activity, and peer review will be graded as Good, Satisfactory, and Unsatisfactory. You will receive feedback that will indicate how you are faring. The final submission will have a letter grade. The grade will be based on thematic focus, appropriate organization, effectiveness of style, and care in editing.

SCHEDULE

Week 1: Introductions;
         Reading: Canagarajah, "Fortunate Traveler" essay
         Writing: Answer questionnaire from Belcher and Connor
         on your literacy development
         Activity: Share questionnaire with peer and interview him/
         her on additional matters of interest
Week 2: Reading: Macaulay excerpt (Ahmad, p.469); Chang, Ch.1
         Writing: Draft 1: My feelings about English writing; out
         line and paragraph
         Activity: Exchange paragraph with peer and suggest
         improvements
Week 3: Reading: Achebe essay (Ahmad, p.425); Chang. Ch. 2
         Writing: Draft 2: Revision of Paragraph
         Activity: Edit revised version of peer
Week 4: Reading: Tan essay (Ahmad, p.502); Chang, Ch. 3

Writing: Draft 3: Attitudes to English and home language: A comparison essay

Activity: Small group discussion of drafts

Week 5: Reading: Grace (Ahmad, p.165); Chang, Ch. 4.

Writing: Draft 4: Revision of "Attitude to English and home language"

Activity: Peer critique and editing of draft 4

Week 6: Reading: Bennett (Ahmad, p.37); Kasaipwalova (Ahmad, p.202); Chang, Ch. 5

Writing: Draft 5: Most striking memory of earliest writing in English

Activity: Collecting Personal Memory Data; send summary of your findings to folder

Week 7: Reading: Brathwaite essay (Ahmad, p.458); Brathwaite poem (Ahmad, p.42)

Writing: Draft 6: Revision of "Most striking memory"

Activity: Peer critique of draft 5; identify and start reading at least three published articles that relate to your literacy experiences

Week 8: Reading: Lovelace (Ahmad, p.214); Chang, Ch. 6

Writing: Draft 7: Explaining my attitudes: A cause/effect essay

Activity: Collecting Self Reflective Data; send summary of findings to folder

Week 9: Reading: McKay (Ahmad, p.82); Keens-Douglas (Ahmad, p.68); Chang, Ch. 7

Writing: Draft 8: Revising "Explaining"; send annotations of articles to folder

Activity: Collecting external data; send summary of findings to folder

Week 10: Reading: Johnson (Ahmad, p.64); Mutabaruka (Ahmad, p.85); Chang, Ch. 8

Writing: Outlining literacy autoethnography

Activity: Review of peer's outline; read summary of peer's research results and help find a thesis for his/her literacy narrative

Week 11: Reading: Malkani (Ahmad, p.348); Mistry (Ahmad, p.232); Chang. Ch. 9

Writing: Draft 9: First draft of literacy autoethnography

Activity: Managing data; read draft of peer and provide comments for improvement

Week 12: Reading: Okara essay (Ahmad, p.475); Chang, Ch. 10
Writing: Draft 9: continuation
Activity: Analyzing and interpreting data; peer critique of partner's draft

Week 13: Reading: Anzaldua essay (Ahmad, p.437)
Writing: Draft 10: Revision of literacy autoethnography
Activity: Review peer's draft

Week 14: Reading: Iweala (Ahmad, p.330); Saro-Wiwa (Ahmad, p. 390)
Writing: Second revision of literacy autoethnography
Activity: Editing your peer's draft

Week 15: Reading: Chosen student essays for general class discussion
Writing: Final edits and submission of final draft of literacy autoethnography

3 Occasions, Sources, and Strategies

Douglas Hesse

How might writers locate themselves in relation to the welter of texts and text-making practices extant these days? That's the framing question for my first-year writing course, "Occasions, Sources, and Strategies."

Devising a single-semester course is clearly more vexed now than it was even twenty years ago. The rise of genre theory and research, the sophistication with which we have rendered "academic discourse," the explosion of the "civic sphere" due to digital culture, the ubiquity of new composing tools and modalities, the economic pressures and social forces that increasingly transform education from a social to a personal good: all these have accreted on "old rhetoric" and "old composition" theories of discourse and pedagogy. Taxonomies have multiplied, fractured, and recombined since the 1980s: from Donovan and McClelland's *Eight Approaches*; to Berlin's four; to Tate, Rupiper, and Schick's dozen; to Fulkerson's analysis of them all. It is not only that the practitioners' house of lore has added new rooms; it's that the whole neighborhood of theory and research has experienced a wild, building splurge in which little gets torn down (though some becomes seedier) and zoning laws are scant—or, in the case of the WPA Outcomes Statement, so prolix that they resist development in a single course. Five questions, then, influenced my drafting of this course:

1. Should the course focus on one general "domain" of writing and, if so, which? Consider four broad domains of writing, each defensible as the focus of a first-year course: academic writing (i.e., the genres of the academy, with a particular emphasis on an ostensible but vexed common denominator of thesis and support), civic writing (i.e., writing to influence opinions and decisions in public realms), vocational writing (i.e., the genres used to transact work in business and professional settings), and aesthetic writing (i.e., writing to create engaging artifacts, from memoirs to poems to literary essays). I figured that deep knowledge and skills in any one of these domains would be elusive, but that a fifteen-week course had a better shot at one than does a course that aspires to all.

Still, there is the problem of representing the selected area. (My money was on civic discourse.) One solution, of course, would be to make the relationships among these four areas the subject of the course, much like that venerable *Four Worlds of Writing* textbook. The challenge, though, is that there are so many differences between and overlaps among these four worlds. Emphasizing rhetoric as the basis of the course promises one common denominator as a solution.

2. What, then, should be the role of rhetoric? Focusing on how a few rhetorical principles are enacted in different writing situations allows students to see how different plausible texts result. Sure, there's some challenge in deciding on whose rhetoric (Aristotle's or Kenneth Burke's?) though it is vital to stick with a few features rather than to have the course rehearse theoretical debates. In the end, I privilege audience, kairos, and delivery. a time lapse — moment where everything happens

3. What should be the ratio of analyzing texts to producing them? Of course, writing a rhetorical analysis, a stylistic analysis, an X-ist analysis of any text produces something, so the binary deconstructs itself. The distinction I make here is between writing done "in the service of a text," laying out its strategies or interpretations, and writing done "to implement a strategy or to address a rhetorical situation." It's the distinction between having students complete rhetorical analyses of photographs or websites and having students make their own photographs or websites. It's the distinction between having students characterize the ethos of a given text and having students construct an ethos in a text of their own making. A cycle of analysis and imitation often characterizes this pedagogy. In any course building conceptual knowledge, analysis is attractive because it promises direct proof that students grasp concepts. When discourse community theory ascended twenty-five years ago, for example, heuristics like James Porter's forum analysis lent themselves to assignment-making; but, to have students only analyze puts them in thrall to other texts and raises questions about transfer: Might analysis without production parallel the problematic relationship between students completing grammar drills and being able (or unable) to avoid error in their own writing? A more subtle issue is affective: Do students perceive performance or analysis as more engaging or authentic?

4. *The analysis or performance of what?* Should texts consist of words only, arrayed in sentences and paragraphs (for example), or should texts consist only of images (still or moving, sound or silent), or of hybrid variants? If the course is fussily constrained as a writing course and only a writing course, possibilities diminish, though there remains a broad swath between sonnets and court decisions. With the recovery and reconceptualization of "composition," words alone seem a meager constraint, one increasingly out of step with how texts are created, circulated, and experienced. Admitting a plurality means apportioning course attention and settling a sequence—hardly a new challenge, since even the venerable modes of discourse require deciding whether each mode gets exactly two weeks.

5. *Theme or not?* Not long ago, writing about literature was a popular scourge of writing courses. One argument against the practice was that the kinds of writing assigned in such courses (generally varieties of literary analysis and interpretation) did not transfer to other writing situations. The larger argument, though, was that "writing about literature" courses inevitably and inexorably became "about" the texts being read and about literariness—not "about" student writing and its development, as Erika Lindemann and others have explained. Poems, plays, and stories were attentional black holes. These days, "literature" has been replaced by "theme," with course goals enacted through a subject matter advertised to would-be students and teaching peers. The recent roots of this practice are in epistemic rhetorics, especially as encapsulated by Bartholomae and Petrosky's *Ways of Reading* pedagogy. The question, "What should students write about?" is far more venerable. In 1935, for example, John Crowe Ransom's textbook noted that the whole problem of freshman English lies in the improvisation of subject matter. The most recent permutation of thematic foregrounding is Elizabeth Wardle and Doug Downs's composition studies as a course focus. As with writing about literature, theme carries the threat that student writing and its development will be eclipsed by topical knowledge. Still, most writers are steeped in a subject matter for a good chunk of their work. So, to ignore content altogether is to ignore how practicing writers really write.

MAJOR GOALS AND OBJECTIVES

The course translates my analyses of the previous five questions into four goals:

1. Students will understand possible reasons why any given piece of writing exists, especially where it came from. Most college students write (and to large extent, read) because someone has obliged them to. For them, certain kinds of writing exist largely because they've been assigned to write. The same applies to a fair amount of reading. Now, students also write because they want to, but these forms differ from school writings: they are text messages, social networking posts, and occasional "creative" works. To be sure, students read works they don't have to, generally things recommended (or linked) through social networks, both physical and virtual. Occasionally, these obliged and self-sponsored worlds of writing merge; but, for most students, there is a mysterious mix of texts that sail under the flag of writing—from psychology textbooks and research papers to Dave Eggers and *The Onion*. A first-year writing class that fails to map the larger writing terrain and locate the course against it, then, risks confusion or contempt. Academic discourse, for example, looks little like the kinds of texts students encounter outside of school. A works cited or references page? Really? Literary non-fiction may seem attractive to some, but is highly impractical to others, especially since it's not a kind of writing they encounter in most classes or expect on a job.

For those reasons, one course goal is to create an understanding in students that text "comes from" different places. Texts exist for multiple, overlapping reasons, certainly. So, for the purpose of this course, I focus on two heuristic poles. Does the writer expect readers to recognize a text as a turn in an ongoing conversation, as a response to a situation? Or, does the writer have to "make a way" for the text, broaching a new and not necessarily expected topic? Of course, most writings that do more than reply to direct questions carry some burden of creating reader attention; and, of course, no writing exists unattached from previous discourse. The main challenge for students, however, is in seeing the ratios of given to new text and in understanding the strategies available when writers assume or command attention (as in tax return instructions), versus those available when writers must create attention.

2. Students will understand how writings are made of different source materials, with some source materials meeting some rhetorical situations better than others. Consider the bi-polar way in which most undergraduates understand "research." On the one hand, research means finding and synthesizing published texts, sometimes in the service of an argument, but just as often in the anatomy of a topic. On the other hand, research means scientists gathering and analyzing data. Since the latter is often beyond the purview of first-year courses, their research papers are primarily the former, leaving a mysterious gap between "real" research as students perceive it, and the dummy runs they're assigned.

Of course, "real research" is possible, even if not the kind that requires Bunsen burners or time on the Hubble telescope. I'm referring to the empirical work of systematically collecting data. How is education portrayed, directly or indirectly, in the top twenty television sitcoms today? Do men and women post different kinds of pictures on social networking sites? (Could a system be devised for coding Facebook photographs by certain subject matters and types, then apply that system to, say, two hundred images, and then report any findings?) What was the main advice about writing students can recall from high school? (Could a survey be created, results pooled, and an interpretation written?) Most handbooks have an obligatory section on "primary" research.

In addition to textual and empirical sources, my students use two kinds of experience, experience they bring to the course and experience they create during the course, to provide them with writing occasions. "Lived experience" is life as it happens, and only later is it perceived as grist for writing. Most obviously the stuff of memoir, autobiography, and personal essays, lived experiences also contain television shows and movies watched, books read, conversations overheard, and so on. These last materials may show up not as the extended narrative of memoir, but in service of other ideas, from the opening gambit of many *New York Times Book Review* pieces to the essayistic flourishes that get writers and readers from one topic to another.

The second I call "created experience": doing something or being somewhere specifically for the purpose of writing. If one looks *back* on lived experience from the *act* of writing, one looks *forward* to created experience through the *prospect* of writing. This is the stuff of journalism, from a brief interview to an extended immersion in a place, from attending an event (a concert, a demonstration, a meeting, a hearing) to hanging out in a place (a shop, a café, a factory, a school)—in each case the purpose is to gather first-hand subject matter. Created experience is also the domain of ethnography, where writers devise sustained observations with the ultimate purpose of interpreting the situation or dynamic they enact.

So, the course has students consider four sources of material for writing: reading, empirical research, lived experience, and created experience. Each source could be further factored and delineated, but four is enough.

3. Students will understand that the context of publication determines many characteristics of a text. This goal contains dimensions of rhetorical situation, the familiar knowledge that successful writers shape texts according to their readers' knowledge and beliefs, to their purposes for writing, and to the nature of the subject matter at hand. The goal further encompasses considerations of genre, albeit at some broad levels of, say, features of academic discourses versus popular discourses. Finally, and most significantly, the goal includes the medium and mode for which a text is produced. For example, what are the affordances and constraints of popular pieces composed to be read online by self-sponsoring readers, versus pieces composed to be read in print by scholars? Even as print scholarship increasingly is read online, what, in fact, is the design palette available to writers, and how can they use it?

4. Students will perform Goals 1–3 in their own writing. This goal has two important aspects. One is to bend the previous three into performance. That is, the earlier goals foreground understanding: students developing knowledge about writing. Goal 4 makes clear that this knowledge is instrumental, and is to be put to use in students' own texts. Second, the goal emphasizes strategies. Experienced writers have considerable craft knowledge, knacks, and techniques they can use not only for invention, but also for shaping, everything from how to synthesize sources to how to design pictures into pages of text. Some of that craft knowledge can be taught, practiced, and learned, and this goal obliges the professor to teach it.

COURSE STRUCTURE

I have organized the course into four main sections. The first two, each several weeks long, parallel each other. During the first chunk of the course, students complete a series of writings and exercises on a common focus (in this case, "introversion"). Then, students complete similar writings during the second chunk, only this time on a subject of their own choosing. During the third phase of the course, students re-purpose an earlier writing (according to audience, genre, or mode) and pursue an entirely original (to them, at least) topic. During the last section, students select and revise pieces for a portfolio.

I imagine a fifteen-week, four-credit course that meets twice a week. In such courses, I customarily expect students to spend about ten to twelve hours per week outside of class on reading and writing, though this will vary. I also presume that students have a laptop and wireless access in class, which is standard and required where I teach. I realize that is unrealistic at many schools, so some of my in-class activities would be adjusted for such those situations. The course is supported by a course management system (Blackboard, in my case), through which I collect and respond to student writings (using Word's comment feature) and share readings, including other student writings as readings.

The first part of the course uses the topic of introversion and extroversion to focus analysis and writing. The specific topic isn't crucial: What does matter is that the topic be current; be treated widely in academic and an array of popular settings, in various modes; and has numerous points of entry for students, including a likely personal connection. I've found it useful to have one substantial text to center this part of the course. Recently, I have used Dalton Conley's *The Elsewhere Society* and Farhad Manjoo's *True Enough: Learning to Live in a Post-Fact Society*. For this course, I've chosen Susan Cain's *Quiet: The Power of Introverts in a World that Can't Stop Talking*. The main advantage of having a common theme, at least for a while, is that by holding subject matter fairly constant, we can focus on different manifestations of that subject matter, including different genres, audiences, source materials, and so on. By controlling the variable of content, we can experimentally manipulate and throw into relief other variables.

Certainly, the course could exploit a single topic the entire term, and I have done so in the past. However, there are two reasons that compel me to change things up. First, students often feel they exhaust a topic after a few weeks; never mind that professors can trod narrow subject corridors for careers, first-year students are not professors.

Second, shifting the topical terrain reminds everyone that the course focuses on writing and that the subject matter is only a vehicle.

During the second phase of the course, students choose another contemporary issue, one that meets the criteria of the initial common one. I'm happy that students choose their own topics; but, given the pace of the course, I don't want them to dither or choose poorly. Therefore, I propose a default list of issues and focalizing texts. Again, I emphasize a current topic, and as I draft this chapter, my list might include Michelle Alexander's *The New Jim Crow*, Daniel Kahneman's *Thinking Fast and Slow*, Eric Klinenberg's *Going Solo: The Extraordinary Rise and Surprising Appeal of Living Alone*, Charles Murray's *Coming Apart*, and Katherine S. Newman's *The Accordion Family: Boomerang Kids, Anxious Parents, and the Private Toll of Global Competition*.

Given that writers learn by writing, and given that there is lots to learn, in the third phase of the course I assign numerous, short assignments rather than a few long ones. I have taught courses in which students write four or five papers in multiple drafts, and I grant the wisdom (and convenience) of this venerable process pedagogy. In this course, however, students submit at least one piece of writing most class meetings, and most of these writings are one to three pages. My response takes the following form: "If you were going to revise and develop this piece, you should consider . . . ." Because process instruction happens mostly "between" tasks rather than "within" them, portions of class meetings function as studio time.

The fourth phase of the course focuses on revision, as students prepare work for a final portfolio by selecting and revising a few pieces into showcase works that are often considerably longer than their initial versions. Each student selects a piece for a fifteen-minute class workshop, attends one fifteen-minute office consultation, and has a voucher for written comments on one draft. Beyond reading and responding to classmates' works in progress, students have no new assignments or readings in this phase.

The final, important element of the course is a set of readings about writing principles and strategies. These are short chapters and related materials that I've written over the years, partly as class handouts (and later, PDFs offered online), and partly as versions of the *Simon and Schuster Handbook for Writers*, which I've co-authored in recent editions. The titles of these materials are available in my syllabus. These readings become the basis of short lessons and exercises, some of them done in class.

ASSIGNMENTS

The following are out-of-class assignments for the course. Because of space limitations, I have omitted many in-class exercises, and I have shortened the wording of these assignments—though not hugely, as I prefer brief assignments—written for students.

1. Common Topic, Diverse Texts. I'm going to give you four texts to consider. List all the possible features these texts have in common. List all the possible ways these texts differ from one another. (As you make these two lists, you may find yourself thinking "these two are like each other, but not like those other two"; or "this text is very different from the other three;" or so on. That's fine.) After you've made your lists, which I'll want you to share and to hand in, select two differences that you think are most important or interesting. Spend thirty minutes writing, trying to help us understand the differences. Further, you can speculate why they differ. For example, is there something about the audience, purpose, place of publication, or writer's identity that accounts for the differences?

2. Your Stake in This Topic. Would you characterize yourself as an introvert or as an extrovert? Please write a page or two in which you help us understand your answer to that question. Your explanation will be clearer if you search recent experiences for a scene or event that illustrates your introversion or extroversion, and then carefully describe and analyze that scene or event. (If you reject such a stark self-label, choose a couple of situations that show your perspectives and write about them.)

3. A Class Bibliography. We need to build a class bibliography. Identify six different writings that deal with introversion in some meaningful way. Choose your writings from four different databases: a Google search, Academic Search Complete, PsychInfo, and the "Notes" section of Cain's book. Identify writings that differ in type (for example, short web page versus long article, or an article directed at an amateur audience versus one directed at an expert audience). You don't need six completely different types, but strive for a range. For each source, write an annotated bibliography that has three parts.

1. A citation in MLA form.
2. A one or two sentence summary of the content.
3. A one or two sentence characterization of the type of source.

*4. **Making Our Own Data**.* Step 1: I've created a SurveyMonkey version of Susan Cain's introversion quiz on pages 13–14. Please complete the quiz. Step 2: Here are the findings from the class introversion quiz. What sense do you make of those findings? We'll discuss this in class, so bring some notes.

*5. **Presenting Modest Findings**.* Write a one-page paper that presents your findings from #4, and explains one interesting finding or implication of the findings. Think of this second element as answering the question, "So what?"

oh, y'd so

*6. **Synthesizing Data: An Exercise in Three Audiences**.* Let's imagine the following situation: Before our class has met for the first time, you've gained access to the class survey findings and to all of the writings that your classmates did for step 1 in Assignment #4 above. As a helpful and thoughtful person, you want to synthesize these findings. What are members of this class like? Are there any trends? What might be the significance of that information: Why might knowing this matter? Keeping this situation in mind, I'd like you to do three different pieces of writing.

1. Write a short text message or email to a friend about your findings in no more than fifty words.
2. Write an email to me about your findings in no more than one hundred words.
3. Write a two or three-page report in which you present these findings and advise me, as your professor, what I should do with that information. For example, how might I use class time, make assignments, respond to drafts, or so on?

*7. **Reader Response**.* Reflect on the reading you've done so far in Cain. What is one aspect of this reading that you find interesting or thought-provoking? Why? Write at least a page. What is one aspect of this reading about which you or someone else might be skeptical or uncertain? Write at least a page.

8. A Writer Repurposing. Here's a link to a TED Talk that Susan Cain delivered in February. Although Cain draws upon the same material as in her book, she obviously makes a lot of changes. Write a page in which you explain both what she chose to present, how she chose to present it, and more importantly, why she might have made the choices she did.

9. Extending a Topic. Cain's book was published in early 2012; however, she likely completed its writing no later than early fall of 2011. Considerable time has passed since then. Write a short article (around five pages) in which you extend—or critique—the ideas in *Quiet*. To do this, you'll need to develop some new material, so use one or a combination of several sources: your own experience (after all, Cain uses hers); selected interviews you conduct; observations of introversion versus extroversion as you see them on display in popular sites, like television shows, music, films, self-help books, and so on; and current scholarship on personality type or introversion—sources she did not consider.

10. Repurposing: Text to Presentation. Return to the writing you did for #9. Create a two-minute presentation, using one or two images or slides. You'll make your presentation during the next class.

11. Information for Decision Making. For the next phase of the course, you will spend five weeks writing about a different topic, one of your own choosing. You'll be doing many tasks that are similar to those you did previously by circling back in order to reinforce skills and strategies. Because you'll be working some time with Topic B (as I'll generically call it), you'll want to make an informed choice; to help this process, I will have the class preview six books. I'll assign you and two others to read the opening chapters of a particular book. Your task will be to introduce this book to your classmates. This writing should accomplish two things. First, it needs to give a sense of what the book is about—its topic, approach, source materials, style, and so on. Second, you need to give readers a sense of what is promising or interesting about it. What kinds of questions or projects might this topic support? Why is this book important or interesting to a group of first-year students, to college students in general, or to American society at the present time? Think of your purpose, then, as to inform and entice.

12. Choosing Topic B. Decide on your topic for the next few weeks of writing, and write one page that explains why you want to pursue that topic. Why, for example, do you see that topic as more important than others? What is your personal connection to it? Why does it matter to you? What do you expect to learn from writing about that topic? If you choose the same book you previewed for the rest of the class, that's fine. Still complete the one-page writing, but, additionally, write a paragraph that explains what would be your second choice, if your first was unavailable. (Don't fret; you won't be compelled to do something with the second choice, though I may use this information to set up response groups, etc.)

Alternative: If none of these six books and topics is sufficiently engaging, you may propose your own; however, that will require some extra work on your part. You'll need to identify a current book (something published in the past year) on your topic, and you'll need to do the preview assignment. Finally, you'll need to write a paragraph that convinces me that your new topic is worthy for the class. This might sound like I'm making you jump through hoops, but my main concern is that you don't disadvantage yourself by choosing a focus that ultimately will not work very well.

13. Once More to Text Types. Follow the same directions you did for #1, only this time you'll need to identify your own four texts for analysis. (See the directions for #3 to help you find appropriate sources; obviously, use your own Topic B book and use a database other than PsychInfo, if it makes more sense.)

14. Academic to Popular. Identify a current, scholarly article related to Topic B. Write two short pieces intended for different readerships. In one piece, write about the article for a popular blog in a way that really tries to "sell" it; make the article seem exciting or important, and use whatever strategies are useful, short of outright lying. In another piece, write about the article for an "intellectual" blog in a way that more cautiously conveys its content. You'll want people to think that the article is worth their while to read, but you'll want to be measured about it.

15. Extending Topic B. The book you've been using as your base work for Topic B was published in early 2012; however, its author completed the writing no later than early fall 2011. Considerable time has passed since then. Write a short article (around five pages) in which you extend—or critique—the ideas in your book. To do this, you'll need to develop some new material, so use one or a combination of several sources: your own experience; selected interviews you conduct; observations of the topic as you see them on display in popular sites, like television shows, music, films, self-help books, and so on; and current scholarship—sources that your author didn't consider. Write for the same audience that read your book for Topic B.

16. Your Choice. What is a current topic or cultural phenomenon that interests you? Perhaps you know something about it, but would like to learn more. Here is your chance to guide readers' attention on a topic that engages you. You'll need to report and discuss some "new" (at least, to your readers) information, so use one or a combination of several sources: your own experience; selected interviews you conduct; observations gleaned from popular media, like television, music, film, self-help books, etc.; and current scholarship. Write a short article (around five pages) aimed at a thoughtful popular audience.

17. Repurposing Once More. Look back on the writings you've done in the course so far. Choose one to repurpose. By that I mean substantially revise the original work so that it reaches a different audience, revise the work into a different genre, or create it for a different medium. For example, turn a traditional paper into a web page, a newsletter, a PowerPoint (a good PowerPoint), a podcast, or a video. Take something written for an academic audience or for a popular audience and flip it. When you turn in your repurposed work, please also include a commentary on what you did and why.

18. Portfolio. Select and revise two to six pieces of your writing in this course to include in a final course portfolio. Your goal is to show your strengths as a writer able to produce different kinds of work. Your portfolio should consist of fifteen to twenty pages of writing. Beyond selecting and revising, please do one more thing: Write an introduction to your portfolio. This introduction should explain the works that follow (what your purpose and audience was for each), should comment thoroughly on how the pieces demonstrate your mastery of the course goals, and will likely need to be two to four pages long. One additional element will enhance your introduction: If you had more time to work on this portfolio, what additional revisions would you make, and why?

CLASS TIME

During any given class time, I tend to use two or three different modes of activity, depending on the project at hand, the needs of the students, and the phase of the semester. The following is a basic menu of five ways I spend class time, followed by an example of two class meetings in a typical week.

Focused Studio/Problem Solving. Students have a brief amount of time to perform a particular task, followed by some sharing of results (in pairs, groups, or the whole class), followed by a discussion of issues raised during the process and, perhaps, my comments on a couple of particularly effective solutions. Generally, focused studio time is preceded by a presentation or by discussion of a technique or concept. For example:

- Here's a quotation and a fact: (1) "We see little use for the 'brilliant' introvert" (Alfred Whitney Griswold, President of Yale in 1950, quoted in Cain, 28). (2) One-third to one-half of Americans are introverts (Cain 3). Write a paragraph that makes use of both pieces, employing one or more of the techniques we have studied.
- You're the afternoon editor of the *Denver Post Online*, and you've come across this article in an academic journal. You think readers will find it interesting—but not in its present form. Write a new opening designed to attract *Post* readers.
- A current textbook describes vocal and energetic leadership as essential to effective management. Imagine that you are Susan Cain. Write a paragraph in which you assess this statement.
- In the course's Blackboard site, you'll find a file that has two photographs and three chunks of writing. Using those materials (but revising them as you see fit), compose a one-page (or shorter) handout in which you present the most effective message you can.

Open Studio Time. Students work on a project that they are either continuing or starting. I circulate the room for short conferences. Students ask questions of me or one another, but if they have none, I pull up a chair for quick conversation, asking, "What are you up to, and how is it going?"

Presentation/Application/Demonstration. This element is closest to lec-turing. I use my best teaching to review a concept or strategy I asked them to read about before class, or to introduce a concept or strategy they will read about afterwards. Illustrations or demonstrations are key. For example:

- Here's a page from the article that Cain cites on page 73. Let's explore how she incorporates that material into her own text. For example, look at this . . . .
- Let me show you how changing a few words and revising some sentences dramatically changes the voice of this passage.
- We've just talked about warrants in Toulmin's approach to analyzing arguments. What do you see as the warrants in this section?

The movement from concept into application or demonstration is also Socratic, as I ask students to identify a strategy in a passage or to create an example using a technique.

Discussion. When everyone in class has read a selection, we spend sev-eral minutes talking about what it means and how we respond to it. Do people like, agree, or connect the selection to something else? Who disagrees with it? If the piece is accurate or true, what are its implica-tions? This kind of discussion differs from analytic discussions of how a piece works. When people say, "We had a great discussion today," they are often pointing to this sort of conversation. I tend to spend less class time in this mode than in others, usually to create interest or to invent ideas for a subsequent writing.

Class Invention or Revising. In this type of class activity, I ask students some of the following: "How might you start this assignment?" or "What are your first thoughts?" Questions like these frequently initi-ate a few minutes' discussion of a particular homework writing task; the point is raising some possible starting places and common ideas so that students do not leave class paralyzed or clueless. The flip side is to bring in some promising drafts or passages and ask the class to gen-erate some ideas for revising it (or sometimes doing a revision them-selves, as a form of focused studio/problem solving). This activity can happen as a full class or in small groups.

RESPONSE AND EVALUATION

I read and respond to everything that students write, though the scope of my response differs in relation to the scope of the task (e.g., a short, in-class writing versus a longer piece drafted over a week). Students turn in work via BlackBoard, and I use the comments feature in Microsoft Word to point out strengths, make revision suggestions, and share my ideas or questions. I write an end comment (or in some cases, a head comment), and I usually include a short rubric that I've tailored to individual assignments so that students can "see how they did" in the way that, alas, often seems most meaningful to them. I find Word's Track Changes feature really cumbersome for editing purposes. Students have difficulty seeing their original text and my edits at the same time, so I often print a page or two, hand-edit, and then scan the result into a .pdf or .jpg file. In any event, I do not edit every page to avoid diminishing returns.

As for the overall course grade, the final portfolio counts most: 40%. It allows students to take risks during the course, but also rewards students who take seriously the previous exercises and papers leading up to that point. I reserve 20% of the grade for in-class activities, both contributions to class discussions and performances on class problems and challenges. (I have developed a guide for evaluating class contributions that works pretty effectively.) Three significant papers in the course count for a total of 20% of the final grade, and all other out-of-class writings count 20%.

CONCLUSION: WHAT'S ABSENT AND WHY

Among the familiar foci explicitly missing from the course I've sketched include: a systematic rhetorical vocabulary (e.g., logos, ethos, pathos, etc.); systematic process knowledge (e.g., invention, drafting, revision); formalist knowledge associated with "academic discourse" and "college writing" (e.g., thesis and support, topic sentences and development, introductions and conclusions, etc.). I introduce these sorts of elements during class meetings, but the course places its main emphasis elsewhere. My students at the University of Denver have met those topics previously, and while they have hardly mastered them, I want students to grasp straight away that levels of writing exist beyond the competencies they already bring. (In annual surveys of over four thousand students since 2007, we have learned that University of Denver students bring a lot of formalistic knowledge about writing as well as experience with process pedagogies.) Faculty at other schools, of course, will have a sense of their own students' experiences and needs.

I also want students to understand how writing they do because professors assign it relates to writing they might do because it engages them. That is, while I'm confident that the strategies they will practice in this course will inform their writing for other classes, I have not devised this course as a "service" course for the academy. Rather, I hope it stands as a service course for writers, connecting them to wider possibilities for texts and text-making.

WORKS CITED

Alexander, Michelle. *The New Jim Crow.* New York: The New Press, 2012. Print.

Bartholomae, David, and Anthony Petrosky. *Ways of Reading.* 9th ed. Boston: Bedford/St. Martin's, 2011. Print.

Berlin, James. "Contemporary Composition: The Major Pedagogical Theories." *College English* 44 (1982): 765–77. Print.

Cain, Susan. *Quiet: The Power of Introverts in a World That Can't Stop Talking.* New York: Crown, 2012. Print.

—. *The Power of Introverts.* Video. TED.com. February 2012. Web. 15 July 2012.

Conley, Dalton. *The Elsewhere Society.* New York: Vintage, 2010. Print.

Donovan, Timothy, and Ben W. McClelland. *Eight Approaches to Teaching Composition.* Urbana: NCTE, 1980. Print.

Downs, Douglas, and Elizabeth Wardle. "Teaching about Writing, Righting Misconceptions: (Re)Envisioning 'First-Year Composition' as 'Introduction to Writing Studies.'" *College Composition and Communication* 58.4 (2007): 552–84. Print.

Faigley, Lester. "Competing Theories of Process: A Critique and a Proposal." *College English* 48.6 (1986): 527–42. Print.

Fulkerson, Richard. "Composition at the Turn of the Twenty-First Century." *College Composition and Communication* 56.4 (2005): 654–87. Print.

Kahneman, Daniel. *Thinking Fast and Slow.* New York: Farrar, Straus, Giroux, 2011. Print.

Klinenberg, Eric. *Going Solo: The Extraordinary Rise and Surprising Appeal of Living Alone.* New York: Penguin, 2012. Print.

Lauer, Janice M., Gene Montague, Andrea Lunsford, and Janet Emig. *Four Worlds of Writing.* New York: Harper and Row, 1981. Print.

Lindemann, Erika. "Freshman Composition: No Place for Literature." *College English* 55 (1993): 311–16. Print.

Manjoo, Farhad. *True Enough: Learning to Live in a Post-Fact Society.* Hoboken: Wiley, 2008. Print.

Murray, Charles. *Coming Apart: The State of White America 1960–2010.* New York: Crown, 2012. Print.

Newman, Katherine S. *The Accordion Family: Boomerang Kids, Anxious Parents, and the Private Toll of Global Competition.* Boston: Beacon, 2012. Print.

Porter, James. "Intertextuality and the Discourse Community." *Rhetoric Review* 5.1 (1986): 34–47. Print.

Ransom, John Crowe. *Topics for Freshman Writing.* New York: Holt, 1935. Print.

Tate, Gary, Amy Rupiper, and Kurt Schick, eds. *A Guide to Composition Pedagogies.* New York: Oxford UP, 2001. Print.

Appendix: Course Syllabus

SYLLABUS FOR WRITING:
"OCCASIONS, SOURCES, AND STRATEGIES"

Section 5: 8:00–9:15 am MW
4 Credit Hours
Professor Doug Hesse
dhesse@du.edu / The University of Denver
Office Hours: 3:00–4:00 MW and by appointment. As Director of Writing at DU, I'm on campus daily from 9:00 am to 4:30 pm. You may drop by my office, but my administrative duties require several meetings, so I recommend appointments.

Overview

You've done enough reading in and out of school to notice intriguing gaps between advice about good writing (for example, that all paragraphs should begin with topic sentences) and realities that many kinds of texts don't seem to play by those rules. There's nothing necessarily wrong with the advice you've received; it's just that there's even more to learn; writing comes in so many shapes and forms, for so many audiences and purposes, that teachers have to compromise for practical reasons, distilling complex ideas into simpler strategies. But now you're ready for more.

This course teaches three powerful concepts to explain distinctions and connections among different types of writing. First, writing comes from different source materials: experiences; readings; data; and observation. Second, writings exist in different contexts, for different readers at different times, whose knowledge, views, and expectations affect writers' decisions. Third, where and how a piece is published shapes the options available to the writer. These concepts determine the characteristics of good writing. Now, if these concepts seem simplistic, don't worry: the course will complicate them. If the concepts are cryptic, don't worry: the course will elucidate them. Developing a deeper understanding of writing is an ongoing, life-long process.

So is developing your writing ability. That last, finally, is the main point of this course. People don't really learn ideas and strategies except by putting them to use in their own writings. "Occasions, Sources, and Strategies for Writing" will give you structured writing practice applying these concepts to your own work, some 40 or 50 pages, with about 15 to 20 of those pages polished and finished.

I've designed the course to take advantage of a common topic, at least at the beginning: current ideas about introversion in contemporary society. To that end, we'll read several chapters of a recent book by Susan Cain, *Quiet*. I've chosen that book because its topic should be accessible and generally interesting to all of us in the class and because it nicely allows us to explore the concepts I've introduced. However, the topic of introversion is a vehicle for understanding writing; the course is not "about" introversion. In fact, you'll see that you have greater choices for writing topics as the course progresses.

I look forward to reading your writing and sharing my knowledge and advice. I inevitably learn from students, and I look forward to learning from you.

Course Goals

Students will
1. demonstrate an understanding of reasons why a given writing exists and the context of its origins.
2. demonstrate an understanding of how writings are made of different source materials and how some source materials meet certain rhetorical situations better than other ones.
3. demonstrate an understanding that a text's publication circumstances determine many of its characteristics.
4. be able to perform goals 1, 2, and 3 in their own writings.

Texts

Cain, Susan. *Quiet: The Power of Introverts in a World That Can't Stop Talking.* New York: Crown, 2012. Print. ISBN: 978–0-307–35214–9.

Hesse, Doug. *Writing and Rhetoric: From Where? With What? To Whom? And Why?* I've produced this collection of readings (I'll refer to it as WR) for students in my writing classes. Individual articles and chapters are available to you free via the course Blackboard site.

Policies

The Writing Program's course policies apply for this course. Please read them at http://www.du.edu/writing/policies.htm. These policies govern Student Engagement and Participation; Absences; Civility and Tolerance; and Plagiarism. My late work policy is that assignments turned in late receive my lowest priority. I reserve the right to provide minimal feedback on late work and to return it much later than timely work; I also reserve the right to hold it to a higher standard. Work later than a couple days, without extraordinary compelling circumstances, will receive a zero. Anything you write for this class is subject to reading or discussion by other class members, but we will do so respectfully and with the understanding that we're mostly looking at drafts.

Accommodations for Students with Disabilities

The Writing Program will provide reasonable accommodations to every student who has a disability that has been documented by The University of Denver Disability Services Program (www.du.edu/disability/dsp or 303.871.2455).

Technology and Blackboard

Please bring your laptop to every class meeting. You'll upload all exercises and writings to Blackboard, which will also contain the most current version of the course schedule and all assignments. Many course readings will be distributed via Blackboard.

Grades

Class activities (discussion, peer work, in-class exercises, and so on)	20%
Writings 9, 15, and 16	20%
All other writings	20%
Portfolio	40%

Schedule

Week	Topics and Readings (Listed below are the out-of-class readings. Omitted are shorter in-class readings, usually examples from different genres.)	Writing Assignments (Assignments are presented at some length in my chapter. In-class exercises are omitted.)
1–Phase 1	WR: "Rhetorical Situations, Ideal and Actual" Cain: Introduction (1–19)	1. Common topic, diverse texts 2. Your stake in this topic
2	WR: "Where Does Writing Come From?" Cain: Chapter 1 (19–33)	3. A class bibliography 4. Making our own data
3	WR: "Sources: Textual, Empirical, Experiential" Cain: Chapter 3 (71–96)	5. Presenting modest findings
4	WR: "Writing About Numbers" Cain: Chapter 7 (155–81)	6. Synthesizing data 7. Reader response
5	WR: "Writing About Reading" Cain: Chapter 10 (244–40), Conclusion (264–66)	8. Writer repurposing
6–Phase 2	WR: "Academic v. Popular, Scholars v. Journalists"	9. Extending a topic 10. Repurposing: Text to present
7	First 2 chapters of Assigned Book (see assignment 11)	11. Information for Decision 12. Choosing Topic B
8	WR: "Writing About Experience and Observation"	13. Once more to diversity 14. Academic to popular
9	WR: "Documenting Sources: Practices and Philosophies"	
10	WR: "Writing and Design"	15. Extending Topic B
11–Phase 3	WR: "Page and Screen"	
12	WR: "Elements of Style"	16. Your choice
13	WR: "Futures of Writing"	17. Repurposing once more
14–Phase 4	WR: "Making a Portfolio"	
15		18. Portfolio

4 A Grade-Less Writing Course That Focuses on Labor and Assessing

Asao B. Inoue

In this chapter, I argue that a productive way to design and teach a first-year writing course is to conceive of it as labor: to calculate course grades by labor completed and dispense almost completely with judgments of quality when producing course grades. This is my ideal writing course that would allow me to cultivate a more critical, democratic community. It shares responsibility and negotiates most of the work (as well as the terms by which that work is done) with students. Finally, it operates from an assumption about assessing writing (in all its forms) that allows students to democratically address difference and see acts of assessing as acts of reading, critical judgment, and writing. I hope to show how this kind of course can be just as rigorous and engaging as other courses that use quality judgments of student writing to grade students, and is perhaps more rigorous than courses that do not engage students more fully in the assessment technology of the course—that is, in the processes, products, discourses, expectations, judgments, and other structures that make up the assessment of student writing—the heart of any writing course.

A course like this is perhaps more responsive to diverse groups of students, students who come to our classrooms with various Englishes and who may have a wide variety of literacy competencies that may not match those the academy promotes. This course does not consider these other Englishes as signs of being "underprepared," "deficient," or "lacking." In fact, I believe that the academy needs courses like this to enlarge its boundaries and to do more than give students the "right to their own languages." Courses like this will allow the academy to incorporate more fully students' languages, create new ways of thinking and communicating, expand its discourses, learn from and change because of its students, and change the destructive, white hegemony that has punished and shunned so many. My courses at Fresno State are filled with students of color. The majority are first generation, working-class Hmong American, Asian American, and Latino/a students who come with a variety of discourses and Englishes. Our first-year writing program uses a directed self-placement system, so my students choose their writing courses from essentially three options (Inoue, "Self-Assessment"). It is from this context that I offer my ideal first-year writing course.

Three questions organize and form the central, ongoing conversations of the course and identify tensions students and I continually explore. I use these questions to organize the course and this chapter. They are:

What is *labor* in our writing class?

How do we know how well we are doing if there are no *grades*?

What does *assessing* mean?

WHAT IS LABOR?

When I say that the course is focused around "labor," I do not mean we will read texts about Marxist theory; although, I suppose that could happen. Instead, I mean that the writing and work of the course is conceived of as "labor," as opposed to being "work" or documents that are due. What's the difference? Work in a writing class can be thought of as items to turn in, documents to submit, and texts to read—this work can be easily thought of as things "of the mind" or tasks done at a desk that may seem purely intellectual. This can be off-putting to many students, who see intellectual activities as foreign, painful, or too difficult and mysterious for them to engage in, especially writing activities that may have been graded poorly in the past.

When I say "graded poorly," I mean this in three senses, all of which affect students' abilities to perform in the classroom and are the subject of class discussions. First, grading writing is hard to do well. Grading writing is often done in courses other than writing courses; thus, it is likely to be done poorly, since most teachers in other disciplines do not study the scholarship of writing assessment, composition theory, or response theory. While many of my colleagues in other disciplines respond to and evaluate student writing well, many students still experience teachers who grade writing poorly, focus on error, do not respond to content or ideas, do not respond at all, evaluate first drafts as if they were final drafts, etc. Second, my students' written documents in school are often graded as poor writing. Students tell me this every semester, explaining almost unanimously that "they are not good readers or writers." Where else would they get these ideas about themselves? Third, my students' writing is often only graded, meaning that the only feedback they receive on their writing is a grade. To experience grading as the primary measure of how well one is developing as a writer is a poor way to understand one's writing and writing practices; it is a poor way to receive feedback.

Notice that all three of these "poor" ways of grading center on a document, a text written by a student. Typically, when teachers grade documents or provide feedback, we neglect the labor and effort that produced those documents. We may even emphasize that we do not, or cannot, evaluate or grade a paper based on "effort" or on how hard a student worked on it. I've said this myself in the past. However, this reason is a bit dishonest and not helpful to a student who not only works hard, but also works from an English that is not considered academic, or what we expect. In short, it ignores the student's labor and, in doing so, disrespects something fundamental about what the course asks of that student and how he or she experiences that work.

At a deeper level, the concept of "labor" is rarely thought of as work of the mind, and I want it to be. Labor is, of course, work and time put into something. It often signals the quantity of time and effort put into a project or an activity. I emphasize time the most in assignment instructions, as U.S. culture usually rewards and defines labor by the hour, and this paradigm of labor's rewards is familiar to my students (they usually work in labor economies). At some point, I want them to question this paradigm, question the idea that the rewards we get out of our labors correlate positively to the time and effort we put into them, that learning is a linear equation, and that more time spent on writing can always be apparent in the development and quality of drafts, or even writers. I do not think this is entirely true, but it is also not entirely false—it is more true than false. So, for the course's purposes, it is safe to say that writing well and producing effective documents take effort and time.

At an even deeper level still, the course's initial discussions use the concept of "labor" to describe and acknowledge the degree of effort expected in the class. When one labors hard, one is often in physical pain or discomfort. This means that just any labor will not do if our goal is to improve or build better practices. One cannot go through the motions in order to have time and effort produce good results. Labor is, by its nature, hard—dare I say "honest"—effort and work. So, labor is often uncomfortable and painful, but at some point, that discomfort gives way to pleasure in a job well done, in feelings of accomplishment, in satisfaction, success, pride, and growth. It signals the quality of work and effort put into something, and my students, many of whom come from families who are seasonal workers, laborers, or are folks whose family members do honorable, hard, sweaty work, understand and usually respect this kind of labor. The academy should, too. My students see—and feel—the value and honor in such labor, and I want to connect writing with that kind of hard, and sometimes painful and sweaty, doing of things, because it should be that kind of labor. The course engages students in discussions about working up a sweat and getting down to painful work that can and should hurt, much like exercising muscles and feeling pain, fatigue, and then soreness; but this labor makes us stronger and better in some way for doing it.

Finally, as a man, the concept of labor can have gender-bending qualities that are productive for my students and for me. If my students labor to birth essays, much like the labor of childbirth, then my role and the roles of my students are that of midwives. We help create the environment and conditions for successful laboring and creation, but we cannot create the writer's child, her essay. We can encourage, describe what is happening, ask questions, but mostly we watch and describe the labor process. Therefore, ongoing discussions, particularly around the reading of colleagues' writing and feedback, draw out the concept of child birthing. We are creating ideas and texts. We should take joy in them as part of us and also as creations that are separate from us. We should also enjoy and understand the process of creation. The process of laboring to give feedback (midwifery) should be as rewarding and painful, and as fundamental and necessary to our growth as writers and readers, as the process of writing itself.

The laboring I describe is a pattern of chronic or weekly labor that students and I design and engage in together. I, as the teacher, create the structure and categories of labor, but students and I develop what they mean and look like. Our labors could be any number of activities, but the following ones are familiar, although my descriptions of them focus on laboring and time as their defining elements.

Reading. These activities occur between class sessions. In the begin- ning of the semester, I provide reading strategies that help students engage with the texts that either I or they choose. Later, students decide on their own strategies or invent them, and use the sources they have researched for their projects (See Project(ing), below). Every act of reading produces a posting on Blackboard (Bb), a list of items, a freewrite/quickwrite done during or after the reading, a focused paragraph response or summary, or an annotated passage from the reading. We define these activities, like all of the activities, in terms of the time spent on the activity and the kind of labor we expect to engage in. Instructions look and sound like process directions or procedures. We often talk about, reflect upon (see Reflecting, below), or debrief from these activities by discussing how it felt to read the texts, what we were thinking about in particular paragraphs, where folks got stuck, which parts were the most painful to get through and why, or what helped us do the work.

Writing. These activities happen at home, and produce documents that are used in class, in groups, or to begin discussions. Depending on what we agree upon or where we are in the semester, our writing activities invent, research, explore, draft, and revise students' semester-long projects. We decide together on the parameters of the labor to help students through writing processes, and much of the direction involves cues for timing (i.e., how much time to spend and what to do in each stage of laboring, how to do the labor, or how the labor should be focused). Again, the parameters look a lot like procedures. On average, we do one activity a week, and that activity may take a few hours to do, stretched over a few days. The emphasis is on writing as laboring, not as documents that are due with particular quality expectations—even though documents are produced and used in class and on Bb, and quality is discussed in class. The documents are simply the results of our labor. The bottom line is that discussions of quality are decoupled from grading and what the assignment is worth.

Reflecting. These are reading and writing activities done each weekend that are discussed in the first class session of the following week. Students read excerpts, and the class sometimes discusses them. Other times we just listen. Reflecting is only used to show the good thinking and questioning happening in the class. At times, students respond to a prompt that asks them to do some metacognitive thinking (e.g., "What did you learn about 'entering academic conversations' from your group this week? How did it come to you? What rhetorical patterns did you find occurring in the most effective written feedback you received?"); at other times, students are free to reflect on anything that is on their minds, and that pertains to our class. This reflective labor is defined the same ways as are reading and writing labors. Students reflect in writing for a set period of time, usually twenty to thirty minutes, and then they spend twenty minutes or so reading others' postings. Finally, they reply to at least three others with something substantive and meaningful.

Assessing. At around week six to eight, the writing groups move into full swing. Each week, students do the reading and writing labors (above) that work toward their projects (below). Assessment activities that I guide ask students to read and articulate judgments in a variety of ways. To guide assessing labors, there are two sets of collaboratively created expectations, or rubrics: (1) a set of project expectations (i.e., what they should demonstrate in a final draft of the project); and (2) labor expectations (i.e., what they should demonstrate in their labors in and out of class to produce the project). Most of the time, assessing means responding formatively, and the activities are structured so that all responses in a group are similar in format and focus, but are different in what they discuss. Students make no overt judgments of quality that sound final (e.g., "This is good," "That is bad," "I like X," etc.); instead, they make what we call descriptive judgments that sound like observations (e.g., "This sentence is clear," "I'm confused in paragraph four," "The statement about Wilson feels judgmental," etc.). These are still quality judgments. While these two kinds of judgments are similar, what I call "descriptive judgments" ask students to explain more, to support, and to reveal assumptions that create the judgment from reading the text in question, such as what constitutes a "clear" or "confusing" text. Following the descriptive judgments, students are asked to support their observations by pointing to their peer's text, explaining why they see the text in that way, and identifying what assumptions they are making to get to the judgment. I ask them not to offer advice on how to revise anything, since writers must decide how to revise on their own after considering all assessments from their peers. Telling someone what to do in a draft tends to prematurely stop the writer from reflecting on the meaning and value of a particular observation about that draft. I ask students to spend at least forty-five minutes to an hour on each assessment (including reading time). We have two mantras: (1) explain to the writer how you experienced his or her text, and why you experienced it in that way; and (2) remember that writers make decisions; they do not follow orders. Near the end of the semester, students write assessment letters to their group members, and their colleagues and I use these letters in final, one-on-one conferences. These letters address three evaluative questions, asking for evidence of each: (1) How would you describe your colleague as a learner and writer? (2) What did you learn from your colleague during this semester? (3) What do you think your colleague can still work on, learn, or continue to develop? I ask students to spend at least forty-five minutes to an hour writing each letter. Typically, each student writes three letters.

Project(ing). For students, these labors are the culmination of all their work in the course. Projects are often traditional-looking research papers, but sometimes students do Youtube video presentations, Web pages, reports, brochures, etc. All projects require the same amount of research and writing, since the course articulates expectations in terms of labor (time and intensity), not documents—that is, students must write and present that writing to their writing group each week, and that writing leads them to the finished product (the project), whatever it may be. Some may produce a twelve-page research paper, while others produce a five-minute video, or an eight-page brochure. In this environment, all labor in the class is the projection of the student's, chosen research topic/question, learning about writing, understanding and articulating of ideas, texts, and writing processes; and the enactment of his or her learning journey to exactly the place that he or she can achieve. My only limitation is that writers have an academic audience in mind and use academic sources to help them engage with their projects.

Most of the reading and writing activities, all of the prompts for the reflecting, and the instructions and processes for assessing and providing feedback in writing groups are contingent on what happens in the course, what students do and produce, and how they respond to previous work. Many class activities invent these assignments from patterns of need and from student reflections each week.

To illustrate the exact nature and amount of reading and writing in this course, consider a typical student, Maria Zepeda, from a recent course—a course I draw on throughout this chapter. (Both students cited in this chapter have given consent to use their names and their work). Maria is a Latina in her mid-twenties, who stated her project's research question as: "How are Mexicans portrayed in California media?" Her project was rhetorical and historical in nature, considering the history of immigration in California, the Bracero program during the 1940s to the 1960s, and contemporary news media's representations of Mexicans as laborers and immigrants in California. During the semester, her labor consisted of

- Researching and reading two academic journal articles, a documentary, two government documents, three academic sources from academic websites, and several news media clips on YouTube;
- Engaging in annotation and other reading activities using her researched sources;
- Drafting a three-page inquiry draft, a two-page annotated bibliography (using three sources), seven separate drafts (five of which were substantively different) of the paper for peer feedback, and a final draft of twelve, double-spaced pages;
- Providing peer feedback, through documents and dialogue a total of seven times for each of her three writing group members as well as for two external group members on a late draft (this incident is discussed below); and
- Writing several reflections on the parts of her project's process.

All of the above is in addition to weekly reflections and activities in and out of class that helped students understand elements of rhetoric or to think through their reading and writing practices. While we did not write labor journals, in an ideal course she would have done a labor journal where she would describe and reflect upon her reading and writing labors (discussed below).

How are labor expectations articulated? How do students know how much labor they must accomplish, and what that labor looks like on any given assignment? In the same course, after two weeks of activities, my students and I produced two rubrics: a project rubric explaining what they will demonstrate in proficient projects, and a writer's rubric explaining what they will do in order to produce those projects. The writer's rubric articulates each students' expected labor for activities related to the project in four areas: researching and reading, using rhetoric, laboring and showing effort, and giving and receiving feed-back. Under the area of "labor and showing effort," students produced the following explanatory statements:

- Show through the writing that both time and effort were com-mitted to the project;
- Produce work clearly and meaningfully (cut out filler informa-tion or repetitive parts);
- Submit all assignments on time; and
- Demonstrate interest in the chosen topic.

Arguably, these statements are just as vague as saying, "show labor and effort," but in on-going classroom discussions, activities, and re-flections, we pointed out the good ways students had articulated and demonstrated these qualities. These statements of labor gained mean-ing contextually, and then changed. For instance, "interest" for some was seen in the way readers responded in writing to drafts, and then in the way they developed new ideas or new sources for writers through group dialogue. Early on, showing labor "through the writing" meant that effort in drafting produced very different drafts from one week to the next, with over half of the drafted material added or changed. Just a week or two later, several students identified drafts that got messier, uglier, or that "got all fucked up" as evidence of deep, sweaty, good labor. Most importantly, I did not encourage consensus on what ap-propriate labor should look like. Yes, the rubric was a guide for discus-sion and reflection, a focus point for us to reference, but I did not want a full consensus on its meaning. I wanted students to rearticulate and revise what productive labor looked like *in medias res* so that defining it would always be on the table, since labor was core to how their prog-ress was conceived and because it needed continual redefining.

Some may question: Isn't this just another way of doing a 1970s-style, process-based writing course? Perhaps, at its face. I do argue for a process-style writing course, but given how assessment is configured in the course, it's not simply process. At a deeper, more significant level, defining the concept of "labor" as time, effort, intensity, and creation that describes the writing we do, how long we do it, the degree to which we suffer in it, and the products that come from it makes "labor" much more than simply process. In my ideal course, *writing is labor*—it is time and increased intensity. Time and intensity involve assessment and reflective practices that allow the writing to constantly evolve.

How Do We Know How Well We Are Doing?

Questions of how course grades are decided, and the relationship of the quality of student writing to course grades, must be discussed carefully and often in a course like this one. Students need a clear sense of how well they are doing. Scholarship on grading is almost unanimous about the unreliability (inconsistency) and subjectivity (in the bad sense) of grades (Starch and Elliott; Bowman; Charnley; Dulek and Shelby; Elbow, "Taking Time"; and Tchudi), and just as much research shows how grades and other kinds of rewards and punishments de-motivate and harm students, hampering their abilities to learn anything (Kohn, *Punished* and *Schools*; Elbow, "Ranking"; and Pulfrey, Buchs, and Butera). However, grades often work in concert with (or against) issues of language diversity and difference (e.g., class, gender, race, religious view, sexual orientation, ability, etc.). These very real and obvious differences show up in students' writing and in their feedback to each other, just as much as they do in a teacher's expectations and feedback. Knowing how well one is doing in a class is important, but as research suggests, letting a student know how well he or she is doing is not the same as giving grades or points. In fact, using grades based on judgments of quality (or comparisons to expected, dominant academic discourse) usually devalues the students' labor, and therefore devalues students' *writing* as experience.

The idea of writing as labor, while intuitive on some level, is not intuitive for many students when it is used to determine course grades or when helping students understand how well they are doing on a task or generally in the course. As Elbow has discussed in a similar way, most students are so conditioned to thinking in terms of documents, page counts, and grades that thinking in terms of labor, quantity, time, and how to do an activity can be disorienting and confusing without constant discussion in class ("Taking Time"; "Ranking").

For this reason, my ideal course starts by asking, "How well do grades explain our performances in writing?" This question is answered quickly, turning into a more productive question: "How do we know how well we are doing?" To answer this question, we look at examples of each assignment, talk about the signs of labor, time spent, effort, intensity, and difficulty that could be seen by length, how the text is put together, or what elements from other places and texts (preparation and research) were used to produce the text in front of us. It could be discussed at the sentence level, at places in the writing where the writer gets tangled up, tries something that seems confusing, or opens up new ideas and questions things in the document.

To help us inquire about labor's time and intensity, we query writers in class, ask how they produced what we see, and build together labor practices that help students do the work of the course most effectively. These discussions may look at labor journals, weekly journals that document time spent on activities, and the level of intensity of that work. Each journal entry may: (1) document how much time was spend on an assignment; (2) describe the intensity of the work; or (3) reflect upon the writing produced by that session's time and intensity, connecting the labor to the expectations identified on the writer's rubric. In class, these journals give us ways to discuss how our particular kinds of labors and their contexts have consequences on the page or computer screen.

Most importantly, all effort and labor must be acceptable, as long as students continue to incorporate the practices of the course, improve and reflect meaningfully on their evolving labor, and listen to colleagues and to me when we ask them for more time or intensity in their work. So, discussing labor's effects is not about creating the linear and hierarchical equation, "more time and intensity equals better quality writing." Instead, I ask students to consider more time on and intensity in the labor of writing as an investment that produces different qualities in writing—lateral and non-hierarchical ones. There is no magic to getting students to do more work, no easy way to get them to spend more time or effort in writing, no creative assignment that produces labor-hungry students. I have found trusting students when they say they have done the work in the manner asked, and describing to them what I see as the effects of their labor in their written documents to be all I can and all I want to do.

If it is not already clear, this course uses a grading contract for a course grade of "B," similar to Peter Elbow's (see Elbow, "Taking Time"; Danielewicz and Elbow; and the Appendix). It articulates writing as labor, helping to begin discussions about grades, meaningful feedback, and how well one is doing in the course. The students and I negotiate the grading contract details in the ways that Shor explains his contract system, promoting a democratic culture in the classroom by providing students a way to help create the course (13-14). In another place, I've examined the ways that grading contracts at Fresno State help students of color, particularly Hmong students, who prefer contracts over conventional grading systems more than all other racial formations (Inoue, "Grading Contracts"). In the same course, a female Hmong student, Amy Vang, offered this instructive response to a reflection activity that asked what she had learned so far in the course (it was about week thirteen in the semester):

> This class is different. With this class I was able to write more freely because what is important in this class is the time and effort that we put into our project. I'm not a very good writer, so my biggest challenge at the beginning of the class was being afraid I wasn't going to meet the expectations of this class. I learned that when you're not judged by how good you can write, you're able to do more with your writing.

All the issues and themes I've discussed thus far show up in this excerpt. A focus on documents in Amy's past makes her feel like she is "not a very good writer." Her comparison is between our class and other courses that grade documents on quality, and she compares a class that allows Amy freedom to write (the current one) by acknowledging and valuing her labor and effort with other courses that do not allow her freedom because "time and effort" were not important in them, at least to the extent that they were not incorporated into the grading of those courses. Freedom, time, and effort are important elements in a writing course for Amy to "do more with [her] writing."

Seeing the contract graded class as one that offers "freedom to write" is a typical theme in end-of-semester, anonymous surveys by Hmong students in the first-year writing program (Inoue, "Grading Contracts" 88). No other racial formation articulates their courses in this way, and this is true for the course this student took. I cannot help but think of the well-known book of testimonies by Hmong refugees, *Hmong Means Free*, published in 1994 by Sucheng Chan. The book recounts several families fleeing oppression and massacre in Laos, and immigrating to the U.S. in 1976. Before coming to the U.S., the lack of freedom in the lives of Hmong punctuates their migration: They flee from the Yellow River Valley to the jungles of China, then to Indochina, and to northern Laos. Several groups have attempted to colonize them, including the Chinese, the French, and the Japanese. It appears that freedom to do anything—to live and prosper, let alone to write—is crucial to many Hmong's sense of well-being, learning, progress, and development.

Finally, I call your attention to the final sentence in the above re-flection and its key adjective: "when you're not judged by how *good* you can write, you're able to do more with your writing." Though it may have been a verbal slip, the adjective "good," modifying the verb "write" in this case, typically modifies nouns. This linguistic slip (or is it?) suggests that using quality to judge how well a student is doing may not help him or her. However in this verbal slip, Amy teaches me some-thing very important about this course and its assessment technology (i.e., the grading contract): Attention to quality, or how good one's documents are judged to be, in grading holds students like her back because judgments of quality restrict her—they keep her from being *free*, from doing, just as much as they restrict her writing and what she can/is able to say. Amy directly associates judgments of quality with a lack of freedom, and associates "time and effort" with the freedom to write and with the conditions that allow her "to do more" with her writing. Is this freedom a freedom of the mind, or of the body? Per-haps, to "write more freely" suggests a connection between how free our students really are to do the kind of laborious writing we ask and the things they feel they can or are able to say in that written act.

My past students' more positive feelings toward their grading con-tracts (Inoue, "Grading Contract") contrast with the student resis-tance that Spidell and Thelin document (40). The difference in racial formations that make up students at Fresno State with those of Spi-dell and Thelin's almost exclusively white student population explains many of the differences in students' acceptance of grading contracts. I also believe that asking students explicitly and continuously about how they know how well they are doing mitigates much resistance, as does the negotiated aspect of the grading contract. How well students are doing in the course and in their writing is a key factor of resistance in Spidell and Thelin's findings (40-42); yet, it's a not a source of re-sistance in my classes. Spidell and Thelin's students suggest that they do not know how well they are doing in the class because they are accustomed to understanding their status in terms of a grade. This is not the case in my classes because we attend to this question explicitly and continuously. One could also argue that such differences in atti-tudes about grading contracts stem from fundamental differences in educational experiences with the grading of writing in previous, con-current classrooms and between white students and students of color, who make up the majority of my students. Students of color do not typically benefit from a grading technology that uses quality to deter-mine grades because the measure of "good" quality usually conforms to a white, middle–class, academic discourse. Many working class and poor students of color do not enter college practicing such discourse.

WHAT DOES ASSESSING MEAN?

In the last, and perhaps most important element of my ideal course, the student and I jointly assess his or her work in conferences where we discuss grading and how we know how well we are doing. In the past, most students have been provided feedback that is attached to grades on their writing, but my course decouples grades from the assessment of writing. This is similar to what Elbow describes, but I take the as-sessment part further by making students the primary agents of assess-ment and by making it a defining process of the course ("Ranking" 196).

The driving engine in any writing course is its assessment mecha-nisms, its assessment technology (Inoue, "Technology"). I define as-sessment technologies as having seven components: power, parts, purposes, people, processes, products, and places. All writing assess-ments have these components, even if teachers and students do not pay much attention to or notice them. Put them together, and you have an assessment technology. In my course, students are a part of each ele-ment in the technology, and they discuss their roles in that technology. A big part of that technology is the grading contract that contextual-izes all our work, but the contract really just sets up an environment that allows us to do the real work of assessment for the course. We spend time in weekly reflections thinking about our roles, duties, and work as readers, assessors, and as classroom citizens, each with a role in the course's assessment technology, and in helping each other and ourselves understand how well we are doing. In other places, I discuss versions of this assessment-based pedagogy that focus on creating with students rubrics and assessment documents in cyclical, semester-long processes (Inoue, "Community-Based Assessment") and ways to teach the rhetoric of assessment as the writing of the course (Inoue, "Teach-ing the Rhetoric"). What is important to understand in conceiving of the classroom environment as an assessment technology is that it reveals all the components of assessment that students and their labor need to be a part of, including: the design of activities, assessment documents, codes and processes for assessing, power relationships created in and from assessments (and discussed when thinking about the construction of expertise), places of assessing, and the purposes of assessment activities.

To illustrate, consider a typical feedback session of a draft, one conducted in a writing group of four or five students. This is a typical activity in most writing courses—except, perhaps, that my students must be agents in the technology of feedback by creating a rubric that: continually explains what those expectations mean, how they are seen in documents, and what labor is required to produce those results; owns the products of feedback (i.e., the written assessments to writers) and the processes that create and revise those products; negotiates power relations among one another through discussions of conflicting judgments by peers; and reflects on feedback activities, including how and why they came to the judgments they did on others' drafts. To contextualize all this, nothing is graded, and I (the teacher) am not a voice in most feedback cycles. There is no anticipation of my judgments or of a grade that signifies completion, acceptance, or quality. They own most of the feedback.

As suggested in the previous Hmong student reflection, when grading systems based on judging and ranking the quality of writing are used in the classroom, teachers and students unwittingly become victims of larger societal structures like racism, sexism, and classism that use (often invisible) whiteness as the default yardstick by which to make judgments on student writing. Using quality as the calculus in determining course grades, or the value of any piece of writing, in a writing course means that some dominant discourse—usually a white, middle-class, academic one—is used to punish students for not being white, middle-class academics. Grades are the vehicle for this punishment, and grading, then, usually harms students of color more than their white counterparts. Really, grading harms everyone because grading writing by comparing it to some ideal, dominant, white, academic discourse means that we lose the ability to value any other discourse, regardless of what we say to the contrary. Subaltern and alternative discourses and perspectives are necessary to critically see the dominant one as such, and as contingent. In short, grading often is a racist project in the sense of being a "racial project" that promotes a racial hierarchy that upholds the status quo, as Omi and Winant define it (55-56). This is also the status quo that writing teachers usually ask students to question in the name of being critical.

I'm not suggesting that I do not teach a white, middle-class academic discourse, or that our rubrics and expectations do not resemble that dominant discourse. They often do. I am saying that I try to teach that dominant discourse without using it as a cudgel to bludgeon students of color or other students because they are not white, middle-class academics. Rethinking grading practices and how assessment functions is the first step in this process, because it is through our assessment technologies that we promote, critique, or change those expectations and discourses. Our responses to each other may make judgments that compare a dominant discourse to what is presented in a student's writing, but if judgments of quality are not used to produce grades, and if grading is calculated by labor only (not quality), then writing assessment is not so easily made a racist project in the classroom. Hierarchies are less likely to be established in such a case because aspects of students' subjectivities, like their histories, cultures, and languages—things they have little control over—are not made a part of their graded success in the class.

Furthermore, learning something and being judged against some ideal of that something are completely different things. The first does not mean that we need to engage in the second, at least not initially. In fact, I find that my class's labors can be more rigorous and more engaging, especially when everyone (including me) stops trying to compare student documents to ideal documents, or those we think that a writer should strive to meet. When we stop trying to "correct" problems (from errors, to logic, to matters of content and convention), we free ourselves to better engage with the writer and his or her labor of writing and meaning-making. We can also begin on better footing in order to see dominant discourse as a set of conventions and behaviors, and compare those with those we use natively. That is, students can engage in more critical reading and judging because they are not using a false yardstick to judge themselves and their colleagues as deficient. This better honors the languages that students come into my classroom with. Reading to correct, or reading to compare to an ideal text in our heads, always means that readers (peers and myself) never really *read* each other as intellectuals, never respect the labor and effort that goes into drafting even a messy draft, never engage well with the writer as a thinker, never engage well with his or her ideas, and certainly never critique the very discourse the writer is attempting to learn and perhaps change. What happens is that we read to look for deficits, not for differences.

Don't get me wrong: We always have ideal texts in our heads, and Richard Haswell's discussion of "prototype" and "exemplar" categorization strategies (246-47) used by writing placement readers can be instructive in designing activities and discussions that examine ideal texts assumed in student and teacher feedback. I'm simply saying that when labor is the goal, and not a particular kind of document, and when grades are decoupled from feedback, then ideal texts do not have to be the yardstick by which completion, success, or failure of an assignment is determined. Ideal texts cease to produce deficit and lack in students' labors and texts because they are no longer the ideal—there is no ideal, just difference. Beyond this, everyone has their own, idiosyncratic ideal text in mind when they read. Even if we believe we should judge students' writing to produce grades or a written evaluation of a student text, the ideal text we judge against is not static or the same across individuals; it is ideal texts that need to be a part of discussions of feedback.

Furthermore, many less experienced writers have difficulty making decisions once they receive contradictory feedback that is inevitably produced from peers. The default is always to listen to the teacher— the teacher gives the grade, and the teacher likely knows the yardstick (the ideal) better than anyone else. In short, the teacher's feedback and ideal text matters the most, but not in my course, since the teacher isn't grading and does not usually give feedback, giving students more agency and power in assessment. In conventional courses, difference created through discordant, peer judgments on a text are never really discussed or deployed to critique the dominant discourse or ideal texts of readers, such as the teacher's ideal text.

In my course, critique is more likely to happen, because dissonant feedback by peers is more clearly an opportunity to inquire about the ways each reader may have good cause to judge in the ways he or she has. Discussions in writing groups are not just about how successful readers feel a draft is, but about readers' assumptions that lead them to judgments. Perhaps there is a finer point here that is difficult to see: A judgment about a student text in my course is not an evaluation of it, at least not in the strictest sense of the term. Students in the course *assess*, but they do not *evaluate*. Assessing and evaluating are meaningful because of their purposes, and since students determine purposes in my ideal course, evaluation does not function as it usually does. Conventional evaluation is not only linked to grading, but is defined by purposes that are dictated by a teacher. Usually, the purpose is clear: How good does your writing look? For my class, assessing demands that judgments are qualified and explained as contingent on a particular reader's perspective and values. That is why it is important to explain the assumptions that lead to judgments, and not to rationalize why a writer has not met a "standard" or has written something "bad" or "good." Assessment, then, is about establishing a dialogue over a text. Stephen Tchudi's description of the four levels of assessing (i.e., responding, assessing, evaluating, and grading) are helpful to me in explaining these reading activities (xii-xiii). He explains that institutional pressure increases as readers move away from responding to a text and toward other categories, with grading having the most institutional pressure. He says that the "degree of freedom" is reduced because codified value criteria become filters for judgments, limiting direction and movement of what a reader can say (xii). The bottom line is that assessing, in my course, is an inquiry into the grounds on which texts are judged and judgments are made, and are also a way to compare more fairly subaltern discourses and perspectives to the dominant one.

Through revisions and reflections, the assessments we do attempt to understand the ways that the dominant discourse, as a set of reading and writing practices and behaviors, is different from and similar to our own. This starts with how quality is understood and used—or not used, or misused—for grades and for valuing writing. By not grading, the white, middle-class, academic discourse can be more safely and openly critiqued and challenged by students and me through the democratic processes of reading, judging, and feedback.

THREE ASSUMPTIONS I STOPPED BELIEVING

Before I can even dream of a course like this one, I must give up some assumptions that may address criticisms. First, I stopped believing that grades are a good motivator for doing writing in a class; research on grades and motivation consistently tells us otherwise (Benware and Deci; Butler; Butler and Nisan; Grolnick and Ryan; Harter and Guzman; Hughes, Sullivan, and Mosley; Kage; Salili et al.). In fact, using grades to motivate or provide any kind of feedback is harmful to students and their learning. Students may not know this, and likely have been tricked by the system into believing that grades help accurately identify something about their writing. In my course, students must confront this fact about grading and consider what alternatives might motivate them to do work. My hope is that the assessment processes and their own insights will motivate students to do work. Ultimately, only students can motivate themselves to do anything. They will do only what they are willing and able to do, only what they see as worth doing, and nothing more, but often much less if we (teachers) give them reason to. Grades are a good reason to do as little as possible in a writing class. Extra credit is more reason to do less.

Second, I started realizing that most students come to us with discourses worth studying and learning from, not ignoring or punishing. So, I stopped believing that my academic discourse held all the secrets to creativity, insight, critical thinking, explanation, and communication. My students' discourses are not signs of deficiency. They are signs of difference from us, from the academic ways we (academics) are accustomed to and come to expect of our students. Most of the time, my students do not speak my brand of the English language, just as I do not speak theirs. Since I am in power, speak the brand of English that is in power, and am institutionally sanctioned to make judgments on their written discourse, it is my responsibility to share that power, not to abuse it. I am responsible for finding ways to bring my students into the decision-making processes of the course, especially ones that determine the value and valuing of their literacies, and them as learners and people. This means that I cannot make all the decisions about what to expect in writing and from acts of writing in the class. My students should articulate with me the kind of discourse(s) worth journeying towards in the class, and how those journeys may look. It also means that I must help them see what they are really asking for when they reproduce dominant, academic discursive expectations (or when they do not).

Third and finally, I started believing that students can be motivated by learning itself, by the doing of writing as an activity worth engaging in because it intrinsically offers something to everyone. The documents and assignments by themselves are not worth doing, but the doing of those documents is worth quite a bit. Not all my students realize this, but more do than one would expect. We are all animals that use language to do all that we do, to define ourselves, to reflect upon our work and lives, and to be and show who we are. When we cheapen the writing in our classes by bribing students with grades and extra credit, we tell them implicitly that the work we are asking of them is not worth doing on its own merits and that it needs a grade attached to it to be worth engaging in. When teachers are the only readers and judges in the assessment technology of a course, it sends other messages to students: Your judgments are not worth much. You don't know anything. You cannot offer anything meaningful to others. Your languages are irrelevant to our work. These are exactly the wrong messages to send, since their opposites are truer.

Grades are also a threat. They suggest, "If you don't do this writing, I'm gonna give you an 'F'" and "If you don't do it the way I want you to, then I'll mark you down." I refuse to threaten or bribe my students, but more importantly, I do not believe threats or bribes work to help students become better writers (however one wishes to define "better"), nor are they good motivators. Instead, I prefer to focus my energy on finding with them ways to make the labors of the class worth doing. It is harder work, but it is more rewarding. I learn more from my students in the process. They gain power in the construction of the class and in their labors, and they see the respect I give them by how I listen and respond and in how the class is run. In a recent course, many students used a reflection activity to criticize the drafting and revising process in their writing groups that they had been doing for several weeks.

"We cannot say anything else to the writers. We've seen their drafts so many times already," one student said.

"It all looks fine at this point," another told me. "Can we do something else?"

"What would you like to do instead?" I asked.

"Can we have others in the class read our papers?"

While a seemingly obvious and simple solution, I had not thought of it because I had not seen the problem from their perspectives. I was focused on constructing different ways for their groups to read and respond to each other; I had not considered that after three drafts, readers may have great difficulty saying anything new or significant to writers, regardless of the method of response. Additionally, that same day, a student came to me and asked that somehow we focus on criticizing drafts in feedback, and not just on explaining our reading experiences of drafts. Our instructions reflected these two ideas: feedback to non-group members and discussing only criticisms (i.e., Elbovian, doubting-game stuff). Their feedback to writers outside their groups ended up being some of the most insightful and engaging feedback all semester.

My students discuss these three sets of assumptions about grades and the labor of assessing writing in the class with me—not all at once, but over the semester. I do not show them the research, but I do tell them about it. I do not threaten, tease, or belittle them for not seeing these issues the way I do (it has taken me quite a while to understand them in this way), but I do ask them for faith in the class, faith in this system, and faith in me. I ask them to go along with the course for a semester. I tell them that the more faith they have, the better they will do.

Closing Words about Workload and Success

Finally, the workload for the course is about the same as a conventionally run writing course, though perhaps a bit more. The nature of the work is, however, very different. Since I only read the writing, and do not grade or even respond to most of it, weekly work goes smoothly and quickly. Most weeks, a class of twenty-five or thirty students would take around three to four hours of reading, since I'm only looking for patterns of issues and examples to use in class discussions. During the weekend, reading reflections may take another hour or so; but, again, I am only looking for examples to show in class. The amount of work for students is demanding and relentless. Many students express concern in the middle of the semester about writing and other assignments due every week and every weekend, but few drop the course (maybe one a semester—maybe), and I rarely have students who do not meet the labor requirements of the course. Those who drop typically do so in the first week or two of class—on average this is one or two students. I think students stay in the class, despite its demanding labor, because they feel valued more in this environment, and because they would rather feel valued than do less work.

In end-of-semester course evaluations, over 60% of my students consistently say that they loved the grading contract. When asked what their attitudes were about grading before our class and after, the vast majority (over 96%, usually only one or two register a concern) say that they liked the contract and preferred it for our class. What is typically at issue for those who find trouble with the contract is the extra work involved in getting an "A" for the class, since so much work is already asked of them. Interestingly, my grade distributions are not different from those in other English classes at Fresno State or in the College of Arts and Humanities. In the course discussed in this chapter, of the twenty-five students in the course, five received A's, eighteen received B's, one received a C, and one dropped the course midway through. That's typical.

Ultimately, I believe that writing courses, more than any other college courses, make an argument to students about their worth and their value as agents in society, in the institution, and in the classroom. How we argue their worth and value happens through how we value their labor—first and foremost—because the bottom line is this: No matter how we create a course, we always ask students to labor, to do work, and to take time and effort. There is no education any other way. Asking students to labor in a writing course, and then judging that labor on its quality, is not just unfair and dishonest—it can be racist. We know that students come to us from very different educational systems that do not equally prepare them. We know that we judge the quality of writing in most writing courses by a white, middle-class standard, one not native to poor, the working classes, or many students of color. We know that our students have no control over any of these factors in their lives, and yet we still say that judging writing quality, particularly for a course grade, is fair. My ideal course says that it is not fair, nor does it help students learn better reading and writing practices. My students deserve better.

WORKS CITED

Benware, Carl A., and Edward L. Deci. "Quality of Learning with an Active Versus Passive Motivational Set." *American Educational Research Journal* 21.4 (1984): 755-65. Print.

Bowman, Joel P. "Problems of the Grading Differential." *The Journal of Business Communication* 11.1 (1974): 22-30. Print.

Butler, Ruth. "Task-Involving and Ego-Involving Properties of Evaluation: Effects of Different Feedback Conditions on Motivational Perceptions, Interest, and Performance." *Journal of Educational Psychology* 79.4 (1987): 474-82. Print.

Butler, Ruth, and Mordecai Nisan. "Effects of No Feedback, Task-Related Comments, and Grades on Intrinsic Motivation and Performance." *Journal of Educational Psychology* 78.3 (1986): 210-16. Print.

Charnley, Mitchell V. "Grading Standards Vary Considerably, Experiment Shows." *Journalism Educator* 33.3 (October 1978): 49-50. Print.

Danielewicz, Jane, and Peter Elbow. "A Unilateral Grading Contract to Improve Learning and Teaching." *College Composition and Communication* 61.2 (2009): 244-68. Print.

Dulek, Ron, and Annette Shelby. "Varying Evaluative Criteria: A Factor in Differential Grading." *The Journal of Business Communication* 18.2 (1981): 41-50. Print.

Elbow, Peter. "Ranking, Evaluating, and Liking: Sorting Out Three Forms of Judgment." *College English* 55.2 (1993): 187-206. Print.

—. "Taking Time Out from Grading and Evaluating While Working in a Conventional System." *Assessing Writing* 4.1 (1997): 5-27. Print.

Grolnick, Wendy S., and Richard M. Ryan. "Autonomy in Children's Learning: An Experimental and Individual Difference Investigation." *Journal of Personality and Social Psychology* 52.5 (1987): 890-98. Print.

Harter, Susan, and M. E. Guzman. "The Effect of Perceived Cognitive Competence and Anxiety on Children's Problem-Solving Performance, Difficulty Level Choices, and Preference for Challenge." Unpublished manuscript. University of Denver, 1986. Print.

Haswell, Richard H. "Rubrics, Prototypes, and Exemplars: Categorization Theory and Systems of Writing Placement." *Assessing Writing* 5.1 (1998): 231-68. Print.

Hughes, Billie, Howard J. Sullivan, and Mary L. Mosley. "External Evaluation, Task Difficulty, and Continuing Motivation." *Journal of Educational Research* 78 (1985): 210-15. Print.

Inoue, Asao B. "Community-Based Assessment Pedagogy." *Assessing Writing* 9.3 (2005): 208-38. Print.

—. "Self-Assessment as Programmatic Center: The First Year Writing Program and Its Assessment at California State University, Fresno." *Composition Forum* 20 (2009a). Web. 22 May 2012.

—. "The Technology of Writing Assessment and Racial Validity." *Handbook of Research on Assessment Technologies, Methods, and Applications in Higher Education*. Ed. Christopher S. Schreiner. Hershey: IGI Global, 2009b. 97-120. Print.

—. "Teaching the Rhetoric of Assessment." *Teaching with Students' Texts*. Ed. Joseph Harris, John D. Miles, and Charles Paine. Logan: Utah State UP, 2010. 46-57. Print.

—. "Grading Contracts: Assessing Their Effectiveness on Different Racial Formations." *Race and Writing Assessment*. Ed. Asao B. Inoue and Mya Poe. New York: Peter Lang, 2012. 79-94. Print.

Kage, M. "The Effects of Evaluation on Intrinsic Motivation." Japan Association of Educational Psychology. Joetsu, Japan, 1991. Address.

Kohn, Alfie. *Punished by Rewards: The Trouble with Gold Stars, Incentive Plans, A's, Praise, and Other Bribes.* Boston: Houghton Mifflin, 1993. Print.

—. *The Schools Our Children Deserve: Moving Beyond Traditional Classrooms and 'Tougher Standards.'* Boston: Houghton Mifflin, 1999. Print.

Omi, Michael, and Howard Winant. *Racial Formations in the United States: From the 1960s to the 1990s.* 2nd ed. New York: Routledge, 1994. Print.

Pulfrey, Caroline, Celine Buchs, and Fabrizio Butera. "Why Grades Engender Performance-Avoidance Goals: The Mediating Role of Autonomous Motivation." *Journal of Educational Psychology* 103.3 (2011): 683-700. Print.

Salili, Farideh, Martin Maehr, Richard L. Sorensen, and Leslie J. Fyans, Jr. "A Further Consideration of the Effects of Evaluation on Motivation." *American Educational Research Journal* 13.2 (1976): 85-102. Print.

Shor, Ira. "Critical Pedagogy Is Too Big to Fail." *Journal of Basic Writing* 28.2 (2007): 6-27.

Spidell, Cathy, and William H. Thelin. "Not Ready to Let Go: A Study of Resistance to Grading Contracts." *Composition Studies* 34.1 (2006): 35-57. Print.

Starch, Daniel, and Edward C. Elliott. "Reliability of the Grading of High School Work in English." *School Review* 20.7 (1912): 442-57. Print.

Sucheng, Chan. *Hmong Means Free.* Philadelphia: Temple UP, 1994. Print.

Tchudi, Stephen, ed. *Alternatives to Grading Student Writing.* Urbana: NCTE, 1997. Print.

Appendix 1: Course Syllabus

First-Year English

California State University, Fresno
Professor: Dr. Asao B. Inoue

Required Texts/Readings

- A good grammar handbook.
- Reserve about $25-$30 for copying throughout the semester. Instead of a textbook, there will be handouts, articles, and other texts that you'll be required to print and bring to class.

Description

Welcome to First-Year English, a writing course designed to fulfill the writing skills requirement for graduation. This course's readings and in-class discussions will involve the study of *rhetoric,* or the art of speaking/writing well, or the art of finding the available means of persuasion, or the practice of being a citizen (in ancient Greek and Roman cultures, but it equally applies to contemporary U.S. society). Our discussions about rhetoric and writing will help us design, investigate, draft, and revise individual projects. In the first few weeks of the semester, we'll design a good portion of the course (about 50%-75% of it), deciding on goals, methods, a major reading, and ground rules for conduct and behavior in our class. We'll also do lots of reading together, discuss rhetoric, and begin building some vocabulary for talking about our reading and writing practices. We'll do lots of writing.

By sometime around week 6, you'll decide on an academic inquiry that interests you (and perhaps that you think will benefit your colleagues in class). This inquiry may focus on the practices of language used in a community, say the language practices in Biology, or in your church, or some other group/community that you belong to (or seek to enter). Your inquiry might take on some other language-related topic that benefits in some way your peers in this class. Another way to think about this project is that it is one in which you ask a question about rhetoric, or about the language/literacy practices of a particular community. This course requires a lot from each student and asks that you also help your colleagues in a number of ways. Doing both of these things ensures your success in class. Not doing one of them puts your success at risk. '

   IMPORTANT: By staying in this class and posting your work on Blackboard, you agree to allow me to use your written work for research purposes only in my own scholarly work in writing studies. Before any uses of your work, I will attempt to contact you, and I will *never* use your work for demeaning or derogatory purposes. All work will be used without identifying information associated to it (i.e., anonymously or with pseudonyms attached). If you do not wish me to use your work, please let me know before the end of the semester. At any time, you may ask me not to use your work in my research.

Course Outcomes

Upon successful completion of this course, each student will produce:
  * All **assignment descriptions and expectations**, which consist of the labor required, the products that that labor produces, how colleagues will read, judge, and produce feedback and assessments of the labor and the products of each assignment;
  * An acceptable **project** that focuses on a question about rhetoric that is of interest to the writer, demonstrates a clear and appropriate purpose (audience benefit) for investigating the topic for the audience chosen, demonstrates a clear understanding of the main issues involved in the topic, and uses integrally appropriate academic research from the library (typically around 6–7 academic sources);
  * Weekly **reflections and activities** that demonstrate an adequate understanding of all assigned readings, concepts, and issues, turned in on time and in the manner asked;
  * Frequent colleague assessments (usually posted on Bb in document form) that apply the concepts and practices covered in the class and improve in effectiveness over the course of the semester;
  * An acceptable **end of semester letter of reflection** that demonstrates a learner, reader, and writer who can assess his/her practices and applies the rhetorical concepts to his/her learning journey (in the course).

Course Policies

In order to do well in this class, you should:

- Take full and active responsibility for your participation, writing, input in discussions, and progress in this course;
- Give courtesy and respect to everyone;
- Help colleagues in the fullest ways possible, which also means taking very seriously peer response and peer assessment activities;
- Participate daily in all in-class activities and conversations;
- Come to class each day and stay abreast of all assignments' criteria and follow them (see "Attendance" section below);
- Complete/Do all assignments as directed and in the spirit they are asked of you.

If you think you will have trouble complying with an assignment's criteria or any of the policies above, please talk to me in class, email, or call me (leave a voice mail) ASAP, and well before any due date. This does not guarantee an extension or changes, but advance notice helps us make better plans for your success.

Attendance

As explained in our course grading contract, **every absence after four** will constitute a loss of a **full letter grade** for this course (see also the "Course Grade" section below). Please double-check your schedules and other activities this semester. If you cannot meet this requirement, you simply will not do well in this course.

Plagiarism

Remember to always quote and cite your sources appropriately, even if they are unpublished or from friends or classmates. An unacknowledged paraphrase, a patchwork from several sources, as well as the submission of someone else's work (published or not), all constitute plagiarism in the eyes of the university and a **failure of this course.** Please ask questions if you're ever unsure BEFORE you turn in work. **Ignorance IS NOT an acceptable excuse.** The University's language on plagiarism and academic honesty is:

> [A]cademic integrity is defined as "a commitment, even in the face of adversity, to five fundamental values: honesty, trust, fairness, respect, and responsibility. From these values flow principles of behavior that enable academic communities to translate ideals to action" . . . All members of the university

community are responsible for adhering to high standards of academic integrity, for actively ensuring that others uphold the Code, and for responding assertively to violations . . . Faculty are responsible for informing students of academic behaviors that are permissible and not permissible and for reporting violations of the code to the proper campus authorities . . . Students shall not give or receive unauthorized aid on examinations or other course work that is to be used by the instructor as the basis of grading. (CSU, Fresno Academic Policy Manual)

You may access a complete statement from: http://www.csufresno. edu/studentaffairs/general/univhonor.shtml.

Disabilities

In all my preparations and planning, I strive to provide an encouraging and dynamic learning environment for all my students and as wide a variety of learning styles as I can. However, there may be better ways I can accommodate those who have special learning needs. Please see me immediately when and if you have trouble fully participating or engaging in the class's activities and work. Additionally, all reasonable accommodations will be available for students who have a documented disability verified through the university. For more information on the University's policy regarding services for students with disabilities see: http://www.csufresno.edu/ssd/fac_staff/fac_staff_responsibilites. shtml.

Course Grade

Your overall course grade is calculated using a grading contract (see the Grading Contract for specifics). If you do all that the contract asks, you will receive the appointed grade. We'll also have a final conference, in which we discuss your work, the final letter of reflection on your work, and your colleagues' assessments of your work. In the final conference, we will decide together how well you met the contract requirements.

IMPORTANT: We'll discuss and revise the grading contract during the first two weeks of class.

You MUST attend and participate in at least 87.5% of the class sessions (you may miss four class sessions without it affecting your course grade) and participate in a final conference with me (during finals week) in order for you to pass this course. Five absences means an automatic "C" course grade.

Work of the Course

We will construct more detailed information on each assignment. The descriptions below are to give you a clear idea of how much work is expected of you, the general expectations from which we'll start, and the structure of work in the course.

In-Class Activities, Daily Work, and Participation: Most in-class work will be unannounced and deal with that day's readings or homework. We'll do individual freewrites, more structured writing, out-of-class assignments, group activities, and class discussion. When we read something together, part of your preparation for each class session will be to come with at **least three questions and/or explorative ideas** that help us discuss and think about the day's readings. Furthermore, you will also be asked to help define and create in-class activities and assignments. If you come in late to class or unprepared, you will not be allowed to make up any work missed. Often our in-class work leads up to or prepares us for the other work. *Save everything.*

I assess all in-class work the same. You may earn full credit (i.e., you've done the assignment according to its expectations), or no credit (i.e., you haven't met the expectations of the assignment).

Weekly Reflections / Labor Journals (total of around 14): By each Saturday you'll post on our Internet bulletin board (Blackboard) a reflection based on a prompt I'll provide for you. Each reflection should be about 1 page if it were printed (usually around **200–300 words**). These will help us rethink our practices, ideas, and readings, revise our work, ask questions to each other, voice confusion or excitement, and theorize as a community of writers/scholars. You are required also to read and **reply to at least 3 of your colleagues' postings** each week in some meaningful and substantive way. These are crucial to our work in this course. We'll usually begin class each week by reading and discussing a few of these. Some weeks I'll also ask you to accompany your reflections with a labor journal entry. These entries are separate from the reflection prompts and ask you to write about three things concerning another writing activity you did that week. Each entry will: (1) document how much time was spent on the assignment, (2) describe the intensity of the work, and (3) reflect upon how effective the activity's time and intensity was. Labor journal entries offer us ways to see, consider, and craft better labor so that we can improve our reading and writing practices.

We'll assess these documents the same way we do the in-class activities (#1 above). You get full or no credit for each reflection/labor journal entry.

Responses/Assessments (total of around 8 formal and numerous less formal ones): You'll respond to and assess various parts and drafts of colleagues' projects, as well as assess the learning journey of your colleagues and yourself at the end of the course. We'll discuss the guidelines for each of these responses/assessments in class. Some will be formal, structured, written responses or assessments, a few less formal. Each may have a different goal or focus, so expect to create guidelines for each response/assessment.

At the end of the semester, you'll also write a letter to each writing group member (and me) that discusses that colleague as a learner, reader, and writer. This letter, which we'll use in your colleague's end of semester conference with me, will include:

- A description of your colleague as a learner, quoting or citing his/her own letter, any document produced by your colleague, or any details you recall from exchanges, class discussion, or group work.
- A discussion of what you think you learned from your colleague, either in class generally, in reflections, in projects, group work, or responses to your work.
- A discussion of the areas of learning and development that you think your colleague could still work on and improve, or that she/he hasn't yet figured out.

The responses and assessments will be assessed much like in-class work and homework. You may earn full credit (i.e., you've done the response/assessment according to its expectations), or no credit (i.e., you haven't met expectations).

Projects (total of 1 or 2): You'll do one project during the semester in order to fulfill the grading contract for a "B." You may do a second special project in order to be considered for an "A" grade; however, just completing project 2 does not guarantee an "A." The same amount of labor is required for project 1 and project 2. Each project could be a traditional research paper, or something more creative (e.g., Web site, a report, a conference presentation for an academic organization, a YouTube video with a written component, etc.). Your second project could be a related empirical study, ethnographic study, or something that helps answer a question revealed in your first project. It could translate significantly project 1 for another purpose and another audience, but would need to add material, or significantly re-analyze the information in new ways. Project 2 may also be a reflective-rhetorical project that looks closely at some question that came up for you when you wrote and revised your project 1. Regardless of what form project 1 culminates in, all project 1s must meet the following criteria:

- Incorporate at least 4 appropriate academic sources and document their use appropriately;
- Focus on a single, significant problem or inquiry that has importance to the academic community of our class (and perhaps others in the larger Fresno community);
- Have a significant written component, which amounts to 8–10 pages in length, or 2,400–3,000 words (or other appropriate length to be determined in special cases).

Project 2 is special, and the exact guidelines will be determined based on what you choose to do, if you choose to do a project 2 (you do not have to). If you do, generally speaking, you'll be expected to produce a project that is approximately the same in labor and depth as project 1 (8–10 pages, with 4 sources, 1 question, etc.).

I'll provide responses to your projects throughout the process of drafting and revising. I will not, however, assess each draft or portion. Your colleagues will provide most of your feedback, but I will shape their feedback. I will read everything and use drafts and activities to form activities for the class.

End of Semester Reflection Letter: You'll write a letter (about 1–2 pages, or 300–600 words) to me and your colleagues in class that discusses what you've learned throughout the entire semester. This letter will reflect upon your learning journey, the specifics, the readings, and the assignments, and assess your learning in the project(s), how much you've figured out, questions you've come to learn to ask now, and the development you see in your thinking and writing. Your letter should discuss the following things:

> A description of yourself as a learner, both in the class generally and as a writer, quoting or citing from your own work in the class. You may ask: What was your journey from start to finish in the course like? How would you describe it? What are the main milestones or benchmarks of learning you passed?

> A discussion of the areas of learning and development that you think you could still work on or improve, or that you haven't figured out yet. We all have places to improve upon, so it is not a weakness to say that you don't know things or that you are still confused about how to do something. In fact, it's normal and expected.

In your final conference with me, you'll read this letter to me, and we'll use it to help us understand what you've learned and how well you've performed in the class, according to our contract. **If you do not do this assignment, you cannot pass this course.**

Course Schedule

Our course schedule may change as the semester develops. Below is a first draft that should give you a good blueprint of what to expect.

		Developing the Course and Our Interests
Week 1		**Reading:** TBA Introductions, syllabus, grading contract, curriculum.
Week 2		**Reading:** from Peter Elbow's *Writing Without Teachers* (chapters 4 and 5) Curriculum; what do we wish to accomplish and how do we wish to accomplish it? What responsibilities will be taken on? **Labor:** New version of the grading contract; assignment description for weekly reflections (how will we do them and what will we expect of each other in labor and products?).

Week 3	**Reading:** *Kairos* handout (mine); Stasis handout (mine) What's the relationship between thought and language? What is *kairos* and how can we use it in our reading of artifacts? What is *Stasis* theory and might it help us read texts? Create inquiry draft assignment. **Labor:** Example of text/artifact in which you see *Kairos*. Assignment description for Inquiry draft.
Week 4	**Reading:** TBA What are logical appeals/proofs (*logos*)? How can they help us read a text? **Labor:** *Logos* handout. Group *logos* handouts (revised from group work). Assignment description for annotated bibliography and proposal assignments.
Week 5	**Reading:** TBA What are ethical appeals/proofs (*ethos*)? How can they help us read a text? **Labor:** Inquiry draft (1–2 pages) posted on Bb by Sun, at 9:00 AM. *Ethos* handout. Group *ethos* handouts.
	Research Projects
Week 6	**Reading:** Sample academic essay from your project; colleagues' annotated bibliographies. What are pathetic appeals/proofs (*pathos*)? How can they help us read texts? Start creation of project rubric (expectations of documents) and writer's rubric (expectations of labor in writing). **Labor:** Annotated Bibliography #1 posted on Bb by class session on Monday. Annotated sample academic essay (from projects) for rubric building activity.
Week7	**Reading:** Colleagues' project proposals. Project proposal feedback and assessment; rubric creation and begin testing rubrics. **Labor:** Project proposal posted on Bb by class session on Monday; formal assessment of group members' proposals posted by class session on Wednesday.
Week 8	**Reading:** Colleagues' drafts; sample academic article (from your project). Midterm conferences; what is judgment for a reader and how do we express it to writers? Finish testing rubrics. What goes into a literature review or a background section? **Labor:** 3–4 pages of background or literature review section of draft on Bb by Saturday at 1 PM. Assessments documents (feedback) due posted on Bb as a reply by class session. Annotated sample academic article (just background or literature review section).

Week9	**Reading:** Colleagues' drafts; sample background sections from project drafts. Midterm course feedback; assessment of projects. Look again at the grading contract (how is it working?). How are we writing our background sections and literature reviews? **Labor:** Half-draft of project 1 posted on Bb by Saturday at 1 PM. Assessments documents (feedback) due posted on Bb as a reply by class session.
Week10	**Reading:** Colleagues' drafts. **Labor:** Draft 1 of Research Project posted on Bb by class session on Monday; formal assessments of research projects posted on Bb by class session on Wednesday.
Week 11	**Reading:** Colleagues' drafts of project 1 and 2. **Labor:** (optional) Project 2 inquiry draft/proposal with bibliography due posted on Bb by class session on Mon.
Week 12	**Reading:** TBA
Week 13	**Reading:** Colleagues' drafts. **Labor:** Draft 2 of Research Project 1 posted on Bb by class session on Monday. If doing a Project 2, post on Bb by class session on Monday.
Week 14	**Reading:** TBA.
Week 15	**Reading:** TBA
Week 16	**Reading:** TBA **Labor:** post letter of reflection on Bb by class session on Monday; (optional) post project 2 final draft on Bb by class session on Wednesday.
Finals Week	Final letters of assessment of colleagues due by Tue, at 5:00 PM on Bb. Final on Wed, at 5:45–7:45 PM. Finish final **conferences** with me (30 mins.) this week.

Appendix 2: Our Grading Contract for First-Year Writing

Dear Class:

In most learning situations in life outside of school, grades are never given. The learning that occurs in Kung Fu dojos, or cooking, dance, or yoga studios do not use any grading. Why? In these "studio" cases, it seems meaningless to give students grades, and yet without any grades, those students get better at yoga, dance, and cooking. These studio learning situations should prompt us to ask some questions: Why are grades meaningless in those settings but seem so important in a school setting? How do grades affect learning in classrooms? What social dynamics does the presence of grades create? In both situations, instructors provide students/participants with evaluative feedback from time to time, pointing out where, say, they've done well and where the instructor suggests improvement. In the studio situation, many students help each other, even rely on each other for feedback.

Using conventional grading structures to compute course grades often leads students to think more about their grades than about their writing; to worry more about pleasing a teacher or fooling one than about figuring out what they really want to learn, or how they want to communicate something to someone for some purpose. Additionally, conventional grading may cause some students to be reluctant to take risks with their writing or ideas. It doesn't allow someone to fail at writing, which is important to do at times. For these reasons, I use a contract for grading in our class.

This contract is based on a simple principle and a few important assumptions, which are not typical in most classrooms. First, the principle: how much *labor* you do is more important to your learning and growth as a reader and writer than the quality of your writing. Our grading contract calculates grades by how much *labor* you do and the manner you do it in. The more you work, the better your grade—no matter what folks think of the product of your labor—but we assume that you'll be striving in your labors to improve, learn, and take risks. The other important assumption that this principle depends upon for success is that we must assume that all students will try their hardest, work their hardest, and not deceive anyone, when it comes to their labor. If we ask for an hour of writing at home, and someone says they did that and produced X, then we must believe them. This is a culture of trust. We must trust one another and know that deception and lying hurts mostly the liar and his/her learning and growth.

So if you're looking to game the system and do the least amount of work to get the highest possible course grade, this is NOT the class for you. You'll only be frustrated, even angry. Things will seem unfair at times. But if you wish to learn and improve yourself as a writer and reader, are willing to do a lot of work to reach those goals, accept the idea that your labor will be rewarded and not the quality of your work (although we will discuss quality and it is important to your success, but not important to your course grade), then this is the class for you.

Finally, taking grades out of the class, I hope, will allow you freedom to take risks and really work hard. Do not be afraid to take risks in your writing and work. Failing or missing the mark is healthy for learners. Good, deep, important learning often happens because of failure—so it's really not failure at all. Failure really only happens in our class when you do not do the work, or do not labor in the ways we ask of you. Most importantly, what looks like failure in writing can show us our weaknesses, misunderstandings, and opportunities for growing and changing. Furthermore, since I won't grade anything, this allows you the chance to rely more authentically on your colleagues and your own assessment and revision advice. This will help you build strategies of self-assessment that function apart from a teacher's approval. I want you to learn to listen carefully to colleagues' differing judgments, assess the worth of those judgments for your work and its purposes, express why one idea is more workable and better than others, and most importantly, make informed, careful decisions in your writing that you can explain to others.

The default grade, then, for the course is a "B." In a nutshell, if you do all that is asked of you in the manner and spirit it is asked, if you work through the processes we establish and the work we assign ourselves during the semester, then you'll get a "B." If you miss class, turn in assignments late, or forget to do assignments, etc., your grade will be lower.

"B" Grades

You are guaranteed a course grade of "B" if you meet all of the following conditions. Please note that in each item below, there are questions that I cannot decide alone, particularly questions of definition. The results/conclusions of our discussions will be put into this contract in the places below.

Attendance/Participation. You agree to attend and fully participate in at least 87.5% of our scheduled class sessions and their activities and assignments, which means **you may miss (for whatever reason) 4 class sessions.** For our class, attendance should equate to participation, so we need to figure out together what "participation" means and when does someone not get credit for it?

NOTE: Assignments not turned in because of an absence, either ones assigned on the schedule or ones assigned on earlier days in class, will be late, missed, or ignored (depending on when you turn them in finally, see the guidelines #4, #5, and #6 below).

Any absence due to a university-sponsored group activity (e.g., sporting event, band, etc.) will not count against you, as stipulated by university policy, as long as the student has FIRST provided written documentation in the first 2 weeks of the semester of all absences. This same policy applies to students who have mandatory military-related absences (e.g., deployment, work, duty, etc.). Again, the student must provide written documentation, stating the days he/she will be absent. This will allow us to determine how he/she will meet assignments and our contract, despite being absent.

Lateness. You each agree to come on time or early to class. Five minutes past our start time is considered late. Walking into class late a few times in a semester is understandable, but when does lateness become a problem (for the class as a whole and/or for the individual)? As a rule of thumb, **coming in late 4 or more times in a semester will constitute an absence**.

Sharing and Collaboration. You agree to work cooperatively and collegially in groups. This may be the easiest of all our course expectations to figure out, but we should have some discussions on what we expect from each other.

Late Assignments. You will turn in properly and on time all essays, assessments, evaluations, portfolio evaluations, reflections, and other assignments. Because your colleagues in class depend on you to get your work done on time so that they can do theirs on time, all late assignments are just as bad as missed assignments. However, depending on what we agree to in the first week or two of the semester, you may turn in a late assignment or two (see the "Breakdown" table below). In order for an assignment to be considered a **"late assignment," it STILL must be turned in, at least 2 days (48 hours) after its initial due date, and it should be complete and meet all the assignment's requirements** (e.g., if an essay was due on Friday, Sept 20 at noon, a late essay must be turned in by noon on Sunday, Sept 22). Please note that a late assignment may be due on a day when our class is not scheduled to meet.

Missed Assignments. A missed assignment is NOT one not turned in; it is one that has missed the guidelines for a late assignment somehow but is still complete and turned in at some point in the semester (e.g., after the 48 hours). Most missed assignments are those turned in after the 48 hour late turn in period (see #4 above). **In order to meet our contract for a "B" grade, you cannot have any "missed assignments."** Please note that assignments *not turned in at all* are considered "Ignored Assignments" (see #6 below). A missed assignment is usually one turned in after the 48 hour "late" assignment deadline.

Ignored Assignments. Any assignments not done period, or "ignored," for whatever reasons, are put in this category. One of these in the grade book means an automatic "D." Two acquired gives you an "F." Additionally, if any of the essays or portfolios become ignored assignments, it constitutes an automatic failure of the course.

All work and writing needs to meet the following conditions:

Complete and On Time. You agree to turn in on time and in the appropriate manner complete essays, writing, or assessments that meet all of our agreed upon expectations. (See #4 above for details on late assignments). This means that assignments are not just done but done in the spirit and manner asked. They must meet the expectations given in class or on handouts.

Revisions. When the job is to revise your thinking and work, you will reshape, extend, complicate, or substantially clarify your ideas—or relate your ideas to new things. You won't just correct, edit, or touch up. Revisions must somehow respond to or consider seriously your colleagues' (or teacher's) assessments in order to be revisions.

Copy Editing. When the job is for the final publication of a draft, your work must be well copy edited—that is, free from most mistakes in spelling and grammar. It's fine to get help in copy editing. (Copy editing doesn't count on drafts before the final draft or portfolio.)

"A" Grades

All grades in this course depend upon how much *labor* you do. If you do all that is asked of you in manner and spirit asked, and meet the guidelines in this contract, specifically the "Break-Down" section at the end of this contract, then you get a "B" course grade. Grades of "A," however, depend on doing advanced projects for both project 1 and 2, which equates to about twice the work or length of the final project documents. Thus you earn a B if you put in good time and effort, do all the work, and do both projects in an acceptable fashion. But you earn an "A" if you do more work in the two projects—that is, do more in-depth projects (described on the project handout and in the syllabus).

While you do not have to worry about anyone's judgments or standards of excellence to meet the grading contract, you are obligated to listen carefully to and address your colleagues' and my concerns in all your work of the class. This means that when you receive feedback you'll use that feedback to help you continually improve your writing. So while others' judgments of your work are not important to your course grade, they are important to your learning and development.

Grades Lower Than B

I hope no one will aim for lower grades. The quickest way to slide to a "C," "D," or "F" is to miss classes, not turn in things on time, turn in sloppy or rushed work, or show up without assignments. This much is nonnegotiable: you are not eligible for a grade of "B" unless you have attended at least 86% of the class sessions (see also #1 above) and met the guidelines above. And you can't just turn in all the late work at the end of the semester. If you are missing classes and get behind in work, please stay in touch with me about your chances of passing the course.

Break-Down

Below is a table that shows the main components that affect your successful compliance with our contract.

Grade	# of Absences	of Late Assigns.	# of Missed Assigns.	# of Ignored Assigns
A	4 or less	3	0	0
B	4 or less	3	0	0

Grade	# of Absences	of Late Assigns.	# of Missed Assigns.	# of Ignored Assigns
C	5	4	1	0
D	6	5	2	1
F	7	6 or more	2	2 or more

Plea. I (Asao), as the administrator of our contract, will decide in consultation with the student whether a plea is warranted in any case. The student must come to the teacher (Asao Inoue) as soon as possible, usually before the student is unable to meet the contract (before breaching the contract), in order that he/she and the teacher can make fair and equitable arrangements, ones that will be fair and equitable to all in the class and still meet the university's regulations on attendance, conduct, and workload in classes. **You may use a plea for any reason, but only once in the semester.** Please keep in mind that the contract is a public, social contract, one agreed upon through group discussion and negotiation, so my job is to make sure that whatever agreement we come to about a plea will not be unfair to others in class. The plea is NOT an "out clause" for anyone who happens to not fulfill the contract in some way; it is for rare and unusual circumstances out of the control of the student.

By staying in this course and attending class, you accept this contract and agree to abide by it. I also agree to abide by the contract, and administer it fairly and equitably (Asao).

Sincerely,
Asao Inoue

5 A Guiding Question, Some Primary Research, and a Dash of Rhetorical Awareness

Paula Mathieu

NOT A HYPOTHETICAL EXERCISE ...

John Trimbur once remarked that a single-course composition requirement is like an only child: too many hopes and dreams get pinned in one place. I find John's comment doubly relevant to my life, as a parent to one child and the director of a one-course composition program. On many days, I can nod my head in agreement with his assertion that with just one writing course, we inevitably try doing too much with too little. On other days, I marvel at the fun and challenge that comes from nurturing just one thing: to make that writing course, or her, the best it or she can be.

I smiled, then, when the editors of this collection sent the following question my way: "If you had the opportunity to teach a semester-long section of first-year composition at your university, and if you knew that course was the only first-year composition course the students in your class would take, what would you include in the course, and why?" I not only have the opportunity to teach such a course every year, but I also direct a writing program with dozens of full-time, part-time, and graduate instructors who teach a one-semester composition course—the only required university writing course. In this article, I discuss the specifics of some of the first-year writing courses I have taught in this setting, followed by how I structure the goals of the writing program to maintain coherence and individual pedagogical innovation. My discussion is grounded in an awareness of the real opportunities and limitations that a single-semester composition course offers.

. . . In a Local Context

As many important writers in our field show us time and again, place matters (Owens; Reynolds; and Mauk). Where one teaches profoundly shapes the how and the why. So, before discussing the what, why, and how I teach first-year writing, I want to explain a bit about where.

I started teaching at Boston College in fall of 2001. The events of September 11, 2001, unfolded on my second day of teaching, and my first-year writing students and I silently watched together, on our classroom's six-foot by six-foot dual-projection screens, as the World Trade Towers collapsed. I had never taught in a classroom so wired with capabilities and technologies before that semester; in that moment, I experienced both the power and the danger such privilege of access offers.

I tell that story because I think "privilege of access" is an apt way to discuss Boston College (BC), a Jesuit university located half within the city lines of Boston and half in the tiny, adjoining city of Newton, Massachusetts. BC has a gorgeous, hilly campus with impressive stone gothic buildings and expansive athletic fields. While not all students are wealthy, many are. While not everyone graduates at the top of their high-school class, most do. Together, this makes for a socially competitive environment that can be very stressful to students, but the climate is also intellectually rich and challenging. At first blush, people might see BC as a rather homogenous campus of more white and Catholic students than not, but the students there possess a diversity of backgrounds, ideas, and ideologies, all of which are important to acknowledge, given that much of it is hidden from view.

I was hired at BC as an assistant professor to teach in the English Department and to be the Director of the First-Year Writing Program (referred to at BC as the First-Year Writing Seminar, or FWS) three years out of every six. The FWS program was developed eight years earlier by Lad Tobin, with whom I would alternate the duties of the director.

The original FWS program had as its goal helping students develop effective processes for composing and revising non-fiction prose. It was a writing-intensive workshop in which students selected many of their own topics and forms to focus on revision, gave and received feedback, and presented or "published" their work within various classrooms, on campus, or on the Internet. The course met for two fifty-minute periods each week, and instructors were required to conference with students for fifteen minutes each on a close to weekly basis. Course guidelines also stipulated that readings primarily be non-fiction (explicitly not academic writing) and in the same genres as those students were writing. The course description stated:

> We are less interested in teaching students the tropes and conventions of particular academic discourses than we are in teaching them general strategies that can apply to any writing task. We are less interested in telling students how to complete any particular writing assignment than we are in giving them the tools and the incentive to keep writing after the course has ended.

The only required text for the course was *Fresh Ink*, an annual publication of twenty-five essays from FWS students (gathered from a pool of up to 500 submissions), edited annually from 1993 to 2004.

I spend time discussing the program as it was when I arrived because I believe that a writing course—or a writing program—should be responsive to the environment in which it resides. Especially when a writing program marks a revision rather than a creation, a teacher or administrator must be sensitive to and work within the existing context. I was unfamiliar with the BC FWS context when I entered it: schooled largely in cultural-studies approaches to composition, I found myself on uncertain terrain in a process-based, conference-heavy, modes course with content largely chosen by students. The administrator in me (a role I would step into two years after my arrival) imagined making immediate changes. As a teacher, I wanted to learn the terrain and try to fit in. I stumbled through my first uncertain semesters and made lots of mistakes, but I also learned from my colleagues and my students.

By teaching the composition course within the existing program, I grew to appreciate certain things about the approach. I learned that having students find their own ways to be deeply invested in their writing makes them more willing to work on and struggle with their work. Through several hundred individual student conferences, I learned to talk less, be a better listener, and help students discover interesting and surprising options for developing their own essays.

Despite my ongoing appreciation for all that this first-year writing program offered, I still desired to make changes. Since the class met for only one hundred minutes per week, much of the substance of the course transpired in conferences, often making me feel like I taught fifteen independent studies rather than a shared writing course. I also wanted my writing course to not only help students love writing, but to also love thinking through new ideas together via writing, and to grow to see writing as an important guide and tool for thinking and learning. Over time, I developed goals for my own first-year course and for the program that could, I hoped, foster enthusiasm for the craft of writing and for the idea of writing as an important intellectual enterprise.

A Course with a Guiding Inquiry . . .

A bedrock belief I hold about any composition course I teach is this: The course must be framed by a guiding question or inquiry. This idea is similar to Joseph Harris's assertion about writing courses: "It seems to me that much as a piece of writing always needs to be about something, so, too, a writing *course* needs a subject, to be centered on some substantive issue or question—on the role of media in society, for instance, or the nature of work, or theories of schooling, or any of a thousand other complex and open issues that a group of writers can explore together" (Harris 8-9). To me, an inquiry is broader than a topic and a question that can open up, for one semester at least, a shared *whatness* that frames a writing course.

I believe in a guiding course inquiry for several reasons: First, I want to encourage students not only to develop their writing skills, but to come to rely on the practice of writing to deepen their own thinking and to help them discover and learn. In order to do that, I want an ongoing, unanswerable question lurking in the background of the class (and many days, the question truly is in the background) so that at the end of the class, I can ask students two kinds of questions: How has thinking about "x" helped you change your skills of writing, and how has writing and discussing this semester changed or deepened your thinking about "x"? Thought and writing are so inextricably linked that I cannot imagine teaching a course without this unity—although

like those

many great teachers do. A second reason for an inquiry is that a guiding question helps me imagine a coherence of the course so that I can understand its architecture well enough to teach it. It recalls what Malea Powell describes about her course planning in the documentary *Take 20*. She seeks a guiding metaphor for each class she teaches, and once she finds it, she plans the specifics for the course. For me, I need my question.

To me, the question is less critical than its existence and momentary interest. As a result, my questions change fairly often. I have taught first-year writing courses in recent years using the following questions: To what extent is language powerful, and to what extent is it not? What do we learn when we explore where we come from? What does it mean to be at a university, and where are we going from here? While exploring language and story, hometowns, or the culture of the university, and while ideally getting excited by those questions, we read and write and learn about writing. Assignments help us take on a different approach, methodology, or corner of the question.

A case for the importance of a guiding course question is made most persuasively by James Zebroski in *Thinking Through Theory*:

> Writing teachers . . . expect students to write unified compositions made coherent by a theme or thesis, and yet the composition course (not to mention composition textbooks) often lacks unity and coherence. We complain about student writing that is choppy, that jumps from one topic to another unrelated topic without transitions, but we find nothing strange or inconsistent about jumping from one mode to another over the semester. . . . If a composition course is going to be more than a hodgepodge, and if student reflections on the writing activities in that course are going to be more than a hodgepodge, compositionists need to attend more closely to the arrangement of assignments and discussions. (18)

What I appreciate about Zebroski's argument is that he shows a need for teachers to model ideas of coherent thinking through the writing assignments we write. For me, an inquiry allows me to create, for myself and (I hope) for my students, course coherence. A common misconception I have found when discussing the idea of a course inquiry is that it gets mistaken for a topics-based course. While I fully support topical courses, especially for research-specific or elective courses, what I mean by an inquiry is not synonymous with a topic. Again, Zebroski elegantly discusses what makes for an appropriate inquiry (what he calls a "theme") in a writing course:

> [It] provides the course with an evident structure that teacher and students keep referring to, a kind of *refrain* that can help the class to *broaden* its activities, to extend its inquiry. This course theme needs to be open enough to open into a variety of related topics and readings which are of interest to the students. The theme, however, also needs to be somehow implicitly linked to writing, which, after all, is what the course is about. By the term's end, it should be apparent to all, if it hasn't up to that point, that the course theme has turned to, but also has always in some sense been about, *writing*. A teacher and the students need to carefully choose a theme for the course that is open-ended, that is a question to be investigated, without any preformed correct answers decided upon in advance. The class then investigates the theme, coming to its own conclusions, which may well be different or even opposed to the teacher's view. (18)

If an inquiry is too narrow, students have no space to write their way into the question based on their own experiences or interests. If the inquiry is too open, it risks having no unity or shared discussion among students to help them develop their thinking. An inquiry should pattern a course and suggest new activities, but it should not make the course any less a composition course. In the end, it's always about writing and the nature of what writing helps us *do*, as Zebroski's meditation makes clear.

WITH AN ASSIGNMENT SEQUENCE AS MEDITATION . . .

While I begin my discussion of my composition class with the idea of inquiry, I need not always arrive at inquiry first. Sometimes I pick one or two assignments I know I want to give, and then back my way into a question that unites them and suggests other assignments. In terms of creating assignments, I create a kind of mental checklist that includes assignment variety and touching on important goals. For my own class planning, inquiry and assignments act as terms in a dialectic process.

For the sake of example, in this article I refer to assignments I planned around the question, "To what extent is language powerful or not?"

I try to sequence assignments such that students typically begin by writing in a descriptive genre for a local audience (e.g., the class or community), then in an analytic genre for an academic audience, and then develop a final research project (described later in this article) in which each writer defines the purpose, audience, and form of the paper based on the project itself and the purpose each writer creates or discovers. In the first assignment, the goal is to have students explore the content of the inquiry—to what extent is language powerful or not—by deploying evidence from their own lives or observations and to practice writing thickly, with clear, vivid descriptions. I asked students to write short, observational sketches first about moments that proved that "the pen is mightier than the sword," and then others that showed that "while sticks and stones may break my bones, names will never hurt me." We debated the relative truths and limitations of these aphorisms as a class, and everyone chose a moment or series of moments to write about that explore language at work as either powerful, insufficient, or a bit of both. This assignment, I hope, interests students in the bigger questions of the inquiry, and allows them to weigh in using their own experiences or observations, while also practicing deploying evidence effectively.[1]

SOME ACADEMIC WRITING . . . BUT ONLY SOME

For my second assignment in this particular course, I shift into writing analytically in an academic context.

A book that has been influential in planning and imagining my writing courses is Lee Ann Carroll's *Rehearsing New Roles: How College Students Develop as Writers.* Her study of how twenty writers at Pepperdine University developed as writers over their undergraduate years usefully points out the value and limits of a first-year course. She asserts that introductory composition courses serve an important role in helping students develop revision strategies, flexibility as writers, and metacognitive awareness about how to adapt writing strategies to other settings (72-73). A limitation that Carroll notes is that many first-year writing courses lack challenging content, and thus do not help students work to achieve a balance between reporting information and constructing their own arguments in a piece of analytic writing (136).

Her findings concur with my own experiences with student writers, and have influenced me to include an assignment that asks students to engage with a challenging text or texts for an academic audience in order to help students "integrate their own ideas with those of others" (Council of Writing Program Administrators; CWPA).

As such, I typically assign one project (usually the second assignment) in which students must come to terms with or forward a key idea or argument from one or two essays we read together as a class. By using the terms "come to terms with" and "forward," I show my indebtedness to Joe Harris's thoughtful approach to academic writing as generous, performative projects that make "interesting use of the work of others" (1). While I do not have students read Harris—instead, I ask all new graduate instructors to read *Rewriting*—Harris's approach to helping students create their own projects that work with the texts of others deeply influences what I do. It makes academic writing seem like neither a mindless exercise nor a querulous drill in dismissing the ideas of another. Rather, Harris's approach invites students to see their own intellectual work as *projects* that *do something*, and using someone else's ideas is one way to do that.

In my course with an inquiry about language and power, we read Richard Lanham's first chapter of *The Economics of Attention*, where he provocatively argues that the idea of things now has more value than things themselves. It's a slippery and difficult argument to fully grasp, and Lanham's use of deceptively simple terms like "stuff" and "fluff" often lead students to initially misread Lanham's argument, or to think Lanham is actually arguing something other than what he does. In the process of writing about this text, the class discusses what exactly is Lanham's argument on the way to discovering how they feel about it and what they can do with it in their own projects. For example, one student who had worked a summer internship at a hospital that was ranked nationally for its cardiac care *used* Lanham's argument to discuss how, in her view, the hospital's desire to maintain its top ranking led, at times, to decisions that undercut actual patient care. Her project led her to *use* Lanham's argument, but to also *counter* it by arguing that Lanham's neutral stance on this cultural shift overlooks the human cost that accompanies valuing names or labels over material results.

Having students work through a challenging text together helps them contend with issues of challenging content—and Carroll's study shows that this is one of the biggest challenges writers face in disciplinary specific courses—in a setting where *writing about* the ideas (not just the ideas themselves) is central. This provides, I hope, a challenging but supportive practice field for writers who will contend with difficult texts and ideas in other courses and throughout their lives.

While I think this phase of my course is important, it is only one phase. I see having students writing in a variety of rhetorical situations and getting involved in primary research projects as equally valuable phases for my writing course. I explore these below.

AND AN EMPHASIS—A FOCUS—ON (PRIMARY) RESEARCH

The first-year writing seminar is the only course at our university in which undergraduate students are formally introduced to the resources available at our university libraries. Some form of secondary research, then, has been a required part of the first-year course since its inception. It is a requirement that I have continued as program director. If students will get only one course in composition, it is imperative to introduce library resources and some independent research, because understanding and working with research is central to university work.

While I think library research is essential for students to encounter and make sense of, I typically ask students to come to such research as part of a primary research project that is based in observation and interview. In recent years, I have had first-year students do place-based, ethnographic projects as well as oral-history projects, as both require an important blend of primary and secondary research. I want students to encounter secondary research as part of their primary research project, because such a gesture helps students see the motivations and ideas behind the library resources they encounter, and because they are engaged in projects similar to those of other scholars.

I also include primary research in my first-year writing courses because I prize assigning an interview, as interviews are comprised of what I believe to be many important intellectual tasks, especially for students at this age and moment of their lives. Interviews ask them to: become deeply curious about someone else, come up with useful questions to ask the interviewee, actively listen and engage with another person, come to terms with how to record or preserve responses, and engage in the complex task of responsibly re-telling a story. Also, to interview well, especially in oral history projects, requires secondary research.

For the final unit in my most recent first-year course, with an inquiry about the power of language and story, I asked students to interview someone older, possibly but not necessarily a family member, to find a story worth preserving and circulating. To prepare for this project, we read Lesléa Newman's short story, "A Letter for Harvey Milk," as a way to think about the stories we tell, the ones we withhold, and the power (and risk) of sharing stories. I also asked students to listen to a number of online interviews from the StoryCorp project as well as other online sources. Through in-class writing and an ideas workshop, students first chose three possible interview candidates, and then narrowed the choice to one.

Most students chose to interview a family member—a parent, a grandparent, an aunt, or an uncle. We talked about how a class assignment is an opportunity to ask questions one is curious about, but never found the occasion to ask about. For example, one student interviewed his father about when he dropped out of college—a time his father had never wanted to discuss with the student before. Another student wanted to interview his mother about her sister, who had died many years earlier from cystic fibrosis (CF). He wanted to learn about his aunt, wanted to ask why his mother often said he was very like her, and he wanted to ask about CF and the role it might play in his life and future decisions about his own family. Having the permission of a school project often allows students to ask questions they might not otherwise. Another student was born in the Dominican Republic; his mother sent him away to be raised by his father in Los Angeles in order to give him a better life. He wanted to interview his mother about that decision, about how her life changed with him gone, and about what made growing up in LA without his mother seem like a better opportunity than a life with her in the Dominican Republic. A fourth student interviewed her grandmother about her decision to leave England and move to rural New Hampshire shortly after World War II, and what that decision meant to her at the time, as well as today. Another student interviewed her Indian father and British mother about their courtship and the adaptations they had made when coming together as a couple.

While each project is grounded in what might be considered personal, primary research, library research is essential in asking the right questions and in understanding the context of the stories the writers learn about. By researching the genetics of cystic fibrosis and decisions that carriers of CF face, the history of the Dominican Republic in the 1980s, Britain during and after World War II and the context of British colonization of India, for example, students learned about important issues and contexts in order to ask informed questions and tell detailed stories. In addition, through help of librarians, we discussed how to ask the right questions related to time, and especially related to issues of technology. For example, the student interviewing her parents about their courtship had a difficult time understanding how her parents had been in New York at the same time shortly after meeting in college, but they did not know it, since they did not know how to contact each other. Only after she researched more about modes of communication at that time (e.g., how long mail took, the state of telephone access, etc.) did their story make sense to her.

Once students conducted their interviews, compiled their research, and discovered the stories they wanted to tell, they then made decisions about audience, genre, and purpose. Many students created mini-books about their family stories to be kept and archived for future generations. One student said, "Someday, I want my grandchildren or my brother's grandchildren to find this book in the attic, about my grandmother, and learn something about her and me." Once such a future audience was chosen, the student's rhetorical task was to help this reader understand a context and a person far removed by time and place. In this, careful description, dialogue, and background research is necessary. The student who researched her grandmother's move from England to New England, for example, wrote a narrative essay full of description and dialogue, and used extensive narrative footnotes to provide historical context. She said that she wanted to include all those elements without losing the thread of the stories. Footnotes were her way of doing that. The student who wrote about his aunt with CF, alternately, said that he was more comfortable writing about this rather personal subject from a researched, academic perspective. He imagined his project as a way to help families who might carry CF think through the challenges and issues—while still remembering the remarkable lives—of those who have lived and died with the disease.

Framed as a final project for the semester, this primary research project asks students to integrate story, research, and context with a specific audience and purpose in mind—one that they define. Best of all, in this process, students often find themselves working on a project that really matters to them. As a result, the acts of researching, drafting, revising, and editing become not just steps toward getting a grade, but necessary moments in creating a meaningful project.

WHILE ENCOURAGING AWARENESS OF RHETORICAL SITUATIONS AND FLEXIBILITY

While I will not pretend that my first-year course can prepare all students for every rhetorical situation they will ever face, I strive to help students understand that every writing task takes place within a rhetorical situation and that not all situations call for the exact same kind of writing: that there is no *one* such thing as good writing. Helping students learn that they should read and suss out what a writing situation calls for is central to my composition classes. This aligns with Carroll's data suggesting that student writers "need the rhetorical skill to adapt to new writing situations and adapt to differing genre conventions" (120).

How much rhetorical reading and adapting one can do in a single semester is debatable, but the short answer is not all that much. I try to show my students that the particular assignments we do are less important than the larger ideas that they represent: that we write better when we care about what we are doing, that different audiences and purposes call for different kinds of evidence and genres, and that we feel less anxious about writing when we understand what is being asked for and why. While early assignments in a writing class tend to specify audience, purpose, and genre, I build toward a final project in which those decisions must be made by the writer.

My assignment sequence typically asks students to write in one genre for a local audience (e.g., the class or the community), in another genre for an academic audience, and to develop a final project in which each writer defines the purpose, audience, and form of the paper based on the project itself and the purpose each writer creates or discovers. I borrow this idea of constraining the topic but leaving the purpose, audience, and rhetorical form open to Jody Shipka's essay, "Toward a Multimodal Task-Based Framework for Composing." In it, she asks students to think deeply and imaginatively about why, what, to whom, and how they write—and the students' writing often takes on unusual forms, such as a series of gift bags delivered to a doorstep or a text to be read alongside a computer program and music. While I lack Shipka's skills in pushing students toward creative exploration, I hope that in their concluding projects for the semester, my students define how and to whom they want to write in mindful and deliberate ways. I also borrow another requirement from Shipka, what she calls a "heads up" statement, in which students must explain their writerly choices—what they were going for and why they did what they did. Such a final project allows students to have a meaningful connection with the writing they do, and to also be accountable and deliberate with the rhetorical choices they make. This kind of work is what Zebroski calls "metawriting," or, "writing that reflects on writing, that examines writing experiences of student and professional writers" (19). I agree with Zebroski's idea that "all this metawriting helps improve 'content' while making students increasingly aware of their own theories of writing" (21).

But No Service Learning

My own scholarship in composition and rhetoric focuses on community-university partnerships, and I spend a good deal of my own research time involved with community-based writing projects. In her study, Carroll finds that students who are involved in experiential-based learning frequently cite those experiences as deeply important and informative in their development as students and writers (104). It might be surprising, then, when I assert that my first-year writing classes do not have a service-learning component.

I do not include service learning in my first-year course for a variety of reasons, those related to timing, complications of planning, and the peculiarities of course registration on our campus. From 2001 to 2012, the composition classes only met for one hundred minutes of course time per week. With such a tight timeframe, I never felt I had the time or the space to fit in a service project for first-year students. Even if I could have found time in the course, finding or developing a project that could productively involve fifteen students for the fourteen weeks that our class met was difficult, if not impossible, for me to imagine.[2] Beyond the logistical challenges, I feel that, ethically, students should choose to do service projects and not have them thrust upon them—and given when and how first-year students register for their courses, there is no guarantee that they would know that they were enrolling into a service-learning course. My commitment to having students choose service learning has less to do with a reluctance to ask students to do something they might not otherwise choose for themselves—teaching a required course, by default, asks students to do lots of things they might not choose—rather, I worry about the fallout for the clients being served when putting students in a situation where they do not want to be. Research by Randy Stoecker, Elizabeth Tyron, and Amy Hilgendorf, for example, shows that many community organizations who host service learners feel that the students do not provide them with beneficial services.

When a service project is conceived well, carefully planned, and collaboratively monitored and evaluated by the instructor and the community group, positive interactions for students and the community members can and do take place. Concocting such a careful recipe is more art than science, and, at least currently in my own teaching of first-year writing, I do not feel I can reliably create such a recipe in a course already saddled with many other goals and expectations. I would not stand in the way of an instructor in my program creating a service-learning component for the course, but it is not a commitment I take on in that setting.

FROM A COURSE TO A PROGRAM: PEDAGOGICAL FREEDOM AND SHARED OUTCOMES

As director of the First-Year Writing Program, I know I need to structure a consistent and coherent program. At the same time, I want to maintain individual instructor innovation. I do this via shared outcomes across all sections. In addition to the WPA outcomes for Rhetorical Knowledge, Critical Reading and Writing, Process, Knowledge of Conventions, and Writing in Electronic Environments, I ask that each section be organized by a guiding question or inquiry, that all sections include research and an introduction to the campus library resources, and that all sections have students read the in-process and polished work by other students. *Fresh Ink* continues as an online journal, and faculty are encouraged to use student examples from other sources, such as the journal, *Young Scholars in Writing*.

What I hope unites any first-year course in my program is a series of interesting and challenging assignments that ask students to think and write in multiple ways and to revise their ideas and their words.

Also, I hope all our first-year courses help writers leave the class with a toolkit of strategies for reading a rhetorical situation, approaching a complex assignment by breaking it down into steps, and seeing their own writing as something that develops over time and via various processes. Rather than focus on one correct approach or question for the course, my goal as program director is to create opportunities for our instructors to share ideas, discuss challenges, and swap assignments.

BEYOND A SINGLE SEMESTER

In reflecting on what I do teach in a typical first-year course, I am confronted by the reality of how insufficient it all seems, how many important ideas, approaches, and media *are not* taught in a given semester. In the course discussed here, for example, I do not specifically emphasize visual literacy or require multimodal composition, even though I, in fact, value visual literacy and encourage students to explore multimodal writing. The point is that, especially in a one-course format, first-year writing can suffer from a crisis of too many (laudable) goals; so, I limit my scope in order to accomplish the few goals I do outline.

While I enjoy teaching first-year writing in its current, one-course instantiation, I believe that one required writing course is insufficient to support students throughout their years of undergraduate writing development. Part of my mission as director of the First-Year Writing Program has been to advocate and develop opportunities for writing support beyond this single course. Primarily, that has taken the form of developing a Writing Fellows Program.

Writing beyond the first year takes different forms at every institution. In my local setting, I knew that proposing curricular change or adding new courses would be difficult, but that many individual faculty wished to assign and teach more writing in the classes that they already teach. To actively work against the myth that a single writing course can give all students what they need to write in any situation ever, I wanted to be involved in actively developing resources to help students develop as writers beyond the first-year seminar. In that setting, a Writing Fellows Program made sense.[3] In 2004, I created a small pilot project, pairing three graduate-student Writing Fellows with a core sociology class of sixty students who were assigned three papers throughout the semester. The students were required to submit drafts of each paper to their assigned Writing Fellow and meet to discuss the project and strategies for revision. Additionally, the fellows would meet with the faculty member to discuss common questions, struggles, or issues students faced to allow that information to come back into the classroom in the form of faculty instruction.

This pilot has grown slowly but steadily. Since 2004, the program has partnered with faculty in accounting, history, business administration, music, education, psychology, sociology, political science, English, geosciences, and theater. Responses from students have been overwhelmingly positive, reporting that they benefited from the discipline-specific writing support. Faculty are also overwhelmingly positive; they sense that they assign and read better papers and are more effectively teaching writing within their content courses. As the WPA, I appreciate that many of the Writing Fellows—who include several first-year Master's students in English—will teach the first-year writing course the following year and are receiving wonderful preparation by interacting with undergraduates and by learning how to give writing feedback. While the program remained a pilot for many years, in the fall of 2012, the program expanded to Phase Two, with a half-time administrator and an expanded budget to work with more classes. Our goal within this phase is to work with 10% of the undergraduate population annually and to expand further in coming years. This program is one way to acknowledge that a thriving first-year writing course is a necessary but insufficient resource for helping students develop as writers within the university and beyond.

NOTES

1. I say experiences *or* observations because, while I value first-person student writing, I never want to put a student into a position in which he or she must reveal personal details about him or herself that might be uncomfortable or private. I am persuaded by Harriet Malinowitz's argument, in *Textual Orientations: Lesbian and Gay Students and the Making of Discourse Communities*, that an assignment that specifically asks students to reveal details about themselves might especially put gay and lesbian students in a bind to either be out to one's classmates or to choose a story that isn't central. To avoid asking students to disclose information they might not want to, I encourage students to think of all that they have observed, read, and experienced as first-person evidence for the assignment. For example, when we did this assignment, it was the week in which Kanye West interrupted Taylor Swift's acceptance speech at the MTV Music Awards, Representative Joe

Wilson yelled "You lie!" to President Obama during his State of the Union Address, and tennis player Serena Williams raised controversy by swearing at line judges at the US Open. Those three instances were thick with implications of the relative power and of the limits of power to language, especially as they are inflected by issues of race and gender. In the end, many students wrote about their own experiences, but a few wrote about something they observed at their school or something experienced by a close friend.

2. See Mathieu, *Tactics of Hope*, Chapter 4, "Students in the Street."

3. For more about the Boston College Writing Fellows Program, including annual reports, see http://www.bc.edu/content/bc/libraries/help/tutoring/writingfellows.html.

WORKS CITED

Carroll, Lee Ann. *Rehearsing New Roles: How College Students Develop as Writers*. Carbondale: Southern Illinois UP, 2002. Print.

Council of Writing Program Administrators. *WPA Outcomes Statement for First-Year Composition*. Amended July 2008. Web. 28 February 2012.

Harris, Joseph. *Rewriting: How to Do Things with Texts*. Logan: Utah State UP, 2006. Print.

Lanham, Richard. *The Economics of Attention: Style and Substance in an Age of Information*. Chicago: U of Chicago P, 2007. Print.

Mathieu, Paula. *Tactics of Hope: The Public Turn in English Composition*. Portsmouth: Boynton-Cook/Heinemann, 2005. Print.

Mauk, Johnathan. "Location, Location, Location: The 'Real' (E)states of Being, Writing, and Thinking in Composition." *College English* 65.4 (2003): 368-88. Print.

Newman, Lesléa. *A Letter to Harvey Milk: Short Stories*. Madison: U of Wisconsin P, 2004. Print.

Owens, Derek. *Composition and Sustainability: Teaching for a Threatened Generation*. Urbana: NCTE, 2001. Print.

Powell, Malea. *Take 20: Teaching Writing*. Dir. and ed. Todd Taylor. Bedford, St. Martin's. 2008. DVD.

Reynolds, Nedra. *Geographies of Writing: Inhabiting Places and Encountering Difference*. Carbondale: Southern Illinois UP, 2007. Print.

Shipka, Jody. "A Multimodal Task-Based Framework for Composing." *College Composition and Communication* 57.2 (2005): 277-306. Print.

Stoecker, Randy, Elizabeth Tryon, and Amy Hilgendorf. *The Unheard Voices: Community Organizations and Service Learning*. Philadelphia: Temple UP, 2009. Print.

Trimbur, John. "Dilemmas of First Year Writing." Boston College. 24 February 2010. Address.

Zebroski, James. *Thinking Through Theory: Vygotskian Perspectives on the Teaching of Writing*. Portsmouth: Boynton-Cook, 1994. Print.

Appendix: Course Syllabus

ENGLISH 010.02: FIRST-YEAR WRITING SEMINAR

Boston College
M/W 11:00 a.m. + Conference/Workshop (to be scheduled)
Exploring Power in Words, Media and Stories
Dr. Paula Mathieu

Course Overview

People write for many reasons—to remember, to learn, to inform, entertain, persuade—and to many different audiences. Writing operates quite differently depending on the time, place and audience for which it is written. Over the next 14 weeks together we will work on writing different genres and for different audiences. What I hope you'll discover this semester is that there is no uniform idea of "good writing." Writing can be either successful or unsuccessful in meeting its objectives, depending on the audience, the approach of the writer, and the time and place of the writing. By the end of this course, I hope you will have learned strategies for understanding a given occasion for writing (known as a rhetorical situation) and engaging in a writing process that feels productive and helps you achieve your purpose. Writing a successful research report is not the same thing as writing a persuasive newspaper article or a funny email or a moving personal story.

I find the best way to practice these writing strategies together is to have a shared inquiry: shared questions or ideas we'll investigate together. This semester our inquiry will focus on exploring the power of words, images and stories. Specifically, we'll explore the role of names and name-calling, we'll investigate what captures our attention on a day-to-day basis, and we'll interview someone older than ourselves to learn and preserve an important story. We'll also explore writing that we do for no other audience than ourselves. In the end, I hope we'll be able to make some tentative conclusions about what we see as the power of words, media and stories in our own lives.

This semester, we will write and read texts that I hope will be enjoyable, challenging, and significant to you. That significance, however, should co-exist with the knowledge that there are many other worthwhile things to read and write. So take what we do together as a drop in an ocean. I hope this course continues your ongoing relationship with writing in fun, useful, and engaging ways.

This class is a bit unusual in that we meet twice a week for 50 minutes in class. Most weeks, we'll have a third meeting—a one-on-one or group conference that we schedule. Other weeks we might attend a play, do a library scavenger hunt, or meet for informal peer workshops. Just remember, whatever we plan for that third class is required each week, and attendance counts for it as with other classes.

Required Texts and Materials

- EN010.02 Coursepack (available in BC bookstore).
- Donovan-Kranz, Eileen, ed. *Fresh Ink: Stories from BC First Year Writing Seminar*
- Faigley, Lester. *The Brief Penguin Handbook.* (2003) Longman.

All are available at the BC bookstore, or the Faigley book can be purchased online (new or used), through Amazon.com or other online bookstores.

There will be other occasional readings that will be available under the "Readings" section of our Blackboard site as PDF documents that you'll be required to print. Please bring hard copies of the reading to class on the day designated on the syllabus.

To access our class Blackboard site, go to http://cms.bc.edu and log with your username and password, then follow the link with the course name. I also recommend having on hand a notebook (used just for this course) and access to a college dictionary (print or online).

Grading and Required Work

In this course, your writing will be divided into four units: you will be graded for each unit, but you can keep revising any of the units until the end of the semester, provided we discuss the project in conference. Each unit will include short online posts due on specific days, longer drafts, and one revised essay. The grading breakdown of this required work is as follows:

Unit One: Name Descriptive Writing	20%
Unit Two: Analysis of Attention	20%
Unit Three: Researched Oral History	30%
Unit Four: Final Portfolio	20%
Participation	10%

In order to pass this course, you must complete all of the required work. The grading I do will be based on the following objectives for the course. For each unit, we as a class will formulate a list of more specific criteria by which the work will be evaluated.

Objectives

By the end of the course, I will evaluate a portfolio of your writing for its ability to demonstrate the following:

Rhetorical Knowledge

- Be able to focus on a purpose and respond to the needs of different audiences.
- Understand that different rhetorical situations (consisting of audience, writer, purpose, time, and culture) require adopting appropriate voice, tone, level of formality, genre, and format,
- Write in several genres.

Critical Reading and Writing

- Use reading and writing as a means of critical inquiry, which means working to understand, summarize, and analyze the ideas of others.
- Understand academic writing assignments as a series of tasks including finding, evaluating, analyzing, and synthesizing appropriate primary and secondary sources.
- Integrate your ideas with those of others.

Processes

- Be aware that it usually takes multiple drafts to create a successful text.
- Develop flexible strategies for generating, revising, editing, and proofreading
- Learn to respond to and critique your own and others' works.

Knowledge of Conventions

- Learn common formats for different kinds of texts, from academic to public, and understand that appropriate formats vary given the rhetorical situation.
- Practice appropriate means of documenting your work.

- Control such surface features as syntax, grammar, punctuation, and spelling.

Due Dates:

> Unit#1 for grading: Monday, Week 5
> Unit #2 for grading: Friday, Week 9
> Unit # 3 for grading: Wednesday, Week 14 (or in final portfolio)
> Unit #4 (final portfolio): Monday, Week 16

Classroom Policies

Conferences: This class meets twice per week in the classroom, and the third class meeting is meant for conferences or other writing-related activities. Most weeks, we will meet in a conference to discuss ideas for your writings, works-in-progress and research projects. The conferences will either be one-on-one or in small groups of your classmates and will take place in my office (431 Carney Hall) or in a café, like the Chocolate Bar or Hillside. Be sure to check the location and time each week; it's your responsibility to make the conference. Missing a conference is considered a class absence. Individual conferences will last about 15 minutes. You will each sign up for a specific time and keep that time for the whole semester. Group conferences will last approximately 45 minutes and will be held around the time of your regular conference.

Attendance: As this class is small and relies on in-class writing, group discussion and work shopping, consistent attendance is required. Coming in late or leaving early will not be appreciated, and if it becomes a pattern, each occurrence will count as an absence. More than two missed classes or conferences will lower your final course grade by a full step; and each additional absence will count as another step (a step is from B+ to B, to B-, etc.). More than five absences from class or conference may result in you failing the course. Missing a conference is considered a class absence. If an emergency arises that causes prolonged absence, contact the first-year Dean of your college. See me if you are unsure who that is.

This semester, we may be faced with many students contracting the flu. If you become sick, please follow the procedures the university recommends: "if you have a flu-like illness, email your academic Dean who will notify your professors. Make arrangements with your professors for any missed classes." So, if you're sick, stay in touch. Also, you'll be handing in your writing via Blackboard, so even if you're sick, you can hand in your work. If you're too ill, just be sure you contact your dean and stay in contact with me. And do us all a favor: get some sleep, don't run yourselves down too much, drink in moderation, and try to keep yourselves healthy. College is a lot more fun when you're not sick!

Plagiarism: According to the BC Policy on Academic Integrity, "Plagiarism is the deliberate act of taking the words, ideas, data, illustrations, or statements of another person or source, and presenting them as one's own. Each student is responsible for learning and using proper methods of paraphrasing and footnoting, quotation, and other forms of citation, to ensure that the original author, speaker, illustrator, or source of the material used is clearly acknowledged." In this course, my job is to teach you the proper methods for citation and attribution of sources. Your job is not to plagiarize or cheat. Any breaches of academic integrity will result in serious repercussions, such as failing the course. (For the university policy on academic integrity see: www. bc.edu/integrity. FYI: submission of the same written work in more than one course without prior written approval from the instructors involved is viewed as a form of cheating under the university policies.

Late Papers: All work is due by the time and date listed on the course schedule. Any late work will receive a lower grade.

Participation: Ten percent of your course grade is determined by in-class participation. Your participation grade will include completion of readings, participation in class discussions, bringing appropriate materials to class, including drafts of essays, and providing detailed feedback to your classmates during peer conferences and group workshops.

Cell Phones, IMs and other Communications: Please turn off the ringers on all cell phones or other PDAs in class. Please refrain from sending emails or IMs during class time. If your cell phone rings or if you're receiving a text or instant message, I get to answer it! The same rule applies for me; if my phone rings, someone in the class gets to answer.

Campus Resources Available to You

Academic Advising

In addition to being your FWS instructor, I am also your academic advisor. That means, I am open to talk with you about your other courses, questions or concerns you have as you pick a major, and any other issues you'd like to discuss. I may not have all the answers immediately, but I am good at finding things out. Please use your conference time or my regular office hours to ask any advising-related questions you have.

We will also have a small budget to get together for a meal or two or an event during the semester. We'll make plans and set a date early in the semester.

Connors Family Learning Center (CFLC): Located in 200 O'Neill Library, this is a place where you can go for one-on-one writing tutoring. A tutor won't "fix" a paper, but can be a great resource if you're feeling stuck or if you'd just like the feedback of another reader. Most professional writers would dream for such a ready resource, and it's available to BC students free. To schedule an appointment call **2–0611**.

Campus Technology Resource Center (CTRC): Located in 250 O'Neill Library, this is a place to access a computer and print documents like the PDF readings from our Blackboard site.

Counseling Services: (108 Gasson Hall). If things seem a bit tough for you at any point, or if you would just like someone to talk to— about feeling homesick, having trouble fitting in, or feeling depressed or overwhelmed—there are great people available to listen and help through the University Counseling Services. Call (617) 552–3310 to set up an appointment or stop in any of their offices at Gasson 108, Fulton 254, or Campion 301. It's free to all students.

Accommodations for Disabilities: If you have a disability and will be **requesting accommodations** for this course, please register with Kathy Duggan [kathleen.duggan@bc.edu], Associate Director, Academic Support Services, The Connors Family Learning Center (learning disabilities or ADHD) or Suzy Conway [suzy.conway.1@bc.edu], Assistant Dean for Students with Disabilities (all other disabilities).

Advanced notice and appropriate documentation are required for accommodations.

Schedule

Readings must be completed by the class day for which they are listed. Writings should be posted to Blackboard by the times stated. While I will try very hard to stick to this schedule, due dates, readings, and class schedule may change during the semester. All changes will be announced in class. You are responsible for updated deadlines.

Week 1 Introducing Ourselves, Course Overview
(W)   Introduction, Course Objectives, Writing Sample
         Write out your schedule for Wednesdays and Thursdays.

Unit One: What's In a Name? Writing Descriptively for a Local, but Unfamiliar, Audience

Week 2
(M)   Reading Due: The entire syllabus!
         Sherman Alexie, Maya Angelou and Nancy Mairs (Coursepack)
         Writing Due: Reading Response (Post on Blackboard):
         Respond to one of the day's readings:
         You can write about what you want, but some things to consider are as follows:
         Why are names important or not to the writers? What in either story do you respond to most strongly? What can you isolate on the page (images, words, description, dialogue) that leads you to your response?
(W)   Reading Due: Ann Lamott "Shitty First Drafts" (Coursepack)
         Sean Casey and Kendra Steele (*Fresh Ink*)
         —Discuss First-Year Convocation
         Writing Due: Writing 1.1 (post on Blackboard by midnight Tuesday)
(TH)   Individual Conferences

Week 3
(M)   Reading Due: O'Brien "The Things They Carried" (Blackboard)
         Rudner "Leader of the Pack and Now She's Gone" (Blackboard)
         Writing Due: Writing 1.2 (Post on Blackboard by midnight Sunday)
(W)   Reading Due: Read all of classes posts 1.3
         Writing Due: Writing 1.3 (Post on Blackboard by 10pm Tuesday)
(TH)   Individual Conferences

Week 4

(M):   Class Workshop
        Reading Due: Faigley, Chapters 5A, 5B, and 5C.
        Writing Due: Full typed draft of 1.4 (Post on Blackboard by 6pm
        Sunday)

(W)   Class Workshop Continued
        Reading Due: Faigley Chapter 5E, 5F
        Writing Due: Workshop Response

Unit 2: The Power of Attention: Writing Analytic Arguments for an Academic Audience

Week 5

(M)   Optional Group Workshop (no class)
        Writing Due: Revised Draft of Paper 1.4 due (posted by end of
        Monday) for grading

(W)   Reading Due: Kirn "The Autumn of the Multitaskers" (Coursepack)
        Faigley 6B: "Critical Reading and Viewing"
        Writing Due: Respond to Kirn: (post on Blackboard by midnight
        Tuesday) Pick one of his claims—what evidence does he use to sup
        port it? Do you agree or disagree?

(TH)   Conferences

Week 6

(M)   Holiday: No Class Meeting

(W)   Understanding the Place of the University in Arguments
        Reading Due: Lanham "Fluff and Stuff" (Coursepack)
        Writing Due: Writing 2.1 Due (post by midnight Tuesday)

Week 7

(M)   What is Summary vs. Analysis?
        Reading Due: Faigley 19E; Chapter 7
        Jenny Choi (*Fresh Ink*)
        Writing Due: Writing 2.2 (post by midnight Sunday)

(W)   Reading Due: Faigley, Chapter 10 "Writing to Persuade"
        Writing Due: Post notes for 2.2 (by Tuesday midnight)

(TH)   Conferences

Week 8

(M)   Writing an Academic Argument
        Reading Due: Faigley, Chapter 26 and 27
        Writing Due: Notes toward 2.3

(W)   Writing Due: Draft of 2.3 (posted to Blackboard by Tuesday at
        midnight)

(TH)   Individual Conferences (Midterm Assessments—Where are we?)

Week 9

(W)   Revised and polished draft of 2.3 posted to Blackboard by midnight

Unit 3: The Power of Oral History for a General Readership

Week 10

(M)   Reading Due: Studs Terkel (Coursepack) and Unit 3 Assignment
       Ron Fletcher "Professor of Soles" (Blackboard)

(W)   Asking Good Interview Questions
       Reading Due: Donald Ritchie (Coursepack)
       Writing Due: Writing 3.1 posted to Blackboard by Tuesday
       midnight

(TH-F) Patricia Riggin play on oral history with BC Employees. Attendance
       in lieu of conferences.

Week 11

(M)   What to Do with Interview Information?
       Reading Due: Holman (Coursepack); Robin Phillips (*Fresh Ink);*
       Faigley Chapter 15

(W):   Asking Good Research Questions
       Reading Due: Faigley 16–17
       Writing Due: Writing 3.2 posted to Blackboard by Tuesday
       midnight

(TH)   Conferences on interview transcripts and research questions

Week 12

(M)   Research Session with BC Librarian
       Reading Due: Faigley 18
       Writing Due: Come with questions you'd like to research

(W)   Making Annotated Bibliographies
       Reading Due: At least one source for your research
       Writing Due: Post to Blackboard bibliographic citation and
       annotation for one source (by class).

(TH)   Conferences

Week 13

(M)   Writing a Seamless Profile
       Reading Due: Carlo Rotella on Deval Patrick (Blackboard)
       Writing Due: Draft of 3.2 (post to Blackboard by Class)

(W-TH) NO Class—Happy Thanksgiving!

Week 14

(M)   Workshop (Complete drafts of 3.4 post to Blackboard by Sunday
       noon.)

Unit 4: Self as Audience and Final Portfolio

(W)   Reading Due: "A Letter to Harvey Milk" (Coursepack)
        Writing Due: (optional) Revised 3.4 for grading (or wait until final
        portfolio)
(TH)   Individual Conferences

Week 15

(M)   Reading Due: Read your entire work for course thus far and bring
        in one essay for more revision
        Writing Due: Reaction to 4.1; Come to class with questions about
        portfolio
(W)   Final Class Workshop (Bring 3 copies of any essay you'd like to get
        more feedback on.)
(TH)   Office Hours: optional conferences)

Final Portfolios to be handed in by noon on Monday of Finals Week.

Writing Unit One: The Power of Words—Writing Descriptively for a Local Audience

Audience: We will post our essays on our class Blackboard site and share our work in class workshops, so your audience is, literally, your classmates and me. Think about this audience as you write. You need to give us enough background and description to understand and appreciate your story. Language need not be overly formal—use of first person, and even written dialogue is encouraged; but it should not be overly colloquial either.

Writing1.1: What's in Your Name?

In this class, we'll be exploring the power of language, images and stories. To kick this off, we'll share a few stories about our names. What is an interesting story behind your name? Is there a special reason you have your first name? Does your family name carry a certain reputation or story in your community, because of older siblings or generations? How do you feel about your name? Have you ever been called a name that hurt you or one that made you feel good? Do you have nicknames, and how did you get them? (Don't feel the need to answer all of these questions—they're just to get you thinking. Feel free to choose one story about your name and tell that.)

Writing 1.2: What Do You Believe?
We have all heard the saying, "Sticks and Stones may break my bones but names will never hurt me." We've also all heard, "The pen is mightier than the sword." These two aphorisms are both common-place, but they argue entirely opposite beliefs about language and its power in the world.

Think about your own life, what you've experienced, read, written, etc., and write an essay arguing which of these statements you believe to be truer. Try to use a few vivid examples from your life and observations.

Writing 1.3: Adding Vivid Description to Your Essay
By now we've read several descriptive essays by writers like Sherman Alexie, Maya Angelou, and Nancy Mairs, in which they meditate about some aspect of words, names, or writing in their lives. You've also drafted an argument using some examples from your own life about the role of language.

Pick one example of something you've written about in 1.1 or 1.2, and vividly describe that situation. Use your senses—not just sight, but smell, touch, sound, and taste. Where is the place this scene took place? Can you include dialogue? Render the scene clearly for someone who didn't share your experience. Allow us to be there through your words.

Writing 1.4: Revision into a Descriptive Essay
Next, revise 1.1 or 1.2 incorporating your vivid description. Can you make it read like one of the essays that we read? It needn't be long— think roughly four pages—but make it rich, filled with description, dialogue, and reflection. I'd rather have you focus closely on one or a few instances than make broad claims or descriptions.

Writing Unit Two: The Power of Our Attention—Writing Analytic Arguments in an Academic Setting

Audience: Our writing for this unit will be geared toward an academic audience, which means writing should be precise, somewhat formal, and all sources should be cited. Since you will be responding to one of the essays we read in class, based on information you gather about your own life, you can use limited first person voice to make your arguments. For example use 'I' when referring to a specific example in your life, but you don't need to repeatedly say, "I think," or "I believe" about the claims you're making. Most importantly, make your claims specific and not overly general.

Writing 2.1: Paying Attention to Your Day
What do you pay attention to? In this unit, we'll be examining two contemporary arguments about multitasking and what we pay attention to in a day. Before we evaluate writers' arguments, we need to gather some evidence about our own lives.

Keep a 24-hour log in which you mark down **everything** you pay attention to, from the time you wake up, until when you are asleep. For example, if when you get up, you're listening to the radio while talking to your roommate and checking email, indicate that. If at breakfast, you're reading and eating and watching people in the cafeteria, indicate that. If you're in class and texting (not this class, of course), note that. If you go to sleep with music or the TV on, indicate that. You needn't go into description of any of these tasks, just **notice** them and **note them down**. Our goal is to gather data on where, what, and how many things we pay attention to during the day. (We will make sample logs in class, so we can all be somewhat consistent with how we record our days.) Be prepared to bring your logs with you to class.

After you've recorded a day, post a response on Blackboard in which you make some observations about your data: How often do you focus your attention on one thing, and how often are you multitasking? How often do you feel well focused, and how often do you feel distracted? What if anything surprised you about your observations? What, if anything, would you like to change about how and what you pay attention to in a day?

Writing 2.2: Understanding and Summarizing Kirn's Argument
Walter Kirn's "Autumn of the Multitaskers" is a humorous article, but in it he's making arguments about our culture today. In one page, write a summary of Kirn's article. A good summary should include the following:

- The full name and title of the article, and where and when it was published.
- What its main argument is, in your opinion.
- How the writer makes that argument (tone, what kind of evidence used, etc.).
- Although your goal here is to **summarize**, it's impossible to get away from some aspect of **evaluation** through the language

you use, etc. And that's as it should be. Thus, your summary can give some indirect indication of the strength and value of the argument.

Writing 2.3: Group Summary of Lanham's Argument

We're reading the introduction to Richard Lanhams's book *The Economics of Attention*. In order to effectively summarize and analyze his somewhat complex argument, we need to be sure we first understand what he's trying to say. So, we'll use the class group to divide up the chapter into equal length excerpts (we'll do this in class). Your job is to read the entire article and do your best to understand his argument. For your excerpt, your job is to understand **every small detail**. This means, you'll look up any unfamiliar words or allusions, be sure you're clear about the terminology he's using (such as 'stuff' and 'fluff'). In your brief (one to two paragraph) Blackboard post, discuss anything that is unclear in your excerpt, a challenging or important passage, or a question you have. Discuss how this excerpt fits into the overall argument. You will be the expert on your section. In class we will create a summary of Lanham's argument by piecing together our understandings, observations, and questions.

Writing 2.4: Analytic Essay Responding to Kirn and/or Lanham

Analysis means using a lens or point of view to evaluate something; by its very nature, which means an analysis is always an argument. Using your data and our class discussion about our observations about what we pay attention to in a day, write an analytic argument in which you either agree or disagree (or partially agree and partially disagree) with either Kirn's argument, Lanham's argument, or both. Be sure to include enough **summary** of your own data and the articles that we read to have your argument make sense of what you're agreeing with and disagreeing with. And be sure to use enough **evidence**, in the forms of examples from your own life, what you've observed or read, to give your argument credibility.

Since this is an academic essay, be sure to use clear, precise language; cite your sources (using MLA documentation), and make sure your arguments are not overly general or broad. Since the evidence you're using will be gathered from your own life and observations (this is called *primary research)* it is appropriate to use first person when referring to this information. The overall tone, however, should not be overly casual or conversational.

Writing Unit Three: The Power of Storytelling for a General Readership

> *"Research is formalized curiosity. It is poking and prying with a purpose. It is a seeking that he who wishes may know the cosmic secrets of the world and they that dwell therein."*—Zora Neale Hurston

Audience: Your audience for this unit will be a general, but educated readership. Think of essays you might read in *The Boston Globe Magazine* or *The New York Times.*

Writing 3.1: Interviewing Someone Older than You

In this unit, you will pick someone older than you—someone you know well, like a family member, or someone you would like to know more about, like a faculty member, a co-worker, etc.—and you will interview him or her about some aspect of history. The goal is to have you find some aspect of his or her life fascinating and to learn as much about a specific time or place as possible. In the past, students have interviewed, for example, a father talking about the year he dropped out of college to travel the country as a singer-songwriter; a grandfather, who as a child, fled the North Koreans before the start of the Korean war; a neighbor who had been a prisoner of war; a mom who worked as an undercover drug cop; a friend who is a recent immigrant from Cuba, reflecting on his view of US culture; a BC custodian who lost his job as a printer during the economic slowdown after September 11, 2001; a staff member at the McMullen Museum who has four children but is pursuing a graduate degree in art history; a boss who runs a local coffee shop that is important to the whole community. Everyone has fascinating stories and aspects of his or her life. Your job is to choose someone to interview, become fascinated in his or her story, and become a historian, documenting some aspect of his or her life. For this first section, select **three** possible interview candidates, and write up **six** possible questions to ask each. Be sure each choice is someone you can actually interview, in person, sometime between now and the end of Thanksgiving break.

Writing 3.2: Interview Transcript

From your list of three, you will select one person that you could interview two to three times, with at least one of these times being face to face.

Complete oral histories strive to transcribe entire conversations with people and then reproduce them in edited form. Rather than doing that, I would ask that by the end of your first interview, you single out some area or aspect of the person's life that you would like to be the focus of your essay. Then transcribe (using quotations, paraphrase, etc., techniques we will discuss in class) as much about this topic as possible.

Include in this transcript additional questions: both to ask the person in a follow-up interview and for your own background research.

Writing 3.3: Background Research

Oral histories combine interview research (also known as primary research) with extensive background research (also known as secondary research) that helps describe the **context** of the story: the time, place, customs, and people relevant in the story. Whatever interests you most in your interviewee's comments will be what you research. For example, a former student wrote about her grandmother's personal friendship with Mother Theresa. In the interview, she described her mother's travels to Rome after Mother Theresa's death, to take part in the Beatification Ceremony for her. She chose to research what Roman Catholic Beatification means and the significance of this ceremony, which became the frame for her story. She might have alternatively researched more about Mother Theresa's life to provide more context to the stories of the time and places where she and her grandmother met, or even researched the U.S. hospital where the two became friends. Your interest and curiosity (along with feedback from class members and me) will help shape the story and your research.

You should be prepared to have a minimum of five sources, for which you provide an annotated bibliography. You need not summarize the entire source, just summarize and provide salient quotes for the relevant information.

Writing 3.4: Integrated Profile Essay

We will read several examples of profile essays, which combine interview, description and background research. Your final draft for this unit will be to write and revise a profile essay drawn from your interviews and research. You should include vivid descriptions, direct quotations, and cited background research (using MLA documentation).

Writing Unit Four: Final Portfolio—The Power of Writing

Audience: This unit you will write for two very different audiences: for yourself, in a letter that I won't see, and then to me, in a portfolio letter that I will read. Only you will know for sure the differences you notice in writing for yourself and for your teacher. But I will be curious to know how changing audiences throughout the semester affects how you write.

Writing 4.1: Writing a Letter You'll Never Send

In a "Letter to Harvey Milk," Harry's teacher asks him to write a letter to someone who was in his past, a letter he would never send. I am asking us all to write a letter to someone (living or not), telling him/her something that you have never ever told anyone before. Write and tell him/her (imaginary friend) something you never ever wanted anyone to know.

YOU WILL NOT BE HANDING IN THIS LETTER, NOR ADDING THE LETTER TO YOUR PORTFOLIO, NOR TELLING ANYONE WHAT YOU WROTE ABOUT.

You are responsible for writing up the process you went through doing this. **Without telling what you wrote about,** you will talk about the process of doing it. Is there a power to writing, even when you are the only reader? What was the effect of writing something you have never told anyone? Did you type or handwrite? What did you do with the document when you were done? Does writing have any power to help us process our lives and heal?

Writing 4.2: Portfolio Letter

In each writing unit in this class, we've written in different genres for different audiences, ranging from our class, an academic audience, a public audience, and just ourselves. We've also tried to explore the power of words, images, and stories in our lives and in the lives of others. Also, I hope, you've learned some things about generating interesting ideas for your writing, researching, drafting, revising, and editing your work.

Part 2: Portfolio Letter

This letter is in many ways the most important element of your portfolio for it affords you the chance to reflect on your writing from the semester and evaluate what you've gotten out of the course. You will need to show that you can evaluate the strengths of your work and that you understand what you do well, what you have learned and improved on over the semester, and what aspects of your writing will continue to require your attention. This moment of reflection is where process and product come together. As one of your readers, I have not witnessed your writing process in its entirety—I haven't watched you write, seen your notes, heard you talk to your friends about your projects, seen you struggle to find that perfect transition. This letter allows you to share with me your process as well as your view on how well you have met the stated objectives of the course.

Your letter should be roughly 500 to 750 words. In it, you should discuss the work you've done in relation to the stated objectives of the course (listed below). Consider and demonstrate **by referring to specific essays you've written** how responding to the works of your peers helped you develop or think about each of the specific objectives. **Try to offer a sense of what you see as your greatest strengths as a writer, what areas you want to develop, what has been most worthwhile in this course, and how you want to work on your writing in the future.**

Be sure to focus on some of the issues and themes we have discussed throughout the semester:

Audience: you wrote for various audiences—our class, an academic audience, a general readership, and yourself only. How does your writing change when your audience changes? What have you learned about adapting your writing to your audience? In what ways did voice, tone, level of formality, genre, or format change when your audience changed?

Genre: We have written descriptive essays, analytic arguments, and researched oral history. What have you learned about the differences in these genres of writing? Where are you most comfortable as a writer and where do you want to develop more?

Critical Reading and Writing: What did you learn this semester as you read and wrote about the power of words, media and stories? What surprised you most? What, if anything, are you curious to learn more about? What did you learn about research and evaluating sources?

Editing and Proofreading: We spent time on editing and proofreading for proper citation and to correct typographical and grammatical errors. What did you learn in this area? What do you want to learn more about?

Writing 4.3 Revised Drafts of Final Essays

Your portfolio will include any additional revisions you make to Writings 1.4, 2.4, and 3.4. Revision is a process that doesn't just 'fix' a draft; it's where you change it, re-see it, develop it. Any changes you've made to your essays should be included in this final portfolio. And be sure to discuss your revisions in your portfolio letter.

6 "Talkin bout Fire Don't Boil the Pot": Putting Theory into Practice in a First-Year Writing Course at an HBCU

Teresa Redd

When I talk about writing, I find myself returning to certain theories again and again, whether I am teaching composition, directing the Writing Across the Curriculum (WAC) Program, or running the faculty development center at my historically black university (HBCU). While teaching my students or preaching to colleagues, I inevitably cite the theories that have inspired me the most during thirty years of teaching—theories rooted in rhetorical analysis, cognitive psychology, social constructivism, sociolinguistics, and critical pedagogy. However, as the African American proverb says, "Talkin bout fire don't boil the pot," so, in the attached syllabus, I demonstrate how I would put these theories into practice in a first-year writing course at my HBCU. I call my course "ENGL 101 Interdisciplinary Explorations in Writing," a culturally appropriate initiation into writing, research, and interdisciplinary learning at my university. Below I explain how theory—along with empirical research, professional associations, classroom experience, and my HBCU's mission—guided my selection of ENGL 101's goals, objectives, content, activities, and assessments.

GOALS AND OBJECTIVES

As the syllabus suggests, ENGL 101 seeks to prepare students—in one semester—for college-level writing, life-long learning, and engaged

146

citizenship. At the same time, it helps students develop my university's core competencies. I do not believe in reinventing the wheel. So for my ENGL 101 syllabus, I have borrowed my goals and objectives from the WPA Outcomes Statement for First-Year Composition, the National Council of Teachers of English (NCTE), the Council of Writing Program Administrators (WPA), and the National Writing Project's (NWP) Framework for Success in Postsecondary Writing, since these position statements are well-grounded in rhetorical, cognitive, social constructive, and sociolinguistic theory. However, I have added to the Framework's goals while also modifying the WPA objectives in the syllabus to ensure that ENGL 101 is culturally appropriate, interdisciplinary, and research-intensive.

Goal 1: To develop students' rhetorical knowledge and sense of authorship so that they can adapt writing to different purposes, audiences, and contexts. One of the reasons I have engaged students in writing across the curriculum, technical writing, service-learning, and journal writing is that the purposes for writing vary widely—from academic, professional, and civic to personal, social, and aesthetic. As Aristotle surmised centuries ago, these purposes shape everything from the writer's thinking, feelings, and composing process to the form, structure, and language of the written product. Therefore, although the English department at my HBCU bears the primary responsibility for preparing students for college-level writing, ENGL 101 cannot limit itself to academic purposes for writing. As the Conference on College Composition & Communication (CCCC) warns, "to restrict students' engagement with writing to only academic contexts and forms is to risk narrowing what we as a nation can remember, understand, and create" ("CCCC Statement on the Multiple Uses of Writing").

Regardless of whether purposes are academic or not, they emerge from what Lloyd Bitzer calls a "rhetorical situation," or the "natural context of persons, events, objects, relations, and an exigence which strongly invites utterance" (385). Bitzer taught me the importance of creating "rhetorical situations" in the classroom. Too often, school writing assignments do not present students with real reasons to write ("rhetorical exigencies") for readers who could be influenced by the writing and who could bring about change ("rhetorical audiences") (386-87). Yet, if students are to negotiate rhetorical situations in the world outside the classroom, they need to develop rhetorical knowledge, especially a sense of audience. Whether the audience is analyzed

[handwritten marginal note: real audience]

or invented, generations of rhetoricians (e.g., Chaim Perlman, Lisa Ede and Andrea Lunsford, and Walter Ong) stressed the importance of adapting writing to an audience. Research confirms that expert writers pay more attention to their audience and other features of the rhetorical situation than do novice writers (Flower and Hayes, "The Cognition of Discovery"). That is why developing students' rhetorical knowledge must be a goal of ENGL 101.

However, rhetorical knowledge will not suffice if students lack a sense of authorship—the belief that they *can* write and that they know something worth writing about (Bartholomae; Berkenkotter). All able human beings can write; as Toni Morrison says, "We do language." Yet, numerous scholars have hypothesized that African Americans cannot write English well because of intellectual deficits, verbally impoverished homes, or dialect interference (Redd and Webb 58–61). Even teachers who reject such hypotheses may question their African American students' ability to write well because of low scores African Americans receive on national, standardized writing tests (ACT; Banchero). Fear of confirming this stereotype may lead some African Americans to perform poorly on such tests, creating a self-fulfilling prophecy (Steele). So ENGL 101 must help African American students develop a sense of authority as writers.

Goal 2: To stimulate critical thinking and interdisciplinary learning through writing, reading, and research. Having directed a WAC Program for twenty years, I repeat almost daily the "NCTE Belief" that "Writing is a tool for thinking." Perhaps E.M. Forster sums up this idea best when he asks, "How do I know what I think until I see what I say?" (99). Beginning with work by James Britton, Janet Emig, and Judith Langer and Arthur Applebee, theory and research suggest that writing enables us to think in ways that are virtually impossible without writing because we can reflect upon our thoughts more easily when we can see and preserve them.

James Britton, however, was the theorist who first opened my eyes to the power of writing as a tool for learning. Since writing facilitates thinking, he argues, it helps students make course material their own; thus, "the process of writing . . . is demonstrably a process of learning" (Britton reported in Mayher et al. 86). Although Charles Bazerman reminds us that we still need to investigate how specific types of writing promote specific types of learning, the body of empirical research suggests that ENGL 101 students should "write to learn," not simply "learn to write." Moreover, ENGL 101 students should "write to learn" and "learn to write" *across* disciplines. Such interdisciplinary learning facilitates the type of "integrative learning" that the Association of American Colleges & Universities and The Carnegie Foundation for the Advancement of Teaching consider critical to success in academic, professional, personal, and civic life.

Given the mission of an HBCU, ENGL 101 should promote, above all, critical thinking and interdisciplinary learning about issues of concern to the African-American community. Thirty years ago, I started teaching writing at an HBCU largely because an HBCU enabled me to pursue such a goal. Since then, Mary Louise Pratt's "contact zone theory" has reinforced my commitment and deepened my understanding of the transformative power of writing. From the perspective of contact zone theory, African American students need to think through issues of concern to African Americans because they live and learn in "contact zones," or "social spaces where cultures meet, clash, and grapple with each other, often in contexts of highly asymmetrical relations of power, such as colonialism, slavery or their aftermath" (4). Nevertheless, Pratt explains, in such zones students can practice the "literate arts of the contact zone," including autoethnography, critique, resistance, transculturation, and bilingualism (11). Consequently, in ENGL 101, I encourage students to write about issues of concern to the African American community so that they can confront and critique the dominant culture and rewrite the story of their own.

Goal 3: To equip students with effective writing and research strategies. We cannot truly teach writing without teaching the process of writing, for it is the development of flexible processes that will enable students to fulfill the wide range of writing tasks they will encounter in the university and beyond. Clearly, there is no magic formula that will work in every situation. Nor is there a linear series of steps, for the composing process is varied and recursive, as decades of research have shown since Linda Flower and John Hayes published their pioneering studies of the cognitive process of writing ("A Cognitive Process Theory" and "The Dynamics"). With its emphasis on the task environment, the writer's memory, and the writing process, Flower and Hayes's cognitive process theory still influences how I teach, compelling me to help students set goals, break down tasks, and monitor their writing processes. It also shows me how to help students handle constraints, such as the need to integrate knowledge or to solve a rhetorical problem. Consequently,

ENGL 101 will help students develop strategies for generating, drafting, revising, editing, and reflecting on how they write. However, the
composing process is not just cognitive; it is also social. As Patricia
Bizzell, Mikhail Bakhtin, Stanley Fish, and others have revealed, texts
are socially constructed; the composing process incorporates not only
the efforts of living collaborators, but also "voices" from texts the writer
previously read. Therefore, ENGL 101 develops in students the ability
to collaborate efficiently and responsibly and heightens their awareness
of intertextuality and its impact on their composing processes.

Since conducting research is an important part of the composing
process, it is also an important part of ENGL 101. However, since my
HBCU is a research university, ENGL 101 does not simply include
research papers and projects. It fosters undergraduate research as it is
defined by the Council on Undergraduate Research: "an inquiry or
investigation conducted by an undergraduate student that makes an
original intellectual or creative contribution to the disciplines." Studies suggest that engaging undergraduates in original research increases
student engagement and retention, especially among African Americans (Brownwell and Swaner 34). Therefore, ENGL 101 seeks to whet
students' curiosity, stimulate inquiry, equip students with strategies for
analyzing primary evidence, introduce them to new research methodologies and technologies, and develop the persistence needed to complete a semester-long research project.

***Goal 4: To empower students to use the appropriate discourse conven-
tions in different cultural and disciplinary contexts.*** I tell my students
that conventions matter because readers matter, and that conventions
matter to readers. Conventions make it easier for readers to comprehend a text, in large part because conventions fulfill readers' expectations. That is why ENGL 101 aims to deepen students' understanding
of conventions—whether the conventions pertain to genre, documentation, grammar, spelling, or mechanics. As the authors of the "NCTE
Beliefs" warn, "Without mastering conventions for written discourse,
writers' efforts may come to naught. Drawing readers' attention to the
gap between the text at hand and the qualities of texts they expect
causes readers to not attend to the content." Worse still, and in the case
of African American English (AAE), readers who expect the conventions of Standard Written English (SWE) may not attend to the content of a text because they wrongly assume that AAE is "bad English"
and, thus, consider the writer incompetent. Therefore, it is important

to empower speakers of AAE to take control of conventions instead of letting conventions take control of them. With this aim, ENGL 101 shows students how to choose appropriate conventions for the purpose, audience, discipline, or genre. At the same time, the course helps students realize how much they already know about academic conventions so that they can tap into that expertise and build their self-confidence.

No one has impressed this point upon me more deeply than "the Ghetto Lady Turned Critical Linguist," Geneva Smitherman. Through her linguistic and rhetorical analyses, she has revealed the communicative competence of speakers of AAE and exposed the language policies that have denied their competence for so long. That is why, in ENGL 101, I seek to *add* discourse conventions to my students' repertoire rather than replace those that students bring from home. In fact, I create contexts in which students may write in AAE (what Suresh Canagarajah calls "safe houses"), because writing in a home language helps some students "express complex thought," "accelerate their acquisition of academic discourses," and "become more invested in school learning" (NCTE, "Resolution on the Students' Right"). Moreover, since both Smitherman ("African American" 185) and Elaine Richardson (104) have documented the effectiveness of an AAE rhetorical style, ENGL 101 encourages students to enrich their academic writing with AAE rhythms, metaphors, proverbs, and word play. In short, students can produce what Bruce Horner, Samantha NeCamp, and Christiane Donahue call "translingual" texts (286).

Goal 5: To develop students' ability to compose in multiple environments, using everything from traditional pen and paper to electronic technologies. As CCCC declares, "The curriculum of composition is widening to include not one but two literacies: a literacy of print and a literacy of the screen" ("Position Statement on Teaching, Learning, and Assessing Writing in Digital Environments"). To be truly literate, students need to choose appropriate technology for their role, purpose, and audience. In addition, they need to evaluate, synthesize, and contribute to what they find online and avoid plagiarizing what they find. At the same time, students need to incorporate technology to save time, paper, and energy. ENGL 101 addresses all of these needs by building upon students' e-writing experiences—inviting students to use familiar technologies for academic purposes and to expand their repertoire of composing tools.

Expanding the repertoires of African American students is critical: Too often African American students enter college with a limited command of composing technologies because of unequal investments in technology in minority schools (Selfe 64). That is not the only problem. From Cynthia Selfe I have learned "the importance of paying attention" to *how* technologies are used in education. As Selfe first warned in the 1990s, although more African Americans than ever have access to computers and the Internet, a racial digital divide still persists in terms of "technology literacy"—the ability to read, write, and communicate in electronic environments in culturally and socially valued ways (10-12). That is why ENGL 101 does not simply require students to word-process, complete online exercises, or consume other people's media. Instead, the course encourages students to use technology to collaborate online, analyze data, and become producers, whether they are designing multimedia presentations, building websites, or posting videos on YouTube. Like Adam Banks, I give African American students the opportunity to use technology "to tell their own stories in their own terms and . . . to meet the real material, social, cultural, and political needs in their lives and in their communities" (138).

CONTENT

Guided by these goals and related objectives, I have selected content that supports a culturally appropriate, interdisciplinary, and research-intensive composition course.

Syllabus Preamble. To develop a sense of authorship (Goal #1), the ENGL 101 syllabus opens with an affirmation of African-American literacy that places African American students squarely in an African American intellectual and rhetorical tradition. Like my department's English Composition 002 syllabus, the ENGL 101 syllabus begins with a reminder that the students are part of a liberating tradition of reading and writing, a tradition dating back to Frederick Douglass's success in writing his own pass from slavery to freedom. To reinforce this point, I include an introduction to pioneering author Zora Neale Hurston, since she not only pursued interdisciplinary research and writing, but also studied at my HBCU.

Theme. To promote critical thinking and interdisciplinary learning (Goal #2), ENGL 101 adopts a theme that changes from year to year, but always focuses on a problem of importance to the African American community. For instance, I recently chose the theme, "In the Wake of Katrina: Exploring the Hurricane's Long-Term Impact on African Americans," a theme that engages students in studying the impact of a natural disaster that had a disproportionate effect on the black and the poor. Adopting a theme also permits students to participate in learning communities with students in other sections or courses that explore the same theme. Educational research has shown that such learning communities are associated with deep learning and with personal and practical gains, and that they are particularly effective for African American students (Kuh 26).

Textbooks and Films. To develop students' rhetorical knowledge (Goal #1) and writing strategies (Goal #3), I adopted Laurence Behrens and Leonard Rosen's textbook, *A Sequence for Academic Writing,* with its digital companion site and access to MyCompLab, a website that provides multimedia lessons, customized study plans, online tutoring, and self-scoring exercises for personalized learning. I chose Behrens and Rosen's book because it eschews the traditional modes for summary, critique, analysis, and synthesis. At the beginning of each chapter, it also demonstrates how these types of writing permeate academic, workplace, and civic writing. Moreover, the book emphasizes research and writing processes, and features both student and professional models. However, to learn from these models, teachers must show students how to read like writers, noting the choices writers made as they constructed their texts.

[handwritten margin note: must be Pearson]

To stimulate critical thinking and interdisciplinary learning (Goal #2) about the Katrina theme, I ask students to read and write a review of one of the books listed on the course Blackboard site (e.g., Michael Eric Dyson's *Come Hell or High Water*). To introduce students to the Katrina story, during the first week of class I ask them to watch Spike Lee's films *When the Levees Broke: A Requiem in Four Acts* and *If God Is Willing and Da Creek Don't Rise*. These films give students enough background information to write the "Diagnostic Position Paper" about issues of race and class in the Katrina tragedy.

Interdisciplinary Virtual Library. To help students respond to Katrina from an interdisciplinary perspective, I have assembled an online library where students can search for information about different disciplines (Goal #2). This virtual library contains videotaped, transcribed, and summarized interviews with professors across the disciplines. The library also includes links to resources such as Marquette University's "Department-by-Department Guide" for writing across the curriculum, where students can read what faculty say about excellent writing in their field (Goal #4). In addition, students find videotaped lectures on Katrina, delivered by professors and professionals in a wide range of disciplines. I also invite guest speakers from other disciplines to the Blackboard chatroom or discussion board to respond to questions about the aftermath of Katrina, and I archive those exchanges.

Research. To develop effective research strategies (Goal #3) and a sense of authorship (Goal #1), much of the content of ENGL 101 comes from the students' own research. While students mine library databases (see "Exercises" in the syllabus), ENGL 101 encourages them to tap two other types of online resources: digital data or archives and online tutorials. On CETLA's Teaching with Digital Data and Archives webpage, students can find primary sources that equip them to generate new research questions and new analyses. Data and archives related to Hurricane Katrina are particularly plentiful, as students see when they begin their online search at the Greater New Orleans Community Data Center and the Hurricane Digital Memory Bank. On the other hand, CETLA's Online Tutorials webpage introduces students to the methodologies (e.g., statistics) and technologies (e.g., GIS) that they may need for their topic.

The Web. Since students compose in electronic environments (Goal #5), the Web is a major source for content in the course. Not only does it provide up-to-date information, but it also facilitates collaboration, puts students in touch with outside audiences, and stimulates active learning through assignments such as WebQuests.

Student Writing. Student writing from the discussion board, group pages, wikis, and textbook constitutes a significant percentage of the texts that ENGL 101 students read and critique. These are opportunities to review and revise other students' writing to help students improve their composing strategies (Goal #3) in multiple environments (Goal #5).[1]

Most of the sources listed above are available in digital format to support my "Green Teaching" efforts. See http://www.cetla.howard.edu/green_teaching/index.html.

ACTIVITIES

ENGL 101 consists of an integrated sequence of activities designed to fulfill Goals 1 -5. Many of the activities are derived from the Mellon Interdisciplinary Undergraduate Research Program and Freshman English for Engineers, two of my most successful attempts to put theory into practice.

Goal 1: Rhetorical Knowledge and Authorship. ENGL 101 engages students in adapting their writing to a variety of rhetorical situations that occur "in a real-world context" and address "real-world needs"— tasks that can increase student engagement and achievement (NCTE, "Writing Now"). For instance, as the syllabus reveals, ENGL 101 students produce a wide range of genres—everything from scholarly case studies or scientific posters to dramatic scripts or spoken word poems. The students also write for diverse audiences, including real readers outside the classroom, such as Amazon.com customers, Wikipedia editors, and judges or spectators at the Undergraduate Research Symposium. In addition, students practice crafting the same message for different audiences (e.g., summarizing what is known about a problem in a literature review for a scholarly audience and, later, in an advocacy pamphlet for a public audience).

Goal 2: Critical Thinking and Interdisciplinary Learning. ENGL 101 activities repeatedly engage students in critical thinking, reading, and writing. For example, students must respond to exercises on the class discussion board that stimulate critical thinking about information from sources: the authoritativeness of a website, the bias of newspaper images, and the manipulation of statistics. Students must also accurately summarize sources before they attempt to write critiques in their book and literature reviews. Likewise, before they attempt to take a stand in their research position papers, students must explore both sides of an issue by composing a dialogue between their opponent and themselves. As for interdisciplinarity, blog assignments challenge students to generate research questions about a problem from two disciplinary perspectives and to search specialized databases from a wide range of fields. In addition, the interdisciplinary analysis assignment requires students to apply definitions, principles, or theories from two disciplines to help a layperson understand the significance of one piece of data they collected (e.g., a statistic or photo). To familiarize themselves with these disciplines, students watch videos and tutorials in the interdisciplinary virtual library, although I still expect them to ask a professor, professional, or graduate student to advise them about methodology and to vouch for the accuracy of their work.

Goal 3: Writing and Research Strategies. Beginning with the first blog assignment ("How do you compose an essay in class and at home?"), ENGL 101 engages students, step-by-step, in the composing process, both inside and outside the classroom. ENGL 101 fosters brainstorming, freewriting, diagramming, outlining, and especially revising, since research suggests that students improve most from revising in response to explicit criteria and focused feedback (Hillocks 166–68). Most assignments are integrated so that students can use documents written earlier to help them compose their research reports. For instance, the book review and annotated bibliography function as a form of prewriting for the research report, while the literature review functions as the first draft of a section of the final report. Thus prewriting and rewriting are built into the composing process, although students are encouraged to generate and rethink ideas at any time. Talk is built into the composing process as well: Students can discuss their ideas and drafts with the teacher and their peers online, in face-to-face team meetings, and at "Writers' Workshops" throughout the process. Proofreading, on the other hand, is emphasized at the end. Citing psycholinguistic research on reading (Smith 3), I show students how readers normally focus on constructing meaning, while proofreaders must pay attention to individual letters, words, and punctuation marks.

As for the research process, ENGL 101 students assign tasks, conduct research, develop timelines, sketch outlines, compose multiple drafts, and give presentations. Blog assignments seek to make this process transparent, since they require students to brainstorm research questions and describe their search strategies. While ENGL 101 requires students to conduct original research, it does not require them to collect primary data on their own. Thanks to online databases and web-based tools, ENGL 101 students can formulate original research questions about the data and archives of other researchers and use that information to conduct their own analyses.

Goal 4: Discourse Conventions. ENGL 101 provides meaningful opportunities for students to practice using discourse conventions in different cultural and disciplinary contexts. For example, as described in the syllabus, students earn extra credit for incorporating "AAE Styling Patterns" in their academic papers; they can use AAE to write some rough drafts, blog posts, and discussion board entries; they learn about the rules, rhetoric, and roles of AAE, and then discuss these on the class discussion board. Most of the time, however, students practice the conventions of the academy and the workplace since "the goal is not to leave students where they are . . . but to move them toward greater flexibility, so that they can write not just for their own intimates but for wider audiences" (NCTE, "NCTE Beliefs"). Therefore, in addition to writing and completing exercises, students familiarize themselves with academic and workplace conventions by consulting discipline-specific writing guides and by participating in reading experiments that allow them to experience what happens to readers when writers violate conventions. Through "Contrastive Analysis" and "Discovery Activities," students recognize the differences between SWE and AAE by using what they already know about language. Although I teach a few grammar lessons (e.g., "The Sentence," "Agreement," and "Punctuation") derived from Joseph Williams' book *Style*, most grammar instruction is personalized (via MyCompLab, conferences, and the Writing Center) so that students can practice only the skills they need based on evidence in their writing.

Goal 5: Multiple Composing Environments. The varying contexts for writing in ENGL 101 compel students to choose the most appropriate means of composing and presenting. For instance, they can produce pamphlets, videos, or digital stories to advocate for causes. Students can also produce prezis, posters, or performances to present research. Through online tutorials, ENGL 101 also introduces interested students to applications for data analysis (e.g., SPSS, GIS, or NVivo). Moreover, ENGL 101 harnesses blogs, wikis, discussion boards, and other social media to facilitate teamwork, class discussions, peer review, collaborative writing, interdisciplinary collaboration, presentations, and publications. ENGL 101 also takes advantage of the Blackboard learning management system to provide "anywhere, anytime" access to information, to facilitate the incorporation of multimedia, to enable students to review and practice until they achieve mastery, to give students time to reflect before participating in discussions, to schedule "just-in-time" online student-teacher conferences, to check for plagiarism, to customize aspects of instruction, and to save time, paper, and energy. In addition, ENGL 101 promotes the use of electronic databases and networks as well as digital data and archives. A librarian is "embedded" in the course so that, online or face-to-face, the librarian can help students locate, organize, and evaluate information.

To sum up, ENGL 101 is filled with activities that the Consortium for the Study of Writing in College says stimulate deep learning: "interactive writing activities" and "meaning-constructed writing" (Anderson et al.). The blog and the portfolio offer students an opportunity to reflect on this learning, thereby reinforcing it.

ASSESSMENT

A course map would show that ENGL 101's activities align with its goals and objectives, but how can I measure students' progress and proficiency as they engage in these activities? And how can I ensure that the assessments are "appropriate," "fair," "valid," and "reliable," as is recommended by the "NCTE-WPA White Paper on Writing Assessment in Colleges and Universities"? Although I have adopted an eclectic approach, I find that Barbara Walvoord's philosophy of responding to student writing is the best guide.

When will assessment take place? First of all, in ENGL 101 assessment is ongoing: It begins with diagnosis, using the students' diagnostic position paper and blog post about their composing processes, and ends with a summative assessment, using the portfolio. However, since assessment helps teachers "decide what and how to teach next" (NCTE, "NCTE Beliefs"), formative assessment takes place throughout the term.

What will be assessed? Whether formative or summative, assessments in ENGL 101 vary in terms of what is being assessed. CCCC points out in its position statement "Writing Assessment": "Best assessment practice uses multiple measures. One piece of writing—even if it is generated under the most desirable conditions—can never serve as an indicator of overall writing ability," since a student's writing ability varies in response to different occasions, audiences, and genres. Therefore, ENGL 101 students produce multiple pieces of writing that vary in purpose, audience, and genre—everything from an informal discussion board post for classmates to a formal research presentation for a scholarly audience. Students also write inside and outside of class and have ample opportunities to read, reflect, and talk about the subject matter before writing.

Not only do the types of writing I assess vary, but the quantity does as well. Although I evaluate some papers individually, I also evaluate a student's body of work via the ENGL 101 portfolio. I assign a portfolio so that I can evaluate each student's development over time in different writing situations. Since the portfolio includes a diagnostic position paper and a revision of the paper, it also facilitates a pre- and post-comparison.

Who will assess? In addition to multiple measures, ENGL 101 engages multiple readers in the assessment process, including the teacher, classmates, and student authors. In ENGL 101, peer review takes place in the classroom, on the discussion board, and in the team wiki; however, I do not leave peer review groups afloat. Having taken heed of George Hillocks' meta-analysis (161), I give peer groups guidelines and/or rubrics for assessing the work of their classmates. Not only do such guidelines or rubrics help peer reviewers give student authors more valuable feedback, they also help reviewers develop a critical eye that they can use on their own work. I facilitate the development of this critical eye through self-assessment in ENGL 101. For example, I ask students to submit completed rubrics with their papers and to assess their progress in their blogs and portfolios so that they can develop metacognition. In addition to teacher, peer, and self-assessment, ENGL 101 enables students to receive feedback from real audiences outside the classroom, including, for example, Wikipedia editors, visitors at the Undergraduate Research Symposium, and Amazon.com customers. In the case of the public service and research presentations, I incorporate peer and visitor feedback into my final evaluation.

How will I evaluate? Like Walvoord, I rely heavily upon rubrics for online discussion, papers, presentations, and portfolios. I prefer rubrics because they compel me to articulate what I consider to be the features of good writing and to be more consistent in evaluating writing. More broadly, rubrics help faculty build consensus and consistency across a writing program. Moreover, rubrics can help students plan and assess their work before submitting or posting it. Rubrics can also guide peer review. In addition, rubrics communicate my standards to other stakeholders, such as administrators, parents, and accreditors. However, rubrics have their limitations. Although the ENGL 101 rubric covers the generic features of course assignments, there is no one-size-fits-all rubric, so I supplement the ENGL 101 rubric with genre-specific checklists, such as a book review checklist to guide students' selection of the content, arrangement, and style for a particular audience and genre.

In ENGL 101, one of the primary tools for assessment is the student-teacher conference—either face-to-face or online. Conferences are critical for diagnosis, especially for AAE-speakers who struggle to write Standard English. For instance, through conferences, I can distinguish what Walvoord calls "performance-based" errors from "knowledge-based" errors (235). Like David Bartholomae, I ask students to read aloud their unmarked papers in my office while I read along. If students correct the errors as they read (e.g., changing "my sister house" to my sister's house"), these are probably "performance-based" errors, so the students need better proofreading strategies. If they *consciously* correct the errors, then I ask them whether, when, or how they proofread. On the other hand, if they *unconsciously* correct the errors, I ask them to reread, showing them how to slow down their eyes so that they see what is actually on the paper. Finally, if the students read the errors as written without acknowledging the errors, then these are probably "knowledge-based" errors, so the students may require an in-depth explanation, practice, or assistance from a tutor. Upon talking with the students, I may also discover the logic of an error: For instance, a student who writes "two boy" may assume that the number "two" suffices to indicate plurality, when Standard English requires a redundant "-s" placed on the end of the noun. On the other hand, I may discover that an error is developmental, that it represents learning in progress, as Mina Shaughnessy observed (5). Thus, an AAE-speaker who says "two boy" might write an inter-dialectal form, such as "two mens," as an approximation of the Standard English the student is learning to write. Like Arnetha Ball, I find that conferences enable me to learn more about the cultural context and intentions that produced such an error (241-44).

Since there is no substitute for a knowledgeable teacher's judgment, I rarely substitute computerized assessment for my own in ENGL 101. The main exceptions are grammar and citation exercises, since the computer allows students to repeat exercises until they achieve mastery. I also enlist Blackboard's Safe Assign program to alert students to instances of plagiarism so that they can rewrite plagiarized passages before they submit a final paper to me.

How will I respond? In ENGL 101, whether I write, record, or digitally embed my comments in a paper or rubric, I vary my response according to the purpose of the assignment, stage of writing, and a student's needs, as Walvoord advises (146-150). Thus, I may choose a holistic, analytic, focused, or detailed response. For instance, if the purpose of a blog post is to stimulate critical thinking, critical thinking is the focus of my assessment. If a student submits a first draft, I may write detailed comments to stimulate revision but write the bare minimum on the final draft. On the other hand, if one student is a "quick study," and another is not, I may bracket a sentence and write "wordy" in the margin for the "quick study" but rewrite several sentences to show the other student how to cut unnecessary words. Sometimes I may not write any comments at all: If I have to struggle to comprehend a student's paper, I may return the paper unmarked or, having written "Stopped Here," ask the student to see a tutor or me. Regardless of the purpose, stage, or student's needs, I strive to find something positive to say before I write constructive criticism on a student's paper, for research suggests that positive comments are especially effective (Hillocks 164). Praise is particularly needed when students stumble while grappling with complex ideas or structures. The authors of "NCTE Beliefs" explain, "This is because their mental energies are focused on the new intellectual challenges. Such uneven development is to be tolerated, in fact, encouraged. It is rather like strength gains from lifting weight, which actually tears down muscle fibers only to stimulate them to grow back stronger."

How will I grade? Although I provide feedback on each paper, I do not grade the team papers (i.e., the literature review, the research proposal, and the research report). Instead, I grade the portfolio, which includes these team papers, but, more importantly, evidence that each student met or did not meet the course's objectives. Moreover, while I grade individual papers (i.e., the book review, the interdisciplinary analysis, the argumentative dialogue, and the revised position paper), I do not grade first drafts—with the exception of the diagnostic position paper, whose grade does not count. I prefer to grade revisions or a body of work so that students have a chance to do their best. Because exercises are for practice, I mark them as pass/fail, with 70% required for passing. However, for computerized grammar exercises, I set a higher pass rate (80% or 100%) so that students will repeat exercises until they achieve mastery. Finally, to encourage students to work hard throughout the semester, I offer extra credit only during the term, and only to the class as a whole.

CONCLUSION

At this point, you may conclude that ENGL 101's goals are too ambitious. Why should a writing teacher strive to engage students in African American studies, primary research, and interdisciplinarity? Isn't teaching writing challenging enough? Indeed it is. However, because writing is a powerful tool for learning and liberation, as Britton et al. and Pratt point out, we owe it to our students—especially those in the contact zones—to empower them through writing instruction. Maybe "talkin bout the fire don't boil the pot," but teaching writing can ignite a fire that will make the pot boil over.

WORKS CITED

ACT. "The Condition of College & Career Readiness 2011." *ACT.* 25 Oct 2011. Web. Web. 7 June 2012.

"Advocacy: About the Council on Undergraduate Research." *Council on Undergraduate Research.* Council on Undergraduate Research. n.d. Web. 1 Feb 2012.

Anderson, Paul, Chris Anson, Bob Gonyea, and Chuck Paine. "Using Results from the Consortium for the Study of Writing in College." *NSSE Institute Webinars.* National Survey of Student Engagement, 17 July 2009. Web. 25 Aug 2011.

Aristotle. *The Rhetoric.* Trans. W.R. Roberts. New York: Modern Library, 1984. Print.

Ball, Arnetha. "Evaluating the Writing of Culturally and Historically Diverse Students: The Case of the African American Vernacular." *Evaluating Writing: The Role of Teachers' Knowledge about Text, Learning, and Culture.* Ed. Charles R. Cooper and Lee Odell. Urbana: National Council of Teachers of English, 1999. 228-48. Print.

Bakhtin, M.M. "Discourse in the Novel." *The Dialogic Imagination: Four Essays.* Austin: University of Texas P, 1985. 259-300. Print.

Banchero, Stephanie. "SAT Reading, Writing, Scores Hit Low." *Wall Street Journal* 15 Sept. 2011. Web. 26 Sept 2011.

Banks, Adam J. *Race, Rhetoric and Technology: Searching Higher Ground.* Mahwah: Lawrence Erlbaum, 2006. Print.

Bartholomae, David. "Inventing the University." *When a Writer Can't Write: Studies in Writer's Block and Other Composing Problems.* Ed. Mike Rose. New York: Guilford, 1985. 134-165. Rpt. *Cross-talk in Comp Theory.* Ed. Victor Villanueva, Jr. Urbana: National Council of Teachers of English, 1997. 589-620. Print.

Bazerman, Charles. *Reference Guide to Writing Across the Curriculum.* West Lafayette: Parlor Press, 2005.

Behrens, Laurence, and Leonard J. Rosen. *A Sequence for Academic Writing.* 5th ed. Boston: Pearson Education, 2012. Print.

Berkenkotter, Carol. "Student Writers and Their Sense of Authority over Texts." *College Composition and Communication* 35 (1984): 312-19. Print.

Bitzer, Lloyd. "The Rhetorical Situation." 1968. Ed. Richard L. Johannesen. *Contemporary Theories of Rhetoric.* New York: Harper & Row, 1971. 381-93. Print.

Bizzell, Patricia. *Academic Discourse and Critical Consciousness.* Pittsburgh: U of Pittsburgh P, 1992. Print.

Britton, James, Tony Burgess, Nancy Martin, Alex McLeod, and Harold Rosen. *The Development of Writing Abilities.* London: Macmillian Education, 1975. Print.

Brownwell, J.E., and L.E. Swaner. "Outcomes of High-Impact Educational Practices: A Literature Review." *Diversity & Democracy* 12.2 (2009): 4-6. Print.

Canagarajah, Suresh. "Safe Houses in the Contact Zone: Coping Strategies of African-American Students in the Academy." *College Composition and Communication* 48 (1997): 173-96. Print.

CCCC Committee on Assessment. "Writing Assessment: A Position Statement." National Council of Teachers of English. Conference on College Composition and Communication, Nov. 2006. Web. 11 Dec 2011.

CCCC Committee on Teaching, Learning, and Assessing Writing in Digital Environments. "CCCC Position Statement on Teaching, Learning, and Assessing Writing in Digital Environments." *National Council of Teachers of English.* Feb. 2004. Web. 12 Dec 2011.

CCCC Multiple Uses of Writing Task Force. "CCCC Statement on the Multiple Uses of Writing." *National Council of Teachers of English.* 19 Nov. 2007. Web. 12 Dec 2011.

Council of Writing Program Administrators, The National Council of Teachers of English, The National Writing Project. "Framework for Success in Post-secondary Writing." *Council of Writing Program Administrators.* January, 2011. Web. 12 Dec 2011.

Council of Writing Program Administrators. "WPA Outcomes Statement for First-Year Composition." *Council of Writing Program Administrators.* July 2008. Web. 6 Nov 2011.

"Department-by-Department Reference Guide." *Marquette University: Writing across the Curriculum.* Marquette University, July 2011. Web. 15 Aug 2011.

Douglass, Frederick. *Narrative of the Life of Frederick Douglass.* New York: Dover Publications, 1995. Print.

Dyson, Michael Eric. *Come Hell or High Water: Hurricane Katrina and the Color of Disaster.* New York: Basic Civitas, 2006. Print.

Ede, Lisa, and Andrea Lunsford. "Audience Addressed/Audience Invoked: The Role of Audience in Composition Theory and Pedagogy." *College Composition and Communication* 35.2 (1984): 155-71. Print.

Emig, Janet A. *The Composing Processes of Twelfth Graders.* Urbana: National Council of Teachers of English, 1971. Print.

Fish, Stanley Eugene. *Is There a Text in This Class?: The Authority of Interpretive Communities.* Cambridge: Harvard UP, 1971. Print.

Flower, Linda S., and John R. Hayes. "A Cognitive Process Theory of Writing." *College Composition and Communication* 32 (1981): 365-87. Print.

—. "The Cognition of Discovery: Defining a Rhetorical Problem." *College Composition and Communication* 31 (1980): 21-32. Print.

—. "The Dynamics of Composing: Making Plans and Juggling Constraints." *Cognitive Processes in Writing.* Ed. Lee W. Gregg and Erwin R. Steinberg. Hillsdale: Lawrence Erlbaum, 1980. 31-50. Print.

Forster, E.M. *Aspects of the Novel.* New York: Harcourt, Brace, 1927. Print.

Greater New Orleans Community Data Center. Nonprofit Knowledge Works, 4 Jan. 2012. Web. 10 Feb 2012.

"Green Teaching." *Center for Excellence, Teaching, and Learning and Assessment.* Center for Excellence, Teaching, and Learning and Assessment, 2011. Web. 13 Mar 2012.

Hillocks, George. *Research on Written Composition: New Directions for Teaching.* Urbana: National Council of Teachers of English and English and Educational Resources Information Center, 1986. Print.

Horner, Bruce, Samantha NeCamp, and Christiane Donahue. "Toward a Multilingual Composition Scholarship: From English Only to a Translingual Norm." *College Composition and Communication* 63 (2011): 269-300. Print.

Hurricane Digital Memory Bank. Roy Rosenzweig Center for History and New Media, 2005. Web. 10 Feb 2012.

Hurston, Zora Neale. *Dust Tracks on a Road.* 1942. New York: Harper Perennial Modern Classics, 2006. Print.

If God Is Willing and Da Creek Don't Rise. Dir. Spike Lee. Prod. Spike Lee and Samuel D. Pollard. 40 Acres & A Mule Filmworks, 2010.

"Integrative Learning: Opportunities to Connect." *Integrative Learning: Opportunities to Connect.* The Carnegie Foundation for the Advancement of Teaching, and The Association of American Colleges and Universities, Jan. 2007. Web.8 Feb 2012.

Kuh, George D. "High-Impact Educational Practices." *New England Association of Schools and Colleges.* The American Association of Colleges and Universities, 2008. Web. 1 Dec 2011.

Langer, Judith, and Arthur Applebee. *How Writing Shapes Thinking: A Study of Teaching and Learning.* Urbana: National Council of Teachers of English, 1987. Print.

Mayher, John S., Nancy Lester, and Gordon M. Pradl. *Learning to Write/Writing to Learn.* Portsmouth: Boynton/Cook, 1983. Print.

Morrison, Toni. "Toni Morrison's Nobel Lecture." Stockholm, 1993. *Nobel Prize.org.* The Nobel Foundation, 07 Dec. 1993. Web. 11 Oct 2011

National Council of Teachers of English. "NCTE Beliefs about the Teaching of Writing." *National Council of Teachers of English.* Nov. 2004. Web. 19 Dec 2011.

—. "NCTE-WPA White Paper on Writing Assessment in Colleges and Universities." *Council of Writing Program Administrators.* Web. 19 Dec 2011.

—. "Resolution on the Students' Right to Their Own Language." *National Council of Teachers of English.* 1974. Web. 19 Dec 2011.

—. "Writing Now." *National Council of Teachers of English.* National Council of Teachers of English: James R. Squire Office of Policy Research, 2008. Web. 18 Dec. 2011.

Ong, Walter J. "The Writer's Audience Is Always a Fiction." *PMLA* 90 (1975): 9-21. Print.

"Online Tutorials." *Center for Excellence, Teaching, and Learning and Assessment.* Center for Excellence, Teaching, and Learning and Assessment, 2006. Web. 8 Jan 2012.

Perelman, Chaïm, and Lucie Olbrechts-Tyteca. *The New Rhetoric: A Treatise on Argumentation.* 1958. Print. Trans. J. Wilkinson and P. Weaver. Notre Dame.: U of Notre Dame P, 1969. Print.

Pratt, Mary Louise. "Art of the Contact Zone." 1990. *Professing the Contact Zone: Bringing Theory and Practice Together.* Ed. Janice M Wolff. Urbana: National Council of Teachers of English, 2002, 1-18. Print.

Redd, Teresa M., and Karen S. Webb. *A Teacher's Introduction to African American English: What a Writing Teacher Should Know.* Urbana: National Council of Teachers of English, 2005. Print.

Richardson, Elaine. *African American Literacies.* London: Routledge, 2003. Print.

Selfe, Cynthia L. *Technology and Literacy in the Twenty-First Century: The Importance of Paying Attention.* Carbondale: Southern Illinois UP, 1999. Print.

Shaughnessy, Mina P. *Errors and Expectations: A Guide for the Teacher of Basic Writing.* New York: Oxford UP, 1977. Print.

Smith, Frank. *Understanding Reading: A Psycholinguistic Analysis of Reading and Learning to Read.* 6th ed. Hillsdale: Lawrence Erlbaum Associates, 2004. Print.

Smitherman, Geneva. "African American Student Writers in the NAEP, 1969–88 and 'The Blacker the Berry, the Sweeter the Juice.'" *Talkin That Talk: Language, Culture, and Education in African America.* London: Routledge, 2000, 163-69. Print.

—. "From Ghetto Lady to Critical Linguist." *Talkin That Talk: Language, Culture, and Education in African America.* New York: Routledge, 2000, 1-13. Print.

Steele, Claude M. "Thin Ice: 'Stereotype Threat' and Black College Students." *The Atlantic.* Aug. 1999. Web. 10 Feb 2012.

"Teaching with Digital Data and Archives." *Center for Excellence, Teaching, and Learning and Assessment.* Center for Excellence, Teaching, and Learning and Assessment, n.d. Web. 15 Jan 2012.

Walvoord, Barbara E. Fassler. *Helping Students Write Well: A Guide for Teachers in All Disciplines.* New York: Modern Language Association of America, 1986. Print.

When the Levees Broke: A Requiem in Four Acts. Dir. Spike Lee. Prod. Spike Lee and Samuel D. Pollard. 40 Acres & A Mule Filmworks, 2006.

Williams, Joseph M., and Gregory G. Colomb. *Style: Toward Clarity and Grace.* Chicago: U of Chicago P, 1995. Print.

"Writing Guides to the Discipline." *References.* CETLA Center for Excellence in Teaching, Learning, and Assessment. Web. 10 Feb 2012.

Appendix: Course Syllabus

Howard University
Department of English

THE MISSION OF THE WRITING PROGRAM

The eloquence of the spoken word and the devotion to writing—the art of language by line—are two of the most highly valued skills manifest in African American culture. African American author James Baldwin succinctly expresses the importance of these values when he tells us, "People evolve a language in order to describe and thus control their circumstances, or in order not to be submerged by a reality that they cannot articulate." You are heirs of a long tradition of peoples who equate reading and writing with the expression of self-identity, self-possession, self-empowerment, and self-esteem. . . . It is the mission of all writing courses in the Department of English at Howard University to carry forward and transmit to you a liberating tradition in reading and writing skills. You may then use these skills in your and the world's best interest.

—Eleanor Traylor, former Chair of the Department of English

ENGL 101: INTERDISCIPLINARY EXPLORATIONS IN WRITING

Dr. Teresa M. Redd
CRN 123456 3 credits
tredd@howard.edu
MWF 11:10am -12:00pm Office Hours: MWF 10–11, 3–4 and by appointment

. . . the force from somewhere in Space
which commands you to write in the first place,
gives you no choice.
You take up the pen when you are told,
and write what is commanded.
There is no agony like bearing an untold story inside you. . . .

> Research is formalized curiosity.
> It is poking and prying with a purpose.
> It is a seeking
> that he who wishes may know the cosmic secrets of the world
> and that they dwell therein.
>
> —Zora Neale Hurston (*Dust Tracks on a Road,* 1942)

As the preceding lines reveal, African American author Zora Neale Hurston loved both research and writing. An anthropologist, folklorist, fiction writer, journalist, and playwright, Hurston discovered her passion for writing and research as an undergraduate at Barnard and Howard. However, it was at Howard that Hurston launched a literary career that secured her place among the literati of the Harlem Renaissance. It was at Howard that she co-founded the *Hilltop* student newspaper. Indeed, it was at Howard that she began to write about Southern Black culture, a subject she would investigate years later as an anthropologist.* The data she collected informed not only her scholarly writing

Zora Neal Hurston. Photo by Carl Van Vechten with permission from the Carl Van Vechten Trust

but her fiction as well. Thus, she remained both an artist and scientist, pursuing her twin passions from an interdisciplinary perspective. Now that you have arrived at Howard, we invite you to follow in Hurston's footsteps during this course by exploring issues, archives, data, and language as you research and write across the disciplines.

COURSE DESCRIPTION

ENGL 101 Interdisciplinary Explorations in Writing is designed to improve your writing while increasing your learning through research and writing. Because writing is an essential tool for thinking and communicating in virtually every field, ENGL 101 builds the foundation

---

*   Valerie Boyd, "Zora Neale Hurston: The Howard University Years," *The Journal of Blacks in Higher Education,*" *39* (2003): 104–08.

for success in upper-level courses throughout the University and for life-long learning and engaged citizenship in the 21st century global community. Thus, this course emphasizes rhetorical and self-awareness, critical and interdisciplinary thinking, reading and research, discussion and debate, cultural and disciplinary conventions, writing strategies and technologies. To develop and integrate these skills and concepts, you will engage in interdisciplinary research—individually and with teammates—on a contemporary issue of special concern to the African American community. You will also join a program-wide learning community that will come together for symposia, exhibits, performances, and field trips related to this year's interdisciplinary research theme: "**In the Wake of Katrina: Exploring the Hurricane's Long-Term Impact on African Americans.**" Consequently, your research project will explore one of the Hurricane's effects on the African American community in New Orleans.

Course Goals

ENGL 101 will help you develop **Howard University's Core Competencies**: critical and creative thinking, inquiry and analysis, oral and written communication, information and technology literacy, teamwork and problem-solving, integrative and applied learning, knowledge of human cultures as well as the physical and natural world, and—depending upon which research project you choose—qualitative or quantitative literacy. Specifically, ENGL 101 pursues five goals:[*]

1. To develop the rhetorical knowledge and sense of authorship students need to adapt writing to different purposes, audiences, and contexts.
2. To stimulate critical thinking and interdisciplinary learning through writing, reading, and research.
3. To equip students with effective research and writing strategies.
4. To empower students to use the appropriate discourse conventions in different cultural and disciplinary contexts.
5. To expand students' abilities to compose in multiple environments, using everything from traditional pen and paper to electronic technologies.

---

[*] Adapted from the *Framework for Success in Postsecondary Writing*

Course Objectives

Upon successfully completing this course, you will be able to do the following:*

Rhetorical Knowledge
- Focus on a purpose.
- Respond to the needs of different audiences.
- Respond appropriately to different kinds of rhetorical situations.
- Use conventions of format and structure appropriate to the rhetorical situation.
- Adopt appropriate voice, tone, and level of formality.
- Explain how genres shape reading and writing.
- Write in several genres.
- Approach writing tasks with a sense of self-efficacy.

Critical Thinking, Reading, and Writing
- Use writing and reading for inquiry, learning, thinking, and communicating.
- Carry out a writing assignment as a series of tasks, including finding, evaluating, analyzing, and synthesizing appropriate primary and secondary sources.
- Integrate your own ideas with those of others, incorporating ideas from more than one disciplinary perspective.

Processes
- Create multiple drafts to complete a successful text.
- Develop flexible strategies for generating, researching, revising, editing, and proofreading.
- Engage in an open process that permits you to invent, research, and rethink to revise your work.
- Develop effective strategies for negotiating collaborative and social aspects of the writing process.
- Critique your own and others' work.
- Balance the advantages of relying on others with the responsibility of doing your part.

---

* Adapted from the *WPA Outcomes Statement for First-Year Composition*

- Use a variety of technologies to handle a range of audiences and research tasks.

Knowledge of Conventions
- Write in common formats for different kinds of texts and contexts.
- Use appropriate disciplinary and cultural genre conventions, ranging from structure and paragraphing to tone and mechanics.
- Document your work appropriately.
- Control such surface features as syntax, grammar, punctuation, and spelling, adapting to the cultural or disciplinary context.
- Describe the relationships among language, knowledge, and power.

Composing in Electronic Environments
- Use electronic environments for drafting, reviewing, revising, editing, and sharing texts.
- Locate, evaluate, organize, and use research material collected from electronic sources, including scholarly library databases; government databases; and informal electronic networks and Internet sources.
- Identify and exploit the differences in the rhetorical strategies and in the affordances available for both print and electronic composing processes and texts.

Instructional Methods

To fulfill the preceding objectives, you will engage in problem- and project-based learning, where one activity builds upon another. Individually or with your teammates, online or on campus, you will participate in a wide range of writing-related activities, including class discussions, personal reflection, team meetings, hands-on training, Writers' Workshops, rubric-based norming sessions, "Language Discovery Activities," and reading experiments.

Textbooks and Other Resources

Most of the resources for this course are digital to facilitate access and to support Howard's *Green Teaching* efforts. These resources consist of diverse media: print, images, animations, simulations, data, archives, virtual tours, audio, and video. To view these media, you will need Acrobat Reader, MS Word, Power Point, Quick Time, Flash, Shockwave, and Real Player.

Books

Given the wealth of Internet resources, there is only one required textbook, the e-book version of **Behrens, Laurence, and Leonard Rosen's** *A Sequence for Academic Writing (5th ed.).* **Boston: Pearson, 2012.** When you purchase the book, you will also gain access to the digital companion site and an online learning resource known as MyCompLab.

  For your book review (described below), you should choose ONE of the 20 books listed under "For Review" under COURSE INFORMATION on Blackboard (e.g., Michael Eric Dyson's *Come Hell or High Water: Hurricane Katrina and the Color of Disaster* and Chester Hartman and Gregory Squire's *There Is No Such Thing as a Natural Disaster: Race, Class, and Hurricane Katrina*).

Films

You should immediately buy, rent, or view on reserve at the Media Center, Spike Lee's *When the Levees Broke: A Requiem in Four Acts* and *If God Is Willing and Da Creek Don't Rise.*

Interdisciplinary Virtual Library

With the aid of a librarian, I have assembled an interdisciplinary online library that will help you complete assignments that ask you to analyze the Katrina tragedy from more than one disciplinary perspective. This library contains videotaped, transcribed, and summarized interviews with professors across the disciplines. The library also includes guides to writing across the curriculum, where you can read what faculty say about excellent writing in their fields. In addition, you will find videotaped lectures on Hurricane Katrina delivered by professors and professionals in a wide range of disciplines. During the semester, I will invite guest speakers from other disciplines to the Blackboard chatroom or discussion board to respond to questions about the aftermath of Katrina, and I will archive those exchanges as well.

Other Resources

For assistance with language, see *Darling's Grammar* and the *Merriam-Webster Dictionary*. In addition to these digital sources, I will assign WebQuests and website reviews so that you and your classmates can find and share web resources. I will also ask you to access two other types of online resources: (1) digital data and archives, where you can find primary sources such as the Greater New Orleans Community Data Center and the Hurricane Digital Memory Bank and (2) online tutorials that can introduce you to the methodologies or technologies (e.g., SPSS or GIS) that you might need to pursue your research. However, you should also find a professor, professional, or graduate student who can serve as your technical advisor.

COURSE OUTLINE

PART ONE: SURVEYING THE SCHOLARSHIP

I. DIAGNOSING
   A. Examining Your Writing (Diagnostic Position Paper)
   B. Analyzing Your Composing Processes (Blog)

II. WRITING A SUMMARY
   A. Reading Critically
   B. Composing a Summary (Book Review Part I)
   C. Paraphrasing vs. Quoting
   D. Citing Sources and Avoiding Plagiarism
   E. Revising: Unity
   F. Editing: The Sentence

III. WRITING A CRITIQUE
   A. Brainstorming (Blog)
   B. Formulating a Thesis for an Audience
   C. Organizing Ideas
   D. Composing a Critique (Book Review Part II)
   E. Revising: Coherence
   F. Editing: Agreement

IV. WRITING AN EXPLANATORY SYNTHESIS
   A. Locating Secondary Sources (Blog)
   B. Evaluating Sources (Team Annotated Bibliography)
   C. Composing an Explanatory Synthesis (Team Literature Review)
   D. Revising: Development
   E. Editing: Punctuation
   F. Presenting an Explanatory Synthesis (Team Public Service Presentation)

PART TWO: CONDUCTING RESEARCH

V. PROPOSING A RESEARCH PROJECT (Team Research Proposal)
- A. Stating the Problem
- B. Proposing a Plan

VI. GATHERING PRIMARY DATA (Blog)

VII. WRITING AN ANALYSIS (Interdisciplinary Analysis)
- A.   Selecting a Disciplinary Framework
- B.   Applying the Framework

VIII. WRITING AN ARGUMENTATIVE SYNTHESIS (Argumentative Dialogue)
- A.   Identifying the Elements and Appeals of Argument
- B.   Accommodating and Refuting Opposing Views
- C.   Avoiding Logical Fallacies

IX. REPORTING FINDINGS
- A.   Composing a Research Report (Team Research Paper)
- B.   Presenting Research (Team Research Presentation)

X. ASSESSING
- A. Assessing Your Progress (Revised Diagnostic Position Paper)
- B. Reflecting on Your Learning (Portfolio)

Course Requirements

Over the course of the semester, (in addition to a diagnostic essay) you will compose **five short, interrelated papers** (2 -5 double-spaced pages) that will prepare you to write an **interdisciplinary research report** that analyzes digital data or archives. *This report will revise, synthesize, and expand what you wrote in the five papers.* You will also give **two presentations**, one for the public and another for a scholarly audience. You are expected to write both in class and out of class, prewrite and rewrite, and complete exercises in a blog, discussion board, and MyCompLab so that you can explore ideas from interdisciplinary perspectives and practice critical thinking, research, and editing skills. At the end of the term, you will submit an **electronic portfolio,** in which you post examples and reflections on your coursework to demonstrate how you have fulfilled your personal and course objectives. Please see COURSE INFORMATION in Blackboard for a sample portfolio, instructions for building your portfolio, and the manuscript conventions and procedures for submitting papers.

Description of Major Assignments (See Blackboard for due dates and sample papers.)

1. *Diagnostic Position Paper*

In a 500-word essay, take a stand on one of the issues presented in Spike Lee's documentary *When the Levees Broke* and *If God Is Willing and Da Creek Don't Rise.* Support and defend your position not only to show me what you already do well as a writer but also to clarify your own thinking. Writing about the films now will help you and your teammates decide what aspect of the Katrina tragedy you would like to investigate later. Since you will have only 50 minutes to write in class, bring an outline or diagram. As long as you complete this assignment, you will earn credit. However, at the end of the term you will revise this paper for a grade to demonstrate your progress.

2. *Book Review*

Write a 500-word review of one of the Katrina books listed on Blackboard. Your teammates should review different books to maximize the number of perspectives that your team can draw upon later for the team research project. However, since you will post the final version of this review on Amazon.com, write for Amazon customers who are looking for a good book to buy. First, compose a summary, then revise it in response to my feedback, compose a critique, and, finally, combine the summary and critique.

3. *Team Literature Review*

Synthesize your team's secondary research in a 750-word literature review that summarizes and evaluates at least ten sources. The primary purpose of the literature review is to build the information base for your public service presentation and your Team Research Proposal. Your sources should come from two or more disciplines (including two scholarly books, two articles from peer-reviewed journals, two news reports or commentaries, and a book you or your teammates reviewed). First, compile an annotated bibliography, using MLA or APA and what you learned about summarizing a few weeks ago. Each teammate should contribute at least two different entries to the group wiki in Blackboard. The annotated bibliography will enable our class librarian and me to assist you at the beginning of your research process. After you receive our feedback, via the group wiki, summarize, critique, and synthesize the sources from your bibliography, following the format of the sample literature review posted on Blackboard. Address a scholarly audience, represented by the librarian and me.

4.   *Team Public Service Presentation*

Design an "infomercial" about your research problem to recruit HU students to go on Alternative Spring Break to New Orleans next semester to conduct needs assessments, collect oral histories, and assist elderly survivors. Convert the information from your literature review into a dynamic presentation that emphasizes visual communication or performance. Choose the most effective medium for your audience, whether it is a pamphlet, digital story, or spoken word poem. Then prepare a 5-minute in-class presentation or submit your presentation to the *Hilltop, The Root.com,* or other Black media outlets.

5.   *Team Research Proposal*

Compose a 1,250 word proposal that (a) states your team's research problem, (2) revises your literature review, (3) poses one or more research questions, and (4) explains how you will gather and analyze primary data sources (i.e., digital data or archives) to answer your question(s). With your teammates, first, list the tasks you need to complete, construct a timeline, and assign tasks. Then draft a proposal in your group wiki. Submit the proposal to your technical advisor and me for feedback. Then submit a revision to the Undergraduate Research Symposium reviewers. This revision will inform the "Introduction" and "Method" sections of your Team Research Report.

6.   *Interdisciplinary Analysis*

Write a 500-word analysis of ONE piece of your research data (e.g., a statistic, graph, photo, map, or testimony). After summarizing or describing your data, apply definitions, principles, or theories from two disciplines to help a layperson understand the significance of your data. Your teammates should choose different data so that you can combine your insights when you compose the "Discussion" section of your team report.

7.   *Argumentative Dialogue*

In 250 words, write a dialogue between you and someone who is skeptical about the conclusions you have drawn from your research. First, state your conclusions. Then, in response to the skeptic's questions, explain why you arrived at those conclusions, citing supporting evidence. Next, allow the skeptic to question your methodology and interpretation of your findings. Accommodate any limitations of your study, but defend your conclusions, citing evidence from your study and other theories or research. Writing this dialogue will prepare you to write the argumentative synthesis known as the "Discussion" section in your Team Research Report.

8. *Team Research Report*

For a scholarly audience, write a team research report of 2,500–3,750 words, as well as a cover letter, abstract, and bibliography. This report should revise, synthesize, and expand what you have written this term. With your teammates, first, draft an outline and abstract of the report. Then assign sections and ask all teammates to post their sections for peer review on the group discussion board in Blackboard. After the group members have used team feedback to revise, the team leader should combine the sections and post the file for the team to review (especially for coherence).

9. *Team Research Presentation*

Prepare a multimedia oral presentation of your research problem, methodology, and findings (e.g., poster, slide show, Prezi, video, or exhibit) for judges, faculty, and students who will attend the Undergraduate Research Symposium.

10. *Portfolio*

Select and reflect on ENGL 101 coursework (e.g., "artifacts") that show how you fulfilled the course and your personal objectives. The portfolio should include not only the first draft of your Diagnostic Position Paper but also a revision for comparison. This portfolio will help you integrate your experiences in this course and document your learning for program, course, and self-assessment. After the portfolio has been submitted to me, you may decide to email a link to your portfolio to admissions officers and/or prospective employers.

Exercises (see Blackboard for due dates, sample papers, and instructions for posting)

Although I may assign some impromptu freewriting and "Language Discovery Activities" in class, you will complete most exercises on the discussion board, your blog, or My CompLab.

Blog Assignments (for teacher-student and librarian-student dialogue, minimum length = 100 words)

1.   Review the ENGL 101 goals and objectives. Which do you share? Are there any missing? Set your personal objectives for this course.
2.   How do you compose an essay at home? In class?
3.   After visiting the Greater New Orleans Community Data Center and the Hurricane Digital Memory Bank, brainstorm five possible topics for a team research project that could use such digital sources to reveal the long-term impact of Katrina on African Americans.
4.   Generate six research questions about the topic your team has selected. The questions should reflect at least two disciplinary perspectives.
5.   Using the assigned databases, search for the following sources related to your research project and then describe your search protocol:
     a.   a scientific article, a dataset, and a technical report
     b.   a government report, directory, data file, law, and testimony
     c.   a historical manuscript, letter, and a map
     d.   a still image, a video, an audio recording, and play-bill from two or more creative and performing arts
     e.   a business report, a foundation report, and an economic analysis.

Online Discussions (minimum length = 150 words for entries, 50 words for replies)

1.   **AAE Forum:** Visit the Linguistic Society of America's website on African American English. Then in a discussion board posting, explain what role African American English plays in your life and what role you think it should play in academe and the workplace. Reply to two classmates' postings.

2.   **WebQuest Forum:** Find a website related to your research topic and, using the Library's checklist, evaluate the site. Post a link to the website along with your evaluation on the class discussion board. Then click the link in a classmate's posting, visit the website, and respond to your classmate's evaluation.

3. **Visual Rhetoric Forum:** Following Behrens and Rosen's guidelines for visual rhetorical analysis, evaluate and discuss the two newspaper images that sparked so much controversy during Hurricane Katrina. Post your opinion and reply to two other postings.

4. **Wikipedia:** With your teammates, locate a Wikipedia article that is related to your research topic and needs improvement. Then submit to the Wikipedia editors corrections, deletions, or additions based upon your research.

My Comp Lab

In MyCompLab, you will practice applying concepts discussed during the lessons on the sentence, agreement, punctuation, and citations. However, most exercises will target a grammatical or stylistic problem that emerges in your writing.

Course Policies

Computation of Final Course Grade
Exercises (including blogposts, online discussion, and MyComp Lab): 1/6
Individual Papers (Book Review, Interdisciplinary Analysis, Dialogue, Revised Position Paper): 1/3
Team Presentations (2): 1/6
Electronic Portfolio: 1/3

Grading Criteria (see all rubrics under COURSE INFORMATION on Blackboard)

Exercises. All written exercises will be graded Pass/Fail (P = 1 point, F = 0 points). A passing score is equivalent to 70% or better. Since these are informal pieces of writing designed to stimulate reading and thinking, I will use a **Rubric for Online Discussion** to assess how well you fulfilled the assigned task. However, since proofreading is an essential editing skill, if I notice a *pattern* of errors in your writing, I will assign you **My CompLab exercises** for practice. If I do, you should repeat these exercises until you achieve mastery (100%) after studying Darling's Grammar or working with a Writing Center tutor. *Note:*

If I invite you to write in your home language (e.g., African American English), this policy will not apply.

Papers. Although I will provide feedback on each paper, I will not *grade* each team paper. Instead, I will grade your ePortfolio (see below). However, I will grade each of the papers that you write on your own: the diagnostic and revised Position Paper, Book Review, Interdisciplinary Analysis, and Argumentative Dialogue, although the diagnostic grade will not count. Using the same multipurpose **ENGL 101 Rubric** that you will use for self and peer review, I will grade these papers on a scale of A = 90–100, B = 80–89, C = 70–79, D = 60–69, F = below 60. However, you and I will also use **genre-specific rubrics** (e.g., a "Book Review Checklist") to confirm that you have chosen the content, arrangement, and style that are appropriate for a particular genre.

Presentations. I will evaluate both of your presentations using the **Presentation Rubric**. However, as I calculate the final score for your team's **Public Service Presentation**, I will incorporate feedback from the class since they will represent the target audience. Likewise, when I calculate the score for your team's **Research Presentation**, I will incorporate feedback from visitors at the Undergraduate Research Symposium.

Portfolio. Your portfolio presents your *self*-assessment of your learning during the course, including your teamwork (Annotated Bibliography, Literature Review, Research Proposal, and Research Report). Therefore, I will evaluate the case that you make through your *selection* of artifacts (e.g., your papers and posts) and your *reflections* about their role in helping you meet the course objectives. While you will earn some points for the design, you will earn the most points for meeting the objectives and writing your reflections (see **ENGL 101 Portfolio Rubric**).

Lateness and Absences

If you are absent, you are still responsible for the coursework, so find a class "buddy" who can keep you up to date. Except in the case of a documented emergency, you cannot make up missed classwork. Moreover, I will not count late homework exercises, although I will gladly discuss such work with you in my office. Also, to be fair to students who submit work on time, I will deduct 10 points a day for late papers and additional points for lack of team participation.

Extra Credit and Other Grading Policies

I offer extra credit only during the term and only to the class as a whole. Therefore, you cannot improve your grades at the last minute by requesting additional work. However, I encourage you to seek extra points *during* the semester by embedding **African-American Styling Patterns** in your papers (see the attachment). Please see COURSE INFORMATION on our Blackboard site for the departmental policies regarding Incomplete grades, withdrawals, and academic integrity.

Support Services

See COURSE INFORMATION on our Blackboard site for information regarding university services that can assist you during this course, including the Writing Center, Blackboard FAQs for Students, and University Libraries. If you need an accommodation required by the **American Disabilities Act**, contact Special Student Services (202–238–2420) immediately. Then document and discuss your disability with me, privately, during the first week of class.

Course Schedule

Go to COURSE IFORMATION to find a table of important due dates. Then click the Unit I—XI buttons in the navigation menu to see the day-by-day lessons and assignments.

Some African American Styling Patterns*

Linguist Geneva Smitherman describes rhythm as one of the distinctive characteristics of the African American verbal style (315). Below are some examples of African American rhythmic patterns that can help you emphasize important ideas in your academic essays. While a number of these patterns share characteristics of Western rhetoric, most have a distinctively African American flavor.

Rhyme

Henry Louis Gates, Jr.: "I think this explains the conservative desire to cast the debate in terms of **the West vs. the Rest**" (12).

---

* All page numbers refer to Teresa Redd's *Revelations: An Anthology of Expository Essays by and About Blacks* (Boston: Pearson, 2002).

A Play on Words

James Baldwin: "The argument concerning the use, or the status, the reality, of black English is rooted in American history and has absolutely nothing to do with the question the argument sup**poses** itself to be **posing**" (319).

Repetition of a Sound

Cornel West: "These institutions have helped create a seductive way of life, a culture of consumption that capitalizes on every opportunity to make money" (459).

Repetition of a Syllable

Randall Robinson: "The initiative must come from blacks, broad**ly**, wide**ly**, implicab**ly**" (453).

Repetition of a Word

Toni Morrison: "Thus my father, distrusting **every** word and **every** gesture of **every** white man on earth, assumed that the white man who crept up the stairs one afternoon had come to molest his daughters . . ." (427).

Repetition of a Conjunction

Alice Walker: "I have fought **and** kicked **and** fasted **and** prayed **and** cursed **and** cried myself to the point of existing" (393).

Omission of a Conjunction

Randall Robinson: "We would begin a healing of our psyches were the most public case made that whole peoples lost **religions, languages, customs, histories, cultures, children, mothers, fathers**" (454).

Balanced Pairs

Ossie Davis: Any teacher **good or bad, white or black, Jew or Gentile**, who uses the English Language as a medium of communication is forced willy-nilly to teach the Negro child 60 ways to despise himself, and the white child 60 ways to aid and abet him in the crime" (168).

Balanced Clauses

Frederick Douglass: "What, to the American slave, is your 4th of July? . . . To him, **your celebration is a sham; your boasted liberty, an unholy license; your national greatness, swelling vanity** . . ." (376).

Negation

Martin Luther King: "The tension in this city is **not** between white people and Negro people. The tension **is**, at bottom, between justice and injustice . . ." (382).

Reversal

Malcolm X: "**We** didn't land on **Plymouth Rock. It** landed on **us**" (407).

7 The Activity of Writing: Affinity and Affect in Composition

Alexander Reid

As director of the composition program at the State University of New York at Buffalo (UB, as we call it), I begin each academic year a week earlier than my colleagues by conducting an orientation for our incoming teaching assistants. I tell them that I view composition as one of the most challenging courses offered by English departments and perhaps across the university. One might describe the challenges of composition in multiple ways. Often, students do not want to be in the course (a problem many required, general education courses face), and there are many institutional demands placed upon the course, specifically the vague and quixotic objectives of "fixing" student writing. However, those are not the challenges to which I am referring. Teaching composition is a challenge because it asks students and instructors to intervene in fundamental processes of thought and symbolic behavior and investigate the ontological foundations of our relations with one another. I realize that composition is not usually conceived in those terms. It is imagined as "basic" in another sense: as simple; as nuts and bolts; as a technological, stylistic skill that carries out already-thought instructions. Of course, in rhetoric and composition, we do not think of first-year composition that way. In the 1990s, in composition programs where I first learned to teach, writing was primarily conceived in terms of discourse and ideology. Following a post-process, cultural studies pedagogy inspired by James Berlin and others, those classes asked students to write essays where they practiced a critical, theoretical understanding of media, representation, and power. If composition textbooks are any indication, such courses remain common in our field.

However, for the past decade, my writing pedagogy has moved in a different direction. I spent eight years teaching in a professional writing major that significantly changed the kinds of writing I taught. I realized in a very immediate way the wide variety of writing that might be addressed in the classroom and the very different pedagogical challenges that writing might present. More importantly, the past decade has seen a revolution in our students' technological capacities to communicate. Today's classrooms are quite unlike those in which I first taught, so it seems obvious to me that my teaching must adapt. Furthermore, such dramatic shifts in communication have demonstrated to me that many of the paradigmatic values of composition in the 1990s (and earlier) were less a reflection of a core ontological basis for communicating than they were a legacy of notions that had accreted over a century of composition instruction. This does not mean that all those practices must be automatically tossed out, but it does mean that many of the underlying assumptions of our disciplinary practices must be interrogated.

In this essay (and in the syllabus that accompanies it), I do not seek to offer a model. One thing that annoys me the most in our discipline is the "heroic pedagogy narrative," so I will offer no story of personal heroism here. If there is one thing I believe our discipline has understood, it is the situated nature of writing and writing instruction, suggesting that such personal stories of pedagogy have limited applicability beyond their specific contexts. That said, as college writing instructors in the second decade of the twentieth century, there are some common contexts we share, including that of our discipline, even though the impact of those contexts upon us may be different. For example, some writing instructors view emerging technologies with great enthusiasm; others view them as a threat. Regardless, wi-fi and cellular signals likely permeate our classrooms, and most, if not all, of our students carry some device that links with those signals. As a scholar who studies digital rhetoric, this shift is of particular interest to me. I do not expect everyone to share that interest; nor do I think such an interest is necessary for teaching writing. Indeed, my other general annoyance is with pedagogues who insist that we must all do as they do, lest the barbarians come crashing through the gate, the university become a dupe for the marketplace, and the humanities shrivel up and die. As such, neither this essay nor the course it describes is fixated upon technology. Instead, my class focuses upon a single, simple

great word

goal

goal: giving students the opportunity to develop a durable, productive writing practice appropriate for the compositional networks in which they operate.

Context

UB is a public research university with nearly thirty thousand students. Most students come from New York State, but there are over five thousand international students who help shape the character of our courses. The result is a fairly diverse campus, with 43% of the student population reporting as non-white and 19% as out-of-state. Our in-state students come from New York City and its environs, from the dairy farmlands and Adirondack forests of "upstate" to the many smaller cities (and their suburban communities) like Albany, Syracuse, and Buffalo itself. However, the students are not particularly diverse in terms of age, with only 17% of the undergraduates being 25 or older. The average SAT critical reading score is 570, placing the average student in the 73rd percentile among test-takers nationally. While I do not personally place much weight on such scores, this is the general demographic information that characterizes our students. In more qualitative terms, UB students have generally been successful in their academic careers. They have succeeded without significant struggle in the writing assignments they have undertaken in high school and on the state writing exams on which their high school curricula are heavily focused. In many respects, they are like students at many public research universities across the nation who, typically, have no great love for writing. They have come to see writing as a rote, mechanical activity. In general, they have had little experience with self-sponsored writing, writing for an audience beyond their teacher, or with doing research. Like many college students born in the 1990s, our students are extensive users of social media and mobile technologies. Many are also gamers. They employ Skype and related applications to keep in touch with family and friends. As such, they are fairly sophisticated consumers of technologies. Generally, though, they do not recognize their texts or status updates as "writing." They also do not tend to have a reflective, rhetorical understanding of the technologies they employ, nor are they particularly experienced with digital production (e.g., building web pages, creating videos, etc.). While there are many other

ways my university and its students could be described, these are some
of the salient characteristics in relation to the syllabus I have created.

COURSE OBJECTIVES

As rhetoricians, it is immediately understandable to us that curricular
objectives be described differently depending on audience, and that
there are many potential audiences for course objectives, including
students in a course, instructors in the program, faculty in one's department, faculty across the university, staff (including writing center
staff, librarians, student advisors, IT support, and so on), administrators, parents and other interested members of the general public,
alumni and other potential donors, and disciplinary colleagues. Here
I am interested in this last audience. If we can agree that writing instruction must be contextualized and situated, then it is not so difficult to also recognize that writing itself is similarly situated. That
is, there is no universal writing pedagogy or curriculum, and, beyond
the basic abilities to speak and later write in sentences that most of us
acquire (at least in our native languages) at an earlier age, there are no
universal writing skills or practices. As such, it would be an error to
imagine a composition course as teaching writing in general. In fact, it
would be an error to imagine teaching *academic* writing in general, for
even the writing done by academics varies widely. This perspective has
been well-presented by David Russell and others. Elizabeth Wardle
and Doug Downs, for example, note that "more than twenty years of
research and theory have repeatedly demonstrated that such a unified
academic discourse does not exist and have seriously questioned what
students can and do transfer from one context to another" (552). My
course begins from the same principle.

   Given the situated, particular nature of writing, most of the general
things we can say about writing are somewhat tautological. However, I
believe they are instructive nonetheless. The first is: "Writers write." A
course that takes as its objective the development of writers must begin
and end with writing as an activity, and the amount of writing that
students do should not be limited by the instructor's ability to respond
to the writing. We all recognize that writing instructors are typically
underpaid and overworked, often teaching multiple sections. As a ten-
ured professor at a research university, I have the privilege of teaching
less, though there are obviously other demands placed on me, includ-

ing serving as the director of our composition program. Regardless of one's workload, the equation to determine how much students write should not begin with how much one can read as an instructor. That said, writing requires a purpose and an audience. Perhaps, for some writers and some situations, an audience of only one's self as a writer is sufficient; however, the first principle of my course's design is that students write regularly and extensively for each other and for larger audiences. Some writing is shorter or more quickly composed, such as writing for online discussion forums or blogs. Other writing projects take shape over longer periods of time and involve multiple drafts. Regardless, the observation that "writers write" indicates that students are asked to participate in regular, ongoing writing practice. To me, this is a common foundation of all writing courses.

The second somewhat circular statement I want to make is: "To become a better writer, one has to want to become a better writer." Students often arrive in their required first-year composition course immediately after completing a compulsory education; this is especially the case at UB, where we teach largely "traditional age" students. Students have generally taken a passive role in their learning by completing tasks set before them, particularly writing assignments, and have rarely taken of a much role in determining the content or objectives of their education. Though they may have been asked to work and have been held to certain standards, issues with motivation were secondary. In my view, this is completely wrong-headed, or at least it is an approach that will not carry students any further. To this extent, writing as a practice or habit is much like fitness: One can hire a fitness trainer to develop an exercise program, take one through the program, and even encourage one to keep it up. Eventually, though, one has to discover a personal motivation to carry on with fitness and make it part of one's life or even one's identity. The same is true of writing: As a writing instructor, I am much like that fitness trainer. I create a program and support students, but eventually they must find their own motivations for writing and for making writing part of their lives and identities. Obviously, no instructor can require a student to want something, even though it is quite ordinary for teachers to play a kind of evangelical role in describing the appeal and value of their subject. In the end, we want to account for agency or a lack thereof: Writers must want to write. I try to make it as clear as possible to students that, at some level, they must make a commitment to writing if they wish to become better writers. In my course, I create opportunities for students to reflect upon their past experiences and current relationships with their writing practices and explore ways to connect their existing educational motivations with writing. Perhaps these two values (that writers must write and want to write) seem to result from obvious and fairly modest educational goals. From my view, a student who is able to recognize or develop a desire to become a better writer (not necessarily writing for writing's sake, but writing in connection with another goal), and subsequently develops a regular writing practice, has had a valuable experience in a composition course. I wish I could say that it was easy to achieve this result in composition. I have not found it easy. The best I can say is that I have created opportunities for students to discover such motivations and to develop writing practices that might continue beyond the end of the semester.

My course has other objectives that are less unavoidable and more a matter of disciplinary perspective than the first two. I agree with Wardle when she observes that a writing course cannot recreate the conditions in which other "real world" or academic genres are composed and that, as a result, composition courses end up creating "mutt genres." Another tautology results, I suppose: One can only write under the conditions in which one is writing, though, some of those conditions are mutable. Setting aside those conditions that are changeable, students who write in a composition course are writing in a composition course, not for a newspaper or a think-tank or a biology lab. As such, one must ask "What are the disciplinary and institutional conditions of a composition course?" These understandably vary with instructors and institutions. In my case, and I don't think this is a particularly uncommon response, the question begins with rhetoric as a mode of investigation and study. That is, I introduce students to rhetoric like other introductory courses introduce students to, say, chemistry or history. Unlike Downs and Wardle, who suggest that such a course might introduce students to works in composition studies, I shape my course around questions I consider as fundamental to rhetoric, such as: "How do I know what this person is telling me is true?"; "How can I persuade my audience of my perspective?"; "How can we improve our lives and resolve disputes in our community through communication?" Noticeably, these are all "how" questions; they are questions of method or practice. I introduce rhetoric in terms of developing critical methods for evaluating communication and that might have applications in al-

[margin handwritten note:] Guiding Ques. Like this

most any rhetorical situation. Like other introductory, general education courses, there is no expectation that students will continue in this
line of study. Instead, the objectives are to offer useful rhetorical methods and to have students understand the general purpose and value of
the academic study of rhetoric.

Finally, my course asks students to operate in a digital, networked
environment. Even though composing in digital environments has become so commonplace in first-year composition that such objectives
are included in documents like the Council of Writing Program Administrator's "Outcomes Statement for First-Year Composition," this
still remains the least standard outcome in my course in comparison
to what is commonly taught across the country. From my perspective,
teaching digital rhetoric and composing should be an integral part of a
composition course. If we are to begin with the premise that writing is
largely a situated practice, we should not make the claim that writing
for print is more fundamental than digital, networked writing. As is
illustrated by many colleagues who are print literate but struggle with
composing in digital environments, one does not necessarily lead to
the other. This does not mean that I eschew print entirely for digital.
We live in a time when both print and digital composing practices
are necessary; indeed, they are not easily separated. Digital composing involves remediation from print, and virtually all print documents
spend time as digital ones. As I note above, UB students, like most
college students, are extensive users of social media and mobile technologies. Most of their daily compositions are digital, and many of
the rhetorical acts most important to them are digital. Of course, they
tend to not connect these practices with writing or rhetoric. As such,
one part of this objective is for students to recognize their existing
network of digital, rhetorical practices and to situate the course's writing practices (and other academic writing they might do) in that context. A typical student's use of Facebook, Twitter, or Google may not
be for educational purposes or occur in conjunction with what we
have conventionally termed writing; however, an increasing number of
academics use social media and the Web as part of their work—as do
many non-academic professionals. This objective feeds back into other
key goals of the course. First, if one goal of the course is to help students develop durable writing practices, then this might begin by identifying and then extending students' existing writing habits in digital
spaces. Second, since the course asks students to write more than I can

thoroughly read, and introduces students to fundamental questions about rhetorical practice, it is useful for students to have a real audience available to them through digital networks. *point taken*

THE RISKS OF TEACHING IN PUBLIC

Once digital composing is introduced into a course, a decision must be made about how accessible such material should be to audiences beyond the classroom. Teaching in publicly accessible online spaces is likely the most controversial component of my course. I do this with all my courses, from first-year composition through graduate classes. I do not believe courses need to be entirely public. Obviously, grades are not public, and I would not make public directly evaluative (i.e., grade-related) comments. I also believe that our default expectation of the privacy of the classroom is more a residue of the technological affordances of the nineteenth and twentieth centuries than it is a carefully considered position. In my class, the public portion might take the form of a group or individual blog, participation on a wiki, or the use of Twitter. As a policy, students can select a pseudonym, though the reality is that virtually all students already have online identities, usually through Facebook. They have already accepted, perhaps tacitly and without reflection, whatever risks may be involved in speaking in public. Admittedly, the course asks students to take on new risks and, as an instructor, I must think carefully about the particular demands I make of students in a public space. Risk is one of my primary interests in teaching in public spaces.

One of the few things we can say about almost every rhetorical act is that it involves risk. Put bluntly, say the wrong thing at the wrong time, and someone might punch you, fire you, imprison you, etc. In my view, much of writing instruction focuses on risk management. *interesting* The years that students spent in school preparing to pass state essay exams did not focus on writing something interesting or even on excelling in this staid, testing context. Instead, such pedagogies focus on devising foolproof methods for generating tepid, acceptable prose. Much of the "writing process" approach has devolved to a similar kind of risk management, using a set of pre-established procedures that all students can follow to compose passable essays. Understandably, students desire such assurances; they wish to pass the class to complete their requirement. They request a definitive list of criteria for "getting an A," and they want models they can replicate. In short, they want to minimize risk. From a certain perspective, this is what rhetoric generally seeks to accomplish. We employ rhetoric to maximize our chances of achieving some purpose and to minimize the likelihood of negative consequences. At the same time, we recognize an inescapable relationship between risk and reward. Students tend to articulate risk and reward in terms of grades because often the only one who reads their writing is their instructor and, in that context, there is little reason to take on a risk that does not correspond to the potential reward of a better grade. In other words, the only risk students can take is to guess what the instructor wants and to seek to minimize that risk by finding out what needs to be done to receive an "A." Composition instructors often try to counter this student strategy by giving assignments with imaginary scenarios; for example: "Imagine you are writing a letter to the editor of a newspaper . . ." If writing is indeed situated, then such imaginary scenarios have little impact, except to the extent that they inform what the teacher wants. Writing in public does not alter the salient fact of the classroom that I will be giving the students grades, but it does create other real audiences and, hence, other real risks (and rewards) for student writing. While students may still care primarily about the grade they receive, they now have other risks to weigh, including the response of other students in the class (who will read some of their writing) and a more nebulous public (that students may or may not encounter).

In my class, the relationship between grades, risks, and the public is further addressed by the approach I take to evaluation. I have observed in my own practice and in the practice of my colleagues for nearly twenty years that a "B" is a *very* common grade in a composition class. If a student completes all the assignments and meets basic, fairly objective criteria (e.g., page length), they will almost certainly get some kind of a B grade. A grade of "C" tends to be used for students who miss some component of the course work, while grades of "A" are reserved for students whose writing stand out. For this reason, I find it justifiable to remove a significant amount of the risk that is conventionally associated with grades. I make it explicit that to receive a B in the class all a student really must do is complete all the work. There is virtually no risk. I made this decision because, in my experience, B students achieve their grades by playing it safe. While it seems unfair to me to punish students for doing what they've always been taught to do, I want to create conditions where it is not necessary to play it safe, where the typical B student can take risks without risking the B grade. Put differently, I tell them that they have little chance of getting an A without taking some risks, and that they have little chance of getting a C if they do take risks. In this context, the risk/reward calculation *Like* becomes less about grades (though grades are always part of the con- text) and more about the real audiences who will encounter their texts. I find this context far more fertile for investigating questions related to my key objectives: developing durable writing practices, finding a personal motivation for writing, understanding introductory rhetori- cal methods, and learning to communicate in digital networks.

ACTOR-NETWORKS AND ASSEMBLAGES

One of the underlying contentions of my research is that theories of written composition and pedagogy necessarily rest upon more capa- cious theories of ontology. That is, one's understanding of how writing is composed is necessarily related to how one understands how think- ing is composed (i.e., how we think) and, furthermore, how things in general are composed. Likewise, pedagogy rests upon more general theories of communication and cognition. Put in those terms, I do not believe these claims are particularly contentious. However, I argue that ontological questions are largely unexamined in our discipline, and *ohh—* many of our conceptions about writing and teaching have been shaped *more* by the industrial and institutional contexts of the nineteenth and *n* twentieth centuries, contexts that are now rapidly changing. When *that* I consider emerging technologies and their role in our work, it is not so much about cajoling my colleagues to get on board with the latest gadget as it is to consider how the legacy concepts of our work were shaped by prior technologies. These matters are only partly about the technologies themselves. While in the field of computers and writing we have studied the role of technologies in composing for more than thirty years, I am less interested in those particular questions than I am with the broader ontologies that have shaped the modern univer- sity and modern rhetoric.

In pursuing this line of inquiry, there are rhetoricians that I have drawn upon. Victor Vitanza and Gregory Ulmer have informed my work since graduate school, but my primary theoretical contexts come from outside our discipline. This is not that unusual. Much of the

post-process movement has drawn upon a variety of French philosophy (e.g., Foucault, Bahktin, Althusser, etc.), feminism, and cultural
studies. While there is certainly a wide variety of positions and methods here, these theories share a common concern with discourse, representation, and ideology. My contexts are slightly different, focusing
on Deleuze and Guattari, Bruno Latour, Manuel DeLanda, Brian
Massumi, and more recently, various schools of speculative realism
(e.g., Graham Harman, Ian Bogost, and Levi Bryant). These thinkers
are not broadly addressed in rhetoric and composition. Within more
mainstream rhetoric and composition, perhaps the closest position to
my work is that done with cultural-historical activity theory (CHAT)
by Charles Bazerman, David Russell, and others. Activity theory
shares some common points with Latour's actor-network theory, and
with the assemblage theory Delanda develops from Deleuze and Guattari, in that it recognizes a network of people, things, and discourses
that shape compositional practices. It also differs in some significant
ways, particularly in CHAT's assumption of the asymmetrical role
played by humans in such networks. That is, humans and human decision-making are the central focus of CHAT. In contrast, actor-network theory and assemblage theory, especially as I employ them, begin
with a flat ontology that assumes that all objects are equally real on an
ontological basis. Certainly, in a given set of relations, one object may
dominate over others, but such asymmetry is not assumed.

How do such fairly abstract philosophies impact the real world situation of composition pedagogy? As I suggest above, it begins with
rethinking writing on an ontological foundation. Rather than asym-
metrically focusing on the student as the determining agent in the
composition network, a speculative realist assemblage theory presumes
a wider, more dynamic network of objects. Perhaps this induces concerns about the agency of the subject, but such concerns would hardly
be new in our field, having long been a worry of post-process composition studies. From this perspective, agency is not simply the property
of an individual or object, but is instead a *capacity* that emerges from
relations with others. That is, I do not have the agency to write within
me; my capacity to write is a networked capacity. As such, learning to
write cannot be only about finding something within, but is instead
about building networks that are productive for writing. This produc-
tivity is partly a technical matter: One can only write in the context
of writing technologies, and the particular affordances of the available

technologies are relevant. However, the network is equally affective. If writing requires some intrinsic motivation, at least in the long term, then the compositional networks we build must produce this affect. Even though this philosophical viewpoint distributes cognition, affect, and agency rather than "empowering" student writers by making them central, recognizing the ontological relations among objects in a compositional network can result in more productive writing practices. Rather than viewing writing as a kind of industrial process that is powered by subjective labor and beholden to cultural or institutional discursive demands, if writing is a networked practice, then, as writers, we can intercede in the network with the idea that a shift in the network can impact the compositional process.

A concrete example of the impact of this shift is found in the role of reflection. Writing reflective pieces on one's process is a long-standing feature of composition pedagogy. I have two concerns with reflection: First, if the focus remains heavily on grading, then reflection always risks being dishonest and performative; the impetus to tell the teacher what he or she wants to hear disrupts the possibility of reflection. Second, when the focus is on the subjective labor of the individual, reflection can quickly verge into an exercise in *ressentiment* (a feeling of resentment or hostility) and bad conscience. As a result, reflection becomes a confessional technology. Students tell stories of how they were once poor writers, but were "saved" through the class. Certainly, reflection does not have to be that. From a network perspective, reflection operates as a part of a feedback loop, offering up information that can be employed to shift the network, the next iteration, or the next composition. Rather than the author reflecting on what he or she did well or poorly, a networked reflection asks one to review the network of objects and operations involved in a composition. Where was this composition produced? What technologies and other objects were involved? How much time was spent? What specific strategies were employed? What choices were available? What informed the choices that were eventually made? This produces a keen sense of the decisions writers make, and hence the opportunities we have to act differently in the future. In other words, writing becomes experimental in the artistic sense, but also in the scientific sense, and the reflection operates roughly analogous to a lab report.

For the purposes of my course, a more significant implication of assemblages lies in the role technology plays in the course. Understandably, communication technologies are a significant part of students' compositional networks. Even though students are often savvy users of mobile phones, social media, and the Internet, when it comes to navigating their social lives and personal interests, such confidence rarely translates to the classroom. In part, this is because most academic uses of digital networks differ from their social uses. However, my students' view of academic writing typically disallows such activities. They have been taught to distrust the Web and to view academic writing as a largely insular activity. This is clear in their inexperience with talking about one another's writing in a peer-group workshop. While digital networks are complex spaces, and evaluating what we find there can be challenging, this is a real-world challenge not just for students, but for us all. When students reflect upon the technologies operating in their compositional networks, they have an opportunity to strategize more productive engagements and to link their academic writing practices with their social ones.

COURSE ACTIVITY AND AFFINITY

Though my course certainly looks beyond current composition theory to investigate the ontological foundations of writing, it also concerns itself with methods that our discipline has left behind, much as Geoffrey Sirc does in *English Composition as a Happening* by paying attention to what composition left behind in its disciplinary turn in the eighties, including compositionists such as Ken Macrorie and also compositional methods from the visual arts and music. In particular, Sirc establishes his pedagogy in opposition to a mainstream teaching he sees as exemplified by David Bartholomae and Anthony Petrosky's *Ways of Reading*. There are other textbook candidates (and Sirc lists some), but it is Bartholomae and Petrosky's approach that he describes as a kind of museum that tries "to continually gloss the canon of our permanent collection, inviting students in to study the great works and contemplate 'the way the text positions them in relationship to a history of writing'" (267). Sirc's quotation of Bartholomae in this passage suggests that his desire is to not position students in relation to a static, curated body of great works, but rather to connect with his students' living cultures and deploy more generative methods that draw upon affect and the sublime, and that do not draw a firm boundary between the poetic and the rhetorical.

In his basic writing course, Sirc describes turning toward hip-hop music and culture, noting that "hip hop is a rubric for some of the most exciting cultural media available to young people today, transcending perceived distinctions of age, gender, race, and ethnicity" (271). While I have never followed Sirc in creating a course around hip hop, I share his departure from the particular curation of academic writing that is characteristic of many composition readers and his interest in student affect. Like Sirc, my course asks students to draw upon their own experiences and interests on issues of education and social media. Admittedly, such topics may not inspire the immediate interest that hip hop might for some students. However, they are subjects in which students are deeply embedded and have existing positions. Students often have strong feelings about their education, both positive and negative, and are obviously embarking on a college curriculum about which they might feel excitement, anxiety, and uncertainty, among other responses. Similarly, students live much of their lives through social media. While they may not have the critical, disciplinary language to investigate social media in academic terms, they have passions and concerns over the roles that Facebook, texting, and other social media play in their lives. In turn, the topics of social media and higher education are two primary sites where public discourse addresses traditional-age college students at UB. Most mainstream media offers critical and skeptical views about social media: Books like Nick Carr's *The Shallows* worry about the effect the Internet is having on our minds as well as more social concerns about privacy, copyright, and even the banal narcissism of the status update. Similarly, public discourse on higher education is also mostly critical, particularly in terms of the humanities. UB students clearly feel the pressure to connect learning to a secure job, a pressure that is often marked in their ambivalence toward the STEM majors they have declared. A significant number of UB students enter in nursing, pharmacy, or engineering, but not many graduate in those majors. While the purpose of composition is hardly to lead students to doubt their choices of majors, this course does ask students to connect their experiences with larger conversations about education and technology.

It would be fair to say that such approaches also typify the post-process, cultural studies composition classroom, where students might read *Ways of Reading* or a similar text. The same might be said of hip hop, for that matter. The difference, then, is not the topics stu-

dents discuss or the research they gather, but rather the activities of
the classroom. A typical cultural studies assignment might ask students to read Foucault on panopticism and then to write an essay on
surveillance in social media. Such an essay would rely primarily upon
a student's understanding of Foucault and his or her ability to apply
the concept of panopticism. The student's experience might come into
play, but it would be subordinated to the theory and the thesis. Rather
than providing a critical lens that creates agency for the writer, here
Foucault's text ironically serves a panoptic function itself, subsuming
the student to its curatorial gaze. This is not a quality particular to
Foucault, of course. As Sirc suggests, composition has become dominated by an approach to "academic" prose that subordinates the student writer. Rather than taking up a conversation of texts in search
of some other understanding, the student writer's typical obligation
is to demonstrate an understanding of readings. Perhaps the defense
of this common practice is that such abilities are expected in other
disciplines. I find this a weak defense. Composition ought to stand
on its own principles rather than some vaguely defined expectations
that come from elsewhere. While I recognize that my students struggle
with reading, summarizing, and evaluating texts (print or digital), I do
not believe there are general reading (or writing) skills. Engagement
through the close reading of essays that is characteristic of composition
(and English Studies in general) might seem strange and inappropri-
ate in other disciplines. Certainly, my course has readings (as well as
videos and other material) and asks students to engage with this material in their writing (including responding to each other), but the goal
is not to develop a particular disciplinary understanding of these texts
or to "position students in the history of writing." Instead, the role of
such materials is to be generative, to serve as objects within the compositional network in which students are working.

More to the point, this course shifts student activity away from
private reading and writing toward a more public and networked activity. In doing so, it connects Sirc's interest in the affective, creative
potential of his students to what James Paul Gee and Elisabeth R.
Hayes term as "passionate affinity spaces," presented as an alternative
to the classroom and its focus on traditional, essayist prose (69). Passionate affinity spaces are easily found online (though not exclusively),
where people gather to share their interests in a particular activity:
"within these spaces people have the opportunity to become lifelong

learners, designers, and knowledge producers" (Gee and Hayes 86). This is precisely the opportunity I seek to offer students in terms of writing, though perhaps the initial reaction of my colleagues and students is that such spaces are incompatible with schooling, as schooling demands a more rigid, disciplined approach to teaching—although, perhaps it is difficult to determine exactly from where that "demand" derives. Sirc recounts classrooms from the sixties, where students sat in the dark on mats, burned incense and listened to Steppenwolf, so the writing classroom has not always been so rigid (1). Passionate affinity spaces update such practices by engaging with the contemporary digital network to facilitate student learning and communication. Clearly, this is not about "required" online participation, but about using networks to connect with others who share one's interests, to communicate with classmates on one's own schedule and as dictated by one's passions, and to create a different relationship to learning than the one developed in traditional schooling. As Gee and Hayes ask, "Does anyone, for example, think that a college organized as a plethora of passionate affinity spaces devoted to academic knowledge and complex systems, spaces with everyone in them (faculty and students alike), would not be as good as, or better than many, perhaps all, of our current colleges?" (88)

One of the challenges of this approach is that it is not really feasible to think of it on the scale of a single course. From the perspective that Gee and Hayes advocate, this would a key institutional limitation of our current situation. As one might rightly observe, one difference between the composition course and an affinity space is, to be blunt, that students generally have little affinity for composition, or at least so they would assert upon arrival in the classroom. They are required to take the class and, at least at UB, are typically block-scheduled into composition courses for the fall semester as part of the freshmen summer registration process. Following Gee and Hayes' vision, one might imagine the entirety of the composition program at UB—about 2,500 students in over 100 sections, taught by approximately 75 instructors each semester—as part of a single affinity space (an obviously online space), where each section serves as a node on the larger network. This conventionally only occurs in the most abstract sense. Each class is a section of the same course number with the same general course description and the same number of credits, and has the same role in fulfilling general education requirements and presumably the same course objectives. However, the courses do not generally communicate. Firewalls exist between courses on the network. Opening those firewalls would significantly alter the roles of instructors and students. Everyone would need to learn new behaviors. In some respects, the challenge would be analogous to learning how to behave in social media. That is, if one imagined one's class of two-dozen students representing roughly one percent of a composition community in which they might be engaged in any number of different writing projects based upon their interests, then clearly one would have to construct one's course differently, because one would have to recognize that even though each student would be part of a common community, he or she would also be working in a unique compositional network with specific affinities. Needless to say, this is already the case with every student enrolled in a composition course; it's just that our institutional pedagogy is designed to stamp out those differences.

COMMUNITARIAN LITERACY

No doubt there is a large number of logistical and institutional problems with teaching in an affinity space on this scale. I do not address those matters here. Instead, I will proceed with a more "realistic," though less satisfying, model of a single course. On this scale, greater rhetorical effort is required of the instructor. Where the now familiar post-process, cultural studies classroom asks the instructor to persuade students to take on certain critical-ideological positions to write traditional academic essays, here the instructor must persuade students to change their writing and learning practices by seeking connections between composing, their interests, and the classroom community that is their primary audience. In making this shift, the fundamental goals of rhetoric or communication are not abandoned. From this perspective, one continues to recognize writing as a practice of discovery and invention, as well as an effort to connect with others, to form community, to persuade, and so on. The shift lies in the ontological basis for this practice and the implications that the shift has for how one understands composing practices and, by extension, composition pedagogies. As I have discussed, my teaching pays special attention to the role of affect and affinity in writing practice. Furthermore, my ontological perspective, which carries me through assemblage and actor-network theories, brings me to view affect and affinity as networked phenomena, as capacities of relations among objects, rather than as isolated characteristics of individual subjects. Though Gee and Hayes do not use this language, their interest in affinity spaces also recognizes this distributed quality. In the classroom, it is not necessary to carry students through these technical, theoretical concepts. The pedagogical task is not to demonstrate or inculcate conceptual mastery, but rather to re-orient writing practice and habit away from the inward-looking, self-controlled author and toward a networked community of actors and objects.

Drawing on Jean-Luc Nancy, Diane Davis suggests that communitarian writers

> . . . do not aim to establish a stable and authoritative ethos nor to put forth an unambiguous message; they aim to amplify the irreparable *instability* and extreme *vulnerability* to which any writing necessarily testifies. . . . Messages and persons must be communicated, of course, but this writing "obeys the sole necessity of exposing the limit: not the limit of communication, *but the limit upon which communication takes place.*" (139)

Like Davis, I recognize that these terms are too demanding for the composition student. It is unfair (and ultimately unproductive) to imagine unmooring people in such an extreme way from their existing practices. More modestly, one might reasonably shift students away from their typical habits of seeking to be finished with writing. As Davis describes, "the stated goal of the essay in such a course would be to hold the door open on this thesis (and so, on one's writing-being), to keep it ex-posed to various encounters, interruptions, contradictions— to resist the urge to turn away from the 'outside' in order to finish off the conversation" (141). In many respects, I see this urge as analogous to one I have seen many times in fiction-writing workshops, where all too often stories end with characters suddenly dying or realizing that "it was all a dream." I have always read such gestures as efforts to get to the end, to force a conclusion. In composition courses, these tendencies manifest in an effort to excise provocative statements in early drafts that demand additional writing or ignoring research that provokes a serious rethinking of one's thesis. The desire to be finished with writing, represented finally in the desire to complete one's college writing requirement, is strong. Writing in the networked affinity spaces I have been describing, however, means encountering an environment where writing is never finished. An assignment is completed, this chapter gets sent to the editors, but writing keeps going on across the network. In the end, the simple tautological fact that writers write is compelling. As I tell my professional writing students, when writing is successful, writers respond with writing; when it is a failure, they respond with writing. When they feel inspired and grasp for the keyboard, writers write. When they are blocked, they write as well. By definition, all that writers can do is to write. As Davis suggests, writing is about keeping that relation open. Of course, we are not *always* writers, even if we decide to expand our conceptual sense of writing beyond the act of inscribing words on paper or on the screen. Writing keeps going on in the networks in which we participate. If nothing else, social media has made this quite clear. Writing involves exposing ourselves to that network, an exposure that has risks that are only matched by its rewards.

Works Cited

Council of Writing Program Administrators. *WPA Outcomes Statement for First-Year Composition.* Amended July 2008. Web. 7 Feb. 2012.

Davis, Diane. "Finitude's Clamor; Or, Notes toward a Communitarian Literacy." *College Composition and Communication* 53.1 (September 2001): 119-45. Print.

Downs, Doug and Elizabeth Wardle. "Teaching about Writing, Righting Misconceptions: (Re)Envisioning 'First-Year Composition' as 'Introduction to Writing Studies.'" *College Composition and Communication* 58.4: 552-84. Print.

Gee, James Paul and Elisabeth R. Hayes. *Language and Learning in the Digital Age.* New York: Routledge, 2011. Print.

Sirc, Geoffrey. *English Composition as Happening.* Logan: Utah State UP, 2002. Print.

Wardle, Elizabeth. "'Mutt Genres' and the Goal of FYC: Can We Help Students Write the Genres of the University?" *College Composition and Communication* 60:4: 765-89. Print.

Appendix: Course Syllabus

ENG 101: Writing I

Alex Reid, English

Course Attributes

Fulfills the General Education Writing Skills Requirement. Reviews essay, paragraph, and sentence development during the first half of the semester. Conceptualizing and conducting original research, culminating in a major research essay using both library and online materials during the second half of the semester. Twenty-five pages of graded, revised writing, excluding first drafts, exercises, and quizzes.

Grading Policies

To receive a B +/- in this course, you must complete the following:
- On-time completion of all 4 major writing assignments (described below), including meeting the requirements of those assignments as detailed;
- Weekly participation in our online discussion and a minimum of 30 posts for the semester;
- Weekly blog posts, minimum 100 words each;
- Submission of final portfolio (described below);
- Satisfying the attendance policy.

Please note that writing assignment requirements include submitting completed drafts and responding to feedback from me and your peers. You may be asked to complete additional revisions to satisfy assignment requirements. Students who meet these requirements will receive a grade from B- to B+ depending upon my judgment of the quality of their work. You will receive ongoing feedback regarding these evaluations during the semester.

Students who do not complete *all four major assignments and turn in a final portfolio cannot pass the class*. However, passing grades below a B- will be given to students who meet these major requirements but fail to complete other elements of the course.

To receive an A- or A (there are no A+ grades at UB) students must first complete B or B+ (but not B-) work, and complete one of the following

- Serve as an editor for our magazine assignment (described below);
- Lead a class discussion, including a brief presentation;

Required Materials

All course materials available via the course website.

Assignment Descriptions

Article and Magazine Project

Summary

The primary purpose of this assignment is for you to think differently about the audiences for whom you write. A magazine article is probably the closest genre to the classroom essay that we typically encounter. They are generally the same length as college essays; they often make an argument (usually in the form of advice); and they incorporate external sources (though the citation format of a magazine article is quite different from the classroom essay). However, magazine article writers, editors, and publishers realize they have to compete for their readers' attention. Unlike the teacher who is paid to read the student's paper, readers pay for magazine articles. They expect to be informed and entertained. In this case, we will be writing articles on the subject of the effects of new technologies on thinking, and we will be reading several articles addressing the issue. This is a topic that has generated a fair amount of interest in recent years as digital media have significantly transformed the lives of Americans and people around the world. Just as the authors we will read discuss their own experiences with digital technologies, you can also draw upon personal experience to help you establish a unique take on the subject.

For the Magazine Project, we will take the articles we have written and produce an online magazine with images and related media. Volunteers will be asked to serve as editors (see grading policy above) who will have additional responsibilities in putting the magazine together. All students will revise their articles based on the feedback they receive and incorporate digital media into their work.

Objectives

Through this assignment, we will be working toward the following goals:

- Developing strategies for writing to different audiences;
- Crafting introductions that grab reader attention;
- Incorporating personal experience with research;
- Articulating a unique point of view on a widely-discussed issue.

Slidecast

Summary

A slidecast offers a different and powerful way to communicate your message. Though we have all experienced boring and confusing slide presentations, a well-designed slidecast can be very successful. The primary problem most slide presentations have is that the slides are designed to serve as notes or an outline for the spoken presentation rather than as a communicative visual element that supports and expands upon the oral message. As we know from elsewhere in our lives, however, images can evoke powerful emotions and serve to make a message more memorable. Part of the challenge though is in learning to think with and through images. Just as the texts we read help to shape our arguments, the images that we find and use in our presentations have an impact upon the messages we compose. As such, through the slidecast assignment, you will have an opportunity to think about your research in a new way. The slidecast will also give you a chance to interest your audience in the final project that you will create, so think of this assignment as a kind of "movie trailer" for your research essay.

Objectives

Through this assignment, we will be working toward the following goals:

- Design effective slides;
- Combine slides with an oral presentation;
- Explain some aspect of your research;
- Generate interest and excitement in your forthcoming work.

Research Responses

Summary

Researchers do a fair amount of informal writing as part of their work. Depending on the kind of research they do, this writing might include lab reports, field observations, notes on primary materials (e.g. historical documents), and summaries of secondary material (i.e. other scholarship in the field). Though this writing may never be made public, it forms an important foundation for the published work that follows. In this assignment, you will be writing about the scholarly material you uncover through library research. Writing about the texts you read is a valuable way not only to articulate your understanding of the material but also to make connections between the texts. More importantly, writing these responses will help you begin to answer the question you have posed with your research project. Unlike some informal writing, in this case, your responses will be available to the other students in the class. Increasingly we see this among professors and other academic researchers who will share informal writing, thoughts on recently published research, and preliminary findings through various online venues. You should think about your research response in this way. It is primarily for your own benefit but should also be addressed to fellow researchers.

Objectives

Through this assignment, we will be working toward the following goals:
  • Demonstrate an understanding of the research you have read;
  • Make connections between the texts you are reading;
  • Evaluate the research you have found for an audience of fellow researchers.

Research Proposal and Essay

Summary

This is the culminating project for this course. The project begins with a proposal. Based upon course readings and class discussion, you will propose a research project. A proposal is fundamentally a question that you want to answer. Your proposal *should not* indicate what you intend to argue. The position that you will ultimately take in your research essay should develop as a result of the research that you do. However, that doesn't mean that you should simply agree with whatever you find in your research. In fact, it is likely that you will find conflicting views, just as we have read conflicting views in class. Your job is review the material and then develop your position.

Your research proposal should refer to our readings but might also draw upon your own experience. It should explain why you are inter-ested in this question and why you think something valuable might result from your efforts. Finally, you should lay out some preliminary plans for conducting your research. Mostly you will do library-based research, but you might also do observations, run surveys, or conduct interviews.

In your research essay, you will adopt a position in relation to your research question based upon the findings of your research. As you will discover, there is rarely a final, definitive answer that results from research, but at the same time there are objective foundations for an academic argument that make it more than a "matter of opinion." There are many ways to do research. In this class we will focus on humanistic methods, which we will discuss. In particular, I will ask you to pay close attention to the texts that you have gathered through research, quote from them, and analyze those quotations. Finally you will construct an essay that considers the breadth of the research you have found, including those positions that disagree with you, and make an argument that seeks to persuade your audience as to why the conclusion you've reached is the best one.

Objectives

Through this assignment, we will be working toward the following goals:
- Identify a viable research question;
- Conduct thorough and productive library research;
- Establish a position in relation to your research question;
- Incorporate research into your essay;
- Lead your audience through the research;
- Explain the value of your research and its implications.

Online/Informal Writing

Students will participate in online discussion forums and maintain a reflective blog. Each week students will write twice on the discussion forum and at least once on their blog. Posts are of an informal nature, usually 100–200 words, and related to class discussion.

Class Work and Participation

This course expects regular participation from students in both small group and class-wide discussion of readings and assignments. Participation in workshops is especially important.

Course Schedule	
Note: Course schedule is subject to change. Notifications of changes will be made in class.	
Meeting Day	**Assignments**
Week One Tu	• First day of class • Article assignment begins
Th	• View Clay Shirky, "How Cognitive Surplus Will Change the World" • Read Kevin Kelly: "The New Socialism"
Week Two Tu	• Read Michelle D. Trim and Megan Lynn Isaac "Re-inventing Invention: Discovery and Investment in Writing"
Th	• Read Nicholas Carr: "Is Google Making Us Stupid?"
Week Three Tu	• Read Dan Gillmor Chapters 1 & 10, http://mediac-tive.com/book/table-of-contents-2/
Th	• In-class workshop • Strategies for revision • Complete drafts of article due
Week Four Tu	• Magazine project assignment begins • Technical matters with WordPress • Submit article
Th	• In-class work on magazine
Week Five	• Classes cancelled for student conferences
Week Six Tu	• Magazine workshop
Th	• Magazine project ends

Course Schedule	
Note: Course schedule is subject to change. Notifications of changes will be made in class.	
Week Seven Tu	• Research proposal • Alexander Reid "Why Blog? Searching for Writing on the Web"
Th	• Matt Barton and Karl Klint "A Student's Guide to Collaborative Writing Technologies"
Week Eight Tu	• Research proposal due • Slidecast assignment begins • Technical instructions on Powerpoint • Style/Delivery: Individual slide design • Microsoft directions for making turning your presentation into a video (in Office 2010): http://office.microsoft.com/en-us/powerpoint-help/turn-your-presentation-into-a-video-HA010336763.aspx?CTT=1 • Microsoft directions for recording narration for Office 2007: http://office.microsoft.com/en-us/powerpoint-help/add-narration-to-a-presentation-HA001230306.aspx
Th	• Genre/Arrangement: What does a slidecast look like? • Invention: Selecting a topic and finding images • Garr Reynold's (author of Presentation Zen and other books) website <http://www.presentationzen.com/> has plenty of good material on slide design and overall presentation strategies. You can also look at his other page: http://www.garrreynolds.com/Presentation/index.html. • Nancy Duarte's (author of Slideology and other books) website: http://www.duarte.com/training/tools/
Week Nine Tu	• Audience and purpose: what does a slidecast do?
Th	• In-class workshop • Complete drafts of slidecast due
Week Ten	• Slidecast due • Class cancelled for student conference

Course Schedule	
Note: Course schedule is subject to change. Notifications of changes will be made in class.	
Week Eleven Tu	• Research project begins • Some history on the academic essay • Read Paul Lynch "The Sixth Paragraph: A Re-Vision of the Essay"
Th	• Read Rebecca Jones "Finding the Good Argument OR Why Bother With Logic?"
Week Twelve Tu	• Read L. Lennie Irvin "What is Academic Writing"
Th	• "Finding Your Way In": Invention as Inquiry Based Learning in First Year Writing by Steven Lessner and Collin Craig
Week Thir- teen Tu	• Research responses complete
Th	• Class cancelled—Thanksgiving Break
Week Four- teen Tu	• In-class workshop • Complete drafts of research project due
Th	• "From Topic to Presentation: Making Choices to Develop Your Writing" by Beth L. Hewett • Strategies for revision
Week Fifteen Tu	• In-class workshop
Th	• Last day of class • Research project due

8 Beyond Text and Talk: A Multimodal Approach to First-Year Composition

Jody Shipka

> *Although an essay might be referred to as a composition, that terminology confused no one. Musicians composed; what we were doing was writing.*
>
> —Lee Odell & Christina Lynn Prell

> *In the traditional freshman English program the term papers written by the students deal with subjects ranging from avitaminosis to Zionism. The fact seems to be an admission that the course lacks a distinguishing content of its own. In history one writes on history; in economics, one writes on economics; in English—or so we now believe— one ought to write on some problem concerning the use of language. This is an idea that gives unified content to the course.*
>
> —Harold E. Briggs

I begin with two epigraphs, each pointing to an important dimension of the first-year composition (FYC) courses I have taught for the past twelve years. While assignments, activities, and the particular texts I assign have changed and will (I assume) continue to change as scholarship, technologies, and students' and my interests continue to also change, what has remained a consistent, non-negotiable aspect of the course are these twinned beliefs: That those teaching first-year com-

211

position should be teaching composition, and that the proper subject matter for composition courses is composition.

In a publication that calls for research on "composing, not just writing—composing" (295), Lee Odell and Christina Lynn Prell point out how the terms "composing" and "writing" are too often, and erroneously, equated. The authors call for a more "comprehensive view of composing" (296), one that attends not just to alphabetic text, but to the "interanimation of words, visual images, and page (or screen) design" (295). To my mind, taking a broader view of and approach to, composing is not just a matter of practicing what many of us profess to teach, theorize, or research. Rather, given the increased materials with which, contexts in which, and purposes for which, students currently make and negotiate meaning, it has become increasingly important that our courses continue to "disturb the marriage between comfortable writing that forms our disciplinary core and the entire range of new media for writing" (Faigely and Romano 49). Like others have argued, I argue here that our courses need to do more to bridge the gap between the texts and practices typically associated with the composition (or writing) classroom and the various other texts and practices students experience beyond the space of the classroom (see also Johnson-Eilola; Millard; Selfe; and Yancey). To ensure that our courses do not become irrelevant—or, depending on one's perspective, to ensure that they do not become *increasingly irrelevant*—we must ask students to examine the design of words on a page as well as the relationships among words, images, codes, textures, sounds, colors, and potentials for movement. We need, in short, to embrace composition. More specifically still, and in keeping with those who advocated a communications approach to the Freshman English course more than a half century ago, we need to create courses and build curricula designed with a mind toward the communicative world(s) that our students "are living in now and will be citizens of in the future" (Dunn 283). The kind of courses I have in mind would

- be grounded in social scientific theories of discourse, underscoring for students both the social and personal dimensions of communicative practice (Dunn);
- focus on the various mediums of communication students encounter (Briggs);

- treat the communicative process as a "dynamic whole," highlighting for students how language and other media are "used by all kinds of people in all kinds of ways" (Dean 81-83);
- require that students attend not simply to what a text says or means, but to what that text *does*—to attend to questions related to how, when, and/or how well that text accomplishes meaning (Briggs);
- encourage a more nuanced understanding of the relationships among words, minds, and things, and acknowledge the roles that bodies, gestures, and environments play in communication practices (Dunn); and
- facilitate greater meta-communicative awareness by asking students to reflect on and assume responsibility for what "one says and writes" (Briggs 328).

In addition to expressing concern that the first-year course was not designed to respond to the current or projected needs of its students, proponents of the communications approach found equally problematic the lack of unified course content. This was a problem Albert Kitzhaber also noted, years later, in his 1963 publication *Themes, Theories, and Therapy: The Teaching of Writing in College*. There, Kitzhaber reported that he had found "a bewildering variety of content" being offered across sections of the first-year course (10). As Harold Briggs argued in *College English* in 1948, when compared with courses in history or economics (to this list we might add many other courses students are often required to take; e.g., psychology, biology, math, etc.), where students are both expected and expecting to learn and to write about history or economics, the "traditional English course" seemed, by contrast, to offer a "hash of strange ingredients" (331). As Briggs writes: "One day one studies punctuation, the next day paragraphing, the next day an essay on the atomic bomb, and the next, an essay on jargon, or frying fish cakes" (331). Proponents of a communications approach proposed instead that the first-year course be "a course in communication *about* communication—that is, a course in communication skills with integrated subject matter" (Malmstrom 23, emphasis added). Instead of looking elsewhere for content, the course would be dedicated to examining the nature of communication: "the elements of which it is composed, the instruments which it used, the processes by which it comes about [and] the obstacles to its achievement" (23). The classroom itself would be fashioned as a "laboratory" of sorts, and in these spaces, students "would learn to exchange ideas and experiences by participating in many reading, writing, speaking, and listening activities" (23).

In keeping with much of what proponents of a communications approach to the first-year course were advocating half a century ago—or, to put a more contemporary spin on things—in keeping with Doug Downs and Elizabeth Wardle's seminal 2007 publication, "Teaching about Writing, Righting Misconceptions: (Re)envisioning 'First Year Composition' as 'Introduction to Writing Studies,'" I too strongly believe that we need to design courses that introduce students to course-appropriate content and that challenge the idea that writing is "a basic universal skill" (Downs and Wardle 553). Further, like Downs and Wardle, I suggest that when we look elsewhere, or when we allow those teaching the course to look elsewhere for course content,

> we silently support the misconceptions that writing is not a real subject, that writing courses do not require expert instructors, and that rhetoric and composition are not genuine research areas or legitimate intellectual pursuits. We are, thus, complicit in reinforcing outsiders' views of writing studies as a trivial, skill-teaching nondiscipline. (553)

A crucial difference between the approach to FYC theorized and described by Downs and Wardle and what I offer here has to do with how the chief aims and objectives of the course point to slightly different, but still, I suggest, overlapping content. Downs and Wardle describe a course that is "topically oriented to reading and writing as scholarly inquiry" and that encourages "more realistic understandings of writing" by having students read and respond to scholarly texts that focus on writing/written discourse (553). The approach I offer has students reading and responding to scholarship that includes, but is not limited to, the consideration of written discourse. More specifically, the content of my course has students reading, thinking, and learning about composition as a course, object, and multimodal communicative practice.

Composed with Words, Images, Genres, Spaces, Feelings, Memories, Hands, Feet, and Other People: Articulating a Tool Kit Approach to First-Year Composition

Given the emphasis my course places on tracing the social and personal dimensions of composing processes, treating that process as a "dynamic whole" (Dean 81), and attending to the various genres and media students routinely encounter, it has proven helpful to ground the course in sociohistoric theory. I have found particular value in adapting for the FYC course what James Werstch has termed a "tool kit approach" to mediated action (94). Rather than attempting to isolate and individually treat the various tools and support one employs while carrying out a particular action, a "tool kit approach" focuses on the complex mix of tools—or, as they are often referred to by Wertsch, *mediational means*—to which people have access. Importantly, the approach requires that we pay close attention to the "patterns of choice [individuals] manifest in selecting a particular means for a particular occasion" (94), and to consider why a particular mix of mediational means (as opposed to any number of others we might imagine having been employed instead) were used while carrying out a particular action or process. This is a phenomenon Wertsch calls *privileging*. Before providing a brief illustration of what a tool kit approach to the FYC course looks like, I clarify what Wertsch means by *mediational means*.

In keeping with the work of Lev Vygotsky, Wertsch's definition of mediational means includes, but is not limited to, what Vygotsky termed "psychological tools"—language, various systems for counting, mnemonic techniques, algebraic symbol systems, works of art, writing, diagrams, maps, mechanical drawings, etc. Maintaining that Vygotsky's work ultimately left underexplored a much wider range of tools and support available to individuals and groups, Wertsch's work expands the category of tools in ways that allow us to consider as well the role played by other kinds of material support, such as hammers, nails, computers, poles, keyboards, pencils, books, and so on.

By way of brief example, a tool kit approach to composing asks students to consider the array of tools, supports, or mediational means they use throughout the process of completing a particular task or objective; say, for instance, while completing a linear, argumentative, research-based essay for a FYC class. The list of supports a particular student draws on throughout the process of completing the task might include, among other things: the instructor's assignment sheet; conferences or informal meetings with the instructor to discuss the task; in-class workshops; conversations with classmates; trips to the library; various books or web sources consulted; knowledge of and adherence to certain writerly expectations (i.e., the use of genres and/or conventions appropriate to the task at hand); the use of the English language; 8 ½ x 11" paper; ink; notes written by hand; time spent entering text into a computer; the experience of having completed a similar kind of task in another context (e.g., for another class, in high school), and so on. If we look to still other supports employed throughout the process—those that do not, on first consideration, seem directly related to the task at hand—the list of supports involved in the production of a single text grows considerably longer: For instance, listening to music or having the television on while one revises their work, preferring to work in specific spaces with one's body positioned in particular ways, taking a break to go running to clear one's head, going to the store to get more paper, asking a family member to proofread a draft, drinking coffee to stay awake during an all-nighter, and so on. From a tool kit perspective, it becomes increasingly apparent just how densely populated, complexly layered, and highly distributed an otherwise seemingly simple and straight-forward task or process can be.

Before attempting to more concretely document how Wertsch's tool kit approach to mediated action informs my approach to the FYC course, I highlight briefly what I consider to be two salient benefits of adopting a tool kit approach. First, asking students to think about the various tools and supports (both human and non-human) that comprise their metaphorical tool kits helps to both populate and externalize something that often feels incredibly individual and internal. Based on conversations I've had with students (and based on much of my own lived experience as a writer/composer), it strikes me that writing—or, more broadly stated, composing—texts seems, indeed, *feels*, like something one does all on one's own. Often the sense is that when something actually happens—when one gets an idea, thinks of something to say, or begins composing a text—those things come from, or happen, inside. It may seem as though the idea or text had suddenly and magically sprung, more or less fully-formed, from the individual's head, heart, or gut. In this way, or so the reasoning goes, one either knows how to write well or one does not; one is a good writer or one is not. Perhaps he or she simply happens to lack that particular skill, knack, gene, or body part. Wertsch refers to this as the "metaphor of possession"—the idea that an individual either has or does not have a specific ability or skill set, and that the outcome of an assessment in one context necessarily predicts assessment in another, or worse yet, in all other contexts. As Wertsch reminds us, as long as the metaphor of possession shapes our understandings, "a basic issue—the different uses or functions of a tool—escapes [our] attention" (94-95). By directing students' attention to the various purposes, uses, and contexts for their work, and by highlighting the array of mediational means they select (or reject) while making and negotiating meaning, a tool kit approach helps combat the idea that the ability to create successful or meaningful texts is simply something one "has" or "possesses." A tool kit approach does this by redirecting our attention to the complexity, contingency, and distributed aspects of composing practices.

In addition to helping populate and externalize something that often feels incredibly individual and internal, the tool kit metaphor also underscores for students that compositions are built, constructed, or crafted things, and thereby help in countering the idea that they somehow magically or suddenly happen for the lucky few. In "Design and Transformation: New Theories of Meaning," Gunther Kress argues that "in the context of multimodal, multimedia modes of textual production in the era of electronic technologies, the task of text-makers is that of *complex orchestration*" (160, emphasis mine). While I quite like the analogy Kress uses here, particularly for the way it directs our attention to modes other than linear/alphabetic, what a tool kit approach affords is the idea of text-making (or composing) as complex, multimodal engineering. While Kress focuses primarily on electronic technologies, the approach to FYC that I offer, as the brief illustration above suggests, considers both new and not-so-new technologies while examining the role that humans and non-humans play in the composing process. To ensure that students closely attend to the built, constructed, crafted, and material dimensions of compositions and composing practices, they are asked to respond to the following questions while creating their own compositions and while responding to those created by others:

- What is it?
- What is it comprised of?
- What work does (or might) it do?

The first question—"What is it?"—requires students to consider conventions of naming or categorizing. How do we know what to call or how to refer to a particular text or process? Is the text a poem, a set of song lyrics, a Web page, an advertisement, an introduction, a scholarly essay, an essay geared to a more general/popular audience, a works cited page, a performance, a photograph, a painting? Here, I urge students to be as specific as possible. If the text is a poem, what kind of poem is it specifically? Is it a sonnet, a haiku, a ballad, blank verse? The second question—"What is it comprised of?"—is intended to not only help students flesh out or justify their response to the first question, but to also closely attend to the specific things a particular text is comprised of—to itemize or catalog, if you will. I caution students that what I look for here is not deep or complex interpretation so much as a listing of the elements that the text-maker used while creating the text—words, sentences, paragraphs, a title, an epigraph, italics, colors, still or moving images, etc. The final question—"What work does it do?"—asks students to consider how the text and its component parts function. What is the text attempting to do for, to, or with its audience? Does it instruct, persuade, emphasize, inform, entertain, caution, acknowledge, move a person into action or feel a specific emotion? Clearly, texts often attempt more than one of these rhetorical objectives, so students are warned to anticipate diversity and much overlap while identifying the work a particular text does.

Although the three questions are listed here in a particular order, they might be approached in any order. Often, in fact, identifying what texts are comprised of helps shed light on the work they do and how, specifically, they are identified and categorized. While I have more to say about the role these three core questions play throughout the semester, I reiterate here that the second question—"What is the text comprised of?"—can prove especially challenging for students, as they tend to imagine that what I'm asking them to identify is far more complex than it is. I have found it immensely helpful to have students work through this question in class, using a common text (usually the first assigned reading of the semester) as the focal text. Placing students in pairs, I ask them to jot down everything they see going on in, on, or around the pages of the reading, beginning with the size, color, and type of paper the text is printed on. I recommend that they work from the top-down, listing everything they can identify with regard to the text's appearance and construction. Nothing, I remind them, is too obvious to note, including the title, the author's name, an epigraph, x-number of paragraphs, use of English language, italics, quotes from other sources, images, captions, hand-written annotations in the margins of the text, works cited, and so on. Taken to an extreme, students could list the number of sentences, words, letters, or marks of punctuation comprising a text, but there is rarely time for, or frankly, the desire to do that. The point of the activity is to get students accustomed to tracking the various items from which, or with which, a text has been composed. Importantly, in asking them to think about texts created by others in this way, the activity invites them to think more about the various ingredients—the specific tools and moves, if you will—that comprise the texts that they create.

On Reading(s)

Like those who insist that the FYC course has a content of its own—whether this means drawing from communication or writing studies scholarship—I choose course materials that include, but are not limited to, the consideration of writing and written discourse. While the specific texts I assign have and continue to change, the content I choose is, for the most part, geared toward having students thinking, learning, reading, and composing about composition as a course, object, and multimodal practice. It is a course in composing about composition. As such, and with a mind toward Odell and Prell's call for a more "comprehensive view of composing" (296), the course materials, combined with in-class activities and discussions, are geared toward facilitating a greater awareness of how writing functions as but one "stream within the broader flows of semiotic activity" (Prior 11; see also Lemke; Medway; and Witte).

When it comes to choosing particular texts for students to engage with in the course, I draw primarily from four areas of scholarship: (1) texts that focus on the FYC course itself (its history, aims, objectives, and development); (2) texts that focus primarily on writing and the production of written texts; (3) texts that concentrate on multimodality, multiple literacies, changing technologies, and newer forms of media; and (4) a category I've termed "other." (See "Partial List of Suggested Readings" in the appendix for examples of texts I've used in the course.) Before illustrating how in-class activities and discussions are geared toward providing students ways of engaging more deeply with texts that are often challenging for them, I'll say a bit about why I include readings from each of the four categories.

I began sharing with students readings about the history, objectives, and development of the FYC course when students began expressing surprise that the course actually has a history or that people (like myself) actually chose to spend time researching, theorizing, and publishing scholarship about it. The readings also proved useful because students often relate to them. Many of the texts are, after all, supposedly about them: who they are, what they know, and what they are supposed to learn, do, and/or experience as a result of taking the course. Because my approach to the course tends not to be what the majority of students expect (many expect, for instance, a course that has them reading popular, controversial, or "hot" topics and writing variations on five-paragraph themes that many students practiced in high school), the readings have helped illuminate for students how my approach to the course relates to, and diverges from, what other scholars and practitioners have identified as the salient goals, objectives, and outcomes of the course. In part, I include a good number of texts that deal with writing and written processes because it is what students (and others) expect to see being read, discussed, and written about in an FYC course. Return once again to Odell and Prell's words: "Although an essay might be referred to as a composition, that terminology confused no one. Musicians composed; what we were doing was writing" (296). Choosing to include this scholarship is not simply about aligning with student or institutional expectations. Rather, if I want students to attend to writing in relation to the other supports and semiotic systems they draw upon while making and negotiating meaning, scholarship that deals with writing and the process of composing written texts strikes me as a necessary component of the course. The choice to include readings that focus on multimodality, multiliteracies, and the changing technologies of communicative practice is a way to extend, enrich, and complicate the readings that deal with written texts and processes. For instance, after reading selections from Margaret Finders' *Just Girls: Hidden Literacies and Life in Junior High*, students are asked to consider how such a study might be impacted or updated by considering still other kinds of (multi)literate practices, such as blogging, Facebooking, texting, and Youtubing. Finally, cognizant that the bulk of the texts I assign for class are print-based, I include the category of "other" for those texts, objects, and performances that cannot be neatly bound in course packs or shelved at the bookstore. Included here are videos I have created, ones that have proven useful to further illustrate or problematize issues that come up in assigned, print-based texts. For instance, "Gonna Make You Sweat" deals with the affective dimensions of composing processes and documents one woman's process of making a dance-based composition. "Other People's Lives" and "Tripping the Decades" are both mash-ups. "Tripping" relates nicely to the FYC readings, as it deals with the history of the discipline and the course, but both videos facilitate conversations about creating arguments with video and problematize notions of individual authorship. Also included in this category are various sample texts composed by former students that I share with students throughout the semester, as well as the various texts students bring to class. In fact, the bulk of the texts comprising the category of "other" are usually suggested, found, or brought in by students. For instance, after reading a chapter from David Levy's *Scrolling Forward*, entitled "A Mediation on a Receipt," students are asked to bring to class a found or authorless text; this might be a coffee cup, receipt, sticker, grocery list, advertisement, or candy wrapper. With our core questions and Levy's treatment of the receipt in mind, students share with each other their found texts, discussing what each one is, what it's comprised of, how it's used, valued, circulated, and responded to. Having said a bit about how content for the course is selected, I offer another example of an activity, one I refer to as "The Textual Olympics," designed to provide students with ways of engaging with assigned readings. I indicated earlier that such activities can be extremely helpful unpacking readings that students find difficult, unfamiliar, or theoretically dense.

Though I often change the readings for the course, I tend always to include, and in fact, begin the semester with the same two readings: A piece by Lex Runciman titled "Fun?" and Andrea Fishman's study of writing in the Amish community, "Because This Is Who We Are: Writing in the Amish Community." Runciman's piece is a wonderful way to introduce students to FYC scholarship and to get them thinking about the affective dimensions of writing and writing processes. Fishman's piece, though it can prove difficult for students not accustomed to reading ethnographic studies, is highly effective in getting students to think about issues surrounding writing and identity as well as how their uses for, and attitudes toward, writing compare with those of the Amish community that Fishman studies. During the class session before these readings are assigned, I ask students to begin comprising a list of all the kinds of texts they know how to produce. They do this as homework, understanding that their list will be discussed in the next class. I am careful to underscore that in using the word "text," I am imagining a broader definition than they may be accustomed to. By "text," I mean something that is purposefully (though not always successfully) engineered in ways that convey meaning to a particular audience. Thus, while some of the texts on their lists may be comprised chiefly of words and sentences, including poems, scholarly essays, the minutes for a meeting, memos, a tweet, a type-written letter, a Facebook status update—others may not be. Some of the texts appearing on their lists might have no alphabetic text associated with them at all, including a painting, a photograph, a well-designed room, or a special meal. Still other texts might feature a mix of alphabetic text, spoken words, images, gestures, and color, including a greeting card, a Web page, a spoken poem, a blog entry, or a monologue. I ask students to be as specific as they can with their lists. Rather than simply listing "poetry" or "research paper," I ask them to think about all the different kinds of poems or research papers they have composed; for example, a research paper for a history class, an English class, a philosophy class, and so on. While composing their lists, students are asked to reflect on how, where, when, and from whom they learned to compose specific types of texts. Did they learn to compose them in school, from parents, from a book or a movie, by watching someone else, or on their own, perhaps by trial and error? I also ask students to consider what makes someone good, proficient, or even an expert at producing the various texts on their lists. Related to this, I ask them to rate themselves and their ability to produce the various texts on their list—hence the "Olympic" part of the activity's title. Students come to class with their lists and having read pieces from Runciman and Fishman. In addition to providing students with a way of comparing how the kinds of texts they produce compare with those produced by the Amish community Fishman studies, the lists allow us to examine how students' uses of, and attitudes toward, the production of texts compare with those of the Amish. With a mind toward Runciman's piece, we consider the affective dimensions of textual production: Which listed items (if any) are fun to compose, and why? Which seem more like punishment, and why? As there is rarely enough time in a single class session to discuss every text on their lists—again, to identify what those texts are, what they are composed of, and what work they do—I ask students to hold onto their lists so we can revisit them in the context of other readings, during other class sessions. I encourage students to continue adding texts to their lists as the semester progresses, as they often prove useful when students receive their major project assignments.

ON TASKS AND ACTIVITIES

Throughout the semester, students complete four different kinds of tasks. In addition to completing two major projects, they must participate in a group presentation, compose summary-synthesis reports for assigned readings, and create posts for Blackboard-based discussions. In keeping with Wertsch's tool kit approach to mediated action, each of these tasks has been designed in ways that require students to think both purposefully and flexibly about their work while also attending closely to the various choices they make while completing these tasks. Students are also required to consider how and why a particular mix of mediational means—as opposed to others they might have imagined employing—was ultimately decided upon while completing a task. Here I offer a brief description of each task type.

Summary-Synthesis Reports. These tri-part, one page, single-spaced reports are due at the start of class sessions when readings have been assigned. Devised as a way to ensure that students are keeping up with the readings and to facilitate class discussion, the summary-synthesis reports serve an additional function by providing me with a better sense of how students are engaging with readings, how they are connecting issues raised in current readings with previous readings, and help to address the kinds of questions students have about the readings. Here, proportion is everything. Students are asked to briefly (in two or three sentences) summarize a point raised in one of the readings. In the synthesis section, they are to make connections between current and previous readings. The synthesis portion should comprise the bulk of report—at least three-quarters. Finally, in the question section of the report, students offer two or three questions about the readings or points raised in the report. I try to steer students away from definitional questions (e.g, "What does Lemke mean by selective contextualization?") and toward questions that work to extend or complicate the readings (e.g., "Finders' study is pretty dated. What might that study look like if it were replicated now? What might it have looked like then had it focused on boys?").

Students bring two copies of their report to class. One is handed in to me, and the other is circulated amongst other members of the class. After spending time reading the reports, the class discusses the readings and questions that are raised at the end of the students' reports. What I like about this task is that having students read one another's reports helps combat the idea that writing and reading activities have one correct answer. It does this by concretely illustrating that different points will be raised, connections made, and questions asked by different people with different interests and investments.

Major Projects. I've described in great detail elsewhere some of the projects assigned to students (see especially *Toward a Composition Made Whole*). Here, I attempt to talk about how, generally speaking, the major project assignments are engineered. In contrast to assignments that allow students to choose their own topic—with the expectation that their final products will all look similar to one another and be experienced in similar ways (i.e., a video, a Web page, or an argumentative, research-based essay)—my tasks routinely specify for students something about the content of their work and leave decisions about the final form of and context for that work up to the students. In this way, when final products are due, they take many different forms. I might receive the URL for a Web page, an essay, a video, or a magazine.

This is not to say that students are free to do what they want, how they want. Each task comes with certain non-negotiable elements. For instance, with a task called "Texts in Contexts," students examine the way a person, place, thing, or belief system (stereotypes work extremely well for this task) is represented in at least six different types of texts. In so doing, a student might choose to examine a film, a scholarly essay, a greeting card, a television show, a bumper sticker, a piece of fiction, a song, and so on. While students are free to choose their subject matter, no two of their source texts are allowed to be of the same type. Students cannot examine, for instance, how the idea of Santa as fat and jolly is represented in six different films. The task is designed to have students closely attend to how the various text sources capitalize on the media, modes, and moves of which they are comprised in order to perpetuate a certain belief or stereotype. Students must also produce 200-word (minimum) analyses for each of their sources. It is up to students, then, to determine an audience for their work, including the specific context in which it will be encountered and experienced, the rhetorical work their project will do, and the form the finished work will take. The major projects are, indeed, daunting. Students often claim that they have no idea of what to do or where to start. In this way, I have found it helpful to share with students examples of what former students have done and to refer students back to the list of texts they generated for the "Textual Olympics" activity.

Equally helpful are the two in-class workshop sessions held one week after a project task is assigned. Unlike workshops in which students pair up and trade drafts of their work, the workshop sessions are always run as large group, whole-class workshops. Rather than asking students to bring full or rough drafts of their work to the sessions, they are required to compose "project notes"—a single-spaced page or two of ideas detailing how they are currently thinking about approaching the task. With the task referenced above, for instance, a student's project notes mention the subject matter or stereotype he or she plans to work with and list the various ideas he or she has come up with for contextualizing and presenting the source analyses for an audience of his or her choosing. Importantly, for each project assigned, students must come up with at least two or three ways of approaching the task. Thus, project notes also treat the various ways students have begun thinking about approaching the task. During workshop sessions, students take turns talking about their ideas and soliciting feedback from their peers. I cannot emphasize enough how incredibly valuable these sessions have proven to be. In addition to illustrating for each other the various ways they go about approaching the task, students often report leaving these sessions with a much better sense of what they will do for the project and how they will go about accomplishing it.

Holding these workshop sessions early—one week after a task is assigned—is incredibly beneficial. Not only are students more willing to consider and work with feedback offered by myself and their peers, but asking students to bring in project notes (as opposed to full drafts) allows them to take more risks, to be more flexible in considering the various ways they might approach a task. To my mind, the best workshop sessions are the ones that end with students changing their approach because, as many have reported over the years, the questions and advice offered during the sessions help them come up with better ideas and/or ones they were much more passionate about pursuing.

Blackboard Responses. Assigned after the second in-class workshop session described above, these mandatory postings require students to continue fleshing out and developing their plans for major projects, solicit advice from classmates, and/or provide input or advice on the evolving projects plans of their classmates. Like the in-class workshop sessions, the Blackboard postings underscore for students that there are many ways of approaching and accomplishing the major projects. I believe strongly that students who are able to see (or, in the case of the workshop sessions, hear about) the ideas, tools, techniques, and strategies their classmates employ while working on major projects benefit tremendously, both in terms of understanding that there is more than one way to accomplish a task and in thinking about how the adoption of similar tools, techniques, or strategies might potentially impact their own work.

Group Presentations. Students are placed into groups of four and assigned the readings and class session for which they will be responsible. As the task sheet makes clear, the group's job is not to summarize the readings for the class; rather, the group's main objective is to find ways of extending, enriching, or even complicating issues raised in assigned texts, usually by way of an in-class activity. This may sound like a daunting task, but, in addition to selecting readings for the presentation dates that are particularly presentation-friendly, I share with students examples of what former students have done with the same or similar readings. Additionally, and long before the first group is scheduled to present, I model the task for students through activities and in-class discussions conducted earlier in the semester. All group members are required to meet with me at least a week prior to their presentation date. During this meeting, after students have already met on their own to discuss the readings and their plans for the session, the group shares their ideas with me. They articulate what, specifically, they hope to accomplish during the session, detail the various ways they have imagined achieving those ends, and generally address how their plans relate to the readings. One week after they present, each group member is required to submit a highly detailed reflection about the experience—something I discuss in more detail below—called a "Statement of Goals and Choices" (SOGC).

RECONFIGURING THE DYNAMICS OF RESPONSE AND ASSESSMENT

In addition to providing students with a more comprehensive approach to composing—one that includes, but is not limited to, examining how talk and how written text impacts composing practices—the course works to facilitate greater meta-communicative awareness. It does this by requiring students to assume responsibility for what they say or write, but also for what they build: for the texts and contexts they engineer throughout the semester. To ensure that students think carefully about the choices they make, they are required to compose highly detailed statements for much of the work they produce during the semester. Designed to provide students with still more experience addressing the core questions associated with the course (i.e., "What is it?"; "What is it comprised of?"; and "What work does it do?"), the Statements of Goals and Choices (SOGCs) require that students provide a list of all the rhetorical, methodological, and material choices they made with their work. Following this, they are asked to explain why they made those choices and to reflect on (or anticipate) how those choices might impact the reception and subsequent evaluation of that work. To ensure that students are putting into the statement the maximum amount of thought and effort, they are worth half the total grade earned for a task.

While the questions students respond to may differ slightly depending on the task, they are always asked to respond to the following questions:

1. What, specifically, is this piece trying to accomplish? What work does, or might, this piece do? For whom? In what contexts?

2. What specific rhetorical, material, methodological, and technological choices did you make in the service of accomplishing the goal(s) articulated above? Catalog, as well, the choices that you might not have consciously made—those that were made for you when you opted to work with certain genres, materials, and technologies.

3. Why did you end up pursuing this plan, as opposed to the others you came up with? How did the various choices listed above allow you to accomplish things that other sets or combinations of choices would not have?

At the end of each statement, students are asked to list all the supports or mediational means (both human and non-human) that played a role in helping them accomplish the task. Similar to the scrolling credits featured at the end of movies, these lists remind students of the individual and social aspects of composing processes, further underscoring just how densely populated, complexly layered, and highly distributed those processes can be.

I see at least two primary benefits associated with requiring students to compose these statements. Firstly, given that students often choose to work with genres, materials, and technologies I am not familiar with, the statements provide me with ways of navigating, responding to, and assessing such texts. In requiring students to discuss why they selected "a particular means for a particular occasion," thereby highlighting their "patterns of choice" (Wertsch 94), the statements also provide me with a better understanding of how the mix of mediational means students employ in their work simultaneously provide shape for, and take shape from, the tasks they encounter in the course. Secondly, as these "precisely defined goal statements" make students increasingly cognizant of how texts are comprised of a series of choices or "moves" that, taken together, afford certain potentials for engaging with those texts (Beach 137-38), students are better prepared to consider if, how, when, why, and for whom their texts might fail to achieve their primary objectives. Instead then of relying on instructors to "tell them what their problems are and how to remedy those problems" (Beach 127), students become more sophisticated and flexible rhetoricians, and are able to describe and share with others the potentials and limitations of their work. This ability to rigorously reflect on their own work—to articulate what they are attempting to do and why—I believe, serves students well, whether in other classes, in the workplace, and/or in other areas of their lives.

The workshop sessions and SOGCs, in particular, serve the purpose of reconfiguring the dynamics and directions of responding to and assessing student work. This is not to say that students are assigning grades to themselves or to each other. In the end, I respond to and assign a final grade for their work. What it does mean, and what I take to be one of the chief benefits of this approach, is that throughout much of the semester—particularly as they begin generating ideas and working through their approaches to tasks and activities—students are not depending on me (i.e., as the class' sole authority) to tell them if something is working well, whether they should pursue other courses of action, or what they should change or revise. While I certainly raise questions and offer input about their work, students also look to one another for ideas, feedback, and suggestions. What's more, they are learning to think even more carefully, critically, and flexibly about the goals they set and the choices they make with their own work.

In her 2004 publication, *Geographies of Writing: Inhabiting Spaces and Encountering Difference*, Nedra Reynolds calls for the development of writing studies that foreground "the sense of place and space that readers and writers bring with them to the intellectual work of writing, to navigating, remembering and *composing*" (176, emphasis mine). In doing so, Reynolds challenges us to develop frameworks that attend to the affective, embodied, and material dimensions of writing—ones that highlight how texts are carved "out of time and space in particular circumstances that differ for each writer" (3-4). What I have offered here is an approach to the FYC course that affords this by providing students with opportunities to examine writing in relation to other supports or mediational means that they routinely employ in their work. It provides them with an opportunity to learn more about composition—as a course, an object, and a multimodal phenomenon. The approach highlights for students the richness and complexity of composition(s) and composing processes, and also prepares them to speak to matters concerning what texts are, what they are comprised of, and the kinds of rhetorical and material work they do.

WORKS CITED

Beach, Richard. "Showing Students How to Assess: Demonstrating Techniques for Response in the Writing Conference." *Writing and Response: Theory, Practice, and Research.* Ed. Chris Anson. Urbana: NCTE, 1989. 127-48. Print.

Briggs, Harold E. "College Programs in Communication as Viewed by an English Teacher." *College English* 9 (1948): 327-32. Print.

Dean, Howard H. "The Communication Course: A Ten-Year Perspective." *College Composition and Communication* 10 (1959): 80-85. Print.

Downs, Douglas, and Elizabeth Wardle. "Teaching about Writing, Righting Misconceptions: (Re)envisioning 'First Year Composition' as 'Introduction to Writing Studies.'" *College Composition and Communication* 58 (2007): 552-84. Print.

Dunn, Thomas F. "A New Freshman Approach." *College English* 7 (1946): 283-88. Print.

Faigley, Lester, and Susan Romano. "Going Electronic: Creating Multiple Sites for Innovation in a Writing Program." *Resituating Writing: Constructing and Administering Writing Programs.* Ed. Joseph Janangelo and Kristine Hansen. Portsmouth: Heinemann, 1995. 46-58. Print.

Johnson-Eilola, Johndan. *Nostalgic Angels: Rearticulating Hypertext Writing.* Westport:: Praeger, 1997. Print.

Kitzhaber, Albert R. *Themes, Theories, and Therapy: The Teaching of Writing in College*. New York: McGraw-Hill, 1963. Print.

Kress, Gunther. *Before Writing: Rethinking the Paths to Literacy*. London: Routledge, 1997. Print.

—. "Design and Transformation: New Theories of Meaning." *Multiliteracies: Literacy Learning and the Design of Social Futures*. Ed. Bill Cope and Mary Kalantzis. London: Routledge, 2000. 153-61. Print.

Lemke, Jay. "Metamedia Literacy: Transforming Meanings and Media." *Handbook of Literacy and Technology: Transformations in a Post-typographic World*. Ed. David Reinking, Michael C. McKenna, Linda D. Labbo, and Ronald D. Kieffer. Hillsdale: Lawrence Erlbaum, 1998. 283-301. Print.

Malmstrom, Jean. "The Communication Course." *College Composition and Communication* 7 (1956): 21-24. Print.

Medway, Peter. "Virtual and Material Buildings: Construction and Constructivism in Architecture and Writing." *Written Communication 13 (1996):* 473-514. Print.

Millard, Elaine. "Transformative Pedagogy: Teachers Creating a Literacy of Fusion. *Travel Notes from the New Literacy Studies*. Ed. Kate Paul and Jennifer Rowsell. Clevendon: Multilingual Matters, Ltd., 2006. 234-53. Print.

Odell, Lee, and Christina Lynn Prell. "Rethinking Research on Composing: Arguments for a New Research Agenda." *History, Reflection, and Narrative: The Professionalization of Composition, 1963–1983*. Ed. Mary Rosner, Beth Boehm, and Debra Journet. Stamford: Ablex, 1999. 295-319. Print.

Prior, Paul. *Writing/Disciplinarity: A Sociohistoric Account of Literate Activity in the Academy*. Hillsdale: Lawrence Erlbaum, 1998. Print.

Reynolds, Nedra. *Geographies of Writing: Inhabiting Places and Encountering Difference*. Carbondale: Southern Illinois UP, 2004. Print.

Selfe, Cynthia. "Students Who Teach Us." *Writing New Media: Theory and Applications for Expanding the Teaching of Composition*. Ed. Anne Frances Wysocki, Johndan Johnson-Eilola, Cynthia L. Selfe, and Geoffrey Sirc. Logan: Utah State UP, 2004. 43-66. Print.

Shipka, Jody. *Toward a Composition Made Whole*. Pittsburgh: U of Pittsburgh P, 2011. Print.

Wertsch, James V. *Voices of the Mind: A Sociocultural Approach to Mediated Action*. Cambridge: Harvard UP, 1991. Print.

Witte, Stephen P. "Context, Text, Intertext: Toward a Constructivist Semiotic of Writing." *Written Communication* 9 (1992): 237-308. Print.

Yancey, Kathleen Blake. "Made Not Only in Words: Composition in a New Key. *College Composition and Communication* 56 (2004): 297-328. Print.

Appendix: Course Syllabus

ENGLISH 100: FIRST-YEAR COMPOSITION

This course is designed to introduce students to techniques that will enable them to engage with a wide range of social texts (including but not limited to those traditionally referred to as "academic") in increasingly active, flexible, responsible, and purposeful ways. In keeping with the course title, we will be examining composition—as a course, object and communicative practice. In so doing, we will explore the complex relationship between speech, writing and other of the rich communicative resources we routinely employ while creating and responding to various types of texts.

Some of the questions the course will explore include:

- In addition to speech and lettered text, what are some of the meaning-making resources upon which we routinely draw while composing texts?

- How do images, movements, gestures, objects, colors, sound schemes, scents, etc. impact our interactions with (and our understanding of the potentials of) talk and text?

- How do we determine which communicative resources are the most appropriate for the task to hand?

- How do we acquire, learn to value, learn *when* and *how* to use these resources appropriately?

- What role does context play in helping us make and negotiate meaning?

- How are new media applications (and the increasing speed at which data can now be transmitted from one machine to another) impacting our curricular and extracurricular routines? For instance, how might time spent on *Facebook,* or time spent creating webpages, blogs, emails, and text messages impact how we write, when we write, where we write, how frequently we write, and what we even think of as writing?

- If print is, in fact, "being pushed off the page" (as Gunther Kress and others have maintained), how might this impact what we do, what we learn to value, and/or how we are assessed in school? In other words, if the experience of reading a web page demands that one negotiates typewritten characters on the page as well as images, sounds, color, design/layout principles, and movement (or at least potentials for movement) on the page, how does this impact what we need to know, consider or do while interacting with multimodal texts?

Course Percentages

Participation: 10%*
Weekly Responses (summary-synthesis reports or Blackboard postings): 30%
Project #1: 20%
Project #2: 30%
Group Presentation: 10%

* A note on participation: I expect that each of you will be here **on time**, and prepared to engage with the course readings, workshops, or other activities we have scheduled. To earn a passing (C-level) mark for participation, you need to do more than prep for class and show up for each class session. This course has been purposely designed to afford you all the opportunity to exchange ideas, to discuss the readings, and your own work as it progresses. I expect each of you to be here, ready to share your ideas on the course materials with others. Anyone arriving unprepared for the class session will be marked as absent. Anyone checking email, text-messaging, etc. in class will be marked as absent.

See the "Partial List of Suggested Readings" below for a sampling of some of the texts, or portions of texts, I've used over the years.

Partial List of Suggested Readings

(arranged by topic/theme)

On the FYC course—History, Approaches, Assignments, Expectations

Bridwell-Bowles, Lillian. "Discourse and Diversity: Experimental Writing within the Academy." *CCC* 43, 1992.

Carroll, Lee Ann. "Pomo Blues: Stories from First-Year Composition." *CE* 59:8, 1997.

Cline, Andrew R. "Reconsidering the Textbook in the First-Year Composition Class" in *In Our Own Voice: Graduate Students Teach Writing.* Tina LaVonne Good & Leanne B. Warshauer, eds. Longman, 2000.

Connors, Robert. "Personal Writing Assignments." *CCC* 38:2, 1987.

Council of Writing Program Administrators. "WPA Outcomes Statement for First-Year Composition." *The Writing Program Administrator's Resource.* Eds. Stuart C. Brown and Theresa Enos. NJ: Erlbaum, 2002. 519–22.

Crowley, Sharon. "Correct English . . . Entrance Exam" (1870) in *Composition in the University: Historical and Polemical Essays.* Pittsburgh: University of Pittsburgh Press, 1997.

Deemer, Charles. "English Composition as a Happening." *CE* 29:2, 1967.

Lambert, Robert. "Freshman Masks." CCC 13:4, 1962.

Larson, Richard L. "The 'Research Paper' in the Writing Course: A Non-Form of Writing." *College English,* 44:8, 1982.

Lutz, William D. "Making Freshman English a Happening." *CCC* 22:1, 1971.

Paull, Michael and Jack Kligerman. "Invention, Composition and the Urban College." *CE* 33, 1972.

Stout, George D. "A Why and How for Freshman Composition." *CCC* 4:1, 1953.

—Plus select 1950 CCCC workshop reports (i.e,. "Function of Comp Course," "Objectives," "Reading/Grading Themes")

On Writing/Writing Studies

Bazerman, Charles & Paul Prior, eds. *What Writing Does and How It Does It: An Introduction to Analyzing Texts and Textual Practices.* Routledge, 2003.

Bawarshi, Anis. *Genre And The Invention Of The Writer: Reconsidering the Place of Invention in Composition.* Utah State University Press, 2003.

Brooke, Robert. "Underlife and Writing Instruction." *CCC* 38:2, 1987.

Bruce, Bertram & Maureen Hogan. "The Disappearance of Technology: Toward an Ecological Model of Literacy" in *Handbook of Literacy and Technology: Transformations in a Post-typographic World.* David Reinking, Michael C. McKenna; Linda D. Labbo; & Ronald D. Kieffer, eds. Routledge, 1998.

Chiseri-Strater, Elizabeth. *Academic Literacies: The Public and Private Discourse of University Students.* Heinemann, Boynton/Cook, 1991.

Corno, Lyn. "What It Means to Be Literate about Classrooms" in *Classrooms and Literacy.* David Bloome, ed. 1989.

Finders, Margaret. *Just Girls: Hidden Literacies and Life in Junior High.* Teachers College Press, 1997.

Fishman, Andrea. "Because This Is Who We Are: Writing in the Amish Community" in David Barton & Roz Ivanic, eds. *Writing in the Community.* Sage, 1991.

Miller, Susan, ed. *The Norton Book of Composition Studies.* W. W. Norton, 2009.

Nelson, Jennie. "Reading Classrooms as Text: Exploring Student Writers' Interpretive Practices. *CCC* 46, 1995.

Runciman, Lex. "Fun?" *CE* Vol. 53, No. 2, Feb., 1991

Wardle, Elizabeth & Douglas Downs. *Writing about Writing: A College Reader.* Bedford/St. Martin's, 2010.

On Multimodality/Multiliteracies/New Media

Baron, Dennis. "From Pencils to Pixels . . ." in *Passions Pedagogies and 21st Century Technologies.* Gail Hawisher & Cynthia Selfe, eds. Utah State University Press, 1999.

Davis, Robert and Mark Shadle. "'Building a Mystery': Alternative Research Writing and the Academic Act of Seeking." *CCC* 51:3, 2000.

Dunn, Patricia. *Talking, Sketching, Moving: Multiple Literacies in the Teaching of Writing.* Portsmouth: Boynton/Cook, 2001.

George, Diana. "From Analysis to Design: Visual Communication in the Teaching of Writing." *CCC* 45:1, 2002.

Jewitt, Cary & Gunther Kress. *Multimodal Literacy.* Peter Lang, 2003.

Kress, Gunther. *Before Writing: Rethinking the Paths to Literacy.* Routledge, 1997.

—. "Design and Transformation: New Theories of Meaning" in *Multiliteracies: Literacy Learning and the Design of Social Futures.* Bill Cope & Mary Kalantzis, eds. Routledge, 2000.

Lemke, Jay. "Social Semiotics: A New Model for Literacy Education" in *Classrooms and Literacy.* David Bloome, ed. Ablex, 1989.

Levy, David. *Scrolling Forward: Making Sense of Documents in a Digital Age.* Arcade Publishing, 2003.

New London Group. "A Pedagogy of Multiliteracies Designing Social Futures" in *Multiliteracies: Literacy Learning and the Design of Social Futures.* Bill Cope & Mary Kalantzis, eds. Routledge, 2000.

Saljo, Roger & Jan Wyndhamn. "Solving Everyday Problems in the Formal Setting: An Empirical Study of the School as Context for

Thought" in Understanding Practice: Perspectives on Activity and Context. Seth Chaiklin and Jean Lave, eds. Cambridge, 1996.

Williams, Sean. "Part 1: Thinking Out of the Pro-verbal Box." *Computers and Composition* 18, 2001.

Wysocki, Anne Frances, Johndan Johnson-Eilola, Cynthia Selfe & Geoffrey Sirc, eds. *Writing New Media: Theory and Applications for Expanding the Teaching of Composition.* Utah State University Press, 2004.

Other

Shipka, Jody. "Gonna Make You Sweat: Composing a History of 'This' Space." www.remediatethis.com/projects.

—. "Other People's Lives: A Projection" in "Master Hands, A Video Mashup Round Table." Eds. James J. Brown Jr. and Richard Marback. *Enculturation* 11 , 2011. <http://enculturation.gmu.edu/master-hands>

—. "Tripping the Decades." www.remediatethis.com/projects.

—Plus samplings of former students' projects (video-, print- and object-based), authorless/found texts, select textbook ads (from different composition journals), children's books (usually focused around the theme of learning or doing school) Flickr and Blogger pages, YouTube videos, and the various texts students bring into class.

9 Working Through Theory in a Community College Composition Classroom

Howard Tinberg

> *If we're good enough teachers, are we only good enough to help students navigate the upward and (sometimes slippery) slope, but not good enough to get them to the summit? Should we, dare we, ask more of ourselves—as teachers?*
>
> —Lynn Z. Bloom

PRELUDE

When I first arrived to teach composition at a public community college, having taught at a private university, I was hell-bent on creating a course heavy on reading, and not just any kind of reading. I required my students to purchase Bartholomae and Petrosky's *Ways of Reading* and to tackle the complex prose of authors such as Paulo Freire, John Edgar Wideman, and Jane Tompkins. I was determined to not use a rhetoric or a handbook, but rather to immerse my students in the thoroughly academic task of "text wrestling." I accepted, uncritically, the notions a) that academic work necessitates reading "against the grain" and b) that my students, regardless of the reasons why they were at the community college, would do well to acquire such skill. Perhaps *I* should have wrestled more rigorously with Bartholomae and Petrosky's assumptions myself. Neither my students nor I knew what to do with these odd essays/readings. After two frustrating semesters, I turned away from the "difficult essays" approach. In retrospect, I had not sufficiently thought through how I might translate the theoretical understandings contained in the *Ways of Reading* to the community college classroom. I neglected to ask and answer questions such as these: What role does reading have in a writing classroom? What level of complexity is appropriate for such reading? Who are my students as readers? What knowledge do my students need to have to work with these readings?

[margin note: good questions]

Aside from these questions, I took from the experience a crucial point: First-year composition must be true not only to the conventions, scholarship, and best practices of Rhetoric and Composition as a discipline, but it must also be true to a whole galaxy of other concerns, including the nature of the institution and the diverse needs of its students. The required composition course at a community college must, it seems to me, conform to the complex and comprehensive mission of the community college itself. In the case of our college's mission statement, we find a particularly telling passage about the programs offered: "These programs are characterized by a strong foundation in liberal arts and sciences; an emphasis on practical, employment-oriented education in allied health, engineering and technology, and business; and workforce development from adult literacy to advanced technology skills" ("Mission Statement").

Given that *all* students in *all* degree, transfer, and career programs are required to take a first-year writing course, and that virtually *all* certificate programs require the same first-year writing course, that course should not only prepare transfer students for the writing that lay ahead, but it must also attend to the needs of students who, through obtaining an associate's degree or receiving a certificate for a skills upgrade, plan on entering (or re-entering) the work place. In another context, I refer to this kind of outcome as "hybrid literacy" as a blending of both "academic" and work-related writing ("What Is 'College-Level' Writing?" 170). Perhaps I am reflecting my fifteen years' worth of experience directing a multidisciplinary writing lab when I note that community college students need to write and think in ways that will promote their success in the work place (in human services or in occupational therapy, to give two examples of popular programs at the college) while, at the same time, enable them to write successfully in general education courses such as history or psychology.

THEORETICAL CONSIDERATIONS: WHAT FORMS
OF KNOWLEDGE SHOULD BE FOSTERED IN
A REQUIRED COMPOSITION COURSE?

Given the enormity of that challenge, it is important to foreground as goals in the course the acquisition of four kinds of knowledge: rhetorical, genre, process, and metacognitive. Here, for the most part, I follow the lead of Anne Beaufort who, in her qualitative studies of undergraduate writers within the classroom and in professions, argues that these three forms of knowledge—taken together with knowledge of the subject and the conventions of a discourse community—bode well for writing success beyond college (*Writing, College*). *Rhetorical knowledge* requires an understanding of the writer's purpose, the message that is being conveyed, and the receiver or intended reader of that message. Such knowledge also assumes a facility in deploying logos, ethos, and pathos when using writing for the purpose of persuasion. *Genre knowledge* entails a clear understanding of the form of the writing and the expectations and actions associated with that form. Writing in the genre of the proposal, for example, requires knowledge of its various components and their effects. In contrast with these knowledge domains, *process knowledge* is rooted not in forms or products, but rather in the means by which ends are produced. Students need to come to value and understand the processes of drafting, revising, and editing their writing. To these domains, I would add one other: *metacognitive knowledge*. In the context of writing studies, metacognitive knowledge has been defined as "Self-awareness of methods of approaching writing tasks and the ability to articulate and assess personal strengths and weaknesses related to these methods" (Walters, Hunter, and Giddens). This habit of mind (the term is drawn from Walters, Hunter, and Giddens), in fact, underlies a great many activities in the course, from peer review to post-writes to the reflective cover letter that introduces students' final project: a portfolio of their best work. In short, a key goal of this course is to develop in students a critical vocabulary about writing. Can students find language with which to discern the elements of effective writing in their own work as well in that of others? Can they come to recognize what elements prevent writing from being effective?

Stated Goals of the Course

As I move from these theoretical considerations to practical goals, I inform my students that by the end of our course, they should be able to

- respond appropriately to an assignment or writing situation;
- state their purpose clearly and stick with it;
- consider their reader's needs;
- understand the genre in which they are writing;
- value and demonstrate a clear understanding of the drafting, revising, and editing processes;
- develop a clear and precise vocabulary about what works and what needs work in a particular piece of writing;
- develop their ideas through the use of appropriate detail;
- provide appropriate and convincing evidence to support their claims; and
- demonstrate a control over language (i.e., grammar, mechanics, and tone). (See the Appendix.)

The order in which these stated goals are offered reveals something about my priorities. For instance, I put a great deal of emphasis in class discussions as well as in my response to student writing on understanding the question that prompts the writing. I see that element as key to grasping the rhetorical situation in which the writing is situated. Of course, considering the reader's expectations should also be part of that situation. As I note later, peer review is a dominant part of the classroom experience in part because I wish students to feel the pressure of a genuine reader (as opposed to the somewhat compromised and complex role I assume as the teacher *and* the reader). Furthermore, the course is very much genre-based. In other words, students are asked to produce writing that spans a great many genres, from an essay for radio to a profile and a proposal. Finally, a critical concern in the class is an attention to process: Students are expected to submit at least two drafts for each paper assigned and to engage not only in editing but also in substantial revision in response to peer and teacher feedback.

The remaining goals reflect somewhat current traditional aspects of my pedagogy: on the specificity of language, on the use of appropriate and relevant evidence, and on the control of language. Why do I specify these items and not, say, pay attention to organization or logic? In part, I regard attention to organization as very much tied to genre specifications and the demands of the writing situation, including an understanding of purpose. Moreover, a quarter of a century's worth of teaching inexperienced college writers has shown me that attention to detail and the use of relevant evidence makes a good deal of sense, given the often generalized and unsubstantiated nature of the writing.

Why the formalist nod to language in these goals for first-year composition? In an open-admissions institution, I will see a range of abilities and levels of preparedness in a typical composition classroom—from students whose fragmented writing seems more like utterance than written prose, to students (albeit, not many) who are technically adept and fluent writers. True to best composition and writing center practices, I attend to matters of mechanics and grammar within the context of students' writing, identifying and glossing patterns of errors and inviting students to become editors of their work rather than taking on the task myself. To be honest, relatively little classroom time is taken up with mechanics and grammar.

Instead, language becomes a more visible concern when seen as an aspect of style and voice. Perhaps my approach is somewhat dated in this respect: I spend a good deal of time arguing that writing engages readers through a consciously accessible style and through an engaging voice. Early in the course, as I explain later, students are invited to establish their "presence" in the writing while, at the same time, becoming more cognizant of reaching out to other readers. Indeed, I assign "an essay for radio" (for the "This I Believe" feature at our local National Public Radio affiliate) to make the points early on that voice is important and that it is possible to be "present" and somewhat personal in one's writing while at the same time establishing a relationship with the public. This notion of a writer's presence looms large in the second half of the course, when students are required to draw from external sources in their writing, when, all too often, the outcome is to vacate the writing out of deference to expert testimony.

A SEQUENCE OF ASSIGNMENTS

I owe this much to *Ways of Reading*, the reader that I discarded early in my teaching career at the community college: It introduced to me the idea of a meaningful and developmental sequence of assignments—a strong feature of the collection. While I do not establish a thematic thread among the various assignments of the course, I do attempt to organize assignments so that students a) learn in a developmentally sound way, reinforcing what they have learned and building new knowledge in the process; and b) experience writing in a variety of genres, each with its own sets of formal constraints, expectations, and purposes.

An Essay of Belief. Initially, students are asked to compose an "essay for radio" that centers on an important belief:

> For this assignment, I'd like you to write an essay, following the format given below (and typed, double-spaced), on a significant belief of your own. While I'd like you to consider a belief that you consider important, please do not feel obliged to be *deadly serious*. You may be funny, too, in this piece (one student last semester wrote that she believed in the "power of make-up," for example). Of course, you may also write about an aspect of a religious belief; although, with this subject as well as with others, you need to consider the possibility that your reader does not share that belief.
>
> Please keep in mind that while the subject of your essay may be quite personal, you must do your best to expand your concerns to *include your readers' interests*. In other words, you need to ask yourselves the question, "How does my experience instruct others?" The most effective essays in this series are those that are both personal *and* public in scope.

This assignment, like others that follow, is accompanied by a checklist of criteria—qualities necessary for successful work. The checklist for this assignment reads as follows:
- Have you included a statement of your belief?
- Have you shown, through an anecdote, in what way that belief has been "tested," formed, or even "changed"?
- Have you provided descriptive detail relevant to your purpose in this essay?
- Have you integrated dialogue and speech into your piece?
- Have you used some of the techniques suggested in our textbook to give your writing voice and style?
- Have you provided closure at the end, preferably one that points to the significance of your belief?

The essay is to be relatively brief, one that can be read aloud in fewer than three minutes.

At the end of the semester, students invariably select this assignment as the most interesting. This is hardly surprising, given that for inexperienced writers, it is far more appealing to write from and about one's own experience than to work with the ideas of others. Also common is the trap that students fall into: essentially narrating a story of personal significance to them, but with little analysis of the meaning of that story for themselves or for others. In addition, students struggle with finding evidence of when the belief was "formed or tested." Doing so requires memory work and metacognitive understanding—in other words, the ability to step out of one's own experience to discern its shape and, in this case, its inception. Nevertheless, I have stayed with this assignment because it produces fluency and a level of comfort early on for my students and because it signals to them that their ideas—their presence—matter. While I have not emphasized this point in the past (though I plan to do so from this point on), I would like to send the message out that it is alright for students to share a religious belief—something that I'm confident they have not been encouraged to do in a classroom context (DePalma). As with other subjects for this assignment, students must be mindful of readers, allowing access to the public as to why this belief matters to the writer and to readers.

An Essay of Application. Students further explore the dynamic between the personal and the public in their next writing assignment: an essay of application. Like the essay about an important belief, this assignment calls for the student to look inward for a subject. Unlike that initial assignment, the essay of application demands that the writer deliberately look outward—at the question being asked (ranging from directive to wide open), the nature of the institution asking that question (public or private, small or large), and the purpose of the writing in the first place (to demonstrate an enthusiasm for application and to reason why the writer is a "good fit" for that particular institution). Students are encouraged to seek out questions from colleges they may wish to transfer to, giving the assignment a genuinely pragmatic quality. The prompt reads as follows:

> It is a fact of life that at some time (likely a few times) you'll be asked to write a letter or essay of application: perhaps for a scholarship, or to transfer to a four-year college, or to get a job. For this assignment, I'd like you to write an essay of ap-

plication, a formal piece of writing, written in multiple paragraphs, addressing a specific question or prompt for a specific audience.

Students are encouraged to research a college or agency of interest, locate its application, and address the questions asked. I offer the following checklist:

- Is the question provided at the top of the essay?
- Is the name of the college or scholarship granting agency provided as well?
- How well does the essay stay on task?
- Are topic sentences provided for each paragraph? If so, please underline that sentence. If not, underline the sentence that you believe could serve that purpose.
- Is evidence provided to support the claim made in the essay? What form does that evidence take (for example, relevant personal experience)?
- What facts are included in the essay to suggest an understanding of the readers or the intended institution?
- Is analysis used? If so, what are the units/themes used for analysis?
- What is the dominant impression left by the essay?

Here we see many formal requirements particular to conventional essays that emphasize staying on task, paragraph coherence, and evidence. Equally important is the focus on the question being asked and the institution asking it. In fact, this early assignment is the first to require some (albeit informal) research: in this case, research into the relevant programs the college might have that are of interest to the student. Slowly, incrementally, I try to bring students to the point of hearing voices other than their own and to work with the ideas expressed by others.

The Profile. The next assignment, interviewing a person of interest and writing a profile of that person, directly compels students to listen to the voice of another. At the same time, the assignment requires that students do more than report what someone else has said. They must offer an interpretive thesis, or "nut graf" (Blau and Burak 488). In other words, students must offer their own *terministic screen*, to use Burke's famous term, and impose order and structure on what they have heard.

The checklist for this assignment renders the criteria clearly:

- A sharp lead that engages the reader's attention;
- An interpretive thesis ("nut graf") that gives your profile a meaningful focus;
- A body that contains a logical development of facts and ideas about your subject;
- A conclusion that leaves a strong, final impression that follows logically from all that;
- Sharp and relevant physical description based on your own observation (of setting and/or your profile subject);
- Skillful use of quotations from your subject (and about your subject, if you choose to interview others as well);
- Anecdotes or brief stories related by your subject to make a pertinent point; and
- Factual information about your subject.

This assignment marks the first time that students are required to listen to others in order to process and synthesize what they have heard and integrate that material within their own writing. I believe that working with sources requires a semester-long effort rather than merely adding a research term paper to the end of a course. The complex challenge of working with sources demands a developmental and staged approach.

The Proposal. The "outward turn" of this course becomes even more decisive when students are asked, in their next assignment, to "produce a proposal addressing a serious but solvable problem in your community (or at this college)." The assignment calls for some rather jarring rethinking on the part of many students, especially those who do not see themselves relationally; that is, as part of a community or social matrix. The assignment and the genre also call into question the familiar view that writing has little consequence beyond the classroom (and receiving a grade).

Writing a proposal requires an understanding of the genre, a solution, the necessary analysis of costs and benefits, and a call to action. Still, many other aspects of the assignment recall concerns that have been raised elsewhere in the course, as this checklist attests:

- Reader: Where have you specified your intended reader?
- Problem: Where have you provided a clear statement of an urgent, *local*, and solvable problem?

- Research/Context: Where have you given evidence, drawn from a reputable news account (obtained via print or an online database), as to the nature and seriousness of the problem?
- Solutions: Where have you offered a practical and clear solution or set of solutions?
- Analysis of Costs/Benefits: Where have you provided an analysis of the costs and benefits of your proposal?
- Call to Action: Where have you offered a specific action or set of actions on the part of your reader?

Students must demonstrate an awareness of readers and establish a clear statement of thesis, here called a "problem." Moreover, they need to bring evidence drawn from research to confirm the seriousness of the problem and integrate that information within their writing.

Annotation of a Scholarly Article. The course now takes a clearly academic turn, in that students are asked to work with scholarly sources (defined as peer-reviewed articles). Realizing that writing with research is extremely challenging for novice writers, I continue my efforts to developmentally stage assignments. Hence, for this next assignment, I ask students to "write an annotation of a scholarly article, at least two paragraphs long, containing both a summary and evaluation of that article." Ideally, students search for an article on a subject they have already written about (in their proposal), or on a subject of interest to them, and the source may also be used for their final project, a research and analysis of a trend. There is no denying the significant challenge here: to find and read an article written by a scholar for other scholars in a field and written in language that is often technical and discipline-specific. Students would be listening-in on a conversation already in progress without the necessary means to fill in the gaps. Summary, as a result, becomes exceedingly difficult: What are the key concepts being discussed? Students must then critique what they read, drawing upon questions given in the assignment checklist:

- Have you included the full citation, in MLA style, at the top of your annotation?
- In the summary, where do you use signal phrases so as to make clear the author's ownership over the ideas expressed?
- In the summary, have you accurately represented the argument of your source?

- In the summary, have you used your own words rather than quoting from the original?
- In your evaluation of the article, where do you answer the following questions:
  - What do I know about the author that would make the article credible?
  - How recently was it published?
  - How credible is the journal in which the essay appears?
  - What audience is the article intended for? How successfully does the article consider that audience?
  - What is the author's purpose? What is his or her bias, if any?
  - What kind of evidence is given? How effective is it?
  - What is not stated in the article that needs to be noted?

sounds like ours

Students typically have never even heard of annotation as a genre, let alone been asked to summarize and critique a scholarly article. Not surprisingly, early drafts from less invested and less confident writers produce somewhat generalized summaries with little in the way of evaluation. *— I feel that's what I did*

Analysis of a Trend. As a final project, one that tries to bring together the various strands of knowledge domains and skill sets introduced in the course, students produce an analysis of a trend—a genre usually associated with marketing and business, not with academe. "This assignment," students are told, "will be based in research. You'll be writing a three-to-five page, typed, double-spaced essay in which you document and analyze a significant trend. (Our textbook defines 'trends' as recent 'patterns in behavior' of a clearly identified social group or culture expressing a change over time (Blau and Burak 518)."

Students are not asked to produce a substantial research paper, but rather one of modest length that requires the use of two quality, scholarly (peer-reviewed) articles. I like this assignment, challenging though it is, because of its streamlined nature and clearly denoted components:

- State clearly a thesis that identifies a trend;
- Document through the use of "statistics, facts, and expert opinion" (Blau and Burak 519) that the trend exists (you may use visual evidence, such as charts and graphs, but if doing so, please comment on the data presented);

- Analyze and discuss the causes and effects of the trend, keeping in mind that a trend typically has multiple causes and effects; and
- Cite your use of sources in MLA style.

Students are challenged to fit their subject to the stated definition of a trend. Some may omit a starting point for the trend, neglect to specify the participants of that trend, or quantify the change produced by the trend. Many students, furthermore, find it difficult to substantiate, in a scholarly way, the trend's existence, preferring—no surprise here—to find evidence via Google.

DEVELOPING A CRITICAL AND PRECISE VOCABULARY ABOUT WRITING

Fundamentally, a required writing course promotes student agency. In other words, it gives students the tools with which they can be successful as writers. I believe that such agency resides in the power of clear and precise reflection on what works and what needs work in a particular piece of writing. Having the words with which to name qualities of their written work enables students to manipulate and re-authorize that work in productive ways. Without that vocabulary, students may simply take their chances on success by unthinkingly rehearsing what seemed to work last time, even though the terrain and the writing task has shifted. They may also leave things to chance or inspiration. I hope to show my students that writing success comes through making conscious choices.

Throughout the course, students are asked to become articulate critics of their own writing and the writing of peers. Each draft, for example, must include a post-write, or writer's memo, that includes responses to these questions:

- How do you feel about the paper so far? Please explain and offer evidence from the work.
- What remains to be done? Please be precise.
- What questions do you have for readers about the piece?

The goal is to be able to answer these questions by referencing the criteria of each assignment. Hence, peer reviews that students are required to submit for each assignment always begin with the instruction: "In your own words, fully and with precision, describe what the assignment is asking the writer (your partner) to do." Students are then asked to draw upon these criteria when describing precisely what aspects of their partner's writing works well and what needs additional work.

In addition, and after I've commented on students' writing (via students' blogs), I require students to comment further as part of their "Talk Back," attending to these prompts:

- Please summarize my comments.
- Do you feel that I have missed something that should have been addressed? Is there something you think worked well, but that I didn't comment on or are you unsure about how well something worked in your paper that you would like clarification about? Please explain.
- Do you feel you can take something of what you've learned from this assignment and transfer that lesson to other writing in this class or elsewhere? Please explain precisely what that transferable element might be.

Building on such work, in-class discussion during workshop weeks (weeks in which students share their work for review) involves a reading and an analysis of writing samples drawn from the class. Students, in small groups and as a class, are asked to indicate at least three aspects of the writing that work, specify the passage, and offer reasons why the writing is effective by drawing upon the criteria for the assignment. The same process holds for aspects of the writing that do not seem to work. All these exercises are geared toward promoting a vocabulary about writing—reflecting, and perhaps enhancing, student metacognition.

WRITING AND RESPONDING TO WRITING IN THE BLOGOSPHERE

For years, I have struggled with how to distribute student writing for discussion in class and for peer review. Making hard copies seemed a significant challenge, given the number of students and the cost of printing. In addition, I have, for most of my adult life, been challenged by painfully illegible handwriting; hence, my written response to student writing often resulted in a "Huh?" response. I would, over the years, try to respond to student writing via the comment function of Word, but the intended reader could not always open the document properly to view my comments and, of course, my inbox would fill quickly.

When a colleague demonstrated the use of a blog in his composition classroom for posting assignments, for student writing, and for responses to writing, I became very interested: With one click of a mouse, I saw the problems of distribution and penmanship disappear. I could have students post their drafts on their blog, and then have readers comment on those postings. It's not a perfect solution, of course. Despite the fact that we live in the age of Facebook, many students are loathe to spend their online time blogging for school. Other students simply don't have reliable Internet access at home (aside through their smartphones, that is). Moreover, blogging usually connotes talky, informal writing about any subject that pleases the blogger and his or her readers. On a blog, students would be expected to focus their writing on the question and to write in a language appropriate to the situation. Finally, students might find it odd that a face-to-face (f2f) course would feature so much online work—that was not what they signed up for.

Despite those obstacles, I am willing to stay with the blog. The advantages, aside from those I named, include the fact that the blog provides a convenient electronic portfolio of students' work over time and over drafts: a mirror from which to reflect on their progress as writers. By the semester's end, students know where their writing is and are able to view quite clearly the distance from which they have come. They have a written record of response to their work that guides them as they revise and edit their writing for their semester-culminating project: the course portfolio (still handed in as hard copy—I haven't gone so far as to go fully digital). Each student's blog contains their peer partner's comments (on first drafts) as well as my own reaction to their drafts (on second drafts).

When it works, the blog provides a truly rich record of conversations between the writer and his or her readers. For example, here's an exchange between a student and me about her essay of application, in which she is prompted to write about her choice of community service. In her post-write, the student assesses the situation:

> I feel good about this draft because, unlike the first, this one is linked to my major. A bit more detail was provided and I think the paragraph organization is better. I think I might have to go more in depth with my reasoning, although I don't know exactly how. How does the bringing back awareness sound? Is it relevant? Should I get rid of it and pay more attention to the other reasonings or keep it this way? Do you have any suggestion and examples on how I can talk about my reasonings more in depth and clearly? (Camilla, "Postwrite")

Then my response:

> I think this reads well and is a reasonably focused response to the question. I'm glad that you tried this one, since I assume you are applying in reality for the scholarship. I wish you luck. You asked about making your reasoning clear. You clearly want to help young children. That comes through well. But might it be helpful if you could say more about your motivation, perhaps expressing through some concrete experience that you've already had? Moreover, I'd like to see a bit more precision when you get to the matter of bringing global "awareness" to this country. That paragraph attempts to do something bigger than the previous paragraphs but seems to need some kind of grounding (you admit the cliché yourself). What do you think? (Tinberg, "Comment")

While her response will not appear in the blog, the student will eventually "Talk Back" to my comment and include that response in her hard copy portfolio. This back and forth about student writing brings huge dividends, as the student gets quick and pointed feedback on her writing and, in the process, refines her own vocabulary of response.

Commenting by way of the blog has also shaped my own response in important ways. Because I am unable to insert my own words within the student's writing, I must offer pointed and precise language so that students know exactly to what passages I refer. Moreover, I must take special care to refer to the question and the situation addressed by the writing as well as the specific criteria of the assignment. My comments, nonetheless, take on a holistic quality given the constraints of the blog: I try to look at the big picture here—at the appropriateness of the response to the question, for example, or the use of evidence.

THE LAST WORD

In composing this narrative of my course design, especially since my voice is virtually the only one expressed in this account, I run the risk of implying that the challenge has been met, that this course has been carefully designed and tested over time, and that I have satisfactorily translated theory into successful practice. Such is hardly the case. I am continually challenged to theorize my classroom practices and render coherent theory from the blur of classroom detail. For me, teaching composition remains a deeply humbling enterprise.

So much is expected from this single course. Likely the only writing-intensive experience that students will have in college, the composition course aims to provide essential skills for writing success—throughout the college curriculum and into the workplace. The course also serves as a gateway or orientation to college itself: demonstrating such important skills as strategic reading and informational literacy. Each of us faculty may choose to focus on a single aspect of these many goals, or we may attempt to meet most, if not all. Regardless of the scope of our intentions, I hope that each of us works through theory to arrive at best practices of teaching composition and that teaching always remains a scholarly and reflective activity.

WORKS CITED

Aviles, Quique. "I Will Take My Voice Back." *This I Believe*, 31 July 2006. Web. 11 January 2012.

Beaufort, Anne. *College Writing and Beyond: A New Framework for University Writing Instruction*. Logan: Utah State UP, 2007. Print.

—. *Writing in the Real World: Making the Transition from School to Work*. New York: Teachers College Press, 1999. Print.

Blau, Susan, and Kathryn Burak. *Writing in the Works*. 2nd ed. Boston: Wadsworth, 2009. Print.

Bloom, Lynn Z. "Good Enough Writing: What Is Good Enough Writing Anyway?" *What Is "College-Level" Writing?* Ed. Patrick Sullivan and Howard Tinberg. Urbana: National Council of Teachers of English, 2006. 71-92. Print.

Camilla. "Postwrite." 2011. Web. 12 January 2012.

Depalma, Michael-John. "Re-envisioning Religious Discourses as Rhetorical Resources in Composition Teaching: A Pragmatic Response to the Challenge of Belief." *College Composition and Communication* 63.2 (2011): 219-243. Print.

"Mission Statement." Bristol Community College, 2012. Web. 12 January 2012.

Tinberg, Howard. "Comment." 2011. Web. 12 January 2012.

—. "What Is 'College-Level' Writing? The View from a Community College Writing Center." *What Is "College-Level" Writing?* Vol. 2. Ed. Patrick Sullivan, Howard Tinberg, and Sheridan Blau. Urbana: National Council of Teachers of English, 2010. 170-82. Print.

Walters, Margaret, Susan Hunter, and Elizabeth Giddens . "Qualitative Research on What Leads to Success in Professional Writing." *International Journal for the Scholarship of Teaching and Learning* 1.2 (2007). Web. 11 January 2012.

Appendix: Course Syllabus

ENGLISH 101: COLLEGE WRITING

Dr. Tinberg

Web Page: http://contentbuilder.merlot.org/toolkit/users/HT/eng11bcc

Course Description

This college-level composition course provides students an opportunity to develop their writing through various stages of composing, revising, and editing. In addition, students learn how to formulate and support a thesis using a number of rhetorical strategies, to conduct research, and to integrate a variety of sources according to the Modern Language Association guidelines. Students write in Standard English with consideration given to audience, purpose, and context.

Prerequisite: Satisfactory performance on the writing skills test or "C" or better in English 10. Passing score on the college's reading placement test or concurrent enrollment in/or prior completion of RDG 10.

You may have some questions. . . .

What will I learn in this course?

I'm hoping that by taking this course you will be better prepared to handle the writing tasks that await you in college and beyond. Specifically, I expect you to be able to

- respond appropriately to an assignment or writing situation;
- state your purpose clearly and stick with it;
- consider your reader's needs;
- understand the genre in which you are writing;
- value and demonstrate a clear understanding of the drafting, revising, and editing processes;
- develop a clear and precise vocabulary about what works and what needs work in a particular piece of writing;
- develop your ideas through the use of appropriate detail;
- provide appropriate and convincing evidence to support your claims; and

- demonstrate a control over language (grammar, mechanics, and tone).

Your grade on particular pieces of writing and in the course generally will depend on how successfully you meet the challenges that I've listed.

How much writing will I be expected to do?

You will be expected to submit formal out-of-class writing (usually 2 to 3 pages typed) about every other week. You will also be expected to keep a weekly reading journal (I'll say more about that in class), which will receive a letter grade. **All out-of-class writing will be considered as drafts and thus subject to change. You are required to submit all drafts when due.** In the last week of the semester, you will be assembling a portfolio of your best work, which should include a reflective component (more about that later) and four pieces of writing, one of which must be writing that uses, and acknowledges, sources.

How will my writing be graded?

Unless you request one, your drafts will not receive a letter grade. **However, each draft will be awarded 100 points if you've submitted that draft by deadline—as hard copies brought to workshop and as e-copy posted on your blog.** Deadlines typically occur on

- *The first day of workshops:* first drafts due as hard copy in class and as electronic copy on your blog (to be read by your workshop partner)
- *The last day of the workshop week:* second drafts are due as electronic copy on your blog (to be read by me, your instructor)

Your point total for the semester will be considered as proof of good "citizenship," which will itself form 30 percent of your course grade. Simply put, I'd like to reward you all for submitting your work on a timely basis.

How much will the writing be weighted?

Your grade for the course will be based on the following:

Portfolio	50%
Reading Journal	20%
Citizenship [timely submission of drafts]	30%

What is a blog?

You'll be posting your papers electronically on a blog (for initial and second drafts as well as commentary on each draft). The blog, which allows you to post messages designed for a select group or the browsing public-at-large, will serve as a place to deposit rough drafts of your writing, as well as receive written commentary from me and from a partner. The blog is a convenient place to store your writing in process.

What is the Portfolio? What will go into it?

At the end of the semester, I will ask you to submit a portfolio, or a collection in hard copy, of your best work. The portfolio that you will hand in will consist of the following:

- A reflective introduction
- A research-based essay using MLA notation (the Trend Analysis)
- Three additional pieces of your own choosing
- *Post Write,* my commentary, and your *Talk Back* for each paper submitted (discussed on our web page)
- A copy of the instructions for each paper.

Please place your writing in a manila folder, with your name, course, section number given on the label) and bring the portfolio to the last class of the semester.

To receive full credit for your portfolio, you will need to have included all the required pieces.

What is the Journal?

You will be asked to keep a weekly journal (the format is included as links on our course web page). Depending on the week, you will either be responding to a chapter in our textbook or offering your commentary ("peer review") on your partner's draft-in-progress. **Journals must be typed and are always due in the last class of each week.**

Is there a Web Page for this course?

Yes. This course has a web page (*http://contentbuilder.merlot.org/toolkit/users/HT/eng11bcc*). On the site, you'll find many documents, including reading assignments, all paper topics, and the template for your journal and peer review responses. **Please note that you cannot access the full web page via Microsoft Explorer, but, instead, will need to use another browser such as Firefox or Chrome.**

Will I be asked to share my writing?

Yes. I don't know of a better way of instilling a sense of audience awareness except through the sharing of your writing with helpful and constructive peers. With each out-of-class assignment, I will ask that you participate in a writing workshop. During the workshop, you will be asked to share your work with others—notably a partner and your instructor. The purpose of sharing your writing is to give you, as the writer, additional perspective on your work. In addition, you'll be posting drafts and receiving feedback via your blog, which will be accessible to classmates as well.

What is plagiarism and what are its consequences?

I expect your writing to be your own. If you use sources without acknowledging them—intentionally or unintentionally—you are likely to face serious consequences, including a grade of failure for that particular assignment.

What book will I need to buy?

I am requiring one book: *Writing in the Works,* 2nd ed. You may buy it at our bookstore or online (www.amazon.com). "Amazon" is the place to start but there are many other sites on the World Wide Web that sell new or used textbooks). Here is the complete info on the required textbook for this class:

Blau, Susan and Kathryn Burak. *Writing in the Works.* 2nd ed. Boston: Wadsworth, 2010. ISBN: 10–547–15151–09

Reading Assignments and Topics for Discussion

Week 1
The Writer's Process (*Writing* 2–49)
Setting up your Blog

Week 2
Keeping a Reading Journal
Writing with Style and Voice (*Writing* 52–71)
This I Believe: Writing for Radio

Week 3
Writing Workshop

Week 4
Application Essays (*Writing* 138–171)

Week 5
Writing Workshop

Week 6
Profiles (*Writing* 458–515)

Week 7
Spring Break

Week 8
Writing Workshop

Week 9
Proposals (*Writing* 302–341)

Week 10
Writing Workshop

Week 11
Reading and Thinking Critically (*Writing* 72–99)
Annotating a Scholarly Article

Week 12
Writing Workshop

Week 13
Research Articles (*Writing* 516–558)

Week 14
Writing Workshop

Week 15
Reflective Cover Letter
Preparing Your Portfolio
Portfolios Due Last Class

10 For the Love of Language: A Curriculum

Victor Villanueva

> *Language is a skin: I rub my language against the other. It is as if I had words instead of fingers, or fingers at the tip of my words. My language trembles with desire.*
>
> —Roland Barthes

A Personal History

It occurs to me that I started teaching composition over thirty years ago as a summer job at a community college in 1980. Like any teacher, over most of those thirty years I experimented with this and with that, until I finally arrived at a particular theoretical or philosophical stopping point, a place where I said, "This is what I believe, truly believe about the teaching of writing and will venture no further." Now, in saying that, I didn't mean that I would never again change my syllabus or that there would be no further revisions to my thinking. "All thinking is revising," I once wrote. I still believe that. What I mean is that I arrived at a firm, guiding principle for the teaching of writing. That principle is that writing is tied to language, that language is the subject matter of a writing course. Let me begin by briefly recounting the journey, how I got to this philosophical home.

I don't remember much about that first teaching stint. I remember hour after hour of commenting on papers and an assignment that has to do with some Bob Dylan poem or other. (I think it was "Memphis Blues.") More clearly than I remember my curriculum, I remember walking in six-inch deep volcano ash. That is the year Mount St. Hel-

257

ens erupted, and I am teaching 250 miles from the eruption, less than two weeks after the first blow. It blows again on the day I receive my first paycheck as a comp teacher. A paycheck and an eerie ash cloud and ash as deep as snow are much more memorable than the first curriculum of a teacher without training.

The training comes a year later, with Professor William Irmscher carrying on about things I don't understand during those few days of orientation before we enter the classroom. When classes begin and we start teaching, he sends us weekly memos, telling us where we ought to be in the curriculum ("You should be on paragraphing at this point"), some notes on theory, and some suggestions for assignments. I don't feel like I am drowning, but I also don't really know what I am doing. I am implementing Irmscher and the notes he converted into a book (or vice-versa)—his *Teaching Expository Writing*. I am also taking classes, discovering rhetoric, discovering composition (putting Kenneth Burke together with Ann Berthoff, Aristotle with Berthoff), discovering the field, and I am not quite clear how to put the theory with the practice, but knowing that that is the way to go. The training then accelerates, as I am put in charge of the English component of the Educational Opportunity Program, a basic writing program. At this point, the reading grows in intensity—Shaughnessy, Friere. Richard Rodriguez and E.D. Hirsch drive me crazy. The program still really belongs to the director, now Charles Schuster, and he introduces me to William Coles's *The Plural I* (re-issued as *The Plural I—And After* a few years later). I will not act on that introduction to Coles until years later. My innovation is to stick with the English 101 curriculum, but to have it extend to two quarters—what Greg Glau will eventually perfect as the Stretch Program (Greg having been a student at Northern Arizona University while I was there, though I don't know if I ever mentioned what I had done as a graduate student; I'm not trying to take credit for his program—I'm saying that I did something like that as well).

It's now 1985, and I move on to be an assistant professor, teaching multiple sections of English 101, writing a dissertation on basic writers, learning all I can, eventually landing on David Bartholomae and Anthony Petrosky, whose *Facts, Artifacts, and Counterfacts* appears the year of my dissertation (a year into my first tenure-track job). I discover a pedagogy of my own, one tied to my sense of obligation about the canon and my intrinsic need—a need that remains—to have students explore racism. Here's how I described it some years back:

Literature can be set up so as to create a dialectic between differing worldviews, between the national-cultural and the critical. Students read Hemingway, for example, as male, white, middle-class as they come, skeptical, perhaps, but no radical. Then they read Buchi Emecheta, *Double Yoke*—a story of a black African woman trying to get through different value systems, cultures, different ways of viewing the world, her struggles at gaining a college degree. Men and women are at issue, black and white; the tribal ways that the main character, Nko, was raised with against the modern Western ways of the university. White students confronting the college community, women, African American students, American Indian students—all have a portion of Nko's pains, and since the story takes place far away, the defense of bigotries does not come up immediately, as it often does in more explicitly African American or Latino or American Indian literature, though often it is good to have these prejudices present themselves. Nko and Hemingway's Nick Adams handle things differently, confront different obstacles. Ideologies peep out of the classroom discussions (which usually begin with moral questions—Nick's sense of responsibility; Nko's integrity). What is it about where the characters come from that causes them to behave and believe in different ways? We can look at Steinbeck and Ayn Rand, Rodriguez and Galarza, Louis L'Amour and Leslie Marmon Silko. Students sometimes shock themselves concerning their own prejudices—anti-color and anti-white. (*Bootstraps* 99)

The theme is less "doing the conflicts" and more "Tradition and Change for Changes in Tradition." The books change, but the principles remain the same. Bartholomae and Petrosky create *Ways of Reading*. The readings are more complex, but the principle can work with that book. All of it works for me. But for me.

THE PRINCIPLES

1995. I assume duties as Director of Composition. With the help of Ms. Anne Maxham, the Associate Director of Composition, the following principles are dictated (and published in *Grading in the Post-Process Classroom*):

1. Language is ontological and epistemological.

The ways humans conduct any business—from the most mundane to the most esoteric, scientific, technological—are founded on our unique ways with language. Other creatures might have and use language, but no other creature has done with language what we have done with it. The manipulation of symbol systems—language, broadly defined—is uniquely and inherently human. It is ontological. The technology which renders language an artifact to be studied, analyzed, criticized is writing—a precise way (though no science) of ordering thought, of bringing to light muddied emotions and fragments of ideas, maybe even the means to producing ideas. Writing is epistemological, in other words. Here's Aristotle on the matter (forgiving his sexism): "It is absurd to hold that a man ought to be ashamed of being unable to defend himself with his limbs, but not of being unable to defend himself with speech and reason, when the use of rational speech is more distinctive of a human being than the use of his limbs."

2. Rhetoric is the root and the business of academic discourse.

The admonition that learning to be conscious of our use of language is more our duty than learning to fight physically can be found in Aristotle's *Rhetoric*. That's our business—the uniquely human literary arts, rhetoric. This is not to denigrate the study of literature. But literature is specialized (for which Aristotle wrote his *Poetics*, for instance). Our business in first-year composition must embrace the entire academic discourse community. Rhetoric is founded on Aristotle's notion (and similar notions from others before him and since) that writing is at least epistemological—a way of discovering what goes on within our minds, a way of learning what we think we know and what we're trying to know. Rhetoric is also a way of communicating those discoveries to ourselves and to others. And rhetoric is a means of engaging in the dialectical process— "dialectical process" meaning that rhetoric becomes a way of engaging in a two-way (at least) communicative process, an exchange which will further learning. In short, writing is a means of discovery, a means of learning, and a means of communicating something to someone.

3. The dialectic process is basic to academic discourse and thereby basic to a first-year writing course.

Writing is considerably more than just a requirement of a university system. But from a most pragmatic position, it is surely that—a requirement, a required ability to manipulate the complex set of cognitive and manipulative skills which is writing to arrive at products that contain certain characteristics: the voice of objectivity or reasonableness, a clear line of argument, substantiation from prior scholarship or research, following relatively predictable patterns and conventions. Our immediate responsibility is to provide an environment, a set of circumstances, which will encourage students to incorporate new information into existing frameworks of knowledge, to look beyond immediate causes for events to less apparent antecedents, to communicate these discoveries to others in writing, within the conventions which this institution—the university—finds meaningful and valuable. The means to that end is to discover writing processes and to enter into dialectical exchanges, pressing issues to the point of questioning, not converting students from what we may believe to be wrongheaded, but to provide an environment which will foster critical reconsiderations of the familiar.

The method whereby students might be brought to consider the possibility of changing their minds about "accepted wisdom" is the dialectic. In teaching circles, the best known is Plato's dialectic, the question and answer method known as the Socratic method. Within the academic community the most revered (apart from the scientific method) is Aristotle's dialectic: disputation, where the aim is to win. But what is better suited to the aims of first-year composition—foregrounding, questioning, coming, maybe, to the point where teacher and student alike begin to question the familiar, begin to consider the possibility of changing perspectives or of knowing the reasons for maintaining long-held beliefs—derives from a careful coupling of several sources which come under the heads of hermeneutics, cultural studies, and critical pedagogy. The method begins with discovering students' prejudices (as in preconceived notions more than bigotries) and having students discuss the sources of those beliefs within them, discussing them, then researching them, to discuss them (best in writing) yet again. The idea is to look to initial sources of ideas, to question them, to see the political or cultural assumptions present in all things, then to write a critical-documented essay—an opinion, backed by substantiation from research, presented in a relatively conventional format.

4. Reading is necessary to writing.

One way to meet the goals implicit in learning that writing is a process, a process of discovery and learning, assisted by a classroom dynamic that is dialectical, is through readings. Readings provide students with challenges which heighten their awareness of questions of culture while enriching their academic experience. Although readings should not be intended as models for students to follow, students should become exposed to the conventions they will be required to mimic in some sense.

5. Writing is a process.

Ultimately, first-year composition emphasizes awareness of writing as a process—from a process of jotting meaningful marks on a page (even if through a computer monitor), to a process of discovery, to a potential process of change (of the self and of others). All of this adds up to first-year composition as a means of introducing students to ways in which writing is an integral—a crucial—element in their achieving their individual educational goals and larger social needs.

6. Responding to student papers is not grading.

> Immediate feedback to student submissions is critical. That feedback should be judicious. Rules of grammar and correctness are many, so that an inordinate attention to such matters becomes the principal cause of writer's block. Confine marking of errors to about three per paper. Otherwise, responses to student papers should be generative and never abusive. By "generative" I mean the kind of response that might prompt revision: paraphrases of what the student wrote ("Are you saying . . . ?) or alternatives ("Couldn't someone argue . . . ?). Whatever the tack, the emphasis should be on stimulating revision, not on justifying a grade. (176-79)

These are the principles that still guide my teaching and my thinking about the teaching of writing—with one exception.

That exception is contained in the reference to prompting revision. Although I still comment on papers in the way I describe in Principle #6, I no longer think in terms of revision as multiple drafts for composition classes, where students are not intrinsically driven to convey a message, and aren't driven to revise. I grew tired of revising my students' papers, insofar as my comments to student papers would be responded to—and *that* would constitute a revision. Following William Coles's *Plural I*, I adopted sequenced or scaffolded assignments. If, as Ann Berthoff says, revision is a matter of thinking again, presenting again, and seeing again (a re-cognition, a re-presentation, and a re-vision), then that becomes the important matter. The matter becomes how best to inculcate that rethinking, that revisioning, in order to come up with a representation rather than a patchwork of additions to a "completed" draft. The trick then becomes making a series of assignments in which each assignment builds on the concepts presented in a previous assignment.

A Disciplinary History and Polemic

The principles worked. Sequenced assignments seemed to work, but the themes didn't. At first I insisted on racism as a program-wide theme for first-year comp. The teachers balked, not because they were racists, but because they feared the theme; they felt ill-equipped to work with the theme. I argued that being knowledgeable of the theme was less important than dialogue about the theme, providing the means with which to compose papers. They still balked. I instituted a series of brown bags: faculty from ethnic studies and from education to discuss critical pedagogy—a pedagogical tool kit. Still they balked. I gave up. The next year, the theme was popular culture. Some would find their way to racism, some to gender, some just to popular movies and TV shows. The following year was ecology. I believed in my principles of writing instruction, but I had lost my imperative for an ethic of composition. That feeling was reflected, implicitly, for the most part, in my 1999 keynote speech at the Conference on College Composition and Communication.

What's more important (and not reflected in that talk) were two realizations: One, that I was Socrates's foil, Plato's Gorgias, advocating a rhetoric devoid of real knowledge. I was arguing that all that mattered was the rhetoric, a persuasive argument, with no one—neither teacher nor student—having a real, deep knowledge of the matters to be written about. Two, that the whole profession (well, maybe an overstatement) is Plato's Gorgias, and that there was a historical reason for that.

Historians of the field of composition (I'm thinking mainly here of Susan Miller) have told us that the birth of composition studies in the twentieth century was to act as a service to literature. In the 1960s, as composition came to realize a purpose larger than simple service to literature, and as it created its genealogical link to rhetoric, it lost its thematic moorings. That is, in breaking from literature, it broke from the literary, even arguing that the only text for a composition classroom was the text that students themselves produced. When composition studies realized that it could not be divorced from reading, the question arose as to what those readings would be, if not literature. Composition needed books to read, things to write about. Whatever we, the teachers, found important became what they, the students, would write about. We became—we remain—a bona-fide discipline that relies on dilettantism.

There is an amateurism that is built into composition studies from without and from within. The institution works on the assumption that anyone who can write can teach writing, and that anyone who is an English major or an English teacher can write. And so graduate students teach writing while some learn more about the discipline, and their professors tell them that they really can't write, quite. Instructors are hired who have degrees in English, though so many are trained in literary studies or in creative writing, asking those in power for opportunities to do "real" teaching (a matter I know intimately as a former department chair). From within, we act as if we have no disciplinary substance for students. There are the exceptions, of course, like Sharon Crowley's *Ancient Rhetorics*, or its predecessor, E.P.J. Corbett's *Classical Rhetoric*. Both argue that rhetoric is the substance of composition. I agree.

Though I have long said that all compositionists should also be rhetoricians, that is not the case. Not all our students, nor all our instructors or our professors of composition are well-versed in rhetoric. Should we mandate rhetoric, we still run the risk of dilettantism. What does join us is language, a love of language—as literary, as poetry, as non-fiction, as the material cause for rhetoric, literature, linguistics, creative writing. As Patrick Hartwell (among many others) told us long ago, what separates the able from the less-able writer is metalinguistic awareness, an awareness of language as language.

The Curriculum

And so to my curriculum. The principles above hold. Sequenced assignments hold. The theme is Language, what students need to think about in order to become better writers, what all of us know something about, and what is at the foundation of discourse, oral and written. This doesn't negate more traditional "themes"; it provides a way into those themes for which we have real expertise, no matter our subspecialty with English studies. The appended syllabi will demonstrate. The theme is "culture."

A note on Assignment #5: The end of a semester is a time when students are cramming and writing like crazy. Accordingly, my most important assignment is the next to last, when students can dedicate more of the time and energy I would wish them to spend. The last is decidedly informal, yet still relies on all that has come prior, during the semester.

We are—all of us who do whatever it is we do as members of writing programs and English departments—lovers of language. Why, then, venture into matters that might be critically important to us, but for which our training tends to be, perforce, limited? For me, at least, the key is in the language.

WORKS CITED

Barthes, Roland. "Declaration." *A Lover's Discourse: Fragments.* 1978. Trans. Richard Howard. New York: Vintage, 2002. 73. Print.

Berthoff, Ann E. "Recognition, Representation, and Revision. *Journal of Basic Writing* 3.3 (1981): 19-32. Print.

Coles, William E. *The Plural I—And After.* Boston: Heinneman, 1988. Print.

Corbett, Edward P.J. *Classical Rhetoric for the Modern Student.* 1971. New York: Oxford UP, 1990. Print.

Crowley, Sharon. *Ancient Rhetorics for Contemporary Students.* New York: Macmillan, 1994. Print.

Glau, Gregory R. "The 'Stretch Program': Arizona State University's New Model of University-Level Basic Writing Instruction." *WPA: Writing Program Administration* 20.1-2 (1996): 79-91. Print.

Hartwell, Patrick. "Grammar, Grammars, and the Teaching of Grammar." *College English* 47.2 (1985): 105-27. Print.

Hirsch, E.D. Jr. *Cultural Literacy: What Every American Needs to Know.* Boston: Houghton Mifflin, 1987. Print.

Irmscher, William F. *Teaching Expository Writing.* New York: Harcourt, 1979. Print.

Miller, Susan. *Textual Carnivals: The Politics of Composition.* Carbondale: Southern Illinois UP, 1993. Print.

Neruda, Pablo. "The Word." *The Poetry of Pablo Neruda.* Ed. Ilan Stavans; Trans. Alastair Reid. New York: Farrar, Strauss, and Giroux, 2003. 621–22. Print.

Rodriguez, Richard. *Hunger of Memory: The Education of Richard Rodriguez.* New York: Bantam, 1982. Print.

Shaughnessy, Mina P. *Errors and Expectations: A Guide for the Teacher of Basic Writing.* New York: Oxford UP, 1979. Print.

Villanueva, Victor. *Bootstraps: From an American Academic of Color.* Urbana: National Council of Teachers of English, 1993. Print.

—. "Bearing Repetition: Some Assumptions." *Grading in the Post-Process Classroom: From Theory to Practice.* Eds. Libby Allison, Lizbeth Bryant, and Maureen Hourigan. Boston: Heinemann, 1998, 176-179. Print.

Appendix: Course Syllabus

English 101–20: Introductory Writing
Fall
Instructor: Dr. Victor Villanueva

Description:

This is a course with a single but complex aim: to enhance your critical reading and writing abilities so that you will be prepared to participate in the ongoing discourse of the communities that matter to you, especially the academic community. Our gaze will always be on **rhetoric**: the conscious use of language, particularly written language, and most particularly the written language of the academic community.

Course Goals:

By the end of the semester students should be able to
1. write an academic critique;
2. perform the research necessary to an academic critique;
3. read and conduct critical analyses of complex written texts.

Procedure:

1. Lecture and discussion on assigned readings;
2. Workshop on assigned writings (papers);
3. Five papers, one formal oral presentation;
4. Focused freewrites on readings.

Attendance:

See grading policy.

Grades:

Workshops and freewrites will be graded on a deficit basis. That is, each absence or failure to take an active part (which includes failing to have a legitimate draft on workshops requiring a draft) will lose points. Negative points are possible. Three missed workshops, for example, would equal *-400 points*). *One late paper* will be accepted without question or penalty. However, a late paper must be submitted before the next assigned paper is due. Later submissions will receive no points. A second or subsequent late paper will receive no points. All timely submissions can be revised through the next-to-last week of instruction. "Revision," however, means more than the correction of mechanical or grammatical errors.

Folders or portfolios are an institutionalized part of English 101. They are advisory: telling you something about how a reader who is not your instructor regards your writing and telling the instructor something about how others regard his or her students' writing. I will take folder results seriously, considering them a major component of discretionary points (see the point scheme, below). Failing to prepare or to submit a folder is grounds for failure.

An **incomplete** will be granted only in the most unusual of circumstances.

Plagiarism is perhaps the greatest taboo of the academic community. Remember to use quotation marks and to acknowledge sources, even when the sources are members of your workshop group. An unacknowledged paraphrase, a patchwork from several sources, as well as the submission of someone else's work (published or not), all constitute plagiarism. Let's be sure to be clear from the outset. Ask questions about the boundaries of plagiarism immediately. Ignorance will not be an acceptable excuse. And the sanctions are severe.

There is a *Writing Center* on the fourth floor of Avery Hall. The Center provides a tutoring system designed to help you with your writing assignments. Use it. You can even get credit for using it, if you elect to enroll for English 102.

ALL SUBMISSIONS *MUST BE* TYPED, double-spaced.

Points

Freewrites & Workshops: 1200 (minus 400 for no shows or no draft)
Papers: 1200 (300 max possible for #1, 2, 3, and 5) 600 (max for #4)
Oral: 500
Discretionary: 500
Final Grade: 4000 x .001

Assignment #1 (to be explained in class)

Assignment #2

18 September—workshop draft

20 September—submission draft

Length: as necessary, but less than three pages would suggest that more could have been done.

Citations: for now, journalistic citation is okay (name, title, page in parentheses directly following the quote).

Background

We can make sense of our experiences through language. Language is a sorting mechanism. Writing is particular use of language that allows us not only to reflect on our experiences but also on the way that we represent that experience to others. We have now been or will soon be introduced to various views of what culture is and how one's culture influences how that person thinks about herself and how she thinks about others.

Heuristics

For this assignment, I want you to write a narrative that presents an experience you have had which shapes your understanding of culture. This experience may be a story that has been told to you; it may be an event that you experienced with your family or your friends; it may be an experience that you have had which is characterized by a clash between cultures; it may be a narrative about something that you have read or observed. What you decide to write about should address your understanding of what culture is and how culture influences who you are. It should address in some way the insights (even if they're insights you would choose to refute) garnered in what you've read. In effect, the essay should add up to an extended definition of "culture."

The Assignment

If there is a guiding set of questions for this essay, they would be: What is culture? And what is it that I have experienced (including experienced through stories heard and things read) that leads me to this idea of "culture"?

Assignments #3, oral, and #4

16 October—workshop draft

18 October—submission draft

Length: this one will be fairly short—two to four double-spaced, typed pages.

Citations: those in the sciences are to use APA style; others use MLA style (see your handbook).

Background

A recent item on NPR (National Public Radio) described a study in which 40% of all fourth graders studied displayed substandard reading. The blame was placed on parents: parents don't read to their children. The item, however, did not offer reasons why parents aren't reading to their children (for which I wonder about the current economy: parents living below the poverty line, single-parent households, two parents who must work outside the home). Still and all, 40% is a startling figure (though we're not told what the "standard" is that this 40% fell below). The figures are always alarming. This isn't the first time the media have set off alarms about America's literacy problems. And it isn't the first time that causes (or solutions) have been remarkably simplistic.

The Assignment

Look to the news media, specifically the print media, and discover what it is they have to say about literacy (keeping in mind cultural dimensions).

1. Go to the library or online.
2. Find a column or an article in a news medium (newspaper or newsmagazine) that deals with a literacy issue.
3. Summarize or paraphrase the column or article.
4. Critique the column or article.
    a. evaluate the validity or the complexity of the cause of the literacy problem, if indeed the article or column describes a problem; do the same if the column or article describes an innovation in literacy instruction.
    b. discuss other factors that might have an effect on the program or the problem being described.
    c. evaluate the overall quality of the description: was it, overall, a fair presentation of the problem or program? why or why not? remember, there are decidedly few absolutes in any issue; the piece being critiqued cannot be all bad nor all good; be sure to point to strengths as well as weaknesses, though deciding which—the strengths or the weaknesses—stand out.

The Oral Report

Due dates—group decision of topic: 16 October
    annotated bib: 25 October
    begin presenting : 25 October
Time: 20—30 minutes

Criteria for Points:

research: quality and compreheniveness of the information, a thorough search for information, contained in an annotated bibliography provided by each member of the group.

presentation: quality of coordination among presenters so as to provide an interesting and engaging presentation which includes a thorough analysis of the synthesized materials (no gimmicks).

dialogue: quality of discussion instigated by and managed by the presenters.

Tasks involved:

1) a division of the labor among presenters;
2) a thorough investigation of the subject (books, academic articles, other newsprint (or popular media) on the subject, at least one expert interview per presenter, each with a different expert, all contained in an annotated bibliography;
3) synthesis of materials, analysis, discussion, coordination of presentation;
4) pose at least two questions which arise from the project with which to instigate audience discussion.

The Assignment:

You've written about your own notions about literacy and culture, have discovered and considered (and we should have discussed as a class) the kinds of things the newsmedia have considered that relate to literacy. Now provide an extended discussion of a particular literacy issue.

Investigate a particular literacy issue in depth. Consider its **history** (when did the issue arise, what were the circumstances that led to it, etc.); consider its **heyday** (when there was the most discussion or exposure to the issue); its **reception** during its heyday (both positive and negative, though assessing which got the greater attention, and from whom); its **present consideration**, either in print or among experts; its **ongoing significance**.

Present this material in a way that will be interesting and informative to an audience which consists, overwhelmingly, of your peers. To do this, you must consider ways of holding the audience's attention without resorting to cheap theatrics. Further, you should have a couple of genuine questions on hand that you believe will spark discussion from and within the audience that is related to the issue you have investigated.

Possible topics (though you are by no means limited to these):
- the French Academy
- Canadian bilingualism
- Swiss multilingualism
- China's official dialect
- National literacy campaigns (Brazil, China, Nicaragua, US, among others)
- Cultural Literacy (as advanced by E.D. Hirsch and Alan Bloom)
- the English Language Amendment to the U.S. Constitution
- English Only/Official English (state propositions)
- Black Americans & language (slavery, Jim Crow, voting, the Ann Arbor Case)
- Censorship in America
- Other Racial or Ethnic Americans & language

Assignment #4—Oral Report

6 November—workshop draft

8 November—submission draft

Length: this is your introduction to what college profs tend to call a medium or moderate length paper—8–10 pages, including Works Cited or Reference pages. (Remember, this paper is worth one third as many points as any of the others.)

Citations: APA or MLA, as appropriate.

The Assignment:

For the oral report, you and your fellow presenters had to come to some sort of consensus in order to provide a cohesive presentation. But what do **you** think, or how was your thinking affected by the discussion that took place leading up to the presentation or during the presentation?

This paper is to be a critique of some aspect of the matters discovered for the oral presentation, bringing in the materials provided by other group members (though with your having to look at some of the materials now), bringing in the kinds of questions or observation that were provided by your peers. And most importantly, the critique is to bring in your analysis and findings of the aspect of the issue you are focusing on.

By "aspect" I mean that you are not to rehash all that took place in the oral report. Rather, you should focus on, say, the reception to the issue at the time it was hot (its heyday); or maybe you would focus on how articles and experts are thinking of the issue these days, how that's different from (or not) its initial reception and what that difference (or lack of difference) suggests about the current state of affairs surrounding that issue; or maybe you want to focus on the present, ongoing significance of the issue, in light of its history. The critique might be best centered on the question "Why is this still important (or Why is this no longer important)?

The format should follow (but is not confined to) the classic critique:

    a) intro
    b) review of the literature
    c) analysis
    d) significance/implications

As always, avoid appearing dogmatic and doctrinaire. Seek the voice of reasonableness in this paper while remaining committed to a particular point of view.

How annotations annote in an Annotated Bibliography (MLA)

Silber, Patricia. "Teaching Written English as a Second Language." *College Composition and Communication* 30 (1979): 296–300.

Because most remedial writers are more proficient in oral discourse than in written and because speaking and writing differ markedly, efforts to teach remedial writing should appropriate methods from foreign language teaching. Silber lists three areas in which this form of dialect interference is most apparent.

Simmons, Jo An McQuire. "The One-to-One Method of Teaching Composition." *College Composition and Communication* 35 (1984): 222–29.

Simmons lists the assumptions and rationale of Roger Garrison's conference method of teaching composition; she describes the procedures and the advantages of his course as well the disadvantages. She includes a list of resources.

Troyka, Lynn Quitman. "Classical Rhetoric and the Basic Writer." *Essays on Classical Rhetoric and Modern Discourse.* Eds. Robert J. Connors, Lisa S. Ede, and Andrea Lunsford. Carbondale: Southern Illinois UP, 1984. 193–202.

Because Basic Writers do not assume learning will occur, they need to be engaged in the overall learning process; classical rhetoric helps Basic Writers because of its emphasis on the whole, its deductive approach, and its emphasis on the power of language.

Assignment #5

6 December—An informal presentation on research, findings, and tentative conclusions.

11 December—An in-class writing

Background

We will have seen that fairy tales and fables are often ways to instruct children on the ways of proper behavior. But we have also seen that what is "proper" reflects particular ways of seeing the world, sometimes ways that some would say might need changes that are reflected in the language used and the ways in which the language is presented (the genre). We have seen authors who have tried to present alternative readings of fairy tales. And I've noted that there are even literary critics and others who devote time and energy to discussing the ways that particular fairy tales or fables reflect social or psychological concerns, the critics using the elevated language of the university.

The Assignment

1. As a group, decide on a particular fairy tale or fable.
2. Go to the library and find stuff on that tale.
3. Discuss the published views and your own (**only rule for your own view: you can't say this is just entertainment for kids**)—always with an eye on the language-as-language.
4. Tell the class what you found and what y'all thought (informal, 6 Dec).

5. Write a paper providing a reasoned response. In other words, using the readings you and others in your group have done and the discussions your group has had about those readings, what seems to you to be a viable way of looking at that particular fable or fairy tale? Keep in mind the viable way can be something entirely different from all others' views (except for the one rule). And keep in mind the major thrust of this class—language.

11 Looking into Writing-about-Writing Classrooms

Elizabeth Wardle and Doug Downs

This chapter primarily focuses on how we each go about enacting the composition pedagogy that we have been advocating for some years now, a "writing studies" or "writing-about-writing" approach that takes declarative and procedural knowledge about writing as the content of the course, and that regards helping students think and learn *about writing* as the appropriate goal of the course (rather than teaching students *how to write*). However, in order to make the best use of our "how do we do this?" discussion, it is essential to start with our rationale for teaching this way. Our pedagogy relies on a set of particular beliefs about the nature of writing that, in turn, impacts what we believe a first-year composition course can and should do. This chapter begins by briefly laying out our understanding of the nature of writing. Then, in light of the understanding we outline, we briefly describe what we believe the role and objectives of first-year composition should be. We then spend the majority of the chapter describing how these beliefs about writing and the goals of composition are enacted in our own classrooms, using a dialogic approach to emphasize areas of similarity and difference.

OUR UNDERSTANDING OF THE NATURE OF WRITING

We understand writing as a process of composing (inventing and designing) and inscribing (arranging and recording on some medium) a language-using text (Prior). Writing processes are unique to a given group of writers and readers in a given writing situation, involving phases of goal-setting, planning, formulation, and controlling (e.g., a feedback/revision loop) (Perrin and Wildi). These phases typically overlap and produce the composing effect Ann Berthoff calls "allatonceness." Because inscription requires use of tools (and because composition is often aided by them), writing is unavoidably technological.

Writing is a kind of symbolic human interaction (the symbols being linguistic), and because such interaction is inherently rhetorical, we understand writing to be a rhetorical activity, meaning that it is *situated, motivated, contingent, material* or *embodied*, and *epistemic*. By unpacking each of these terms, we end up with a reasonably thorough description of our understanding of "the nature of writing."

First, writing is *situated* in specific contexts and reasons-for-being that are unique to each act of writing. Writing is driven by exigence: people do not write unless some need exists for the writing they're producing (including writing produced to fulfill a private, psychological need for self-expression). Meaning, convention, form, and success of texts are dependent on, influenced by, and in return, always influence the communities, systems, and groups whose work is mediated by them. Our two dominant ways of understanding this social dimension of exigence are in terms of activity, where writing is a tool used by groups of people to help accomplish some task, and also in terms of genre, where recurrent forms of writing are dynamically shaped by the situation. To say that writing is situated is to say that a text is understood differently when taken out of the context in which rhetors originally produce and read it; stated another way, what a text means and how it is composed and produced will inevitably depend on the context and circumstances in which it is composed and read.

Second, because writing is situation- and exigence-driven, it follows that it is *motivated*: Rhetors have motives for writing what they write and how they write it, and also for reading texts in the ways they do. The production of texts and the meanings rhetors make for them, then, unavoidably depend on motivations. Because there is no unmotivated writing, there is no objective, neutral, unbiased, or impartial writing or text.

Third, given that writing is situated and motivated, its nature and processes are therefore *contingent* on the rhetorical situation and the motives that situation encompasses. The answer to any question about how a text "ought to be" is: "It depends." Because the shape and quality of a text are contingent on a situation and its conventions, there are almost no universal, "hard-and-fast" rules available for how to write.

Instead, the common ground we find across writing situations—the guidelines and principles writers constantly begin with and return to—are *questions*. What is the exigence for what you're writing? What do you need it to accomplish? How will readers use it? What are readers' expectations for what you're writing, and what are their values for what will make your text "good"? How do those values arise from the activity the text is meant to help accomplish? What genre does the situation suggest or require, what are the typical elements of that genre, and what modifications does this situation suggest for that pattern? What conventions—from word choice to design to style and mechanics—should the text follow? These and other questions are the most stable, "universal" aspect of writing.

Fourth, writing is *material* (as rhetoric itself is *embodied*). Because writing is in one sense a recording of *ideas,* it's easy to lose sight of how writing actually plays out on material objects and how it results from material (not just ideational) labor. It is this aspect of writing's nature that is most closely associated with its technological aspect. Writers are proficient with certain kinds of material practices and objects, and usually we understand that the wider a range of materials a writer can work with, the greater their ability as a writer. To write is to be able to work with the technologies and materials of writing.

Lastly, writing is *epistemic,* by which we mean that writing is an activity that generates new knowledge. That statement may seem unremarkable until we recognize that in most corners of Western culture, writing is understood more as the recording of *existing* knowledge: First we learn something, then we "write it down"; or, first we do research and reach findings and conclusions, and then we "write up" our research, the implication being that we learn nothing new during and through the act of writing itself. In this way of thinking, only the *inscribing* aspect of writing is noted; the *composing* aspect of writing is elided. In both theory and practice, we find that writing is generative, not simply scribal. In theory, we believe that what people experience as reality constitutes and is constituted by language: How we understand our world depends in large measure on the language we use to describe and talk about it, so that our expressive choices generate (understandings of) reality. In practice, writers find that the act of "writing down" the ideas they already have usually gives them ideas they didn't have before. That writing is epistemic has direct implications for how writers experience the act of writing. Because the process of writing is one not only of recording ideas, but also of having them, texts develop iteratively through revision, each new version incorporating ideas gained during the writing and reading of preceding versions. Revision is not the punitive act of "fixing" poorly done writing, but the inevitable, inherent, *healthy* process of developing the text from the beginning.

To summarize, we understand writing as a complex, situational activity in which a writer, in collaboration with other writers and readers, simultaneously and iteratively manages the development of ideas, the choice of the most fitting language related to those ideas, the design of the text to be inscribed, and the production of the text itself—all in response to and formation of a situation that creates particular constraints, conventions, and demands for the text, to the end of creating texts readers will use to accomplish particular activities, and which texts, in turn, continue to shape future situations, activities, and texts.

We take as axiomatic that people's behaviors are shaped by their conceptions of what is appropriate to do in a given situation, and by their perceptions of that situation. What we do in any given moment depends on what we think we are supposed to be doing—what the moment calls for and what seems to be the best way to meet that call. We might say, in other words, that how one plays the game depends on what game one thinks one is playing. When we apply this principle to writing, it is clear that the story we tell ourselves about the nature of writing—our conceptions of what writing is and how it ought to work—will powerfully shape how we go about doing it.

The Role and Objectives of First-Year Composition

Given these beliefs about what writing is and how it works, the purposes and, indeed, the very existence of first-year composition become deeply problematic. From its inception, this course has been imagined as existing for the sole purpose of "teaching students to write" in general: for no audience or purpose in particular, but instead for any future audience or purpose in general. Its purpose has long been understood by college administrators and faculty across the country as 1) correcting faults in previous learning as evidenced by mechanical errors in students' writing, and 2) preparing students for the rigors of "college writing," which is taken to be an undifferentiated, academic writing that David Russell has called "universal educated discourse" (60). In both functions, college writing instruction is essentially an inoculation: a one-shot, "fix it all now," get-it-out-of-the-way attempt to treat writing as a basic, fundamental, universal skill that can be permanently mastered. Further, composition is usually taught by teachers with training in one particular set of disciplinary practices and purposes (i.e., English Studies, broadly understood). Its content—once literature, later student texts, later cultural studies, sometimes anything at all—is understood not as central to the course, but as an occasion to practice writing and attempt various forms of writing (or, sometimes, to encourage "critical consciousness" about issues of race, class, or gender, for example).

The ability of such a "general" writing course to accomplish any useful, long-term, writing-related goal is called into question if we accept that writing is situation- and exigence-driven, and that the motivations of rhetors deeply impact the production and meaning of texts. This concern is not new. Indeed, entire volumes have been devoted to it (see Petraglia, for example), along with critiques such as Wardle's of genres assigned in such courses ("'Mutt Genres'").

We could say much more about why the beliefs about writing we have outlined call first-year composition into question; but, for the purposes of this chapter, suffice it to say that we accept that first-year composition cannot accomplish the goals it was created to accomplish. In our own classrooms, we have laid those goals to rest. Instead, we imagine first-year composition as only an entry point to a comprehensive, vertical writing education that extends across students' time in college (and not only in the classroom), and we believe that part of our role as writing scholars and writing program administrators is to advocate for the creation of such vertical writing structures at our institutions so that composition can fulfill a more realistic and ultimately more useful role. If composition is understood as an entry point rather than as an inoculation, it can focus on accomplishing an obtainable goal that lays groundwork for the remainder of students' writing education: *teaching students flexible and transferable declarative and procedural knowledge about writing.* Such a course can focus on broadening students' conceptions of what writing is: helping them see texts as tools collaboratively produced and used in communities of practice; understanding writing as generative, not merely scribal; experiencing writing as situated and thus contingent rather than rule-driven; understanding genres as dynamic rather than fixed, rigid forms; and considering writing expertise as being both developed over time and situational, rather than universal. Finally, and perhaps most difficult, an effective first-year composition class can enforce accurate conceptions of writing through its pedagogical procedures. For example, in addition to teaching students that genres are flexible responses to recurring rhetorical situations (declarative knowledge), assignment descriptions and scaffolding themselves treat genres this way, and ask students to engage in activities that reflect such an understanding of genre (procedural knowledge).

Approaches that take up these goals have come to be labeled as "writing-about-writing" composition courses. Yet, the fact that these goals have garnered a name should not lead readers to conclude that there is only one way to enact them. To the contrary, there are many ways to enact a classroom with these as stated goals. In our own classes, we often find ourselves changing approaches, assignments, sequences, and activities (not to mention readings), depending on the students in the class, our recent experiences, and the work we have seen our colleagues doing in their own classrooms and programs via the Conference on College Composition and Communication (CCCC) Writing-about-Writing SIG and the related Ning, listserv, and newsletter. We want to stress this point because we have often heard colleagues talk about *the* Wardle and Downs curriculum. We see a writing-focused approach as an end, with many possible means and, even in our own classrooms, we do not enact one, static curriculum over time. In the next section, we discuss some of our own teaching practices for writing-about-writing courses, but we want to be clear that we are *not advocating one way* to reach the goals described above. Rather, we illustrate *some ways* that we have been recently enacting the pedagogy.

ENACTING A WRITING-ABOUT-WRITING PEDAGOGY: A DIALOGIC OVERVIEW

We are not one person; we are very dissimilar in many respects, as anyone who has ever met us both can attest. In fact, we have never taught at the same school, or even observed one another teach. So writing one chapter about how we conduct "our classroom" has been a challenging experience (please pardon this moment of meta-commentary). As we've talked over our classroom practices for this project, we've come to recognize a number of shared philosophies and practices, as well as some areas where we were surprised to learn of some deep-seated beliefs and practices where we differ. To be as fair to our differences as we can, while still abiding by the constraint of length for this book chapter, in this section we discuss some of the major areas of importance to our teaching: designing a course around outcomes, giving thorough assignments and using modeling (or not), deeply integrating reading into a writing course, and using writing as a means of learning, whether through in-class or out-of-class writing. When we come to places in the text where we need to speak in separate voices, we break out into individual, dialogic exchanges.

Outcomes. Regardless of differences in our daily classrooms and on some philosophical issues, we share a deep agreement about the purposes and desired outcomes of our first-year composition classrooms, as the previous discussion suggests. Our primary goal is for students to gain flexible and transferable declarative and procedural knowledge about writing. We both find this goal made more achievable by the fact that students come to our classes with extensive experience as readers and writers in and out of school, and with many questions and ideas about their experiences. Their ideas, coupled with additional, declarative knowledge about writing, can benefit all of us—including the teachers and scholars who often talk about students rather than dialoging with them. (See Downs and Wardle, 2010, for more on what we believe first-year students can contribute.)

This larger goal is broken down into smaller objectives that can be explicitly listed as we draft the course syllabus. These include helping students broaden their conceptions of what writing is and how it is done, thinking explicitly about the affordances and constraints for the writing they face, seeing themselves as writers, understanding the contributive and conversational nature of both reading and writing, and understanding writing rhetorically. We also share a desire to help students create and explore open research questions about writing and learn how to engage in the "moves" of academic inquiry.

As a result, much of the classroom apparatus we design to help students achieve these outcomes uses writing-to-learn activities of various sorts. We both design our assignments, reading lists, and classroom activities to reach forward toward the outcomes, and we try to sequence activities so that students are scaffolded into learning and building toward the skills and experiences needed to engage in the next activity and achieve each outcome. One example of this type of scaffolding is illustrated in our 2007 article in *College Composition and Communication (CCC)*, where we teach invention and move through source searching, summarizing, synthesizing, and data collection and analysis. But many such scaffolded sequences are possible.

Elizabeth. As I design the assignments at the beginning of the semester, I focus very much on writing to learn: What are we reading and talking and thinking about that I would like students to explore further in writing? Given the topics and learning at hand, what should those assignments look like? In a recent semester, I loosened up the structure we described in *CCC* so that students had more time for invention, and I assigned multiple "Thought Documents" that students shared with me and also with one another. They also blogged, did research and analysis together in class and posted about it on the class blog and in EverNote. Eventually, they got to a class project. The assignments weren't really "the thing" in 1102, the second of our two required FYC courses, but rather the impetus for making the moves that people make when they really want to learn more about something, as this was a primary course outcome. In 1101, our first required course, I have a similar philosophy: Help students use the writing assignments as a way of learning about the ideas under discussion. They might explore their own writing processes or those of others and write narratives about them, analyses of the data they collect, or they might even compose more multimedia (even documentary) descriptions of what they learn. They might conduct their own discourse community ethnographies, or they might take up a theoretical point and argue with Swales, Gee, and Harris based on their own experiences. Again, the assignment forms are not "the thing," but are a means of exploring ideas and learning declarative concepts about writing that can help expand their conceptions of writers and of writing.

Doug. Like Elizabeth, I see every shred of writing students do as connecting to one or another learning outcome. For me, many of these outcomes are essentially about shifting students from existing misconceptions of writing to more accurate or usable conceptions. So I find that I design course activities and assignment sequences to explicitly try to connect with and complicate those misconceptions. For example, students often believe that knowledge is simply given, rather than constructed, and they don't connect research to the very real people whose curiosity led them to conduct it and share their findings with others.

My students' experiences with texts and research tend to have been fairly limited, and their ideas about writers tend to come straight from fantasy: that good writers are people for whom writing is quick and easy. So I try to design assignments that speak to these ideas and experiences so that engaging in a given assignment creates the experience that guides students to think about a given conception and offers evidence that might re-shape it.

For example, I can combine a reading like Margaret Kantz's "Helping Students Use Textual Sources Persuasively" with a prompt for a short response writing that asks, "Which of the students in Kantz's article do you most identify with, and why?" Writing that response has students reflect on their previous experience and their current thinking as it relates to course outcomes like understanding writing rhetorically or understanding the conversational nature of reading and writing.

Assignments and Modeling. Starting from outcomes and working backwards to design the class helps us keep in mind a central principle we draw from Erika Lindemann and Daniel Anderson's *A Rhetoric for Writing Teachers*: For any given assignment, find out what knowledges, abilities, and rhetorical moves it will demand, and then make a specific plan for teaching each of those to students. We both tend to write fairly comprehensive assignment sheets (from one to two single-spaced pages) that serve not only as guides for students, but also as reminders for us about what we should teach, how we should respond to drafts, and how we should assess final texts. We give specific rationales for an assignment, describe its goals, and provide a narrative description of how to accomplish the assignment (usually in phases over time, a nod to our desire to emulate as much as possible the ways that working writers really work, outside of school settings; see Appendix 1 for examples of two assignments).

We use writing assignments—small and large, low stakes and high stakes—as learning tools throughout the class, emerging from the purposes and content under consideration. Because content is central to the course, writing in the classroom can function as it does in many other fields: as a means of learning concepts and ideas, demonstrating that knowledge, sharing it with others, and contributing to the conversation on those ideas. Our response to such writing-to-learn assignments helps students learn both procedural and declarative knowledge about writing, rather than serving as error correction or editing.

When giving assignments, we encourage students to consider what "working writers" actually do in varying situations, and to reflect on how they might engage in relevant and useful practices themselves; we strive to avoid teaching a sterile, formulaic process that fails to reflect actual writerly practices. This strategy influences everything from the openness of assignment design (for example, not requiring a specific number of sources, since no working writer sets out to write an article with an exact number of sources) and to process requirements (for example, not requiring a specific number of revisions or a particular invention and drafting process, since these are always situation-, text-, and writer-dependent).

Yet we find that no matter how carefully scaffolded assignment sequences are, and no matter how clearly assignment sheets are written, writing assignments never really "rest." Different students struggle with different skills or ideas required in an assignment, and we struggle to find a happy balance between model or target texts that aid writing and formulaic examples that reify genres or reduce them to modes.

Doug. Most of our divergence here goes to models, which we discuss shortly, but I want to make a point on writing-to-learn versus writing-to-communicate. The introduction suggests that we consider the majority of writing in our classes to be writing-to-learn, but I'm not sure that's true for me. In my classes, some of the main assignments, like a literacy narrative or a writing self-study, are essentially written for students themselves—for their own self-reflection and learning. The assignments are not framed as writing that helps anyone else accomplish anything else (thus, "writing-to-learn.") Other assignments, particularly research reports that culminate in half-semester or full-semester projects that also involve primary research, are explicitly framed as intended to generate and share knowledge with other researchers. The best of them, for example, could be submitted to *Young Scholars in Writing* or similar venues.

My sense is that I use a few more communication-based assignments, and a few less learning-based assignments than you, Elizabeth, and this might parallel differences in how we handle genre and modeling. At the same time, I hesitate to make too much of a dichotomy between learning-writing and communicating-writing. It's a writing course; ultimately, it's all "writing to learn." Still, I'm intrigued by the different teaching demands the two kinds of projects tend to create.

Elizabeth. Doug, I think you are on to something when you question the dichotomy between writing-to-learn and writing-to-communicate. I am coming to see these as inextricably intertwined in a class about writing, both declaratively and procedurally. I start with the learning aspect, because what will students communicate if they aren't first learning something, engaging in a conversation about something? So, I offer many smaller assignments that are primarily used for learning and thinking, but those almost invariably morph into communicating—with me, with peers, with the conversation they are reading and thinking about, and possibly for an audience like *Young Scholars in Writing* or our University of Central Florida (UCF) publication, *Stylus*.

This complication of learning and communicating might account for some of why I have struggled for many years to find a balance between giving models of text types that can serve as aids and guideposts, without sliding into assignments that make a particular genre sound formalistic and reified. In a composition class that is supposed to be a bridge to writing elsewhere, this latter practice is especially dangerous. Students are being told, implicitly and otherwise, that what they are learning will help them and will apply somewhere else. If the assignments are for learning and engaging with others around that learning, then we must be cautious of stunting that learning too soon with examples of rigid text types. Equally as important, if we assign a text with rigid and formulaic expectations (like a "report" or a "research paper" or a "memoir") and then students run into a text with the same name but different conventions elsewhere, we have undermined the credibility of anything we might have told them. If part of what we tell students is that genres are flexible responses to recurring rhetorical situations, but what we show them is quite the contrary, we confuse and frustrate them as well as undermine the declarative concepts we try to teach them.

I try to contextualize and complicate every assignment in my own classroom: How many sources? It depends. How long? It depends. What citation style? It depends. Students discuss why it depends and how they can make a good choice, since they have to make a choice (and then defend it). If I assign a literature review, for example, we look at a lot of examples of literature reviews and figure out where they show up. We examine other texts that a literature review is similar to.

We talk about other names it might go by, and what they can learn from writing one that could be re-purposed later, even if they never write another literature review.

Doug. I like what you say in that last point about showing lots of kinds of models. That is part of the reason I'm apparently not as conflicted as you are on this question. Writers need "goal texts"—they've got to be able to visualize an image of what they're trying to create. To the extent that we are, one, asking them to do activities they have never even imagined before, or, two, struggling to get them re-conceptualizing genres they're already familiar with, we've got to show them something of what's possible. Thus, models are a central pillar of my writing courses. I find that showing students multiple models that are quite different from one another not only reduces the possibility of formulizing the genre, it also quite strongly makes the very point that genres are flexible responses to a rhetorical situation; they are *dynamic* and new every time.

It's definitely a challenge to help students understand models not as "directions" or recipes, but only as instances of how an assignment has been done before, each with a unique set of strengths and weaknesses, admirable and unfortunate aspects and features. I may assign students to read models prior to class discussion, or have them read them live, in the classroom (displayed on-screen), and I typically present models in a "strengths and weaknesses" framework. Doing so helps students see good things to do and good things not to do. I often blend professional models and student models: professional writers tend to model specific processes or approaches well, while previous students have created multiply-revised, fairly polished versions of the specific assignment and documents I ask students to create.

Elizabeth. Just to be clear, I do work with examples, but I tend to back into them rather than start with them. The longer I teach, the more meta-discussion my classes have about what they are trying to accomplish, with whom, and what genres and conventions could help students in accomplishing their communicative purposes—all before I ever provide a model or sample text of any sort. During these analyses, students sometimes hit on genres that are fairly common and have consistent conventions across situations. Other times, they point out that the world is changing, and the genre they need doesn't quite exist yet. Last semester, one student, Joe, explored the impact of technology on writing via observed writing tasks, writing logs, and interviews. During our discussion of purposes and conventions, he very rightly pointed out that a simple, text-based article would not nearly be as rich for readers as would an interactive, online article that allowed readers to see sample texts, listen to parts of the interview, and examine the writers' logs. Had I simply provided a couple of traditional model texts at the beginning of the assignment, I might have closed off the students' thinking, and Joe might have never considered that new technologies and research methods could converge to create new hybrid genres.

I've also watched teachers teach an assignment that is really a writing-to-learn assignment—such as a writing autoethnography, a genre that doesn't really exist anywhere in the world, and doesn't need to look one particular way—and, over time, those teachers have taught the assignment so often that it starts to look reified and static. If one goal of the course is to help students understand the contextual nature of writing and the stabilized-for-now nature of genres (thank you, Cathrine Schryer), then the message of such a static and rigid assignment with "models" from previous students completely undermines this message and keeps students from achieving a primary outcome of the class.

I think models are useful and necessary, but that they also have the potential to completely undermine the entire message of a writing-about-writing classroom. "Use models with caution and a large dose of meta-reflection," is my mantra.

Doug. My mantra on this issue tends to be: "Surprise me!" I completely concur that, even as we use models, we have to help students think beyond them. That is extremely difficult. Never, *ever*, in my classrooms do we work with a model without me saying, "Remember, this is not *what you are supposed to do*. This is *a way this has been done*." Saying this lets us talk about the difference. For this reason, I also shy away from the "best" possible models I've seen or can imagine—I usually show pieces that can be improved, and then help students figure out how. We usually take class time to revise and edit a model, with me asking students, "How could this be better? What would you have done on this problem?" The resulting conversations are productive. The few times I use an exceptionally good model, I pair it with a weaker one to, again, teach by comparison.

Ultimately, I never work without models (except on brand-new assignments; I very rarely use the teacher trick of writing a version myself), but I simultaneously try to help students see what the models don't show and what I don't know about the assignment. This brings us back to the exploratory element of the course: When students ask how an aspect of a piece should be, I most often tell them, "I won't know that for sure until I see what you all write—then I'll find out some things that seem to work, some that don't, and I'll feed that back to all of you to consider as you write the next version of your piece." Students seem more comfortable with that kind of non-direction, especially if it's accompanied by models that show them past approaches to an assignment.

Reading. We both ask students to engage with rigorous texts about writing. This is not because we focus on reading over writing, but rather to help students use those texts to learn relevant and transferable declarative knowledge about writing. Such texts also provide students with jumping off points to explore their own experiences, sites of expertise, and pressing questions about writing. In addition, assigning such readings demonstrates that writers, particularly in a college setting, are always interacting with texts and streams of data (some of them difficult to make sense of initially), and are always finding ways to use and respond to them. We recognize that within a traditional process paradigm, an easy objection to a reading- and discussion-based class is that one doesn't learn writing by talking about writing, but *by writing*. While we agree that students do need to learn about writing by writing, we disagree that talking about writing is unhelpful. As we've already indicated, we see teaching declarative knowledge about writing as central to our classrooms. Such declarative knowledge is learned, at least partially, through reading content that students themselves cannot provide: carefully researched, specialized knowledge about the nature of writing, writers, and writing processes; tales of professional writers writing; and content accessed via scholarly and professional texts.

As with every other aspect of the course, when choosing readings we start with our desired outcomes and consider how to help students achieve those outcomes. A wide range of texts work in the approach. We've used, for example, John Dawkins's "Teaching Punctuation as a Rhteorical Tool," Shirley Brice Heath's "Protean Shapes in Literacy Events," Tony Mirabelli's "Learning to Serve: The Language and Literacy of Food Service Workers," and Christina Haas and Linda Flower's "Rhetorical Reading Strategies and the Construction of Meaning."

✓ check out

(For a longer list of texts we use, see our textbook, *Writing about Writing: A College Reader.*)

We both build explicit reading instruction and assessment of reading abilities into our classrooms, recognizing that most students have not received such instruction for many years. (Doug has written elsewhere (see "Teaching First Year Writers to *Use* Texts") on principles for getting and keeping students reading difficult scholarly work that is well beyond their understanding.) We spend time specifically talking about how to read a kind of text students have rarely encountered before, and we practice some reading "moves" with the entire class. For example, we ask students, in small groups, to identify Swales' three introductory moves in an article they have all read. We provide pre-reading support (e.g., definitions of key terms and jargon, a preview of the problem the reading addresses), hold students accountable, and check for comprehension through written reading responses of about one to two pages, or through in-class writing that responds to focused questions and prompts to help students learn where to focus on a reading. We also have realistic expectations for what first-year students can achieve when reading difficult scholarly texts. The readings provide some language that hooks into ideas that can help students in their daily lives and that they can interpret in light of their own personal experiences. Thus, it's okay if they don't get every detailed nuance of Brandt's "Sponsors of Literacy," for example. They need to get the concept of literacy sponsorship and what that means and looks like for them and for other students, and they need to consider the implications of the very different kinds of sponsorship different students have had. Most important here is that we consciously teach students that what we do as readers is to test statements that writers make against our own prior knowledge and lived experience, and that, as readers, we have the right to call shenanigans when a text fails to match (or help us understand) our experience.

Despite all these shared goals and practices, we do not use the same readings, nor do we always even use readings from our own book.

Elizabeth. As I choose readings, I want to tap into recent scholarship about writing that might appeal to students, and also respond to some of the problems or ideas my students have had during the previous few semesters. In one recent semester, I wanted to help students broaden their conceptions of what writing is and how it is done, and get students thinking explicitly about the affordances and constraints for the writing that they face now and will face in the future. Discussing the technologies of writing has been a good way into this conversation because, as soon as we start talking about Facebook or texting, students immediately imagine writing in a broader way than they had before. I've also found that some students really latch on to discourse communities or activity systems as helpful, explanatory theories for what they have experienced but have been unable to explain in their writing lives. Sometimes, students very much want to talk about issues of identity, authority, and power in their writing lives. Other times, they don't. I usually start with a set of readings that I think will meet students where they are and will get them talking and thinking. I adjust the readings as frequently as necessary to go where the students' questions, ideas, and expertise take them. Recently, I started with the Stanford and WIDE studies of writing (Grabill), a chapter by Danielle DeVoss, an article by Kevin Roozen, and a thesis chapter by one of my MA students, Autumn Shrum, who was finishing up case studies of student writers at UCF. While I expected students to latch on to the technologies of writing, most were far more interested in Roozen and Shrum's findings, so we added readings about discourse communities, genre theory, identity, and authority during the semester.

Doug. It really is interesting to see where students' interests tend to land, among the readings I ask them to encounter. I'm not as flexible in my reading list as you're describing, Liz. I wind up keying readings pretty tightly to assignments, and because the assignment list is fixed when the semester begins, the readings tend to stay so, too.

The obvious challenge this creates is, as you say, meeting students where they are; that gets trickier when the reading list won't necessarily follow students' intrinsic interests. In lieu of that flexibility, I find myself working a lot with rationales (e.g., "Why would I ask you to read this piece, at this time, in a course like this, when we all know it would bore you silly?") and, in any given reading, stretching the envelope of what ideas can be developed from that reading. I find that a lot of my classroom work in discussing readings is in taking students from wherever they start from in a reading and helping them see the connections I want them to see in the piece.

An example is a frequent student reaction to Robert Tierney and David Pearson's "Toward a Composing Model of Reading." The reason I assign the piece is to help students begin to see writing and reading

Look up

as two expressions of the same textual activity, endlessly intertwined and relying on surprisingly similar strategies. This is usually students' first encounter with reading scientists who say, flat out, that individual readers construct individual readings of a text, and why. (They explain a psycholinguistic, schema-based model of textual processing.) Students frequently descend, then, into unrestrained relativism—people can interpret texts "any way they want to," and thus what people take from students' own writing is "completely up to them." When many students in a class take this meaning from the reading, our class discussion of it definitely starts from where they are and will explore the possibilities of what's interesting to them about this reading; but of course I work to help the discussion call into question overly relativistic interpretations of the legitimacy of relativism while, at the same time, try to make sure my own "here's what's important" points are made.

I add here that students are often most interested in the technology and literacy/discourse readings and that I must work a little harder to get them interested in the writing process readings with which I originally began teaching the course and still, to some extent, use (though I tend to use fewer than I used to). I also find myself using almost no purely theoretical readings—students handle empirical work much better because it tends to be more grounded and readable for them.

How Writing Is Used In and Out of the Classroom. Since the beginnings of the process movement in the early 1970s, composition pedagogy has tended to split writing instruction into two camps: one camp concerned mostly with *what is written about*, and another camp concerned mostly with *"how to write"*—*how writing happens and comes to be.* Richard Fulkerson articulates four axiologies or paradigms for writing instruction that break along these lines: mimetic and critical/cultural studies courses that focus on using writing to learn particular subject matter; and expressivist and rhetorical courses that emphasize personal writing processes and how to write convincingly for audiences, respectively. (Fulkerson also describes a fifth, "formalist" axiology that is irrelevant to our dialogue here.) Using student writing in the classroom—both reading it and writing it there, using classroom time—has tended to be a hallmark of the expressivist and rhetorical approaches, while mimetic and CCS approaches tend to focus more on other writers' texts.

We find it interesting to look at our own uses of student writing in the classroom through this lens, because the results are more mixed than might be predicted. We have previously suggested that writing-about-writing integrates Fulkerson's mimetic, rhetorical, and expressivist axiologies (see Downs and Wardle, "Re-imagining the Nature of FYC"). Its focus on content—in this case writing studies—is its mimetic aspect; yet, as we compare our uses of writing in the classroom, we find ourselves making the same uses of student writing as do expressivist and rhetorical approaches. We don't, though, go about it in quite the same ways.

Elizabeth. In my classroom, we try lots of activities with writing in class that we also reflect on. I'm sure this is linked to what I said earlier about writing to learn both procedural and declarative knowledge about writing. We write homework and we freewrite; we share ideas with partners, who write them down and give them back to us; we use recordings to get our ideas out; we write in the dark to practice getting ideas out without correction; and, sometimes, we even practice yoga breathing before we write. These are definitely strategies reminiscent of expressivist writing classrooms, but I find this focus on invention is every bit as necessary in a truly rhetorical writing-about-writing classroom. Expressivist invention is part of the process, not an endpoint, as it might be in an expressivist classroom.

Doug. I'm again sensitive to the risk a writing course takes by spending too much time talking about writing and not enough time *writing*. My students are the first to say that there's no shortage of writing in my writing courses. I find equally great value in talk about writing, because it lets me get at the being and nature of writing in ways that simply writing cannot. So there's no denying that my classrooms can look pretty barren of the activity of writing itself; I have the vast majority of the writing happen out of class to save time in class for talking about writing. However, a recent wildcard here is online discussion boards, where "talk about" writing happens in writing, outside of class. Then, in class, we display that writing and talk about it.

Elizabeth. I was surprised to learn this about your classroom, actually. I certainly share your sense that talk about writing is very important, but I make sure that the writing happens in class as well as out of class, because I'm just not sure students would try some of the things I want them to try unless we do them together. (Will they really go home, turn out the lights, and do some yoga breathing before they write as a homework exercise?). I take your point, though. The discussions *about* all these in-class writing activities are very important. We can't just do them and then not reflect on why we did them and on what happened (more meta is very important to me because of its apparent role in transfer of knowledge). What is writing to learn? What is invention? What is low-stakes writing? What happened when you did this versus that? Would you do it again? When is it useful and when is it not? Every activity every day includes analysis and explanation of it, what we learned from it (or not), and how it relates to what we've been reading and discussing. This is writing about writing and discussion about writing, and because the reading content of the class is about writing, we are not side-tracked by discussions of the death penalty or of global warming.

Where and how does invention for your assignments come, if not via in-class writing?

Doug. I like this focus on invention because it seems to me to be one of the places where talk and writing most fluidly meld—when writers need most of all to be back and forth between (or in and amongst) both activities. When we're working on invention activities in class, I use either small-group brainstorming discussions (if we're starting from scratch) or, more often, small-group reading sessions of freewrites or thought pieces that students have already written outside of class. While I have students do a lot of reading and discussing each other's texts in class, it's pretty rare for me to have students use class time to do that initial writing. Those rare exceptions are moments with, for instance, a literacy narrative, where I give a short prompt, like "think back to the earliest writing you can remember, and describe that scene." I let students write for five to eight minutes on that and then, crucially, place students in groups and read what gets written. I don't do that too often, because that writing time *in the classroom* feels a little inefficient to me, compared with starting from a freewrite written earlier and using that writing as a basis for reading around and discussion.

Elizabeth. I can see why you might feel that putting a lot of written invention into class time might seem inefficient. I'm all for efficiency, but I find that the longer I teach, the more I loosen up on things I used to be pretty inflexible about—for example the reading list and use of class time to write and follow ideas. I'm guessing that this goes back to my increased focus on the writing-to-learn aspects of a composition class. All of my students' in-class writing is central to invention and writing to learn—a necessary step on the road to communicating and engaging in an ongoing conversation. We don't just engage in invention. We also talk about it a lot, and we explicitly discuss the concepts of writing to learn and low-stakes assignments as we work through ideas. We consider and try various processes that seem to work for students in the class (for learning and for drafting), for other writers we read about, and even for me.

This is directly linked to the role of what is generally called "peer review." I am leery of a calendar that has one day for peer review, and then teacher reads and then grade. I couldn't produce an extended written document like that, so I don't ask students to do so. We try to unpack and lay bare all the ways that writers plan and invent long before the pen hits the page (or the fingers hit the keyboard) on the document. We talk about these things, but we also do them together. After readings and class discussions, we consider an upcoming assignment and spend a few minutes freewriting or brainstorming together ways to attack that assignment or arguments that might be made in the assignment. I try to ensure that by the time an official drafting day comes around, students have notebooks or blogs or EverNote notebooks full of ideas and snippets of text. Their minds have been mulling things over long before the assignment "draft" needs to be written. Peer review is not so much review as invention. Pairs might talk about their ideas and write them down for each other, or pairs might work on parts of a developing draft, asking, "Is this idea interesting? Where is it going? What would you say about this?"

Doug. I am right there with you on peer review as invention work even more than as revision work. I've always sort of abhorred the term *peer review* in part because "review" sounds, to me, like "I'm checking what you've done." Instead, if I use instead a term like *reader response*, then I hear something more like "I'm experiencing what you're doing." It seems crucial to me to use students' texts in this way less for the *writer* and more for the *reader*. In reader response sessions, I emphasize that the first reason for the session is for readers of drafts to get ideas about what they ought to do in their own drafts. For the writer of the draft, formative feedback is actually a secondary consideration, mostly because we also emphasize that the reader isn't responsible for improving the paper—the writer does that. The reader simply helps the writer know where and what to work on by relating the reader's experience of encountering the writing.

Those reading response sessions, by the way, are "emergent" in my classrooms. I mean that, within those goals for the sessions I just recounted, students run the show about what to look for in the texts. I've never quite been able to bring myself to go into the session with a pre-made reading rubric for students to work through, though I've seen other faculty use such reading guides to great effect. Rather, we start the session with "harrowing tales of drafting this nasty beast" (asking, "What was it like to try to write this?"), and then move to "So what do you need your readers to focus on as they read your piece?" or, in other words, "What are you concerned about with the piece right now?" That lets us construct a reading guide on the spot from actual writerly concerns that are specific to the particular writing experience.

Parting Thoughts

Our writing prompt for this chapter was something along the lines of, "So you talk a lot about teaching writing, but what is it actually like in *your* composition classrooms?" We hope our discussion here has provided some of that flavor. We conclude with these final reflections on our classrooms.

Doug. I really got in my groove with teaching college writing when I came to see that it is hard to screw up once you understand: (1) the point, and (2) how writers learn. The point is to change the way students have been taught, culturally and in previous education, to think about writing. Doing so changes the ways students go about writing. The way they're going to learn is by immersion in a world of writing, a world I and they collaborate on creating in our classroom, a world where we are ceaselessly reading and thinking and talking and writing about writing.

I say that writing-about-writing is hard to screw up because, within that ballpark, there really isn't a wrong way to do things; there are a practically infinite number of good ways. My daily teaching plan is typically quite general: It usually lists two to three main "segments" for the day, particular activities I intend for us to do during a given segment (e.g., "small group discussion on X," "whole-class edit of draft on-screen,"), and any key ideas (usually three or four) that I absolutely want to make sure come up during the day's discussion. It's almost never more specific than those few steering notes—and there are days, either through my own negligence or because I don't yet know what students have produced, where I have no teaching plan at all. What makes this comfort (with general planning and with letting the class unfold based on where students take it) possible is that I enter the classroom every day with the certainty that there is a world of writing to be discussed and reflected on, and that the corner of it we happen on that day doesn't matter—we can always learn something important about writing.

Elizabeth. Over time, I think that a move to a writing-about-writing approach has meant that I have increasingly turned my attention to writing to learn. When procedural and declarative knowledge about writing is the focus of the course, then writing about ideas about writing and using a variety of written practices to do so become natural and constant foci. For example, writing becomes a means not only of learning to write a particular genre, but also of learning about genres and why and how they function, come to be, and change. Not only that, but writing in any genre becomes a means of learning more about the ideas we've been reading and discussing; deciding on a genre in which to write becomes an exercise in learning about how to dialogue with interlocuters in a way that makes sense to them.

Several times recently, we have heard ourselves referred to as "post-process theorists," a term I feel the need to object to here, now that we've gone on at some length about the processes in our writing courses. Putting writing at the heart of a writing class leads to an ecological and theoretically sound sense of what writing is and how it works, including all of the possible processes that writers use to engage with ideas and with others. If this approach has to be labeled at all, I hope it can be labeled as a full return to the roots of rhetoric, where invention was central.

WORKS CITED

Berthoff, Ann. *The Sense of Learning*. Portsmouth: Boynton/Cook, 1990. Print.

Brandt, Deborah. "Sponsors of Literacy." *College Composition and Communication* 49 (1998): 165-85. Print.

Dawkins, John. "Teaching Punctuation as a Rhetorical Tool." *College Composition and Communication* 46 (1995): 533-48. Print.

Devoss, Danielle, Gail E. Hawisher, Charles Jackson, Joseph Johansen, Brittney Moraski, and Cynthia L. Selfe. "The Future of Literacy." *Literate Lives in the Information Age: Narratives of Literacy from the United States.* Ed. Cynthia Self and Gail Hawisher. Mahwah: Lawrence Earlbaum, 2004. 183-210. Print.

Downs, Doug. "Teaching First Year Writers to *Use* Texts: Scholarly Readings in Writing-about-Writing in First-Year Comp." *Reader: Essays in Reader-Oriented Theory, Criticism, and Pedagogy* 60 (2010): 19-50. Print.

Downs, Doug, and Elizabeth Wardle. "Re-imagining the Nature of FYC: Trends in Writing-about-Writing Pedagogies." *Exploring Composition Studies: Research, Scholarship, and Inquiry for the Twenty-First Century.* Ed. Kelly Ritter and Paul Kei Matsuda. Utah State UP, 2012, 123-44. Print.

—. "Teaching about Writing, Righting Misconceptions: (Re)Envisioning 'First-Year Composition' as 'Introduction to Writing Studies.'" *College Composition and Communication* 58 (2007): 552-84. Print.

—. "What Can a Novice Contribute? Undergraduate Researchers in First-Year Composition." *Undergraduate Research in English Studies.* Ed. Laurie Grobman and Joyce Kinead. Logan: Utah State UP, 2010. 173-90. Print.

Fulkerson, Richard. "Composition at the Turn of the Twenty-First Century." *College Composition and Communication* 56 (2005): 654-87. Print.

Grabill, Jeffrey, et al. "Revisualizing Composition: Mapping the Writing Lives of First-Year College Students." *Writing in Digital Environments Research Center*, 2010. Web. 3 Mar. 2012.

Haas, Christina, and Linda Flower. "Rhetorical Reading Strategies and the Construction of Meaning." *College Composition and Communication* 39 (1988): 167-83. Print.

Haven, Cynthia. "The New Literacy: Stanford Study Finds Richness and Complexity in Students' Writing." *Stanford University News Service.* 12 Oct., 2009. Web. 7 Mar. 2012.

Heath, Shirley Brice. "Protean Shapes in Literacy Events: Ever-shifting Oral and Literate Traditions." *Spoken and Written Language: Exploring Orality and Literacy.* Ed. D Tannen. Norwood: Ablex, 1982. 91-117. Print.

Lindemann, Erika, and Daniel Anderson. *A Rhetoric for Writing Teachers.* 4th ed. Oxford: Oxford University Press, 2001. Print.

Mirabelli, Tony. "Learning to Serve: The Language and Literacy of Food Service Workers." *What They Don't Learn in School.* Ed Jabari Mahiri. New York: Peter Lang, 2004. 143-62. Print.

Perrin, Daniel, and Marc Wildi. "Statistical Modeling of Writing Processes." *Traditions of Writing Research.* Ed. Chuck Bazerman et al. London: Routledge, 2010. 378-93. Print.

Petraglia, Joseph, ed. *Reconceiving Writing, Rethinking Writing Instruction.* Mahwah: Earlbaum, 1995. Print.

Prior, Paul. "Tracing Process: How Texts Come into Being." *What Writing Does and How It Does It: An Introduction to Analyzing Texts and Textual Practices.* Ed. Charles Bazerman and Paul Prior. Mahwah: Earlbaum, 2004. 167-200. Print.

Roozen, Kevin. "From Journals to Journalism: Tracing Trajectories of Literate Development." *College Composition and Communication* 60 (2009): 541-72. Print.

Russell, David R. "Activity Theory and Its Implications for Writing Instruction." *Reconceiving Writing, Rethinking Writing Instruction.* Ed. Joseph Petraglia. Mahwah: Earlbaum, 1995. 51-78. Print.

Shrum, Autumn. "Crossing Literate Worlds: Exploring How Students with Rich Identities as Writers Negotiate Multiple Writing Contexts." MA thesis. U of Central Florida, Orlando, 2011. Print.

Schryer, Catherine. "Genre and Power: A Chronotopic Analysis." *The Rhetoric and Ideology of Genre.* Eds. Richard Coe, Lorelei Lingard, and Tatiana Teslenko. Cresskill: Hampton, 2002. 73-102.

Tierney, Robert J., and David P. Pearson. "Toward a Composing Model of Reading." *Language Arts* 60 (1983): 568-80. Print.

Wardle, Elizabeth. "'Mutt Genres' and the Goal of FYC: How Can We Help Students Write the Genres of the University?" *College Composition and Communication* 60 (2009): 765-88. Print.

—, and Doug Downs. *Writing about Writing: A College Reader.* Boston: Bedford/St. Martin's, 2011. Print.

Appendix 1: Assignment Sheets

RHETORICAL ANALYSIS OF A WRITING EXPERIENCE (DOWNS)

Think back: What's the most memorable piece of writing you've ever done? Now: what was the situation? And how did that situation help shape the writing? In this 4–5 page rhetorical analysis of a memorable writing experience, your task as a writer is to reflect on how that particular writing experience was a result of the particular situation it was related to, how the situation helped determine what you wrote, and why.

Assignment Rationale

Writers are always responding to the situations they're writing in, from, and for, more or less consciously. One of the tasks of this course is to give you a beginning understanding of rhetoric as a theory of communication and to explore its implications. One of those implications is that even when you're not aware of it, you're responding to rhetorical situations. The purpose of this assignment is to show you how you've already been doing that, and to spur your thinking about what possibilities writing holds if you do it more consciously.

Assignment Description and Instructions

Your rhetorical analysis will be based on some significant piece of writing or writing experience that you've had in the last several years. That writing could have been for school, work, family, or your personal life. It could have been completely private (like a journaling experience) or all-the-way public, like a blog or other online post. It could have been a single short document, like a poem or song lyrics, or it could have been an extended project or experience that involved multiple pieces of writing. The key requirement here is that it has to have been a memorable or important enough experience that you can clearly remember *the circumstances surrounding the writing.*

Once you know what experience and writing you want to focus on, you need to *reflect on and analyze that experience and writing from a rhetorical perspective.* What's that mean? Based on the principles

Grant-Davie demonstrates as well as our workshops in class, you'll learn what particular *questions to ask of* the experience you had and the circumstances surrounding it. They will be questions like these:

- Why did you *need to write* to begin with? Since it's easier not to write than it is to write, for most people, there had to be some reason or purpose behind your writing, some problem to be solved or addressed. What was that?

- Where did that need *come from?* What gave rise to it? This is a *historical* question: to understand the circumstances that demanded writing, you need to know what led to those circumstances.

- What *constraints* did you face as a writer? What were the *givens* in your situation—the aspects of it you could not change that controlled what you could do with your writing?

- Who was meant to *read and use your writing* and *what did you mean them to do with it?* How was your writing supposed to do something for, to, or with the readers you imagined it for?

The answers to all of these questions, and others, will help you talk about *why* this piece of writing took the shape that it did.

- In order to make your analysis most meaningful and clear both to you and to other readers, it will need to include at least the following features:

- Some *description of the writing* or experience itself. Ideally, you might include an electronic copy of the writing you're talking about, if one is still available, but in many cases that may not be possible. Whether you can do that or not, take whatever space is necessary in your analysis to describe as clearly as possible what this writing and experience were.

- An extended discussion of the questions above in order to *describe and analyze the rhetorical situation* in which the writing or experience occurred.

- A *conclusion including implications* of your reflection: what do you learn from this? What principles can you draw to help you in future writing situations?

Thought Document #1 ENC 1102H (Wardle)

Purposes and Audience

There are multiple purposes for this thought document:

- To synthesize what you have read so far;
- To analyze the data you have collected so far (in this case, the writing logs);
- To begin to explore some implications, consequences, possibilities, and research questions/projects based on what you have read and thought about so far.

You will, as with almost everything in this class, share your thought piece with the other class members so that you can all pool your thinking in order to work toward the final class project.

Given the above, this text is primarily what writing researchers call *"writing to learn."* But it is also *writing to communicate* with others, so you should do some organizing and editing before you turn it in.

You will, of course, turn the Thought Document in to me and receive a grade for how well you have achieved the purposes and conveyed your ideas in a clear and organized manner.

Contents

The above purposes and audiences should guide everything about how you write this Thought Document. Toward that end, here are my suggestions for the parameters of the document:

1. Keeping the CARS model of research introductions in mind, *tell us about some of the research you have read so far in and for this class.* Synthesize this research instead of just summarizing one article after the other. For example, you might note that "writing researchers are interested in X, Y, and Z and have recently concluded A, B, and C about the literacy practices of today's students." You might also discuss various research methods that have been used: "Researchers have come to these conclusions using methods as varied as A, B, and C."

2. *Analyze the writing logs we have kept for this class and tell us about your findings,* being sure to link them to the findings from others that you synthesized. You could try making the transition by "creating a niche" (again, CARS model) and

then filling it. For example, "Others have examined what students write at Stanford and Michigan State. Building on that work, our class examined. . . ."

3. *Spend some time mulling over (thinking) about the implications, consequences, problems, interesting projects related to the above.* Given what you've learned so far, what can you conclude? What do you want to know more about? What are the questions you finding interesting right now? What data would you like to collect to help you try to answer your questions? What would you like us to be reading in order to learn more about your questions?

4. If you have any ideas for the final class project, tell us about them.

5. *Include a works cited page,* correctly formatted in either MLA or APA. Use your *Everyday Writer* or the Purdue OWL to help you format correctly.

Getting Started, Drafting, and Revising (Your Writing Process)

To start writing a thoughtful piece that accomplishes the above tasks, you will need to:

- *Review all the reading* we have done for class, as well as the reading that your classmates have posted on Diigo. You don't have to cite all of it, but you should cite a good amount of it.
- *Analyze the writing logs.* We did a practice analysis in class, but now you will need to analyze the full set of logs available in EverNote from all of your classmates. You can decide what you want to analyze for—type, amount, audience, purpose, etc— any of the things we tried or discussed in class. But you'll need to do your own analysis for this Thought Document, and do it carefully. Since we all have the same data set, it will be fairly obvious if you don't do a good and careful analysis of the logs.
- *Start drafting in sections* if that is a helpful strategy for you. For example, I would draft the synthesis of existing literature first, trying to highlight main points and interesting conclusions across articles. Then I would try to summarize what I found in my writing log analysis.

- After you've read, analyzed, and done a first draft, then *get serious about revision and organization.* How do you want to order information? Are your main points clear? Have you carefully transitioned from one idea to the other? I like to use headings when I write because they help me stay organized and focused. If you've never tried headings before, you might try them out here and see if you like them.

Don't wait until the night before to start writing. A good thought document is going to require some actual thought. I suggest doing the reading and taking notes one day, drafting that section another day, analyzing the logs another day, drafting about the logs another day, and then revising the entire paper another day. This is about 5 days of steady work, working 1–2 hours a day, maybe more or less on some days. So I suggest getting started right away and then keeping up the steady pace until next Wednesday.

General Expectations for Length, Etc.

The name of this document says it all: *Thought* Document. I want to see you *thinking* about what we have read and collected, and saying smart things about it. I care much more about quality of your thinking and analysis at this point than I do about anything else. I have a general sense that good thinking about so many articles and a data set will likely be around 5–8 pages. However, I am not terribly concerned with page count. If you write 20 pages of thoughtless BS, that is not going to be impressive. If you write 3 brilliant pages, I will be so swept away by your ideas that I won't care about the page length. So start writing without a concern for page length and see where you end up.

While the focus here is on content and ideas, you do have an audience: your classmates and me. We need to be able to understand you, and you want to have some credibility with us. So do spend some time revising and organizing and editing before you turn this in. Otherwise, you might end up with something that is really smart but doesn't make a lot of sense to anyone but you.

Grading

- This Thought Document is worth 40 points.
- I will likely grade each subsequent Thought Document more rigorously, as you learn more and have more experience with the ideas and writing style appropriate to those ideas.

- At the end of the semester you will turn in all of your Thought Documents and your final class project as part of your Class Portfolio. You may revise the Thought Documents for the portfolio if you would like, although you are not required to do so

APPENDIX 2: ELIZABETH WARDLE'S COURSE SYLLABI

ENC 1102
Dr. Elizabeth Wardle

Course Description

ENC1102 is a course intended to help students understand research as genuine inquiry. In this course they are expected to ask difficult questions and explore them using appropriate primary and secondary research methods (library research, historical analysis, rhetorical analysis, survey, interview, and so on).

In ENC1102 students are invited into the research "conversation" on their topic and asked to carefully read what others have said on the topic before they jump in.

Students in 1102 receive instruction in how to find, evaluate, and read difficult material. They learn how to use this material to frame their own research questions, and also how to integrate sources carefully and effectively.

Course Method

The course is about doing, not lecturing. I'll help you with some hard concepts and readings, but the success of this class depends entirely on your willingness to jump in and do things. All of our in- and out-of-class activities are designed and sequenced to help you think, learn, and make regular progress the final course project.

Course Objectives

By the end of this course, students will be able to
- Read, analyze, and respond to difficult texts
- Understand texts as claims and test those claims
- Ask meaningful questions and seek answers to those questions
- Gather and analyze data of various kinds

- Use technologies to help achieve writing and research goals
- Thoughtfully discuss the literacies required in the 21st century
- Convey ideas and research findings effectively in writing as appropriate for various audiences and purposes
- Explain writing-related concepts such as intertextuality, genre, originality, plagiarism, technology, writing, and research.

Course Texts & Resources

- Lunsford, *Everyday Writer,* 4th edition for UCF
- Articles (links are posted on Webcourses in MyUCF):
    - Greene, "Argument as Conversation"
    - Kleine, "What is It We Do When We Write Articles Like This One?"
    - Haven, "The New Literacy: Stanford Study Finds Richness and Complexity in Students' Writing"
    - Grabill, et al, "Revisualizing Composition: Mapping the Writing Lives of First-Year College Students" (The WIDE Study)
    - Roozen, "From Journals to Journalism: Tracing Trajectories of Literate Development"
    - Shrum, draft of thesis chapters ("Case 1" and "Case 2")
    - Wardle, "Identity, Authority, and Learning to Write in New Workplaces"
    - McCarthy, "A Stranger in Strange Lands"
    - Johns, "Discourse Communities and Communities of Practices: Membership, Conflict, and Diversity"
    - Penrose & Geisler, "Reading and Writing Without Authority"
    - Kain & Wardle, "Activity Theory for Students"
- Diigo: http://groups.diigo.com/group/enc1102-wardle-fall-2011 (you'll need an account and I will send you an invitation to join our group)
- Evernote: www.evernote.com (you'll need an account and you'll need to grant the class members access)
- WordPress Blog: http://enc1102hf2011.wordpress.com (you'll need a WordPress account and then I will add you to this private site)

Course Assignments & Point Values

Homework	Responses to readings, interviews & transcriptions, writing log, Diigo contributions, bringing required texts to class, etc. Note that most written homework will be posted to WordPress, but all data collected will be posted to EverNote, and source annotations will be posted on Diigo. *While some homework can be missed, the other course assignments cannot be done unless you have done most of the homework and done it on time.* If you make a habit of skipping homework assignments, I will suggest you drop the class.	80 points
Thought Documents (2)	In each unit we will collect some data and analyze it together. Afterward, you will write semi-formal, documented "thought pieces" that reflect on the data analysis and discuss it using in and out of class readings. These "thought pieces" will give you the chance to think about the data, the readings, and your ideas and help you think about how to present them. You will draw on these for your Final Course Project. *Both Thought Documents must be turned in for you to pass the class.*	80 points
Final Project: Writing Lives of UCF Students	Drawing on the research, reading, and thinking you do this semester, the class will determine the form, purpose, and audience of a final project that conveys relevant information about the literate lives of UCF undergrad students. While the full class will produce the complete project, you will be responsible for at least one formal aspect of the project yourself (for example, the class might create a magazine and you might write one article).	140 points
Portfolio & Framing Thought Document	At the end of the semester you will turn in all of your homework, thought pieces, and contribution to the final project with a framing reflection discussing what you have learned and accomplished this semester.	40 points

Publication Opportunity

The Department of Writing and Rhetoric publishes a journal for outstanding writing produced by Composition students called *Stylus.* You may find the student work published in this journal helpful during our exploration of writing this semester. Also, you should consider submitting your own work for publication. Students published in *Stylus* become eligible for the President John C. Prize for Excellence in First-Year Writing, a $450 book scholarship awarded annually. To submit your work, simply email your essay to me as a Microsoft Word-friendly attachment and I'll send it to the editors. To see previous issues and learn more information, visit the *Stylus* website at http://writingandrhetoric.cah.ucf.edu/stylus/

DETAILED ASSIGNMENT DESCRIPTIONS

"Homework"-Type Assignments (80 points)

Written Homework on WordPress (30 points)

Will not be graded for grammar and polish, but instead for depth of thought and engagement with the ideas. You should write a page or two in direct response to the day's text(s) and the prompt on the daily calendar. Post your written responses before class on WordPress.

There will be 7 WordPress Homework Entries by the end of the semester (due dates are on the daily calendar, and these end after Week 11).

7 entries X 5 points each=35 points but I will drop the lowest grade, so 30 points.

Diigo Entries (10 points)

We have created a class Diigo site (http://groups.diigo.com/group/encl1102-wardle-fall-2011) where we can post and annotate resources relevant for our class project. You are expected to post and annotate (5–10 sentences) no fewer than two useful and credible resources for each of our three main class "units" (students and literacy, literacy and technology, and genres/rhetoric/intertextuality). The purpose of these postings is to share resources that the class can use as they consider these topics and think about the final course project. Don't post just to post. Post things that speak to what we read about and discuss in class.

You should make at least 4 annotated Diigo Entries by the end of the semester, two for each unit.

5 points for each unit's entries X 2 units=10 points

Writing Log (4 Weeks, 4 separate week-long logs) on EverNote (20 points)

You will keep an ongoing writing/literacy log for this class, which will be used as data (along with your classmates' logs) to get a sense of the breadth and depth of the writing that UCF students do. In this log you should record everything you write every day and how long (roughly) you spent writing it. For this log to really "work," you will need to broaden your definition of "writing" to include all the texts that you write—IM, texting, Facebooking, emails, grocery lists, class notes, homework, cards, gaming. As we read and think more together, you will expand this log to specifically mention the various technologies that mediate your writing.

Once a week by class time you should post your writing log for the previous week on EverNote so that we can all access the logs that all class members have kept. You'll post a new Writing Log every week for Weeks 2–6, so there should be five full, week-long logs. These logs will be used for analysis by the class.

4 logs X 5 points each=20 points

Classmate Interviews & Transcriptions on EverNote (10 points)

During Unit Two you will learn how to write research questions, conduct interviews, transcribe interviews, and analyze interview data. Toward that end, you will conduct two interviews with classmates, transcribe them, and post them to EverNote. These will be use for analysis by the class.

You will post two Interview Transcripts to EverNote.

Two interviews and their transcripts X 5 points each=10 points

Genre Postings on EverNote (5 points)

You will post two documents to EverNote, examples of genres you don't write but think you will need to write later. These will be used for analysis by the class.

2 document sets X 2.5 points each=5 points

Research Project Proposal (5 points)

On October 5 you will turn in a 1-page research proposal describing in as much detail as possible your plans for the final research project. What is your research question? What data will you collect to try to answer that question, and from whom? When will you do the work?

Thought Documents (2) (80 points)

In each unit you will read about some aspect of student literacy as well as collect and analyze some data. At the end of each unit you will write a "thought document" that pulls together what you have read and analyzed. These sorts of documents are commonly used by researchers to gather their thoughts and think through ideas as they conduct research. The audiences for these documents are you, the instructor, and your classmates. Thus, they need to be organized, readable, and edited. However, they aren't going to be perfect because they are thinking (writing to learn) documents. You might write them as memos, short essays, etc, and we will talk about this further as we see what happens in class and what your personal writing and research processes are. But general parameters for this are:

- About 5–8 pages
- Documented (citing outside sources appropriate in text and in a works cited at the end of the text)
- Organized
- Thoughtful, interesting, exploratory considering the ideas and data we've worked with as a class, as well as considering where you would like the research to go and the questions that interest you.

2 Thought Documents X 40 points each= 80 points

End of Semester Course Project: Writing Lives of UCF Students (140 points)

You will end the course by creating some sort of project out of all of the reading, data collection, and thinking the class does all semester. At this point it is impossible to anticipate where you as a class will end up, and that is the beauty of genuine research and inquiry—you will go where your questions and interests and data take you. We will discuss this end of course project repeatedly during the semester and when you as a class have made up your mind about what you want your project to be, we will write up some guidelines, parameters, and grading expectations for it. Don't worry; I won't leave you to guess about the expectations. But I can't say much about what they are now; you all will decide.

Below are a few ideas about what this project should likely include:

- Share your research findings and ideas with an audience or audiences who need to hear about them
- Share your ideas and findings in genres appropriate to your audiences and purposes
- Explore mediums that help convey your message and reach your audience.

Each student will contribute something he/she has written, although some parts of the project might be written by the entire class or groups of students.

A wild guess about a possibility:

The class might decide to write a variety of articles describing literacies of UCF students. These might include case studies of specific students, overviews of the practices of a group of students, and so on. And all of these might be framed by a proposal written by the class to UCF administrators or legislators arguing for a different approach to writing education for students. All of this might be conveyed in a website, or in a magazine, or in a wiki. There might be visuals, hyperlinks, activities.

Don't worry too much about this right now. You'll all figure out what you want to do as we move through the research and thinking, and I'll help you.

Grading:

Your independently written research project: 100 points

The full group project as a deliverable: 40 points

Portfolio & Final Course "Thought Document" (40 points)

At the end of the semester you will turn in all of your work for the course—homework, thought pieces, and the parts of the final course project to which you contributed. You will frame all of this with a reflection of your learning and accomplishments this semester. This reflection should really be your last Thought Document. It should talk about your reading, research, and ideas from the semester, talk about your understanding of both research in general as well as of the literate practices of students today. This sort of reflection is an essential part of "learning transfer"—if you want to use what you've learned this semester, you need to reflect on it and think explicitly of how you want to integrate it into your scholarly, personal, or professional life going forward.

The portfolio is also an opportunity to revise anything from the semester in an effort to raise your overall course grade. If you didn't do a very good Thought Piece 1, for example, you could revise it and include it in the final portfolio to demonstrate your growth as a writer/thinker/researcher.

Depending on where and how you end up writing and collecting your work, we might try electronic or paper portfolios.

Appendix 3: Doug Downs' Course Syllabi

WRIT 101 *College Writing I: Writing with Authority in College*

Dr. Doug Downs

Course Description and Objectives

WRIT 101 is a writing course which takes as its object of study the activity of writing in college and how students participate in that activity. We do not, in other words, simply *practice* writing—rather, we *investigate* it, exploring how writing has been for you in the past and what differences you can expect in transitioning from other kinds of writing (high-school, workplace) to college-level writing appropriate to the written work you'll be asked to do in many of your other courses. Put simply, this course aims to change the way you think about writing and the way you understand the game of writing. By the end of the course, you should

- Understand the nature of writing, and your own experiences with writing, differently than when you began;
- Increase your ability to read rhetorical situations and make rhetorical choices awarely in your writing;
- Know what questions to ask when entering new rhetorical situations in order to adjust your approach to writing to meet that situation;
- Be a more reflective writer;

- Build your ability to collaborate in communities of writers and readers;
- Gain comfort with taking risks in new writing situations;
- Increase your control of situation-appropriate conventions of writing; and
- Expand your research literacy.

Required Texts

The following articles (listed in the order to be read) are available as PDFs in the password-protected Readings section of our course website:

Stuart Greene, "Argument as Conversation: The Role of Inquiry in Writing a Researched Argument." *The Subject Is Research,* ed. Wendy Bishop and Pavel Zemliansky. Portsmouth, NH: Boynton/Cook, 2001. 145–64.

Mark Richardson, "Writing Is Not Just a Basic Skill." *Chronicle of Higher Education* 55.11 (7 Nov. 2008): A47.

Keith Grant-Davie, "Rhetorical Situations and Their Constituents." *Rhetoric Review* 15.2 (1997): 264–79.

Christina Haas & Linda Flower, "Rhetorical Reading Strategies and the Construction of Meaning." *College Composition and Communication* 39.2 (1988): 167–83.

Margaret Kantz, "Helping Students Use Textual Sources Persuasively." *College English* 52.1 (1990): 74–91.

James Porter, "Intertextuality and the Discourse Community." *Rhetoric Review* 5.1 (1986): 34–47.

Mike Rose, "Rigid Rules, Inflexible Plans, and the Stifling of Language: A Cognitivist Analysis of Writer's Block." *College Composition and Communication* 31.4 (1980): 389–401.

Carol Berkenkotter, "Decisions and Revisions: The Planning Strategies of a Publishing Writer," and Donald Murray, "Response of a Laboratory Rat—or, Being Protocoled." *College Composition and Communication* 34.2 (1983): 156–72.

Donald Murray, "All Writing Is Autobiography." *College Composition and Communication* 42.1 (1991): 68–74.

James Paul Gee, "Literacy, Discourse, and Linguistics: Introduction." *Journal of Higher Education* 171.1 (1989): 5–17.

Ann Penrose & Cheryl Geisler, "Reading and Writing without Authority." *College Composition and Communication* 45.4 (1994): 505–20.

Lucille McCarthy, "A Stranger in Strange Lands: A College Student Writing across the Curriculum." *Research in the Teaching of English* 21.3 (1987): 233–65.

Coursework

In addition to engagement in class discussion, individual conferences, and workshops, you will complete the following assignments:

Thought Pieces (an average of one per week)

One-page reading responses that reflect on what you found interesting, useful, or problematic in a given reading. You are welcome to use thought pieces to reflect on any aspect of class currently of interest to you, though usually you'll use them to respond to the focusing question that accompanies a given reading. The purpose of the thought piece is to say what you think—not necessarily, or even usually, to come up with "answers" to the focusing question. They need not know, seek, or tell "the Truth"; they need only say what's in your mind in response or reaction to the readings.

Rhetorical Analysis of a Writing Experience (weeks 1–2)

Think back: What's the most memorable piece of writing you've ever done? Now: what was the situation? And how did that situation help shape the writing? In this 4–5 page rhetorical analysis of a memorable writing experience, your task as a writer is to reflect on how that particular writing experience was a result of the particular situation it was related to—how the situation helped determine what you wrote, and why.

Rhetorical Summary of a Scholarly Article (weeks 3–4)

As a college writer, you need to make rhetorical reading (a la Haas & Flower) completely natural. To read texts rhetorically is to read them as if they're people talking to you, people with motivations that may not always be explicit but are always present. It means talking about not only what a text *says* or what it *means,* but what it *does.* (Start a war? Make a friend smile? Throw down a gauntlet? Refocus everyone's attention? Woo a lover?) When you read a text trying to figure out what it does or why a person would bother to write it, you're reading rhetorically. The rhetorical summary gives you practice rhetorically reading a scholarly article and forwards your research project. Write a 4–5 page summary of one of our course readings arguing what the article attempts to accomplish, and how.

Writing Process Analysis (weeks 5–8)

Your task in this assignment is to investigate some aspect of writing process by comparing published research on it to your own experience, in a 5–6 page analysis. You can look at the writing process as a whole, or select just some aspect or feature or experience of it. This assignment combines a few different goals. First, this course in some ways wants to make writing "strange" to you—to look in new ways and open new questions for you about how writing works. (And, possibly, provide some answers.) Studying process is one way to go about that. This course also means to crack open the door on the world of university research, both that which searches for existing research via library resources, and that done to get direct, firsthand answers to your questions (we call that *primary* research). So this assignment introduces you to library resources that help you search, and lets you practice writing about your own, firsthand experiences *in the context of* other people's work that will give a particular perspective on your experiences, and vice versa.

"Good Writing" Study—Collaborative Project (weeks 9–12)

What counts as good writing, and what makes writing "good," in the fields of study you'll be entering? In this assignment you'll address these questions through collaboration with three other students and with primary research, interviewing faculty on campus and members of professions related to your major. As a class, we'll develop a shared set of interview questions, and each team will write and present a 5–6 page report on findings from the interviews it conducts.

List of 10 (weeks 13–14)

Create a list of ten questions that as a writer you've learned to ask when entering any new rhetorical (writing) situation—ten things you understand you must have answers to before you'll know how to write in that situation. Each question will be followed by a paragraph giving the rationale for the question: why is this question an important one to ask? If you could only ask ten questions, why must **this** one be on the

316 Looking into Writing-about-Writing Classrooms

list? Your list should reflect the principles you've learned throughout the rest of the semester both through our course readings and through your writing projects.

Final Portfolio (weeks 15–16)

Your portfolio will contain a collection of your polished writing for grading—the only graded writing you'll do in the course. It is a showcase that allows you to revise your writing to the best of your ability, and to reflect on your learning in the course. Its overall purpose is to make an argument about what you've learned in the course and demonstrate it via the writing you've prepared. It will include a reflective letter, your revised List of 10, and revisions of any two of the four other major writing projects.

Method: A Community of Inquiry

All the assignments and class meetings in this course work toward giving you new, more accurate, more professional ways to understand and strategize writing. Unlike your previous writing classes, the subject (not just the activity) of this course is writing. As each member of the class does reflective work and firsthand research *on writing itself,* we become a group of researchers working together on the same questions—a community of inquiry. All you need to bring is an open, inquiring attitude and engagement, and a willingness to thoughtfully connect your experience and existing knowledge with the new ideas you'll encounter in the course.

All writing you do in the course will receive credit, but only writing in the final portfolio will be graded. Major assignments in the course will be drafted, read by others in the class, revised, and read by me. Portfolio assignments will be further revised based on my feedback and on what you learn during the course. The course should stretch you, but it should create a safe environment where experimentation is not punished and where it's okay to try something new and not get it right the first time.

Evaluation and Grading

Your course grade (100 points) will be comprised of three elements:
I. Engagement: 40 points
   (Thought pieces—20 pts—10 pieces, 2 points each)

(Workshops—15 pts)

(Other class contribution—5 pts based on discussion and in class writing)

II. Writing Assignments: 25 points (5 points for drafting each of the 5 main assignments)

III. Final Portfolio: 35 points (see assignment sheet for grading details)

In this course, I judge writing quality by considering the following categories:

- match to intended genre and/or assignment guidelines
- audience awareness and appropriateness of document for them
- clarity of argument and strength of support for it
- source use appropriate to genre, assignment, and writer's needs
- careful crafting of writing and document design
- editing and proofreading

A writing shows little or no weakness in any of these categories.

B writing shows some weakness in some categories.

C writing shows some weakness in most categories, or great weakness in some.

D writing shows some weakness in all categories, or great weakness in most.

F writing shows great weakness in all categories.

Course Policies

- **Your work in this class is always public.** Don't submit writing you can't let other students read.
- **Out-of-class work will be submitted via e-mail attachment**; it must include **your name and a short assignment title** in the filename. Please only use an e-mail address that you check frequently, for this class.
- When I specify that a revision is to be **submitted with drafts or changes tracked, I won't read it without them.**
- **Revision** is substantive development of a piece, not fine-tuning occasional wording. (That's editing.)
- **Collaboration is highly encouraged**—real writers write with readers and other writers.

- Writing that was or will be **submitted for assignments in other courses** will usually not be accepted here too. You may work on the same problems, but not double-dip the writing itself.
- If an **assignment is lost or missing**, you must provide another copy no matter whose fault it is.
- I decide whether to accept **late assignments** case-by-case. Check with me if you need to submit work late.
- **Attendance is required.** Missed workshops or presentation sessions **count against engagement**; excessive **tardiness** counts as absences. **More than 4 absences (two weeks of class) limits your course grade to a maximum of C.**
- You're welcome to **chat** with me about class business at **downs-doug@gmail.com**. You can find me on **Facebook**, but I don't do class business there because of privacy and archival issues.
- **Plagiarism:** You are always responsible for acknowledging source material and ideas in your writing. Cheating—whether by claiming others' work as your own (fraud) or fabricating material—will result in a course grade of F and report to the Dean.
- **ADA:** If because of a documented physical or psychological disability you are unable to meet the requirements outlined in this syllabus, you must tell me immediately. Accessibility Services (phone, address) will document your disability and coordinate any resulting accommodations. If you have questions, please ask me.
- I reserve **final discretion** in adjusting grades to account for unanticipated circumstances.
- I may use **copies of your work**, anonymously, for samples in future classes or for research.
- **Your continued enrollment in this course constitutes your acceptance of this syllabus and its policies.**

Manuscript Style and Conventions

Skilled writers show awareness of the look and feel of their documents and the mastery of their technology to control that look and feel, ensuring that their documents follow conventions appropriate to the situation for which they're writing. Default formatting for electronic academic manuscripts (which you should use in the absence of other necessary designs) include 1-inch margins, double-spacing, serif font (e.g, Times New Roman, Garamond, Cambria) for body copy, bolded subheadings, no gaps or lines skipped between paragraphs, and one line skipped between sections. Please note that many of these are not MS Word's default settings.

Using Reviewing Tools / Change-Tracking in MS Word

Throughout the course, I will expect you to "track changes" from workshop drafts to drafts submitted to me and then submitted in the portfolio.

- In Word versions pre-2007, locate these controls under the Tools menu with Track Changes, which will bring up the "Reviewing" Toolbar (you can also access this under the View menu—> Toobars).
- In Word versions 2007 and later, locate these controls on the Review tab on the Ribbon.
- In OpenOffice current version, locate these controls under the Edit menu as "Changes." If you use OpenOffice, please save documents by using the Save As (not just Save) command and setting "Save as Type" to "Microsoft Word 97/2000/XP." Your tracked changes will be preserved and viewable in Word.

In addition, my comments on your document will be made using the Comment function in the Track Changes system. I'll demo these systems in class before the first paper is due that requires change tracking.

Tentative Semester Calendar

Week	Readings Due	Assignments Due
1 Tues		
Thurs	Green, Richardson	Thought Piece 1
2 Tues	Grant-Davie	Thought Piece 2
Thurs	Haas & Flower	Workshop Draft, Rhetorical Analysis
Week	**Readings Due**	**Assignments Due**
3 Tues	Kantz	Thought Piece 3; Revised Rhetorical Analysis
Thurs	Porter	Thought Piece 4
4 Tues	Article for Summary	Workshop Draft, Rhetorical Summary
Thurs		Revised Rhetorical Summary

5 Tues	Rose	Thought Piece 5
Thurs	Berkenkotter & Murray	Thought Piece 6
6 Tues	Murray	Thought Piece 7
Thurs	Researching Writing Process Analysis	
7 Tues		
Thurs	Workshop Draft, Writing Process Analysis	
8 Tues		
Thurs	Revised Draft, Writing Process Analysis	
9 Tues	Gee	Thought Piece 8
Thurs	Penrose & Geisler	Thought Piece 9
10 Tues	McCarthy	Thought Piece 10
Thurs	Researching Good Writing Project	
11 Tues	Good Writing Draft Presentations Teams 1 & 2	
Thurs	Draft Presentations—Teams 3 & 4	
12 Tues	Draft Presentations—Teams 5 & 6	
Thurs	Revised Good Writing Study	
13 Tues	Workshop Draft, List of 10	
Thurs	Begin Portfolio Revision Revised Draft List of 10; Portfolio Workshop	
14 Tues	Portfolio Workshop	
Thurs	Portfolio Workshop	
15 Finals Week	Final Portfolio Due	

12 Attempting the Impossible: Designing a First-Year Composition Course

Kathleen Blake Yancey

I'm sure I'm not alone when I say that in designing and teaching first-year composition, we find ourselves in an impossible situation. On the one hand, as the research shows (Hansen et al.; Beaufort; Yancey, "The Literacy Demands of Entering the University"), and as this volume no doubt makes clear, first-year students need such a course; on the other hand, what the course needs to accomplish cannot be achieved in the time given to it.[1] Regardless of where composition is "delivered" or how, what we think we need to accomplish continues to be broad.[2] When I began teaching in the 1970s, for example, our curriculum was already overly full: in addition to helping students develop as writers, we helped them acclimate to college and to campus, to think critically, to develop wider horizons, and to begin a journey in review of received truth. Indeed, as important as writing was to that English course, it was more vehicle than outcome.

Since then, our curricular efforts seem to be contradictory. Seen from one perspective, it's now easier to narrow our aims, and to do so relative to a sense of national aims (at least in some limited ways), given the development and influence of outcomes generally in higher education, and specifically in writing via the (WPA) Outcomes Statement—with its five inter-related dimensions of focus: Rhetorical Knowledge; Critical Thinking, Reading, and Writing; Processes; Knowledge of Conventions; and Composing in Electronic Environments. Seen from another perspective, the promise of such focus—making the planning of a first-year composition (FYC) course take place in the context of a national framework—is contested by three tendencies. First, the WPA

321

Outcomes are often adapted by campuses to their local circumstances; as a consequence, campuses often take the narrow outcomes focus and extend it outward to include their own specific foci. Arizona State pays attention to argument, for instance, and the University of Illinois at Chicago includes the local, urban life of Chicago itself. Second, as of 2010, the WPA Outcomes are now situated relative to another, de facto set of outcomes, ones developed by the Council of Writing Program Administrators (CWPA), the National Writing Project (NWP) and the National Council of Teachers of English (NCTE): the Framework for Success in College Writing. The Framework outlines "habits of mind and experiences that are critical for college success":

Habits of mind refers to ways of approaching learning that are both intellectual and practical and that will support students' success in a variety of fields and disciplines. The Framework identifies eight habits of mind essential for success in college writing:

- Curiosity—the desire to know more about the world.
- Openness—the willingness to consider new ways of being and thinking in the world.
- Engagement—a sense of investment and involvement in learning.
- Creativity—the ability to use novel approaches for generating, investigating, and representing ideas.
- Persistence—the ability to sustain interest in and attention to short- and long-term projects.
- Responsibility—the ability to take ownership of one's actions and understand the consequences of those actions for oneself and others.
- Flexibility—the ability to adapt to situations, expectations, or demands.
- Metacognition—the ability to reflect on one's own thinking as well as on the individual and cultural processes used to structure knowledge.

Interestingly, as admirable as these "outcomes" are, they expand what seems to be a narrower focus of my goals back in the 1970s—and beyond.

Third, but not least, campuses often have their own initiatives that they "assign" to FYC, sometimes because they see the initiatives as related, and sometimes because they see FYC as an empty vessel available for other projects, especially those related to student retention.

[oh yes]

Most notable among these local efforts may be the "one book" program, in which students read a book together and work with it in some way in their FYC classes (e.g., University of North Carolina, University of Texas at Arlington, and Clemson University). All of this is before we think about "alternative" or complementary offerings to FYC, including: freshman interest groups (FIGS); first-year experience groups (FYE); first-year seminars (FYS), and the like. All of *this* is before we think about individual teachers and the ways that they enact their own outcomes for a given set of students.

In sum, it feels like we're still locked into a 70s model, still trying—through first-year composition—to be all things to all students at all times, providing all kinds of preparations for all contingencies. Given this context, it's fair to ask, what *is* the appropriate focus of FYC?[3]

[yes it is overwhelming]

* * *

A recent trend in the teaching of FYC is what's called the writing-about-writing or "Introduction to Writing Studies" approach. As described by Downs and Wardle in 2007, such an approach seeks to foster "rhetorical awareness" in students as they both practice and study writing as an object—although, it is fair to note, as Wardle and Downs have in a recent book chapter ("Reimagining"), that this curriculum comes in various forms, in part because taking writing as an object of study could mean many things. In the course design presented here, it's a mechanism for helping students learn

> Though we complain about public misconceptions of writing and of our discipline, our field has not seriously considered radically reimagining the mission of the very course where misconceptions are born and/or reinforced; we have not yet imagined moving first-year composition from teaching "how to write in college" to teaching *about writing*—from acting as if writing is a basic, universal skill to acting as if writing studies is a discipline with content knowledge to which students should be introduced, thereby changing their understandings about writing and thus changing the ways they write (Downs and Wardle, "Teaching" 2007).

about writing as a part of their becoming composers. Such an approach is congruent with recent trends in higher education more generally in that we now believe that learning requires both theory and practice: assigning tasks *and* explaining the logic of the tasks are a necessary condition for their successful completion.

[sounds like it's including andragogy]

One heuristic for thinking about this approach, as enacted in this course design, is made available through a revised version of Bloom's taxonomy, where there are four dimensions of learning. Students learn *facts*: for example, writers are not born, at least not biologically; we become writers through knowledge and practice, through response and experimentation. Students engage with *concepts*: in this case, the key terms we use to describe writing, to create our map of writing, and to frame new writing situations. Students *practice*: the composing processes that the research says we are good at helping students develop (our stock in trade since the 1970s); in this course, practice is keyed to three spaces of composing—print, the screen, and the network. Students *reflect*: engaging in meta-cognitive practices is a means through which students articulate what they think they have learned—about writing as an object, about writing as practice, and about themselves as writers.

* * *

I'm persuaded by the research reported in *How People Learn* of the power of key terms, of the ways we use them to create mental maps of given phenomena, and of the enactment of those key terms reiteratively as a way of understanding the terms, making them our own, and enhancing practice (Bransford). I've been interested in this approach since at least the 1990s, when I observed how key terms helped even small children play soccer; first and second graders weren't asked to kick a soccer ball—rather to *dribble* it, *pass* it, or *cross* it—in the process to link the kind of kick to its effect. The language mattered, and the children picked it up quickly as they attempted the action. So too with vocabulary in composition, a point I made in *Reflection in the Writing Classroom*: Both genre and reflection were two terms that were central to the course, I thought. More generally, I saw how important those key terms were in helping students create their own maps of what James Moffett described as a *Universe of Discourse*. One question, then, is which key terms we include *as* key terms: Research shows that we need to include a sufficient number for critical mass, but if we include too many, they don't stick (Yancey, Robertson, and Taczak). Another question is how we ask students to link these key terms in literal and metaphorical maps for the purpose of framing their next writing tasks.[4]

key terms

My list of key terms includes *rhetorical situation, composing process, discourse community, genre, literacy,* and *reflection.* The influence of Beaufort's model, outlined in *College Writing and Beyond,* is obvious in these choices. We begin with the term *literacy.* The first day of class, students are asked in a homework

> Being literate means that a person can understand which way to turn a map, which way right and left are, which way North and South are. Literate people know . . . how to rotate a map relative to their position in order to find out the right way to go. . . . When given a map, literate people are perfectly capable of finding their way to any destination they desire. —Jason

assignment to identify an object they associate with literacy and to write a one-pager explaining what they understand about literacy as suggested in the object. Given the course's focus on writing as theory and practice, such an informal assignment seems appropriate. *Love this assignment* Through this assignment, the course commences by tapping students' prior knowledge as a mechanism for setting the stage for the course.

* * *

The first formal assignment in this course design focuses on narrative. Given the course's commitment to writing as theory and practice, it might seem strange to begin with an assignment that seems to fall into a more expressivist version of FYC, but the advantages of beginning with this assignment are four (at least). First, as the research reported in *How People Learn* makes apparent, prior knowledge is the default *schema* option for all learners, including writers. Given their experience with literature in high school, students entering college bring with them a familiarity with narrative. In addition, many students bring *life experience* with narrative through playing video games and watching television and movies. In this sense, too, the narrative assignment invites students to build on what they know, even if they can't necessarily make that knowledge explicit—at least not at first. At the same time, this assignment brings to life genre as a *concept*: narrative is not, in this sense, a filling out of slots, but (in Carolyn Miller's famous formation) a response to a recurring situation. We think in terms of the conventions of a specific narrative in the context of narrative-qua-genre. Second, thinking of narrative inside the frame of a rhetorical situation challenges students' school-based understanding of narrative, as indicated by the line of research on writing in high school conducted by Applebee and Langer. In high school, these researchers explain, the most significant influence on writing is the national and state testing regime that specifies Britton's teacher-as-examiner audience and that makes test-writing the only composing game in town. As Applebee and Langer remark, "Given the constraints imposed by high-stakes tests, writing as a way to study, learn, and go beyond—as a way to construct knowledge or generate new networks of understandings . . . is rare" (26). Engaging students in thinking about narrative as a genre operating inside of a rhetorical situation moves them from the familiar to the unfamiliar, as it asks them to think about the rhetoricity of narrative in their composing of one.

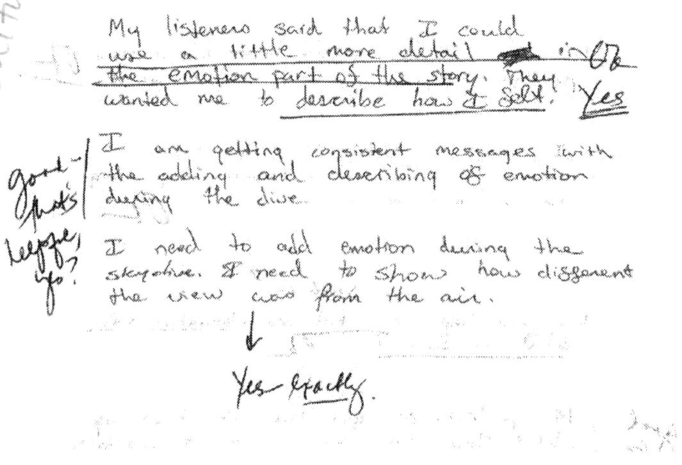

Image 1.

Third, inviting students to write about their own experience validates that experience. As Marcia Baxter-Magolda points out, validating students' experience is a key move in helping students learn. It is important, in a Vygotskian way, that the assignment asks students to revisit an experience of their own choosing so as to make meaning of it for others. Fourth, and not least, the assignment helps students see new ways of approaching material *and* organizing it. Focusing on a scene as the unit of discourse—rather than on the paragraph as the discourse block or on the essay as (familiar, five-paragraph) genre—students develop it out, then repeat the process with another scene, then decide how to connect scenes, and then decide how to make a full composition. In this process, they learn how to compose from scenes, sending them back to the scenes: it's not a linear process. It is a building from the ground up that, in nearly all cases, is very different than what students expected or have experienced, yet very like practices of other narrative composers who work from the small to the narrative arc: think of Jennifer Egan developing a short story for the *New Yorker* through the discourse bloc of a tweet. As students enact this composing, it helps them see how language and genre are synthetic; through working with language and genre, we create both meaning and agency. Last, but not least, in reflecting on the practices they engaged in and on the final text they made, students create another kind of making: composing knowledge for themselves. Here, it's a very different kind of inventing the university than the one David Bartholomae described.

As important, each assignment is itself located in its own archive: a set of texts, scenes, drafts, peer reviews, and reflections that students create through a multiply layered set of practices.

* * *

I've made the argument elsewhere that part of what we do when we teach is to replicate positive experiences or correct our own negative experiences. Too often, we see our students as ourselves; of course, they aren't. My students are younger, with very different life experiences than mine simply by virtue of our diverse chronologies. At the same time, what I design for them as curriculum bears traces of what I might have designed for myself. Entering college as resistance to the Vietnam War was widening and influenced by my own background, I was quite certain—alas, dogmatic even—about our need to contain the Communist dominoes that would (allegedly) fall if we withdrew from Vietnam. A year later, I was protesting the war on the same campus, a very conservative campus, where the protestors were outnumbered, if we trust numbers and eyewitness accounts, about one hundred to one. That, of course, is part of the point: What evidence do we trust? Another part of the point is how we evaluate and decide: how *do* we decide if, or when, we should intervene—in Rowanda, in Bosnia, in Iraq, in Libya? What's the logic, what's the rationale, and what's the endgame?

Later in my undergraduate career, I took what was called a math course that focused on the philosophy of science. We read trade books explaining the development of models seeking to explain the solar system and the universe itself. Coming into college, I certainly understood the shift from an earth-centric model to a sun-centric model, but it had literally never occurred to me that models provide us with a mechanism for understanding and explaining physical phenomena, that such models, like Kepler's, changed over time. In this formation of epistemology, as I would put it now, facts weren't really facts at all, as I had understood them.

Such learning takes more than one course, but it needs to begin in a course. If we think of composing, in the language of Applebee and Langer, *as a way to study, learn, and go beyond—as a way to construct knowledge or generate new networks of understandings*—FYC is one such eligible course.

* * *

Another assignment is what I call an inquiry assignment; its purpose is to engage students not in making claims, not in exploring their interests, but rather—and not simply—in thinking. I'm aware that as Marra and Palmer demonstrate, college students don't understand how knowledge is made, how facts become facts, or how facts are framed as understandings. This finding is echoed in Samuel Wineberg's research on students' understanding of history, and it is echoed again in the University of Washington Study of Undergraduate Learning (SOUL). My hope is that the inquiry assignment moves students toward an understanding that knowledge is in flux, and that specific practices contribute to what we consider knowledge. I'm also aware that many students enter college as dualistic thinkers, seeing the world as a platform for dichotomies, seeing their role as taking and holding one side. When we approach a topic most of us know very little about, we have an exigence, an occasion for inquiring and considering together, for undertaking and pursuing the larger and more philosophical questions that contextualize the specific.

We take as our topic World War II, a war that my father fought in but that is as distant to my students as the Revolutionary War is to me. It's an interesting war, one alive in popular culture through movies like Clint Eastwood's pair of documentary-like accounts, *Flags of Our Fathers* and *Letters from Iwo Jima*, and books like Tom Brokaw's *The Greatest Generation*. Given the Holocaust, World War II seems like the proverbial "good" war, one that was reasonable, justifiable, and even required. Given more current reckonings, it's a war FDR manipulated us into. Given the performance in battle of African Americans and Japanese Americans, it's a war that forwarded civil rights, a claim evidenced by the new roles that women played during the war: Rosie the Riveter was more than a public relations pin-up girl. Any reckoning of the war would also have to include the atom bombs we dropped on Japan. Was there no other way to end the war swiftly, as Truman claimed? Has dropping the bomb functioned as a deterrent since then? What does all this tell us about war generally, about if and when there is a time to go to war, or about how to behave once we are in war? Is this last consideration merely the musings of someone who has never experienced war, and who has the luxury of musing? These, then, are the kinds of questions we take up during the inquiry assignment; students who have been rewarded for claim and evidence for most of their K-12 testing lives now need not to claim, not to argue, but rather, to *inquire*. It's a shift in thinking as well as in genre.

[handwritten margin note: yes—there was]

There are dangers in this approach. Some students become so engaged in exploring that they want to continue exploring; it's engaging, they say. Going forward into the next assignment, they would rather explore; they do not to want to stake a claim and supply evidence— even though there are times when claiming and evidencing is what is appropriate. I worry too that this assignment is too close to my own interests, that it will divert students' attention, that the issues of war will displace our focus on writing.

[handwritten margin note: As a different topic—]

* * *

An advanced writing course I developed at Clemson was intended to help undergraduates work as Studio Associates in the new Class of 1941 Studio for Student Communication. Given the intent of the Studio to help students compose in multiple spaces, I built in specific attention to two such spaces: the page and the screen. Later, at Florida State, I expanded this idea as we developed an advanced writing class as part of our new major, Editing, Writing and Media. The advanced writing course, "Writing in Print and Online" (WEPO, as we call it) is designed explicitly for three composing spaces. Put another way, course outcomes include the successful creation and editing of several texts, including 1) in print; 2) on the screen; and 3) for the network. In addition, at least one of these texts is to be re-purposed for another medium; that is, revised and rewritten to take advantage of the affordances of the medium, and students are expected to conclude the course by creating a digital portfolio, a site that is congruent with the multiple kinds of writing the course fosters.

If we are preparing students for the future, we cannot wait until they are juniors before introducing them to the multiple composing spaces available to them. Indeed, one might make the argument that Bitzer's rhetorical situation should include a consideration of such spaces. In such a class, the portfolio can play a different kind of role. Rather than asking students to compile or assemble a portfolio at the term's end—the conventional practice—we can introduce it early in the term—as a site for archiving informal and formal texts, for reflecting upon texts and experiences, for tracing connections to other kinds of composing and compositions (Yancey, "Electronic Portfolios" 2012). In constructing the portfolio as a site for thinking as well as for presentation, we integrated into the course several advantages of the portfolio that are not otherwise included. One: students begin thinking early on about their portfolio and about the ways they can represent themselves and their composing as they *begin* doing so, and they can do so by including texts from the FYC class, from other classes, and from outside school. Two: students create an archive, and it is through working with the extensive materials in an archive that students engage in making the fullest meaning. Third: early on, students have the opportunity to learn about the technology they want to use so that, as they progress, they can focus on the portfolio itself (Yancey, Graziano, Lee, and O'Malley).

In fact, I think of such a course less as a course culminating in a portfolio, and more as a portfolio course.

* * *

There's a theory that each discipline has its own signature pedagogy. My own theory is that each instructor has his or her own signature pedagogy, too—a way of teaching that distinguishes their instruction. Like others, I try to design a course for a given group of students; I understand, however, that students change class-to-class and year-to-year, not to mention campus-to-campus. I've designed this class for the students I've taught at various campuses—land grants Virginia Tech, Purdue, and Clemson; urban institution UNC Charlotte; former Florida College for Women, now R1 Florida State University. Though the institutions were different, the students were very similar. Still, I try to design for the students whose learning I currently support.

One practice that crosses campuses is what I call "finger exercises," or what I compare to a practice that piano players engage in. The point is to warm up, sound the keys, and rehearse informally: so too with finger exercises in my class. For narrative writing, we use finger exercises for drafts of scenes. For inquiry writing, finger exercises provide accounts of the war—first for college students, then for children, then for twelve-year-old Japanese students, and then in the voice of someone living through the war. In the portfolio, finger exercises help students consider what has been learned so far and reflect on their understanding of genre, its conventions, and on writing itself.

Often, students write brilliantly in the finger exercises; a challenge is to help them write as brilliantly in longer, more sustained writing.

* * *

A now classic assignment in first-year composition is the source- or evidence-based argument. At one point, scholars in the field called it the academic essay, but given what we know about genres and disciplinarity, it's increasingly difficult to argue (ironically) that such an essay is anything more than a school-based genre. Still, being able to identify evidence and employ it to make a point is valuable—whether one is applying for a job, deciding on a candidate to vote for, or writing one's way through college. This assignment, "The Writing Project," asks students to build on inquiry: to inquire into a question, as before, but in this case, to use inquiry to make a claim and to provide evidence for the claim. There are two other caveats to the assignment: 1) it must teach us all something about writing, as it is one of the more understudied fields in the academy; and 2) it must be shared publicly so that the research benefits others.

In thinking about this assignment, I can cite several of my own questions.

My grandmother was born in 1893, an observation that is made possible only by the note of her birth in the family bible; she was the oldest of three, and the names and dates of birth of the three siblings— Olive, William, and Ira—announce themselves on this page, just inside the cover. Nearly sixty years later, my grandfather, an attorney, filed the paperwork required to secure a birth certificate for my grandmother. It went all the way to the California Superior Court for approval and is filled with the language, stamps, and forms that speak to government and regulation. In this small story is one account of writing during twentieth century America: informal, community-based practices of recording significant events through writing were transformed as government—sometimes local, other times state, and still others federal—took charge. Handwritten signatures on a valued familial book were replaced by official government forms. That's not a value judgment per se, I'll note; it is a claim about the role of writing in the twentieth century and how it has changed—a claim that can be evidenced.

Question: When it comes to ways that writing has changed during the last century, is this one example anomalous, or is it synecdoche?

Postcards were created originally in Europe in the nineteenth century; in the U.S., they were originally used for commerce, but toward the end of the century, the government began reducing its restrictions, and individuals began sending them everywhere, sometimes as a testament to travel, sometimes as a substitute for writing a letter, and sometimes to record a significant event. When a specific Brownie camera was invented in 1903, people began creating their own postcards with photographs, now called "Real Photo Postcards."

Question: Where did people learn to write postcards? How did writing postcards influence their view of writing? How did they value postcards? How have postcards represented places and issues, and what difference (if any) have such representations made? What was the relationship of postcards to other genres, like letters and business cards? Is email simply the modern version of postcards? When it comes to answers to these questions, how do we know?

In World War II, a group of five young Japanese-American women began writing to Japanese-American soldiers. The twenty-something year old who founded the group was leading a Sunday school class and conceived of the idea with some of her female students, girls who were only a few years younger than she. This was at the Santa Anita Reassembly Camp, and the girl was Mary Nakahara, whose given name was Yuri, and who married Bill Kochiyama; she is now called Yuri Kochiyama. The young women—but they were really teenage girls, the five of them—pledged to keep writing to the soldiers as they left for internment camps spread out across the Midwest and western U.S. The list of soldiers they wrote grew and grew until they couldn't write letters anymore—there were too many soldiers—so they wrote newsletters that could be duplicated and mailed. Over time, the list of soldiers they were writing grew to five thousand; postcards became letters became newsletters. The role of writing here, in part, was to create a network, a community over space, for support. In fact, the young women who wrote these newsletters theorized them, calling them "mixed up newsletters."

Question: What did the young women write about, and why? Were these newsletters more like letters? More like newsletters? What can we learn about community and about writing from reviewing these? As important, other communities may have participated in similar practices; is this so? If so, who are those communities, who began them, what genres of writing did they employ, and for what purpose and to what effect?

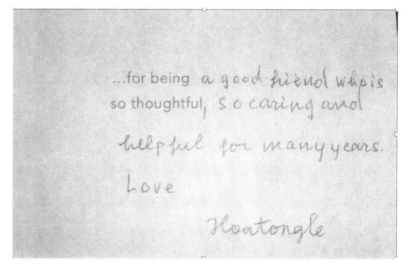

Image 2.

In 2010, a used bookstore in Alexandria, Virginia, gave me all the materials they had retrieved from the used books they had purchased prior to shelving them, including a shoebox full of materials dating from 1942 to 2008. The materials ranged widely: greeting cards, postcards, letters, bookmarks, a jury summons, a menu, a large photograph of U.S. soldiers and European civilians in World War II, a swim club card, a car repair bill, a "Facing Death without Fear" brochure, some pressed flowers, and one leaf. One of the interesting features of both postcards and greeting cards was the kind of additions that writers made to the "given" card: drawings, personal notes, extensions and extrapolations to the greeting card greetings. In fact, both cards and postcards—regardless of the date they were written—seemed to function as a kind of prompt, something for the writer to use not as a substitute for his or her own writing, but as a beginning to say something else, something more.

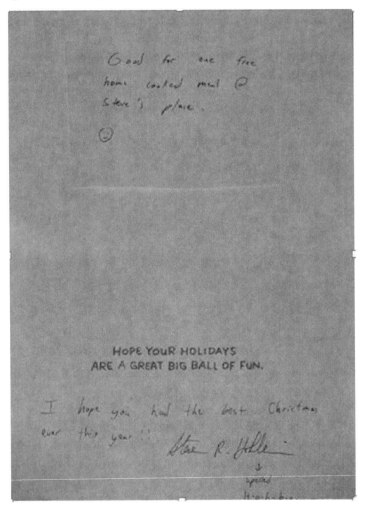

Image 3.

Question: Is this the way we typically use cards and postcards, to write over, around, and beyond the given message? Is this practice a kind of repurposing that predicts the repurposing of today? When people buy cards now, do they think in advance of how they might expand the message, or talk back to it—or does this adaptation or repurposing happen in the process of signing the card?[5]

I have asked students in several courses how they learned the genres they write, from letters and postcards to emails, texts, and tweets. The pattern has changed: In 2006, students had learned to write the newer genres on their own; today, some of them report that they have learned them in school.

Question: How are students learning newer genres? Which ones do they use, why those, and how do they value them? Do all students report the same experience, or does the experience differ across lines of gender, ethnicity, age, major, or some other or combination of factors? Is such a study important, and if so, why?

In taking up questions like these—many of which may well be located at the nexus of personal interest and academic interest—and pursuing them in a source-based way, students engage in inquiry; learn about the function of writing and its contexts in a given situation, field, or event; make a claim about this function and evidence it—all from a position of expertise they are developing. Students can engage in this exploration singly or collectively; on a class blog, we keep track of our progress, raise questions, and help each other; as members of a classroom community, we collect our knowledge about writing and its influences.

Because this area is so under-studied, we have much to learn and much to share about writing itself, about how to write, about how to share what we have learned and can claim and can evidence.

kind of cool to study writing as a process + function in communities

* * *

My interest in reflection began with my interest in portfolios, a practice I first began in 1979. Later, I defined my terms and tried thinking more systematically about reflection itself—as part of a portfolio, yes, but also apart from a portfolio as well—in *Reflection in the Writing Classroom*. More recently, I've been very impressed by new practices in

would be better than death penalty + abortion essays!

reflection that I've seen through my participation in the Inter/National Coalition for Electronic Portfolio Research (I/NCEPR).

One lesson I've learned is that reflection can point in any number of directions: Do we mean meta-cognition, for example, or an account of process? Or perhaps we mean self-assessment generally, or self-assessment in terms of outcomes. Alternatively, we could mean account of learning, synthesis, or exploration. Often, we mean connections— between prior and new knowl-

> Sociolinguistic Content and Process: Reflect back on the content covered in this course. Do you consider geography a social science or a physical science? Why? How do you think other people view geography? Do you feel the things you've learned in this course will be helpful in future courses and your career? If so, how? Do you think your friends, employer, or parents understand the value of geography?

edge, between what we don't know and what we need to know. I use the term too loosely as well: it refers to a rich set of practices, and as a teacher, I'm hungry, wanting them all in my classroom. But perhaps the one that's most important to me is reflection as theorizing— about writing—what it is and why; and about writers—who I am as a composer and why.

One of the questions we've asked participants in the I/NCEPR focuses on prompts: What types of prompts elicit the most reflective thinking? In their work on reflection, the team from the University of Akron used Cranton's model, one that divides reflective thinking into three types: epistemic, psychological, and sociolinguistic (Cranton). What they found was that to encourage the richest reflection, they needed to engage students in all three domains. Later, extending this work, we asked another group in the I/NCEPR to think about reflection by creating a prompt and by observing students creating a portfolio. What they found was that student reflections were especially rich when taking place at the intersection of two of the domains.

Might this be true for writing as well? Is this the logic we call on when we ask students both to define writing and to define themselves as writers?

* * *

The last assignment, apart from the portfolio, asks students to compose a composition in three genres. This is an assignment I adapted from

Liane Robertson and Kara Taczak in their "Teaching for Transfer" course.

MAJOR ASSIGNMENT # 3: COMPOSITION-IN-THREE-GENRES PROJECT

For this assignment you will move from researching and analyzing your topic, as you did in the Writing Project, to creating a composition that uses different genres to communicate to a targeted audience about that same topic. You will use your previous research, along with new sources, to inform your creative strategy and help you make the rhetorical choices necessary to create an effective composition. Your genres are your choice. . . . In this assignment, you will be relating your topic to audience even more than you did in the Writing Project, incorporating additional evidence and new arguments designed for audience expectations. You will target your audience(s), consider the rhetorical situation, and develop genres to communicate to that audience based on the knowledge you have from developing the research essay. You will also develop a rationale to communicate the strategy behind your genre choices, and a reflection on the process. This assignment requires you to engage your critical thinking, your rhetorical awareness, and your reflection capabilities in order to most effectively communicate to your audience.

Of the three genres, there is one genre that is required: a webtext for Florida State University's Center for Everyday Writing, which has as its general mission the study of everyday writing. Through this assignment, students write themselves into expertise from a position of expertise, contribute to a larger archive available to the world, and join a company of other students, scholars, and everyday writers.

Image 4.

* * *

The continuing/culminating project is an electronic portfolio, one that students have been keeping since the beginning of the class. I learned about this kind of portfolio from Julie Hughes at Wolverhampton University in the U.K. In her teaching, Julie had constructed a portfolio not as a final project, but as an environment similar to a CMS, but with additional features (e.g., a blogging tool) and as a place where her students archived, recorded, and reflected upon their learning together. In addition, her students—who are student teachers—continue working in the portfolio as they take up jobs, so the portfolio also serves as a kind of transitional space.

My students are different. They haven't all signed on to the same major, and I can't assume (and I certainly can't require) that they continue with the portfolio, but I can assure that they have a very good experience with it. To do that, I design a portfolio that is integral to the course, a place where they record, archive, think, and share. I create one myself so they can see what mine looks like, and I refer them to others. In terms of grading, this is where the rubber hits the road. We work on a set of guidelines together; each student needs to include his or her goals, and we include development as well as accomplishment.

Image 5.

Grading itself merits discussion. This is a writing class, so the majority of the grade comes from the portfolio—ordinarily about 80%—and the rest comes from class participation and homework. The logic is twofold: First, the portfolio, deferring grading, as Irwin Weiser explained over twenty years ago, gives students—all students—the gift of time. Second, the portfolio provides space for an archive, and it is through working with materials in the archive—including drafts, reflections, responses, and texts from outside the class—that students make meaning from their texts, of their experiences, and with their own reflections. Periodically, over the course of the term, I respond to the portfolio as a member of the audience to let students know what I see, how I'm seeing, and what questions occur to me. At the end of the term, though, the institution has its way; a grade is required, and we move from the formative assessment of responses to writing and to the portfolio to the summative assessment of grades.

For years I used a scoring guide for the portfolio. It is no different with an ePortfolio, though the criteria should be (Yancey, "Electronic Portfolios"; Yancey, McElroy, and Powers). Partly, it's an exercise in survival: Portfolios come in late, and grades are due early. Partly, it forces us to articulate criteria and benchmarks: What is expected begins to become defined. Partly, when put into dialogue with a portfolio, expectations become tangible. More recently, I've seen the guide less as mechanism for summative assessment, and more as heuristic, as a way of prompting a kind of discussion about a writer's development, achievement, understanding, and knowledge. Seen this way, the guide, especially when we all contribute to its making, frames a concluding conversation about the writing we've engaged in all term. What, we can ask, has been learned about writing as knowledge and practice? How has the writer developed? What are the next steps in this development?

* * *

I began this text—is it an essay, an article, a series of short notes strung together, punctuated by images and textboxes?—by saying that first-year composition is an impossible course to design given all that it needs to do. Perhaps this is so for all our courses, but for some reason, it seems especially so for FYC. That's evidenced by what's here, by how I developed what I have here designed—the product of a kind of curricular and pedagogical bricolage, with bits of curriculum stolen from one source, bits of pedagogy borrowed from friends and colleagues, the sum something of a collectively individual design. But the importance and impossibility of FYC is also evidenced by what I haven't included; those absences—of reading strategies, of evaluating sources, of considering how research is made in multiple fields—are a presence providing a small index to what we need to include. Some of those items, I do include. Others: I only wish. So yes, this is an impossible task, I concede, but in the *same* breath, I have to say: It's an important task. And that just because it's impossible doesn't mean we shouldn't try. And that when we try, we should try both individually *and* together.

This design, then, is one effort in the larger constellation. I look forward to learning what you make of it.

NOTES

1. In this sense, my response echoes Edwin Hopkins's view in the inaugural issue of *English Journal* when he, now famously, asked "Can Composition Be Done under the Current Conditions?" and answered: "NO" (1).

2. The range of "delivery" options for first-year composition is wide indeed. See *Delivering College Composition: The Fifth Canon*.

3. The two volumes devoted to this question are one good place to think about this issue. See Sullivan and Tinberg, *What Is "College Level" Writing?* and *What Is "College Level" Writing II?*

4. The metaphor of a map is in fact more than metaphor. As we explain in *Writing Across Contexts*, the kind of map students create has everything to do with how they see the world of writing:

> What's interesting here, relative to writing, is how the mental model of writing that students develop—or don't develop—can affect how they approach writing tasks. One way of thinking about it is to say that a mental map is very like a larger road map that allows one to see different locations and routes to those locations (and connections among those routes); with such a map, one has a fair amount of agency in deciding where to go and how, at least in terms of seeing possibilities and how they relate to each other—precisely because one can see relationships across locations. Instead of maps, of course, many people now use a GPS device, which can be enormously helpful in getting from A to B and, depending on the model, can offer various routes from A to B (the quickest, the most scenic); traffic alerts; and alternative routes. Still, all a GPS offers is the route from A to B: one doesn't have much sense of how the route is situated or its relationship to other routes or places. The analogy, though imperfect, is probably self-evident: at some level, without a large road map of writing, students are too often traveling from one writing task to another, using a definition and map of writing that is the moral equivalent of a GPS device. It will help students move from one writing task to another, but it can't provide them with the sense of the whole, the relationships among the various genres and discourse communities that constitute writing in the university, and the accompanying agency that a fuller map contributes to—nor will the GPS support the development of expertise.

5. These examples are drawn from my forthcoming *The Way We Were: Everyday Writing in 20th Century America*.

IMAGE SOURCES

Image 1: Student writing and my response; used with permission. Source: Kathleen Blake Yancey.

Image 2: Greeting card with handwriting. Source: Kathleen Blake Yancey.

Image 3: Greeting card opened up with handwriting. Source: Kathleen Blake Yancey.

Image 4: Screenshot of website. Source: Kathleen Blake Yancey.

Image 5: Screenshot of electronic portfolio. Source: Kathleen Blake Yancey.

Works Cited

Applebee, Arthur, and Judith Langer. "A Snapshot of Writing Instruction in Middle Schools and High Schools." *English Journal* 100.6 (2011): 14-27. Print.

Beaufort, Anne. *College Writing and Beyond: A New Framework for University Writing Instruction*. Logan: Utah State UP, 2007. Print.

Beyer, Catharine, Gerald Gillmore, and Andrew Fisher. *Inside the Undergraduate Experience: The UW Study of Undergraduate Learning*. Portland: Jossey-Bass, 2007. Print.

Bransford, John. "Learning and Transfer." *How People Learn: Mind, Brain, Experience, and School*. Ed. John D. Bransford, Ann L.Brown, and Rodney R.Cocking. Washington, DC: National Academy Press, 2000: 51-78. Print.

Downs, Douglas, and Elizabeth Wardle. "Teaching About Writing, Righting Misconceptions: (Re)Envisioning 'First-Year Composition' as 'Introduction to Writing Studies.'" *College Composition and Communication* 58.4 (2007): 552-84. Print.

—. "Reimagining the Nature of FYC Trends in Writing-about-Writing Pedagogies." *Exploring Composition Studies: Sites, Issues, Perspectives*. Ed. Kelly Ritter and Paul Kei Matsuda. Logan: Utah State UP, 2012: 123-44. Print.

Hansen, Kristen, Suzanne Reeve, Richard Sudweeks, Gary L. Hatch, Jennifer Gonzalez, Patricia Esplin, and William S.Bradshaw. "An Argument for Changing Institutional Policy and Granting A.P. Credit in English: An Empirical Study of College Sophomores' Writing." *WPA: Writing Program Administration* 28 (2004): 29-54. Print.

Hopkins, Edwin. "Can Good Composition Teaching Be Done under Current Conditions?" *English Journal* 1.1 (1912): 1-9.

Krebs, Paula. "Next Time, Fail Better." *Inside Higher Education*. 6 May, 2012. Web. 8 Jan. 2013.

Marra, Rose, and Betsy Palmer. "Epistemologies of the Sciences, Humanities, and Social Sciences: Liberal Arts Students' Perceptions." *The Journal of General Education* 57.2 (2008): 100-18. Print.

Magolda, Marcia B. Baxter. *Making Their Own Way: Narratives for Transforming Higher Education to Promote Self-Development*. Sterling: Stylus, 2001. Print.

Miller, Carolyn. "Genre as Social Action." *Quarterly Journal of Speech* 70 (1984): 151-67. Print.

Moffett, James. *Teaching the Universe of Discourse*. Portsmouth: Heinemann, 1987. Print.

Sullivan, Patrick and Howard Tinberg. *What Is "College-Level" Writing?* Urbana, IL: NCTE, 2006. Print.

Sullivan, Patrick, Howard Tinberg, and Sheridan Blau. *What Is "College-Level" Writing?* Vol. 2. Urbana, IL: NCTE, 2010. Print.

Weiser, Irwin. "Portfolio Practice and Assessment for Collegiate Basic Writers." *Portfolios in the Writing Classroom: An Introduction.* Ed. Kathleen Blake Yancey. Urbana: NCTE, 1992. 89-102. Print.

Wineburg, Samuel. *Historical Thinking and Other Unnatural Acts.* Philadelphia: Temple UP, 2001. Print.

Yancey, Kathleen Blake. "A View-from-a-Room Perspective: The (Designed) Influence of Culture on ePortfolio Practice." *English in a Globalized World: International Perspectives on Teaching English.* Ed. LouAnn Reid. London: Routledge, 2013. 266-78. Print.

—. *Delivering College Composition: The Fifth Canon.* Portsmouth: Heinemann, 2006. Print.

—. "Electronic Portfolios and Writing Assessment: A Work in Progress." *Assessment in Writing. Assessment in the Disciplines Series.* Vol. 4. Ed. Marie C. Paretti and Katrina Powell. Tallahassee: Association of Institutional Research, 2010. 183-205. Print.

—. "The Literacy Demands of Entering the University." *Handbook on Adolescent Literacy.* Ed. Leila Christenbury, Randy Bomer, and Peter Smagorinsky. New York: Guilford, 2008. 256-270. Print.

—. *Reflection in the Writing Classroom.* Logan: Utah State UP, 1997. Print.

—, Liane Robertson, and Kara Taczak. "Writing Across Contexts: Transfer, Composition, and Cultures of Writing." Forthcoming. Utah State UP, 2013. Print.

—, Stephen McElroy, and Elizabeth Powers. "Composing, Networks, and Electronic Portfolios: Notes toward a Theory of Assessing ePortfolios." *Digital Writing Assessment and Evaluation.* Ed. Heidi McKee and Danielle DeVoss. Logan, UT: Utah State UP. Web.

—, Leigh Graziano, Rory Lee, and Jennifer O'Malley. "Reflection, ePortfolios, and WEPO: A Reflective Account of New Practices in a New Curriculum." *Reflection and Metacognition in College Teaching.* Ed. Matthew Kaplan, Naomi Silver, Danielle LaVaque-Manty, and Deborah Meizlish. Washington, DC: Stylus Press, 2013. 175-203. Print.

Appendix: Course Syllabus

FIRST-YEAR COMPOSITION[*]

Kathleen Yancey (kyancey@fsu.edu) M 6:45–9:30
Spring
Hours: Mon 4–6 and by appointment

Purpose: The primary purpose of this section of First-Year Composition is to help you continue to develop as a writer. To do that, we'll read, write, talk, develop a language that will help us talk about our reading and writing, reflect on our communications with each other, use email, revise, blog, revise again, share writing, and laugh—though not in this order. If we succeed in this effort, you'll find that you are writing differently, with a fuller sense of the interaction that writing initiates.

Texts: Your own writings (including a flash drive)
Three issues of *National Forum*
The McGraw Hill Handbook
Articles in pdf, on the web, and via the library's electronic journals
Handouts

The Nature of the Course: Reading and writing and talking and listening are all part of communication; in this course, we'll use our talents in three of these arts to focus on writing. Just as there are many rhetorical situations in which we write—different occasions and audiences and purposes—there are different genres—forms of writing—and we will work in several of them. We will write individually, and we will write together, as a class and in partnerships and groups. As we

---

[*]   A complete version of the syllabus is here http://kyancey.wix.com/fsufyc#

compose, we will reflect on our writing experiences, thinking analyti-cally and holistically about what works for us and when, about what we are able to see by framing material in different ways, and about how rhetoric is always at the heart of that framing. Through this reflection, especially on the key terms defining writing, we'll create a theory of writing that you'll find helpful as you take up writing tasks in new situations, both inside and outside school.

Requirements: The course requires that you
- participate in class and online
- read material as it is due
- write homework assignments when they are due
- present formally your oral assignments, with visual communi-cation as stipulated
- create an electronic portfolio and submit it at the end of the term with interview materials
- submit compositions when they are due: in addition to a port-folio, there are four of these
    - **narrative
    - **inquiry
    - **source-based argument/claim and evidence
    - **composition in three genres

I may also ask that you attend the Reading/Writing Center or Digital Studio and/or that you complete other supplementary assignments.

Attendance, Assignments, and Due Dates: You'll need to come to class; and if we all participate, you'll want to come to class. This read-ing and writing is engaging, a point of intersection where we learn about ourselves and the world, about people we create, about subjects we create, about knowledge we create. If you have to miss class, please let me know in advance. If you miss more than 2 classes, your grade will be lowered, and you may fail. Assignments are due when they are due. Enough said? They are listed on your course schedule.

Some Axioms: This course is intended to help you develop critical literacy, which is itself a function of one's ability to read, to critique, to articulate, to share, to reflect, to revise. Critical literacy also suggests a kind of ability at adaptation, a kind of flexibility that allows a person to function in many kinds of situations. It's a literacy worth having academically, professionally, and personally.

Evaluation:
Class Participation: 10
Reading SRR (Summary, Respond, Reflect): 20
Portfolio: 70

Academic Integrity: Since we are here to learn, I assume we won't cheat or plagiarize. If you have any questions about whether your work could be construed in either of these ways, please let me know.

Concerns or Questions: If you have them, please let me know. I'm here to assure that you have the best experience possible. If my hours aren't yours, let me know; we'll find a time that works.

The Syllabus is subject to reasonable modification, given the needs of the class. I'll keep you posted.

A YANCEY ACADEMIC USER DOC/GLOSSARY

Class Participation *means what you think it does: prepare for class, be ready to discuss issues and raise questions; when prompted to, discuss in the same way online.*

SRR's come in three forms:

- *First, a general SRR=Summarize; Respond; Reflect (connect to class, readings, other classes/experiences; raise questions)*
- *Second, a focused assignment with its own directions*
- *Third, a collaborative SRR, focused on a specific question and composed with one or more colleagues in class*

Submit=send to KY

Share=put on blog; responding on the blog=provide context; connect your observations/post to earlier ones and to readings; help us all see anew → http://fsufyc.blogspot.com/

Collab Share=as above, but with a partner/s

Electronic Portfolio *typically means a compilation model showcasing someone's work created through collecting, selecting and reflecting that is completed at the end of a given period of time—a unit, a course, a program, even a degree. In this class, we'll work in a different kind of portfolio model, an environmental portfolio providing space for you to* *archive work and to reflect upon it as we go. Think of it as a materially rich thinking space.*

Composition *means: we'll decide this together ;)*

Other than the ePortfolio, all work should be submitted in e **and** *print formats.*

Key Terms: All disciplines and fields of inquiry are defined by their vocabulary, and a map of these terms, created by an expert, is a defining feature of expertise. Our key terms in this course include *composition, composing process, drafting, revision, peer review, editing, rhetorical situation, genre, families of genres, audience, discourse community, context, medium/ia, reflection, knowledge, and theory.*

13 A Cornucopia of Composition Theories: What These Teachers Tell Us About Our Discipline

Deborah Coxwell-Teague and Ronald F. Lunsford

As we have read and reflected on the theoretical statements of the thirteen composition scholars represented in this study—and then examined the syllabi that demonstrate how they apply their theories in their own teaching—we have found an impressive agreement among these teacher/theorists as to what they could wish to accomplish in a one-semester composition course, and an equally impressive range in the choices they make in their courses, given a fact they all point to: namely, that no one writing course can do all that its teacher, its college or university, and its clientele (in the broadest sense of that word) would like it to do. Such a beginning might prompt one to repeat the oft-quoted lament that the first-year composition (FYC) course is expected to be all things to all people. The teachers represented here are not, however, attempting to offer courses that do that. Before we turn to those matters that our teachers would like to see done in FYC, we call attention to a few issues/concerns these teachers do not accept as part of the mission of this course. Obviously, the list of things a group of thirteen teachers do not do would be infinite; we call attention to the following issues because, for some teachers of writing in the United States, they either are or have been important goals of writing instruction.

First-Year Composition Does Not Focus on Grammar. Many of the teachers represented here have nothing to say about grammar and mechanics. In Chapter 11, "Looking into Writing-about-Writing Classrooms," Elizabeth Wardle and Doug Downs seem to speak for those who do mention this issue in their account of the role that "fixing" has played in the early history of writing instruction in the U.S.[1]

> Its [The FYC course's] purpose has long been understood by college administrations and faculty across the country as 1) correcting faults in previous learning, as evidenced by mechanical errors in students' writing and 2) preparing students for the rigors of "college writing," which is taken to be an undifferentiated academic writing that David Russell has called "universal educated discourse" (60). In both functions, college writing instruction is essentially an inoculation: a one-shot, "fix it all now," get-it-out-of-the-way attempt to treat writing as a basic, fundamental, universal skill that can be permanently mastered. (Ch. 11)

a shot

In making this claim, however, neither Wardle and Downs, nor the other teachers in our study, deny the importance of conventions in any writing situation. As the questions Wardle and Downs ask their students indicate, those conventions must be a part of the understanding of rhetorical situation, genre, and discourse that the FYC course should be helping students to develop:

> What is the exigence for what you're writing? What do you need it to accomplish? How will readers use it? What are readers' expectations for what you're writing, and what are their values for what will make your text 'good'? How do those values arise from the activity the text is meant to help accomplish? (Ch. 11)

Even those teachers in our study who are most attuned to the fact that a racist and classist society may well use issues of grammar and mechanics as cudgels against their students are careful to make it clear that their courses will be much more than "fix-it" shops. In Chapter 9, "Working Through Theory in a Community College Composition Classroom," Howard Tinberg speaks about the role of conventions in his writing courses, stating:

> True to best composition and writing center practices, I attend to matters of mechanics and grammar within the context of students' writing, identifying and glossing the patterns of errors and inviting students to become editors of their work rather than taking on the task myself. To be honest, relatively

little classroom time is taken up with mechanics and grammar. (Ch. 9)

In Chapter 6, "'Talkin bout Fire Don't Boil the Pot': Putting Theory into Practice in a First-Year Writing Course at an HBCU," Teresa Redd talks about the connection she sees between issues of convention and rhetorical situation: "I tell my students, conventions matter because readers matter, and that conventions matter to readers. Conventions make it easier for readers to comprehend a text, in large part because conventions fulfill readers' expectations."

In Chapter 4, "A Grade-less Writing Course that Focuses on Labor and Assessing," Asao Inoue speaks about the role of conventions in a first-year course with large percentages of non-native English speakers.

> This course does not consider these other Englishes as signs of being "underprepared," "deficient," or "lacking." In fact, I believe that the academy needs courses like this to enlarge its boundaries and to do more than give students the "right to their own languages." Courses like this will allow the academy to incorporate more fully students' languages, create new ways of thinking and communicating, expand its discourses, learn from and change because of its students, and change the destructive, white hegemony that has punished and shunned so many. (Ch. 4)

Inoue goes on to explain that he is "not suggesting that [he does] not teach a white, middle-class academic discourse, or that [his] rubrics and expectations do not resemble that dominant discourse"; instead, he is determined not to use editing conventions "as a cudgel to bludgeon students of color and other students because they are not white, middle-class academics."

First-Year Composition Does Not Focus on Persuasion. If we think of persuasion in terms of Aristotle's finding the available means of persuasion in a particular case, or in terms of Kenneth Burke's concept of "consubstantiality," or in terms of Stephen Toulmin's claims and warrants; or, if we think of persuasion as debate-style exercises in which students tackle hot-button issues of the day, then persuasion is noticeably absent in the theoretical statements and syllabi of these teachers. For the most part, they do not even refer to persuasion in these senses. That is not to say that they do not deal with claim and support as an important tool for critical thinking; they do, almost to a person. When it comes to that kind of argument/counter-argument that has been a mainstay of many composition practitioners anxious to help move their students up the rungs of William Perry's ladder, as outlined in *Forms of Ethical and Intellectual Development*, these teachers are noticeably silent. Those who do deal with this issue do so not in terms of persuasion but rather in terms of inquiry and the construction of knowledge. In Chapter 10, "For the Love of Language: A Curriculum," Victor Villanueva explains Plato's dialectic as it is practiced in the Socratic method, and then describes how he helps his students use dialectic as a method of inquiry:

> The method begins with discovering students' prejudices (as in preconceived notions more than bigotries) and having students discuss the sources of those beliefs within them, discussing them, then researching them, to discuss them (best in writing) yet again. The idea is to look to initial sources of ideas, to question them, to see the political or cultural assumptions present in all things, then to write a critical-documented essay—an opinion, backed by substantiation from research presented in a relatively conventional format. (Ch. 10)

In speaking of her inquiry project in Chapter 12, "Attempting the Impossible: Designing a First-Year Composition Course," Kathleen Blake Yancey notes that many students "enter college as dualistic thinkers," seeing "the world as a platform for dichotomies and their role as taking and holding one side." Rather than asking those students to engage in debate-style exercises that might exacerbate their dichotomous thinking, Yancey asks students to inquire into a topic they know very little about, thereby providing the student "an exigence, an occasion for inquiring and considering together, for undertaking and pursuing the larger and more philosophical questions that contextualize the specific." Yancey goes on to compare the kind of instruction she provides with academic claim- and argument-based instruction:

> A now classic assignment in first-year composition is the source- or evidence-based argument. At one point, scholars in the field called it the academic essay, but given what we know about genres and disciplinarity, it's increasingly difficult to argue (ironically) that such an essay is anything more than a school-based genre. (Ch. 12)

Yancey concedes that "being able to identify evidence and employ it to make a point is valuable," but she believes that these skills can be taught through inquiry; as she puts it, students may be asked "to inquire into a question, as before; but, in this case, to use inquiry to make a claim and to provide evidence for the claim."

First-Year Composition Does Not Focus on the Improvement of Writing. If we think of the writing process classroom as one in which students are encouraged to think of writing instruction as a series of instructions in, and applications of, writing strategies and stages (from pre-writing, to drafting, to revision, to, perhaps, more pre-writing and invention and more revision, with a final product resulting at some point in the process); and if we assume that those final products will, in most cases, be "better" than earlier drafts; and if we think that the body of work presented in a semester-ending portfolio will, in most cases, show a trajectory of writing improvement over the course of a semester, we do not find these assumptions evident in the work presented in this study. Rather, these teachers focus their attention on the rhetorical nature of effective writing, seeking to help students learn basic principles of rhetorical analysis that should prove useful to them in their professional and personal lives. We see this focus in a comment Paula Mathieu makes in Chapter 5, "A Guiding Question, Some Primary Research, and a Dash of Rhetorical Awareness": "While I will not pretend that my first-year course can prepare all students for every rhetorical situation they will ever face, I strive to help students understand that every writing task takes place within a rhetorical situation and that not all situations call for the exact same kind of writing: that there is no *one* such thing as good writing."

In Chapter 1, "Writing, Language, and Literacy," Chris Anson comments on the importance of helping students develop rhetorical awareness: "Research on transfer in various contexts shows that learning to write is highly situated and depends on immersion in communities of practice where the conventions of writing, imbricated with complex aspects of rhetorical purpose, local histories, and subtly evolving norms, are unfamiliar to outsiders."

In the following two excerpts, the writers make it clear that their courses are designed to help students learn how to assess and negotiate writing situations, not just move lockstep through stages in the writing process. The first is taken from Suresh Canagajarah in Chapter 2, "ESL Composition as a Literate Act of the Contact Zone": "I also do not think that there are certain codes or literacies that can be treated as generic or foundational to prepare students for the communicative challenges they will face later. What is generative and foundational are the underlying practices—i.e., writing process, language awareness, and rhetorical sensitivity—that the course focuses on."

The second comes from Alexander Reid in Chapter 7, "The Activity of Writing: Affinity and Affect in Composition."

> If we can agree that writing instruction must be contextualized and situated, then it is not so difficult to also recognize that writing itself is similarly situated. . . . As such, it would be an error to imagine a composition course as teaching writing in general. In fact, it would be an error to imagine teaching *academic* writing in general, for even the writing done by academics varies widely. (Ch. 7)

The clearest statement that the overall quality of writing in students' finished products is not the coin of the realm in his first-year composition class may come from Asao Inoue. He communicates this fact to students in his class syllabus:

> This contract is based on a simple principle and a few important assumptions, which are not typical in most classrooms. First, the principle: how much *labor* you do is more important to your learning and growth as a reader and writer than the quality of your writing. Our grading contract calculates grades by how much *labor* you do and the manner you do it in. (Ch. 4)

[handwritten margin note: liked the labor idea]

WHAT SHOULD STUDENTS LEARN? HOW DO THESE TEACHERS FACILITATE THIS LEARNING?

Obviously, no analysis or synthesis of the syllabi and discussions in this text can capture the individual voices of these teachers as they explain the theories of writing they have constructed from many years of research in writing and literacy issues; nor could we hope to do justice to the many exciting reading and writing assignments and classroom activities described in the syllabi offered here. Each syllabus and each theoretical statement is as unique as the teacher/theorist who has constructed it. If the discipline of Composition Studies or Writing Studies (to name two of the most common terms used for it) has be-

gun to assume a discernable form, then there should be evidence of
that form in the work presented here. To be sure, we have other evidence of such a discipline in agreed-upon goals for first-year composition, as set forth by such professional organizations as the National
Council of Teachers of English and the Council of Writing Program
Administrators. However, it is one thing to set forth a list of goals; it
is quite another to create a course and then explain what exactly will
be done in that course and why. That is what these teachers have done
here. We believe their work constitutes *prima facie* evidence of this
discipline, and makes an important contribution to it.

As we have attempted to get a glimpse of what this work tells us
about composition theory, it has proven useful to sort our findings
into four large, imaginary bins that we can represent by four questions:

1. What do these teachers want their students to learn about lan-
    guage and writing?
2. What do these teachers do in their classrooms?
3. What kinds of response to writing do these teachers provide?
4. What forms of evaluation do these teachers employ?

In the remainder of this chapter, we will look into each of these bins,
labeled "Course Content," "Classroom Activities," "Response to
Writing," and "Evaluation," in hopes of at least touching all the parts
of the elephant that is first-year composition.

Course Content

As more and more writing teachers have focused attention on language
and writing as the content for their courses, others have questioned
whether the course should focus on learning "about writing" or learning "to write." The teachers in this study suggest that we are dealing
with a paradox—not a contradiction. One theme sounded by these
teachers is that writing is both a subject and a technique—a way of
knowing and a way of doing. Elizabeth Wardle and Doug Downs deal
with this paradox by separating the knowledge they are attempting to
help students construct into two types, what they refer to as "declarative knowledge" (knowledge about writing/language) and what they
refer to as "procedural knowledge" (experiential knowledge that comes
from applying basic principles of writing/language). According to
Wardle and Downs, an effective writing course "can focus on broadening students' conceptions of what writing is" (declarative knowledge) and, at the same time, "enforce accurate conceptions of writing

through its pedagogical procedures" by asking students "to engage in activities that reflect . . . an understanding of genre (procedural knowledge)" (Ch. 11).

For many of the teachers here, the key to this paradox is the role that reflection plays in their teaching. In a fashion reminiscent of an Escher painting, the teachers want students to read and write about texts (in many cases, texts that deal with reading and writing) and then to reflect on their own writing in ways that increase their mindfulness about the role of language in their lives. In the passage below, Paula Mathieu provides theoretical support (in one case, from another member of this study, Jody Shipka) for her understanding of the way students' reflections can help them construct knowledge about writing and develop their abilities to apply those principles.

> I . . . borrow . . . from Shipka . . . what she calls a "heads up" statement, in which students must explain their writerly choices—what they were going for and why they did what they did. . . . This kind of work is what Zebroski calls "metawriting . . . writing that reflects on writing, that examines writing experiences of student and professional writers" (19). I agree with Zebroski's idea that "All this metawriting helps improve 'content' while making students increasingly aware of their own theories of writing" (21). (Ch. 5)

Alexander Reid speaks of the power of reflection from a slightly different perspective; he asks a series of questions that are designed to help students see their writing in the context of the network within which it exists, and then explains what this approach will do for them.

> Where was this composition produced? What technologies and other objects were involved? How much time was spent? What specific strategies were employed? What choices were available? What informed the choices that were eventually made? This produces a keen sense of the decisions writers have made and hence the opportunities we have to act differently in the future. In other words, writing becomes experimental in the artistic sense, but also in the scientific sense, and the reflection operates roughly analogous to a lab report. (Ch. 7)

Howard Tinberg uses reflective writing assignments as a means of helping students develop the vocabulary needed to articulate their understandings of what it means to use language purposefully and, thereby, gain agency in the process.

> I believe that such agency resides in the power of clear and precise reflection on what works and what needs work in a particular piece of writing. Having the words with which to name qualities of their written work enables students to manipulate and re-uthorize that work in productive ways. Without that vocabulary, students may simply take their chances on success by unthinkingly rehearsing what seemed to work last time, even though the terrain and the writing task may have shifted. (Ch. 9)

In the passage below, Kathleen Blake Yancey begins by talking about the various roles that reflection can play, but ends in pointing to the important role it plays in helping students "theorize" about writing and about themselves as writers:

> One lesson I've learned is that reflection can point in any number of directions: Do we mean meta-cognition, for example, or an account of process? Or perhaps we mean self-assessment generally, or self-assessment in terms of outcomes. Alternatively, we could mean account of learning, synthesis, or exploration. Often, we mean connections—between prior and new knowledge, between what we don't know and what we need to know. I use the term too loosely as well: it refers to a rich set of practices, and as a teacher, I'm hungry, wanting them all in my classroom. But perhaps the one that's most important to me is reflection as theorizing— about writing— what it is and why; and about writers—who I am as a composer and why. (Ch. 12)

Clearly, then, reflection is a tool these teachers use as a means of learning: Students write to learn about writing. As we indicated above, though, they fashion courses that deal with more than just learning about writing. They broaden the scope of this course so that it is accurate to say that the real subject is language. Chris Anson speaks to this point in saying: "Both the content and processes of the course turn around language; just as the students explore language as a uniquely human activity, they are also reflect on the ways they use language in the course to communicate their explorations with others" (Ch. 1). In speaking of the various ways in which all teachers of writing, regardless of their backgrounds, approach writing courses, Victor Villanueva says, "What does join us is language, a love of language—as literary, as poetry, as non-fiction, as the material cause for rhetoric, literature, linguistics, creative writing" (Ch. 10).

Language certainly entails writing, but it entails much more. To a person, the teachers represented in this study include instruction in reading as part of their charge. Elizabeth Wardle and Doug Downs speak to the purposeful way that they approach reading instruction in their teaching: "We both build explicit reading instruction and assessment of reading abilities into our classrooms, recognizing that most students have not received such instruction for many years" (Ch. 11). However, neither Wardle and Downs nor the other teachers represented here offer instruction in finding the "correct" meanings of texts. Rather, as Doug Downs articulates, they are at pains to aid students in discovering the connections between reading and writing and, in doing so, to understand the construction involved in all uses of language. According to Downs, his aim is to "help students begin to see writing and reading as two expressions of the same textual activity, endlessly intertwined and relying on surprisingly similar strategies" (Ch. 11). He notes that when he introduces students to constructivist concepts about reading, it is "usually students' first encounter with reading scientists who say, flat out, that individual readers construct individual readings of a text, and why" (Ch. 11). Downs goes on to discuss the difficulties involved in presenting these complex concepts to students, and the ways in which he deals with such complexities in his teaching.

In Chapter 8, "Beyond Text and Talk: A Multimodal Approach to First-Year Composition," Jody Shipka offers students a new perspective from which to see reading, one from which a text becomes something of an artifact to be studied. Here she describes the way students work together to unravel the complexities of texts:

> Placing students in pairs, I ask them to jot down everything they see going on in, on, or around the pages of the reading, beginning with the size, color, and type of paper the text is printed on. I recommend that they work from top-down, listing everything they can identify with regard to the text's appearance and construction. Nothing, I remind them, is too obvious to note, including the title, author's name, an epigraph,

x-number of paragraphs, use of English language, italics, quotes from other sources, images, captions, hand-written annotations in the margins of the text, works cited, and so on. (Ch. 8)

We see then that the subject is language; the method for helping students learn about this subject is to provide opportunities for them to read, write, and to use reflective writing in the service of creating a "mindful" approach to the subject. What, then, are the basic concepts about language that these teachers want their students to grapple with? There are many, of course, but the following topics appear throughout the writings of these teachers: *process, community, multiple modalities, learning,* and *power.* Since the courses these teachers envision use writing to help students construct knowledge for themselves, we use headings below that focus on the role of writing in helping students interrogate these language-related concepts.

Writing to Learn About Process. Though some theorists have pronounced us "post process," the teachers here are committed to providing opportunities for their students to learn about their writing processes. However, in a statement from Douglas Hesse in Chapter 3, "Occasions, Sources, and Strategies," he rejects a linear, step-by-step process in favor of one in which students tend to move from one relatively brief piece of writing to another in assignments that are sequenced in order to help students learn about process and many other language-related issues:

> Given that writers learn by writing, and given that there is lots to learn, in the third phase of the course, I assign numerous, short assignments rather than a few long ones. I have taught courses in which students write four or five papers in multiple drafts, and I grant the wisdom (and convenience) of this venerable process pedagogy. In this course, however, students submit at least one piece of writing most class meetings, and most of these writings are one to three pages. My response takes the following form, "If you were going to revise and develop this piece, you should consider . . ." Because process instruction happens mostly "between" tasks rather than "within" them, portions of class meetings function as studio time. (Ch. 3)

We see a move here toward brief, sequenced writing assignments that might be given by a theorist such as William E. Coles, Jr. That same approach is found in a comment by Teresa Redd. She begins by saying that she offers students "step-by-step" instruction that comprises "brainstorming, freewriting, diagramming, outlining, and especially revising," but she goes on to explain that her assignments are integrated so that "students can use documents written earlier to help them compose their research reports. For instance, the book review and annotated bibliography function as a form of prewriting for the research report, while the literature review functions as the first draft of a section of the final report" (Ch. 6).

In the statement below, Victor Villanueva articulates the problems attendant upon a writing process approach that has become formulaic, and cites writing theorists that inform his approach to process and revision:

> I no longer think in terms of revision as multiple drafts for composition classes, where students are not intrinsically driven to convey a message, and aren't driven to revise. . . . Following William Coles's *Plural I*, I adopted sequenced or scaffolded assignments. If, as Ann Berthoff says, revision is a matter of thinking again, presenting again, and seeing again (a re-cognition, a re-presentation, and a re-vision), then that becomes the important matter. . . . The trick then becomes making a series of assignments in which each assignment builds on the concepts presented in a previous assignment. (Ch. 10)

each assignment builds on the last

Writing to Learn About Community. It comes as no surprise to those who have tracked the social turn in composition during the last several years that the teachers represented here emphasize the communal nature of writing—or, for that matter, of all uses of language. This focus can be seen most prominently in their approaches to collaboration and discourse/situation/genre.

When we say that writing is a collaborative endeavor, it is usual to think about writing situations in which official collaboration is found (for example, when texts have two or more co-authors), or to think of the ways in which a writer may solicit and receive feedback in producing a composition. However, as Suresh Canagarajah explores collaboration with his students, in what he refers to as the "contact zone" between cultures, the voices of readers/listeners (as they are internalized by writers) play a role in helping a writer co-construct a text.

> Students also learn that writing products are shaped socially
> and contextually. Not only do they generate ideas collabora-
> tively, in relation to what others think and write, but they also
> shape the structure, organization, and genre conventions in
> relation to the uptake of others. Though students may initial-
> ly come with some strong preferences on what to write, they
> renegotiate their products in relation to the preferences and
> suggestions of their peers and the instructor. (Ch. 2)

Canagarajah wants his students to come to understand that their
texts will be shaped by readers' expectations; he also wants them to understand that a writer must learn to form his or her texts in light of the
needs and expectations of groups of readers that comprise discourse
communities. What counts as knowledge in one discourse community (e.g., personal experience) may not be acceptable in another. As
Canagarajah puts it, "Multilingual students must realize that the
knowledge represented in their writing must be negotiated in relation
to the intellectual traditions meeting in the contact zone."

Asao Inoue frames his inquiry assignment around issues of language as they relate to discourse communities. His assignment suggests ways students might explore these issues in the school-related
and personal discourse communities with which they may come into
contact.

> This inquiry may focus on the practices of language used in a
> community, say the language practices in Biology, or in your
> church, or some other group/community that you belong to
> (or seek to enter). Your inquiry might take on some other lan-
> guage-related topic that benefits in some way your peers in
> this class. Another way to think about this project is that it is
> one in which you ask a question about rhetoric, or about the
> language/literacy practices of a particular community. (Ch. 4)

In addition to these types of collaboration, our contributors want
their students to see the incorporation of sources, both primary and
secondary, as a type of collaboration. They are especially invested in
helping students incorporate primary sources—such as interviews and
questionnaires—into their texts, and they want students to understand the ways primary and secondary sources may work together to
help shape texts.

somewhat

Paula Mathieu tells us that she includes primary research because it comprises what she "believe[s] to be so many important intellectual tasks, especially for students at this age and moment of their lives" (Ch. 5). She goes on to note that even in primary research, such as conducting interviews, "library research is essential in asking the right questions and in understanding the context of the stories the writers learn about."

Howard Tinberg also talks about the importance of primary and secondary research, and of the ways that students can gain expertise in one via the other. In particular, he encourages students to learn to develop their writing voices as they write about matters they have experienced first-hand (in essays like his "This I Believe"), and notes that such work is valuable in writing that "draw[s] from external sources in their writing, when, all too often, the outcome is to vacate the writing out of deference to expert testimony" (Ch. 9).

Teresa Redd wants students to come to understand the rich variety of traditional secondary and primary sources available to them electronically. In her course that uses the theme of the aftermath of Hurricane Katrina, Redd encourages her students to mine library databases for traditional sources and to use digital data and archives (Ch. 6).

Another key theme that runs throughout this collection is the situated nature of writing. Wardle and Downs speak to this theme below:

> First, writing is *situated* in specific contexts and reasons-for-being that are unique to each act of writing. Writing is driven by exigence: people do not write unless some need exists for the writing they're producing (including writing produced to fulfill a private, psychological need for self-expression). . . . To say that writing is situated is to say that a text is understood differently when taken out of the context in which rhetors originally produce and read it; stated another way, what a text means and how it is composed and produced will inevitably depend on the context and circumstances in which it is composed and read. (Ch. 11)

Teresa Redd responds to her sense that students need an exigence for writing by asking students to produce "a wide range of genres—everything from scholarly case studies or scientific posters to dramatic scripts or spoken word poems," and to write for "diverse audiences, including real readers outside the classroom, such as Amazon.com customers, Wikipedia editors, and judges or spectators at the Undergraduate Research Symposium" (Ch. 6). She focuses her students' attention on the connection between genre and situation by asking them to craft "the same message for different audiences (e.g., summarizing what is known about a problem in a literature review for a scholarly audience and, later, in an advocacy pamphlet for a public audience)."

Some of the teachers in this collection cite recent work on "transfer" in talking about the ways in which they approach the situated nature of writing. Chris Anson says that this research shows "that learning to write is highly situated and dependent on immersion in communities of practice where the conventions of writing . . . are unfamiliar to outsiders" (Ch. 1). Kathleen Blake Yancey creates a research assignment, adapted from Liane Robertson and Kara Taczak's "Teaching for Transfer" course, in which she asks students to create "a composition that uses different genres to communicate to a targeted audience about that same topic" (Ch. 12). Once they have done so, students are asked to "develop a rationale to communicate the strategy behind [their] genre choices, and a reflection on the process."

Writing to Learn About Multiple Modalities. When we decided to title this collection "First-Year Composition," rather than "First-Year Writing," long before we received essays from our contributors, we did so because of our understanding that twenty-first century texts make use of various media in addition to print. Our contributors obviously share this vision of text as much more than words on a printed page.

Douglas Hesse believes that we will diminish possibilities "if the course is fussily constrained as a writing course and only a writing course," adding, "With the recovery and reconceptualization of 'composition,' words alone seem a meager constraint, one increasingly out of step with how texts are created, circulated, and experienced" (Ch. 3).

Teresa Redd creates a course in which students

> use technology to collaborate online, to analyze data, and to become producers, whether they are designing multimedia presentations, building websites, or posting videos on YouTube. Like Adam Banks, I would give African American students the opportunity to use technology, "to tell their own stories in their own terms and . . . to meet the real material,

social, cultural, and political needs in their lives and in their communities" (138). (Ch. 6)

Alexander Reid articulates his understanding of the importance of digital media in today's composition course in the following comment: "If we are going to begin with the premise that writing is a largely situated practice, we should not make the claim that writing for print is more fundamental than digital, networked writing. . . . This does not mean that I eschew print entirely for digital. We live in a time when both print and digital composing practices are necessary" (Ch. 7).

Perhaps the most expansive statement about the important role of multimedia in the composition course is given by Jody Shipka. She discusses her comprehensive view of what "composition" means in the twenty-first century.

> To my mind, taking a broader view of and approach to, composing is not just a matter of practicing what many of us profess to teach, theorize, or research. Rather, given the increased materials with which, contexts in which, and purposes for which, students currently make and negotiate meaning, it has become increasingly important that our courses continue to "disturb the marriage between comfortable writing that forms our disciplinary core and the entire range of new media for writing" (Faigely and Romano 49). . . . To ensure that our courses do not become irrelevant—or, depending on one's perspective, to ensure that they do not become *increasingly irrelevant*—we must ask students to examine the design of words on a page as well as the relationships among words, images, codes, textures, sounds, colors, and potentials for movement. We need, in short, to embrace composition. (Ch. 8)

In listing the items that she considers texts, items such as "a painting, a photograph, a well-designed room, or a special meal," Shipka makes it clear that she has expanded text to include the product of any human semiotic system.

Writing to Learn About Creating Knowledge. The insistence of epistemists that writing is a means of learning is still very much a tenet of the teachers represented in this study. Paula Mathieu tells us that she wants her students "to come to rely on the practice of writing to deepen their own thinking and to help them discover and learn," and she goes on to say that "Thought and writing are so inextricably linked that I cannot imagine teaching a course without this unity. . . ." (Ch. 5). Elizabeth Wardle and Doug Downs contrast the received understanding in western culture that writing is a "recording of existing knowledge" with the "epistemic" view that "writing is an activity that generates new knowledge" (Ch.11). They go on to offer their belief that

> what people experience as reality constitutes and is constituted by language: How we understand our world depends in large measure on the language we use to describe and talk about it, so that our expressive choices generate (understandings of) reality. In practice, writers find that the act of "writing down" the ideas they already have usually gives them ideas they didn't have before. (Ch. 11)

Kathleen Blake Yancey makes a very similar comment about what she hopes to accomplish in the inquiry assignment she offers her students:

> I'm aware that as Marra and Palmer demonstrate, college students don't understand how knowledge is made, how facts become facts, or how facts are framed as understandings. . . . My hope is that the inquiry assignment moves students toward an understanding that knowledge is in flux and that specific practices contribute to what we consider knowledge. (Ch. 12)

Writing to Learn About Power. These teachers want their students to understand that language is integrally connected with power. Language is an important tool used by those who wish to exercise control over others. Our students should come to understand that language is never neutral, never innocent; doing so will empower them to resist the unethical use of language by other individuals, by governments, and by themselves. Elizabeth Wardle and Doug Downs connect the issue of power to another important theme found throughout this collection: motivation, or exigence:

> [B]ecause writing is situation- and exigence-driven, it follows that it is *motivated*: Rhetors have motives for writing what they write and how they write it, and also for reading texts in the ways they do. The production of texts and the meanings rhetors make for them, then, unavoidably depend on motiva-

tions. Because there is no unmotivated writing, there is no objective, neutral, unbiased, or impartial writing or text. (Ch. 11)

Asao Inoue sees a direct connection between the language students bring to a composition course and the grades they often receive in those courses. Inoue believes that as long as the "quality" of student writing is equated with achieving mastery of the dominant discourse, and as long as composition instructors purport to be grading their students on the "quality" of their writing, the "dominant discourse--usually a white, middle-class academic one" will be used to "punish students for not being white, middle-class academics" (Ch. 4). Suresh Canagarajah uses the term "contact zone" to refer to a classroom, or any other arena, in which ways of using language are in conflict. According to Canagarajah, "a contact zone writing pedagogy treats languages, genres, and knowledge as always contested" (Ch. 2). However, rather than suggesting that his students succumb to the language of the dominant discourse, his "pedagogy . . . includes faith in the negotiability of norms" (Ch. 2). Teresa Redd uses the contact zone theory to talk about her sense that her "African American students need to think through issues of concern to African Americans," and she encourages her students "to write about issues of concern to the African American community so that they can confront and critique dominant culture and rewrite the story of their own" (Ch. 6).

Classroom Activities

College and university administrators see the first-year composition course as a special place, though many of them focus on its contributions to student retention more than on its academic substance. Because it is seen as a place where teachers know their students by name and interact one-on-one with them, administrators have looked favorably on pleas made by writing program administrators for courses to be kept small. It is assumed that small classes are places where students should be engaged in active learning, rather than being subjected to lectures about writing and language.

The teachers represented in this collection share this assumption. Several speak at some length about what goes on in their classrooms and why. After speaking about the importance of active learning in general, and specifically for a writing course, Chris Anson details the workings of what he calls "course delivery reversal" or "course flipping." Anson explains that the affordances and availability of new technology allow him to provide students with readings, videos, recordings, and even podcasts to deliver information he might otherwise have to deliver as class lecture. Students are asked to read, listen, and/or watch these texts and then write various types of responses in preparation for class. As Anson explains, "When students come to class, the lecturing is over; almost everything students do involves active learning with the supervision of the teacher, who is the orchestrator of knowledge integration and no longer the sole source of that knowledge" (Ch. 1). Anson notes that he may use class time for brief presentations

> to set a context for students' work or remind them of various concepts or principles; but the time in class is decidedly not used for teacher-dominated talk. . . . Class time is devoted to large-group discussion (using student-centered methods . . . small-group work, brief writing episodes, peer-group brainstorming and revision conferences, oral mini-presentations, poster creation and "gallery walks," problem-solving through cases and scenarios, and other activities. (Ch. 1)

Douglas Hesse offers strategies that are quite similar to those of Anson. Hesse tells us that a typical class period might see the class engaged in two or three of the following activities:

> *Focused Studio/Problem Solving.* Students have a brief amount of time to perform a particular task, followed by some sharing of results (in pairs, groups, or the whole class), followed by a discussion of issues raised during the process and, perhaps, my comments on a couple of particularly effective solutions. . . .
>
> *Open Studio Time.* Students work on a project they're either continuing or starting. . . .
>
> *Presentation/Application/Demonstration.* This element is closest to lecturing. I use my best teaching to review a concept or strategy I asked them to read about before class, or to introduce a concept or strategy they will read about afterwards. . . .
>
> *Discussion.* When everyone in class has read a selection, we spend several minutes talking about what it means and how we respond to it. . . .
>
> *Class Invention or Revising.* In this type of class activity, I ask students some of the following: "How might you start this as-

signment?" or "What are your first thoughts?" Questions like these frequently initiate a few minutes' discussion of a particular homework writing task; the point is raising some possible starting places and common ideas so that students don't leave class paralyzed or clueless. . . . (Ch. 3)

Like Anson and Hesse, several others in this collection devote a good deal of class time to writing. Suresh Canagajarah mentions various activities that take place in his writing classes, "such as idea generating, research, peer reviewing, and serial revision," but he labels his course as "practice-based," and states his belief that "students learn about writing primarily by writing" (Ch. 2). Elizabeth Wardle also allows much classroom time for writing:

In my classroom, we try lots of activities with writing in class that we also reflect on. . . . We write homework and we freewrite; we share ideas with partners, who write them down and give them back to us; we use recordings to get our ideas out; we write in the dark to practice getting ideas out without correction; and, sometimes, we even practice yoga breathing before we write. (Ch. 11)

Elizabeth's co-author, Doug Downs, notes in Chapter 11 that while he allows time for in-class writing, he finds "equally great value in talk about writing" and that, as a result, at times his class "can look pretty barren of the activity of writing itself." He goes on to add that "the vast majority of the writing happen[s] out of class to save time in class for talking about writing." In response to Doug, Elizabeth says that while she remains devoted to in-class writing "because I'm just not sure students would try some of the things I want them to try unless we do them together. (Will they really go home, turn out the lights, and do some yoga breathing before they write as a homework exercise?)," she recognizes the importance of classroom reflection and discussion; she adds: "We can't just do them and then not reflect on why we did them and on what happened (more meta is very important to me because of its apparent role in transfer of knowledge)."

Other teachers in the study speak about the need to "do" writing in class and then talk about what they learned about language and writing from that "doing." Howard Tinberg mentions the various writing and reviewing activities he promotes in his class, and concludes by saying, "All these exercises are geared toward promoting a vocabulary about writing—reflecting, and perhaps enhancing, student metacognition" (Ch. 9).

Response to Writing

Given the assumptions that these teachers make about the communal nature of writing, it would follow that a writer's text will be shaped, in part, by the community for which he or she is writing. As a part of these communities, the teachers represented here understand the key role they play in responding to, and thus helping shape, their students' writing. However, they also understand that a community in which one person gets to say what is good or bad, or what works or doesn't work, in a given text is not a real community. They are, thus, at pains to find ways to help students develop communities in which they can become respondents to one another's texts. In doing so, students can provide feedback that will help peers adjust their writing to fit the needs of the situations in which they are writing.

As all writing teachers know, this balancing act in which teachers play the roles of writing mentor, on the one hand, and authority figure who gives grades, on the other, calls for skills worthy of Houdini. A good many of the teachers in our study make gallant attempts at pulling off this magic act. Howard Tinberg requires students to perform peer reviews of one another's papers for each assignment, though he is very much aware of students' classic response when asked to do such reviews: It's the blind leading the blind. As a means of helping students teach themselves how to respond to others' work, he begins each review session with this task: "In your own words, fully and with precision, describe what the assignment is asking the writer (your partner) to do?" (Ch. 9). He then asks reviewers "to draw upon these criteria when describing precisely what aspects of their partner's writing works well and what needs additional work" (Ch. 9). Teresa Redd also provides opportunities for her students to respond to one another's work. Like Tinberg, she is aware that they will need guidance in this process, and assures us that she will not leave her students "afloat." She goes on to say that she provides students with guidelines or rubrics that will not only "help peer reviewers give student authors more valuable feedback, but also . . . help reviewers develop a critical eye that they can use on their own work" (Ch. 6).

Other contributors are less willing to attempt this balancing act. Victor Villanueva believes that the traditional writing process that moves from draft to draft, with teacher response to drafts in progress, takes agency away from students: "I grew tired of revising my students' papers, insofar as my comments to student papers would be responded to—and *that* would constitute a revision" (Ch. 10). Villanueva still responds to his students' writing, but rather than sandwiching response between drafts of a paper, he has adopted a (William) Colesean sequence of "scaffolded assignments." He explains that the "trick then becomes making a series of assignments in which each assignment builds on the concepts presented in a previous assignment" (Ch. 10).

Like Villanueva, Asao Inoue sees problems with the traditional role of teacher as responder and grader. For Inoue, these problems are not removed when student critiques are added to the process; in fact, in many cases they are exacerbated when students' critiques contradict each other. According to Inoue, when this happens, "The default is always to listen to the teacher—the teacher gives the grade, and the teacher likely knows the yardstick (the ideal) better than anyone else" (Ch. 4). This does not happen in Inoue's classes because of the moves he has made from the beginning to remove himself as the authority figure in the course. Rather than grading students on the "quality" of their work, or even on the degree to which assignments conform to guidelines in prompts, Inoue constructed an evaluation system that rewards students for the labor they do in the course. With this structure in place, he can help students build a community in which they can not only respond to one another's writing, but also negotiate with one another as to what works and why. Inoue explains that his

> students must be agents in the technology of feedback by creating a rubric that continually explains what those expectations mean, how they are seen in documents, and what labor is required to produce those results. . . . To contextualize all this, nothing is graded and I (the teacher) am not a voice in most feedback cycles. There is no anticipation of my judgments or of a grade that signifies completion, acceptance, or quality. They own most of the feedback. (Ch. 4)

Chris Anson offers a somewhat different approach to response. Recognizing students' lack of knowledge in methods of response, Anson creates a course in which "response" becomes one of the subjects studied. As Anson describes the course:

> Students learn about research on response: they read drafts, consider videotapes or transcripts of student response groups, look at the revised texts for evidence of where the response

worked or failed, and provide frequent response on each other's emerging texts. Digital media also play a role here: Both I and the students provide response using video screen-capture programs to demonstrate some of the ways that digital media are changing the nature of reading, writing, and communication. (Ch. 1)

Yet another perspective on response is provided by Elizabeth Wardle and Doug Downs. Like Villanueva, Wardle is "leery of a calendar that has one day for peer review, and then teacher reads and then grade" (Ch. 11). Rather, she designs class activities in which students discuss the ways writers plan and invent, and in which they discuss an upcoming assignment and, perhaps, freewrite or brainstorm as a class about how that assignment might be approached. The result of this kind of work, according to Wardle, is a shared history that allows students to approach peer critique not as "review," but as "invention." Wardle goes on to explain that in those sessions, "Pairs might talk about their ideas and write them down for each other, or pairs might work on parts of a developing draft, asking 'Is this idea interesting? Where is it going? What would you say about this?'" Downs agrees with Wardle that the goals of a writing assignment should be "emergent" in the discussion that transpires in the class and that, as a result, response takes the form of invention rather than review. Downs also elaborates on a point Redd makes in passing, namely, that student reviews of others' papers may, in fact, prove useful to the reviewer in his or her writing. As Downs puts it:

> I emphasize that the first reason for the session is for the readers of drafts to get ideas about what they ought to do in their own drafts. For the writer of the draft, formative feedback is actually a secondary consideration, mostly because we also emphasize that the reader isn't responsible for improving the paper—the writer does that. The reader simply helps the writer know where and what to work on by relating the reader's experience of encountering the writing. (Ch. 11)

We see a very similar emphasis on the role responding can have in the responder's development as a writer in the following comment by Jody Shipka:

I believe strongly that students who are able to see (or in the case of the workshop sessions, hear about) the ideas, tools, techniques, and strategies their classmates employ while working on major projects benefit tremendously, both in terms of understanding that there is more than one way to accomplish a task, and in thinking about how the adoption of similar tools, techniques, or strategies might potentially impact their own work. (Ch. 8)

Evaluation

We suspect that most, if not all, of the contributors to this collection agree with Asao Inoue that "the driving engine in any writing course is its assessment mechanisms, its assessment technology" (Ch. 4). This is not to say that, in a perfect world, they would believe this should be the case; we would guess that every contributor would wish it weren't, that students would find their own exigence in every writing assignment, and that the ways in which teachers propose to go about evaluating the work they do in the course would be inconsequential to them—or at least, of secondary importance. Since the teachers represented here do not assume this will always be the case, most of them have attempted to create courses in which they can perform the delicate balancing act (in fact, the same one alluded to in our discussion of "response" above) involved in offering students occasions for which they will want to produce real writing addressed to situations they (the students) help create and, at the same time, provide a mechanism for arriving at a final grade for the course.

The key pedagogical tool for achieving this balance is the portfolio. While the role the portfolio plays in the courses outlined here differs from teacher to teacher, it plays an important role for nearly every one of them. Most of these teachers weight the grade of the portfolio high, relative to work done in the process of building it. Douglas Hesse tells us that his portfolio counts for 40% of the student's grade, with 20% given for in-class activities, 20% for out-of-class work, and 20% for the three major papers done during the semester (Ch. 3). Howard Tinberg uses a similar system, with the portfolio accounting for 50% of the grade, a reading journal for 20%, and what he calls citizenship, timely submission of drafts, etc., for 30% (Ch. 9).

Other scales are similar, though a few teachers, notably Kathleen Blake Yancey, place even more weight (80% in Yancey's case) on the portfolio. As noted above, one reason to do so is, in Yancey's words, to give students "the gift of time" (Ch. 12). There are clearly other benefits. According to Suresh Canagarajah, the portfolio is a place where students will post "drafts, journal entries, and other course work" for the teacher and for other students to comment on (Ch. 2). Canagarajah explains that the portfolio "provides a record to students on how their own and others' writing is developing," and allows them to "examine the ways in which their ideas and writing are taking shape" (Ch. 2). Like Yancey, Doug Downs puts a great deal of the course's grade into the portfolio (calling it the "only graded writing you'll do in the course") and tells students it is a "showcase that allows you to revise your writing to the best of your ability and to reflect on your learning in the course" (Ch. 11). He goes on to add that "Its overall purpose is to make an argument about what you've learned in the course and demonstrate it via the writing you've prepared" (Ch. 11).

We get the most complete statement about the role of the portfolio in a writing course from Kathleen Blake Yancey. She tells us that she thinks of her writing course "less as a course culminating in a portfolio, and more as a portfolio course" (Ch. 12). According to Yancey, "Rather than asking students to compile or assemble a portfolio at the term's end--the conventional practice--we can introduce it, early in the term, as a site for archiving informal and formal texts, for reflecting upon texts and experiences, and for tracing connections to other kinds of composing and compositions."

Yancey details the numerous affordances and advantages of the portfolio, but most interesting, from our perspective, is what she says about its role in assessment. To this point in our discussion of the portfolio as a tool of assessment, we have focused on the portfolio as a means of collecting work that students can reflect on and continually revise as they work their way toward a grade that is put off as long as possible, via the portfolio process. We have said little, though, about how that grade is arrived at once that reckoning day finally arrives. Yancey speaks eloquently to this issue in her explanation of how portfolios work in her classroom. Calling grading the place "where the rubber hits the road," Yancey goes on to explain that during the portfolio process, she and the class work on a set of guidelines together, and each student includes her or his own goals, including those for "development as well as accomplishment" (Ch. 12). How exactly are these guidelines created? As the following quotation indicates, this has been an evolving process for Yancey:

> For years, I used a scoring guide for the portfolio It is no
> different with an ePortfolio, though the criteria should be
> (Yancey "Electronic Portfolios"; Yancey, McElroy, and Pow-
> ers). . . . More recently, I've seen the guide less as mechanism
> for summative assessment, and more as heuristic, as a way of
> prompting a kind of discussion about a writer's development,
> achievement, understanding, and knowledge. Seen this way,
> the guide, especially when we all contribute to its making,
> frames a concluding conversation about the writing we've en-
> gaged in all term. What, we can ask, has been learned about
> writing as knowledge and practice? How has the writer devel-
> oped? What are the next steps in this development? (Ch. 12)

Yancey's system goes a long way toward achieving the balance between our desires to move students beyond conversations about evaluation as grades, and our acceptance that, at some point, the teacher
must transition from formative to summative response. Not all the
teachers represented in our collection are comfortable with this institutional constraint, however, as we see in examining the assessment
practices of Asao Inoue and Alexander Reid.

We quoted, above, Asao Inoue's contention that assessment is a
driving force in writing courses. After making that statement, Inoue
goes on to explain that in the traditional writing class, where the quality of student writing is used in determining grades, "teachers and
students unwittingly become victims of larger societal structures like
racism, sexism, and classism that use (often invisible) whiteness as the
default yardstick by which to make judgments on student writing"
(Ch. 4). Inoue's solution to this problem is to construct a course in
which students' grades are based on their labor; in addition, his course
empowers students to grapple with, and answer, three crucial questions that determine whether they will judge one another as having
performed the labor required in the course:

1. What is *labor* in our writing class?
2. How do we know how well we are doing if there are no *grades*?
3. What does *assessing* mean?

Once these definitions have been put in place by the class, student
responses to one another's work—together with final conferences between Inoue and each student—result in a determination as to whether the necessary labor was performed. If so, the student receives a "B"
for the course. If not, there are various ways of determining whether

the grade is lowered, or whether the student fails the class—one assumes that these determinations do not need to be made often. If a student wishes to achieve an "A" for the course, he or she may do an extra project that will be assessed in a similar manner to the way other work is assessed.

Alexander Reid comes at assessment from a slightly different perspective than Inoue's. He is not entirely opposed to quality of writing as part of the calculus in determining which students are awarded an "A" in his class, but he is convinced that the reason many students settle for mediocre writing is that their previous experiences have punished risk-taking. Reid believes that there is an inherent connection between risk-taking and good writing, and he attempts to create a climate that encourages students to take risks. In talking about students' fear of risk, he says:

> For this reason, I find it justifiable to remove a significant amount of the risk that is conventionally associated with grades. That is, I make it explicit that to receive a B in the class all a student really must do is complete all the work. There is virtually no risk. I made this decision because, in my experience, B students achieve their grades by playing it safe. While it seems unfair to me to punish students for doing what they've always been taught to do, I want to create conditions where it is not necessary to play it safe, where the typical B student can take risks without risking the B grade. (Ch. 6)

This theme that a willingness to take risks is connected with progress in one's writing is found in statements made by other teachers in this study. Chris Anson describes his forums as places that " provide a space for students to experiment with language, react to ideas in the course, write about their own experiences, or dialogue with other students about theirs" (Ch. 1). Jody Shipka encourages students to consider feedback early in the writing process because, at that stage, doing so "allows them to take more risks, to be more flexible in considering the various ways they might approach a task" (Ch. 8).

CONCLUDING REMARKS

We began this chapter by saying that no one writing course could do all that we would want it to. We then noted a few things that the teachers in our study do not think a writing course should do as a way of signaling some of the important ways that writing instruction has changed in light of the evolving discipline that studies composition. That left us with the task of examining the chapters and the syllabi here in an effort to identify those things that should, or might, be done in a first-year composition course.

We like "might" a lot better than "should." Were we to say that these teachers believe students should know *x* or *y* about writing, or that students should experience *a* or *b* in their own writing as they journey through first-year composition, we would be committing teachers to an impossibly long list of things to accomplish in any one composition course. Rather, we believe that our contributors agree that the outcomes offered here are ones that—given world enough and time—they "might" strive for. As was often the case, one of the writers in the study makes this point better than we can, and so, we will give Kathleen Blake Yancey the final word about what we might hope to accomplish in teaching first-year composition:

> I began this text . . . by saying that first-year composition is an impossible course to design given all that it needs to do. Perhaps this is so for all our courses, but for some reason, it seems especially so for FYC. That's evidenced by what's here, by how I developed what I have here designed. . . . [T]he importance and impossibility of FYC is also evidenced by what I haven't included; those absences—of reading strategies, of evaluating sources, of considering how research is made in multiple fields—are a presence providing a small index to what we need to include. . . . So yes, this is an impossible task, I concede, but in the *same* breath, I have to say: It's an important task. And that just because it's impossible doesn't mean we shouldn't try. And that when we try, we should try both individually *and* together. (Ch. 12)

NOTES

1. Since we quote liberally from our contributors in this chapter, it would be cumbersome to cite every page referenced. We provide the chapter number and the title in our text for a contributor the first time we quote his or her work. Thereafter, we will provide chapter numbers at the end of quota-

tions, unless the chapter has been referenced in text immediately preceding the quotation.

   2. Sources cited in quotations from a contributor's chapter may be found in the Works Cited page for that contributor's chapter.

WORKS CITED

Perry, William G. *Forms of Ethical and Intellectual Development in the College Years: A Scheme.* San Francisco: Jossey-Bass, 1998. Print.

Contributors

Deborah Coxwell-Teague currently serves as director of Florida State University's First-Year Composition Program. In this capacity, she is involved in the training and supervision of close to 150 individuals who teach approximately 350 sections of FYC annually. She has also served as director of FSU's Reading/Writing Center and has taught composition at both the high school and community college levels. Deborah's research interests focus on teacher training and composition. Her publications include *Finding Our Way: A Writing Teacher's Sourcebook*, co-authored with the late Wendy Bishop, and *Multiple Literacies*, a composition textbook co-authored with Dan Melzer.

Ronald F. Lunsford is Professor of English at the University of North Carolina at Charlotte, where he teaches courses in composition theory, rhetoric, and linguistics. His administrative posts include Director of Rhetoric and Writing at Clemson University; Head of the Department of English at Missouri State University; Chair of English, Assistant to the Provost, and Director of Graduate Programs in English—all at UNC Charlotte. His publications include the following co-authored works: *Twelve Readers Reading: Responding to College Student Writing*, *Noam Chomsky*, *Research in Composition and Rhetoric*, *Linguistic Perspectives on Literature*, and *The Longwood Guide to Writing*, now in its fourth edition.

Chris Anson is University Distinguished Professor and Director of the Campus Writing and Speaking Program at North Carolina State University, where he teaches courses in composition theory and literacy studies and supports faculty-development across the institution. He has published fifteen books and over one hundred articles and book chapters and has spoken widely across the U.S. and in twenty-seven other countries. http://www.ansonica.net

Suresh Canagarajah is the Erle Sparks Professor and Director of the Migration Studies Project at Pennsylvania State University. He teaches world Englishes, second language writing, and postcolonial studies in the departments of English and Applied Linguistics. His early education and teaching was in the war-torn region of Jaffna, Sri Lanka. He has taught in the University of Jaffna and the City University of New York. His book, *Resisting Linguistic Imperialism in English Teaching* (Oxford UP, 1999) won Modern Language Association's Mina Shaughnessy Award for the best research publication on the teaching of language and literacy. His subsequent publication, *Geopolitics of Academic Writing* (University of Pittsburgh P, 2002) won the Gary Olson Award for the best book in social and rhetorical theory. His edited collection, *Reclaiming the Local in Language Policy and Practice* (Erlbaum, 2005) examines linguistic and literacy constructs in the context of globalization. His study of world Englishes in writing pedagogy won the 2007 Braddock Award for the best article in the *College Composition and Communication* journal.

Doug Downs is Associate Professor of Writing Studies and Director of Composition in the Department of English at Montana State University, where he also designed the department's Broadfield writing major. He studies composition and research pedagogy through lenses of cultural and personal conceptions of writing, and his most recent research examines student reading practices in the current age of screen literacy. With Elizabeth Wardle, he is author of *Writing about Writing: A College Reader*, an anthology of writing studies research that supports the writing-about-writing pedagogies the two first wrote about in their 2007 *CCC* article, "Teaching about Writing, Righting Misconceptions: (Re)Envisioning 'First-Year Composition' as 'Introduction to Writing Studies.'"

Douglas Hesse is Executive Director of Writing and Professor of English at the University of Denver. He is a past Chair of the Conference on College Composition and Communication, and a past President of the Council of Writing Program Administrators. Among other things, he has published, with Becky Bradway, *Creating Nonfiction*.

Asao B. Inoue is an Associate Professor of Rhetoric and Composition in the English Department at California State University, Fresno, and currently serves as the Special Assistant to the Provost for Writing

Across the Curriculum. He was awarded Fresno State's 2012 Provost's Award for Excellence in Teaching, the highest award given to a faculty member. He has published numerous articles on validity theory and first-year writing program assessment, as well as writing pedagogy. His recent co-edited collection, *Race and Writing Assessment* (Peter Lang Publishers, 2012), is the first collection that directly looks at racial formations in writing assessments and its scholarship. He is currently finishing a manuscript on writing assessment as technology.

Paula Mathieu is Associate Professor of English at Boston College, where she teaches courses in composition pedagogy, nonfiction writing, rhetoric as cultural study, and homeless literature, while also directing the First-Year Writing Program and the Writing Fellows Program. With Diana George, she has co-authored several publications about the rhetorical power of dissident press publications for venues like *College Composition and Communication* and the collection, *The Public Work of Rhetoric*. She is author of *Tactics of Hope: The Public Turn in English Composition*, and co-editor of *Beyond English, Inc.* and of *Writing Places*. She began working with homeless writers in 1997 in Chicago, where she founded a writing group and learning center for homeless vendors of the newspaper, *StreetWise*. From 2003 to 2006, she was Deputy Chair of the International Network of Street Papers.

Teresa M. Redd is a Professor of English at Howard University, where she directs the Writing across the Curriculum Program and the university's faculty development center. A recipient of the university's teaching excellence award, she has published numerous articles about teaching composition as well as two books: *Revelations: An Anthology of Expository Essays by and about Blacks* and *Introduction to African American English: What a Writing Teacher Should Know* (with Karen Schuster Webb).

Alexander Reid is Associate Professor of Rhetoric at the University at Buffalo, where he teaches digital rhetoric and theory and serves as Director of Composition. He has published *The Two Virtuals: New Media and Composition* and co-edited *Design Discourse: Composing and Revising Programs in Technical and Professional Writing*.

Jody Shipka is Associate Professor of English at the University of Maryland, Baltimore County, where she teaches courses in the Communication and Technology track. She is the author of *Toward* *a Composition Made Whole,* and the editor of *Play! A Collection of Toy Camera Photographs.* Her work has appeared in *College Composition and Communication, Computers and Composition, Enculturation, Kairos, Text and Talk, Writing Selves/Writing Societies,* and other edited collections.

Howard Tinberg is Professor of English at Bristol Community College in Fall River, Massachusetts. A former editor of *Teaching English in the Two-Year College,* he has published in a variety of scholarly journals, including *College English, College Composition and Communication, English Journal* and *Pedagogy.* Professor Tinberg was awarded the 2004 U.S. Community Colleges Professor of the Year by the Carnegie Foundation for the Advancement of Teaching and Council for Advancement and Support of Education. He was program chair for the 2013 Conference on College Composition and Communication.

Victor Villanueva is Regents Professor in English at Washington State University. He is the author or editor of numerous books and articles, the 1999 Rhetorician of the Year Award winner, and winner of dozens of honors. He is a former chair of the Conference on College Composition and Communication and was honored with the organization's 2009 Exemplar Award. All of his efforts have centered on the connections between language and racism.

Elizabeth Wardle is Associate Professor and Chair of the Department of Writing and Rhetoric at the University of Central Florida (UCF). She regularly teaches first-year composition and composition theory and pedagogy. She served as Composition Director at UCF from 2008 to 2013. In 2013, UCF's Composition Program won a CCCC Writing Program Certificate of Excellence. She publishes on transfer, genre theory, and the content of composition. With Doug Downs, she co-authored *Writing about Writing: A College Reader,* now in its second edition.

Kathleen Blake Yancey is Kellogg W. Hunt Professor of English and Distinguished Research Professor at Florida State University, where she directs the Graduate Program in Rhetoric and Composition. She has served as President of the National Council of Teachers of English, as Chair of the Conference on College Composition and Communication, and as President of the Council of Writing Program Administrators. She co-founded and co-directs the Inter/

National Coalition for Electronic Portfolio Research. Editor of *College Composition and Communication*, Yancey has authored or co-authored over seventy articles and book chapters, and authored, edited, or co-edited eleven scholarly books, including *Portfolios in the Writing Classroom*, *Reflection in the Writing Classroom*, *Situating Portfolios*, *Delivering College Composition: The Fifth Canon*, and *ePortfolios 2.0*.

Index